YOUTH, EDUCATION, AND ISLAMIC RADICALISM

CONTENDING MODERNITIES

Series editors: Ebrahim Moosa, Atalia Omer, and Scott Appleby

As a collaboration between the Contending Modernities initiative and the University of Notre Dame Press, the Contending Modernities series seeks, through publications engaging multiple disciplines, to generate new knowledge and greater understanding of the ways in which religious traditions and secular actors encounter and engage each other in the modern world. Books in this series may include monographs, coauthored volumes, and tightly themed edited collections.

The series will include works that frame such encounters through the lens of "modernity." The range of themes treated in the series might include war, peace, human rights, nationalism, refugees and migrants, development practice, pluralism, religious literacy, political theology, ethics, multi- and intercultural dynamics, sexual politics, gender justice, and postcolonial and decolonial studies.

YOUTH, EDUCATION, AND ISLAMIC RADICALISM

RELIGIOUS INTOLERANCE IN CONTEMPORARY INDONESIA

MUN'IM SIRRY

University of Notre Dame Press

Notre Dame, Indiana

Library of Congress Control Number: 2023946564

ISBN: 978-0-268-20763-2 (Hardback)
ISBN: 978-0-268-20764-9 (Paperback)
ISBN: 978-0-268-20762-5 (WebPDF)
ISBN: 978-0-268-20765-6 (Epub)

CONTENTS

TABLES

ACKNOWLEDGMENTS

When I joined the Notre Dame faculty in 2014, Professor R. Scott Appleby trusted me to develop a research group focusing on Indonesia. This research group emerged as one of several research units of the Contending Modernities initiative (CM) based at the University of Notre Dame. Founded by Appleby and co-directed by Ebrahim Moosa and Atalia Omer, Contending Modernities seeks to "generate new knowledge and greater understanding of the ways in which religious and secular forces interact in the modern world." Through a variety of innovative engagements, including working groups titled Science and the Human Person, Global Migration and the New Cosmopolitanism, Authority, Community, and Identity, and Madrasa Discourses, as well as scholarly interventions on its blog, Contending Modernities intends to foster public deliberations and open new paths for constructive collaboration across religious communities and between religious and secular actors. For more details, please visit https://contendingmodernities.nd.edu, which highlights the perspectives of scholars, opinion leaders, and students working across differences to accomplish shared goals.

This book is the result of my role as the coordinator of Contending Modernities' Authority, Community, and Identity working group. The geographical focus of this working group is Indonesia: a complex case study of cultural diversity, with over three hundred ethnic groups, more than seven hundred living languages, and six officially recognized religions (i.e., Islam, Protestantism, Catholicism, Hinduism, Buddhism, and Confucianism). Indonesia is the largest Muslim-majority country in the world, with the fourth-largest population on the planet, scattered across six thousand inhabited islands. Indonesia offers rich opportunities for research on the preconditions for, and obstacles to, peaceful coexistence.

I am so grateful for the trust put in me and the opportunity given to me by the CM co-directors (R. Scott Appleby, Ebrahim Moosa, and Atalia Omer) to lead the Indonesian research group, which involves some of the best researchers from Indonesia and the West. This book would not have been possible without their support. The Contending Modernities program manager, Dania Maria Straughan, has been very helpful in the whole process of writing this book.

The data collection for this book has involved a group of fine researchers from the University of Airlangga (Unair) in Surabaya, Indonesia, led by Professor Bagong Suyanto. I would like to express my deepest gratitude for their hard work and professionalism. Pak Bagong has been so kind as to allow me to use their research data for this book. My stay at the Post-Graduate School, Sunan Kalijaga State Islamic University (UIN), in Yogyakarta, provided me with the initial idea to embark on this book project. For that, I am thankful to Professor Noorhaidi Hasan, the director of the Post-Graduate School, and Dr. Moch Nur Ichwan, vice-director, for their generosity in hosting me as a visiting professor during my sabbatical leave (2017–18). I also owe a debt of gratitude to Tim Matovina, the chair of the theology department here at Notre Dame, for his tireless support. I am blessed to be around wonderful colleagues in Malloy Hall at the University of Notre Dame, a place where you can meet with great scholars, theologians, and philosophers.

A special thanks goes to Mark Spinnenweber for his editorial help. His magic hands have enormously improved my prose. For any errors or inadequacies that may remain in this work, I alone am responsible. Finally, I would like to thank the Liu Institute for Asia and Asian Studies and the Institute for Scholarship in the Liberal Arts (ISLA) at Notre Dame for their support.

Introduction

In the past few years, we have witnessed increasing attention to education both as an attractive setting for extremist recruitment and as a key location for anti-radicalization work. Concern about the attractiveness of university students as potential recruits and of educational institutions as places for extremist groups to disseminate their ideologies has featured in security discussions about contemporary terrorist threats. Because of the frequency of educated youths' participating in terrorist attacks in the West or joining radical groups abroad, a simple assumption has been made: that school is a significant environment, trigger, or hotbed for radicalization. Both practitioners and researchers began asking whether radicalization has a causal relationship with education and how to prevent religious extremism through education. In March 2015, the European Union held its first meeting of education ministers, which adopted the Paris Declaration. The Paris Declaration carried with it a clear political signal that the European ministers wanted to boost EU-level cooperation on educational priorities in countering religious radicalization.[1] In the United Kingdom, for instance, the most extensive counter-radicalization measure, known as "Prevent," was introduced with a focus on "developing youth and community programmes targeted almost exclusively at Muslim communities in the UK; but over time, its anti-radicalization agenda increasingly moved into and across the entire UK education sector."[2] Anti-radicalization in education is not limited to the UK and the EU. Parallel developments have taken place throughout Western countries.

While the link between education and radicalization has been a subject of much discussion, most of it is focused on the West. This book represents the first scholarly attempt to address the phenomenon of religious intolerance and radicalization among high school and university students in Indonesia. Drawing on theoretical frameworks for modeling youth radicalization developed by scholars, here I offer a theoretically informed discussion of the complex factors that have shaped the views of young people on religious diversity, as well as the ways in which they have become radicalized in the first place. I also discuss how, in some cases, they have deradicalized themselves. The question of radicalization among educated youth in Indonesia is interesting not only because Indonesia is one of the world's most diverse countries in terms of religion, ethnicity, and socioeconomic status, but also because of the complexity of its education system. In this book I show that the infiltration of radical ideologies into Indonesian educational institutions has taken place in a manner that has been neither a result of indoctrination, as it has been with radical madrasas in Pakistan and Bangladesh, nor mainly due to online radical content, which has been a dominant factor for radicalization in Western universities. I analyze and document, based on testimonies given by radicalized students, those who have deradicalized themselves, or those who have been exposed to radical ideologies but rejected them, nonlinear processes of youth radicalization. Tracking these processes is crucial to identify youths' motives for joining, or sympathizing with, radical networks. By revealing the forces that have driven them to become radicalized, in this study I aim to offer nuanced explanations as to why one person becomes radicalized while another does not. The diversity of motives also suggests that radicalization may not necessarily result in violent terrorism, as has commonly been assumed.[3] Most radicalized youths examined in this study have rejected violent means to achieve their goals, despite their extremist views, such as supporting the caliphate system, rejecting the pluralist Indonesian ideology of *Pancasila*,[4] or exhibiting intolerant attitudes toward non-Muslims and other minority groups.

What distinguishes this book from other studies is the scope of the findings I present in it, which are drawn from original empirical research into both secondary and tertiary education. Most studies on the vulnerability of educated youth focus either on high schools or university campuses, without tracking possible connections between the two. In Indonesia, for instance, several surveys conducted by research think tanks have found that intolerant views were widespread in high schools. As I discuss in this book, the Setara Institute, Wahid Institute, and Center for the Study of Islam and Society (PPIM, Pusat Pengkajian Islam dan Masyarakat) showed that a significant number of high school students held radicalized religious views. At the university level, the Indonesian Institute of Sciences (LIPI, Lembaga Ilmu Pengetahuan Indonesia) and Alvara Research Center found that radical networks have infiltrated campuses and an increasing number of students have experienced radicalization. In its 2018 findings, the National Agency for Combating Terrorism (BNPT, Badan Nasional Penanggulangan Terorisme) referred to seven prominent state universities as having been impacted by radicalism. The Indonesian government established BNPT following the 2009 hotel bombings in Jakarta.[5] My research findings confirm this increasing phenomenon of the radicalization of youth in educational environments, as detailed in subsequent chapters. What is it in education that makes it attractive for extremist recruitment? What shapes students' views? Under what circumstances have the radicalization and deradicalization of educated youth taken place? Addressing these and similar questions is my major concern in this book.

THE INDONESIAN EDUCATION SYSTEM

Before delving deeper into the current state of the art in the scholarly discussion on education and radicalization, perhaps it is useful to briefly highlight the nature of the education system in Indonesia. The history of education in Indonesia can be traced to the Majapahit kingdom before 1300; however, education for the masses did not begin until the colonial period. Beginning in the early fourteenth century, Islamic boarding schools, called *pesantren*, were established following the spread of Islam, especially in rural Sumatra and Java. This type of education was centered on Islamic teaching, with a pedagogy consisting of lecturing and the recital and memorization of texts.[6] In the sixteenth century, the first European missionary schools were established by priests who came to the Spice Islands with the Portuguese and Spanish to spread Catholicism. When the Dutch defeated the Portuguese and Spanish in the seventeenth century, education was provided to children of locally employed European families and children of the aristocratic elite.

However, as M. C. Ricklefs noted, the Dutch had never been interested in educating the local elite, at least until the early twentieth century with the introduction of the Ethical Policy, which favored an increase in education for Indonesia.[7] After achieving independence in 1945, Indonesia witnessed the rapid growth and expansion of public education in the increase of student enrollments and school buildings.

Today, Indonesia has a wide array of educational institutions, a mixture of public and private, at the primary, secondary, and tertiary levels. It has the third-largest educational system in Asia and the fourth-largest globally (behind only the People's Republic of China, India, and the United States). The Indonesian educational system's current structure is based on the 2003 Law of National Education System, which stipulates that all the country's regular public education is to be managed by the Ministry of Education and Culture (MoEC). Additionally, religiously affiliated public schools, or *madrasah*, are managed by the Ministry of Religion (MoR). About 80 percent of schools are under the MoEC, and the remaining 20 percent are under the MoR. Of the 20 percent of *madrasah* under the MoR, only 8 percent are public; the other 12 percent are private.[8] Public schools tend to attract more students than private ones. For instance, according to the data issued by the MoEC for the academic year 2017/18, the number of public and private *madrasah* was almost even (6,732 public and 6,763 private); however, new student enrollments in public *madrasah* were almost three times larger than those in private schools: 1,182,687 new students in public schools and 431,292 new students in private schools.[9]

The situation with religiously affiliated schools is different. Public *madrasah* are indeed more attractive to students. However, as only 8 percent are public, the largest number of high school students attended private *madrasah*. It should be noted that private *madrasah* education differs from the more traditional *pesantren* education; the majority of the curriculum is focused on topics similar to those studied in public schools. As *madrasah* grew in popularity, many *pesantren* schools began to change and adopted the *madrasah* system by offering similar courses.[10] According to the Central Statistics Agency (BPS, Badan Pusat Statistik in 2019–20), the number of students enrolled in private *madrasah* is 965,358 students; only 439,106 students attend public *madrasah*.[11] This split between secular and religious education systems reflects an ideological conflict between Islamists and nationalists that has existed since the nation's early history. Lyn Parker and R. Raihani note that "the structural dualism in Indonesian education that continues today has its roots in the colonial era. *Madrasah* are currently administered by the Ministry of Religion (MoR) and general (secular) schools by the MoEC."[12] Well-established civil and religious organizations, such as Nahdlatul Ulama (NU) and Muhammadiyah, managed their own education systems. Today, these two largest Muslim organizations claim to have over 23,000 schools (13,000 NU schools and 10,500 Muhammadiyah schools).

The government has made several attempts, especially during the Suharto regime (1966–98), to place private *madrasah* and *pesantren* under their jurisdiction. The most notable integration effort was made in 1975 through a three-minister joint decree that required private *madrasah* to implement the national curriculum. On this development, Muhammad Zuhri writes, "Since then, the *Madrasah Negeri*s (state madrasahs) which have been instituted prior to this decision, became models for private *madrasah*s. Consequently, the government did not recognize any Islamic education institution that did not use the government curricula."[13]

Under this joint decree, 30 percent of the *madrasah* curriculum consists of religious education and 70 percent of secular education. Private *madrasah* were under pressure because their graduates would not be eligible to continue their education at public schools or universities unless they implemented the state curriculum. The 2003 law enshrines this integrated national education system by formally recognizing both state schools and private *madrasah* as one "educational unit" (*satuan pendidikan*). Some critics expressed their concerns that "the increased government support for independent *madrasah* may erode the schools' traditional community support base."[14]

As a result of the integrated education policy, beginning in the 1980s a large cohort of *madrasah* graduates began entering public universities. In 1975, about 260,000 students were enrolled in tertiary education, and a decade later, in 1985, the numbers rose to 1.52 million. Since then, more than 1 million students have been added every decade. The number has increased significantly since 2002, when the Indonesian Constitution required the government to allocate at least 20 percent of its budget to education. According to the Central Statistics Agency, in 2018, about

8.5 million students were enrolled in higher education institutions, both secular and religious.[15] Indonesia's tertiary education enrollment rate is 32 percent, higher than that of the Philippines, Vietnam, and Laos, but lower than that of Malaysia (36 percent) and Thailand (51.2 percent).[16] Due to colonial-era neglect, higher education in Indonesia emerged relatively later than in neighboring countries, beginning only in the second half of the twentieth century, with most of the growth occurring in the last quarter of that century. Like primary and secondary schools, secular institutions are administered by the MoEC, religious institutions by the MoR. The 2003 law, along with ministerial regulations issued by the MoEC and MoR, restricted the institutional autonomy to such an extent that institutions could not develop study programs without the governing ministry's approval. "International evidence shows," argue Daniel Suryadarma and Gavin Jones, "that tertiary education institutions need autonomy and academic freedom in order to thrive."[17]

Compared to some of its neighboring countries, like Singapore and Malaysia, in Indonesia higher education has been lagging. With the large number of higher education institutions and very limited sources, it would be unrealistic to expect all tertiary institutions to be research-based. It is no secret that the research and development (R&D) budget in Indonesia is meager: about 0.09 percent of gross domestic product (GDP).[18] This low level of research and publication, coupled with a long history of educational underdevelopment, has caused the Indonesian higher educational system to be internationally isolated. Hal Hill and Thee Kian Wie rightly note that "leading universities are internationally connected institutions,"[19] but the Indonesian government seems to reinforce this isolation with complex regulations requiring faculty and students to study abroad.[20] The internationalization of higher education is one of the most important tools for increasing quality. Some universities have attempted to collaborate with prominent universities abroad, but yet, say Hill and Wie, "the country's investment laws discourage a more substantial foreign university presence, of the type now expanding rapidly in several ASEAN countries, especially Malaysia and Singapore."[21]

While it is true that Indonesian higher education institutions do poorly in international rankings, a handful of "elite" universities, mostly public, aspire to join the rank of internationally recognized institutions. In Asia, some of those universities would be ranked fair to middling, although no Indonesian university is highly placed among the various rankings of world universities. In the 2020 QS (Quacquarelli Symonds) Asian University Ranking, ten Indonesian universities were ranked as follows: Three universities were ranked in the top 100 (the University of Indonesia [UI] was placed at number 59, Bandung Institute of Technology [ITB] at number 66, and Gadjah Mada University [UGM] at number 70); three universities ranked between 100 and 200 (Bogor Agricultural Institute [IPB] at number 132, Airlangga University [Unair] at number 171, and Sepuluh Nopember Institute of Technology [ITS] at number 198); three universities ranked between 200 and 300 (Bina Nusantara University [Binus] at number 234, Padjadjaran University [Unpad] at number 236, and Diponegoro University [Undip] between numbers 281 and 290); and one university (Brawijaya University [UB]) ranked between numbers 301 and 350.[22] Interestingly, seven of these prominent universities were identified by BNPT as having been infiltrated by religious radicalism, namely, UI, ITB, IPB, Unair, ITS, Undip, and UB. In its 2018 nationwide survey, BNPT found that 39 percent of university students subscribed to beliefs that could be considered "radical."

It should be noted, however, that BNPT does not explain how or why these campuses become hotspots for radical activism. Most research—if not all—that has been conducted on student radicalization in Indonesia is based on quantitative data. While my research was prompted by the findings of several think tanks that have highlighted the phenomenon of student radicalization in the country, I expand the coverage to include both university and high school students.

DATA AND METHODS

In writing this book I used both quantitative and qualitative methods for data collection. A mixed-methods design provides a better understanding of a research problem than does either one alone.[23] For instance, while quantitative research has great strength in data analysis because the result is presented with a certain degree of certainty and specificity, it is often criticized for its weakness in explaining the nuanced contexts or settings in which a study is conducted. In contrast, qualitative research produces a holistic picture of the question at hand; however, it limits the generalizability of the findings because of the small number of participants it involves. In this study I aim to understand religious intolerance and radicalization among high school and university students by exploring various factors affecting their views of and involvement in radical networks. Considering the multiple dimensions and contexts in which students develop their intolerant and radical views and attitudes, both within and outside of educational environments, neither quantitative nor qualitative methods alone are sufficient to illuminate their complexities. Alan Bryman justifies the combination of quantitative and qualitative methods as "complete" because they "bring together a more comprehensive account of the area of inquiry."[24]

In 2018, along with researchers from the University of Airlangga (Unair) in Surabaya, I researched seven public universities identified by BNPT as having been afflicted with radical ideologies, namely IPB in Bogor (West Java), ITB in Bandung (West Java), ITS in Surabaya (East Java), UI in Depok (Tangerang), Unair in Surabaya (East Java), Undip in Semarang (Central Java), and UB in Malang (East Java). We started with a quantitative survey to obtain a general picture of student radicalization, which involved 100 students from each institution mentioned above. The total number of respondents was 700 students, 69.6 percent female and 30.4 percent male. The criteria for their selections were as follows: (1) They were students of the seven public tertiary institutions; (2) within the past year they had been exposed to religious group activities that had a radicalized element; (3) they owned personal electronics, and within the past year had accessed online radical content, either passively or actively. Some 56.8 percent of respondents were 18–20 years old, 42.6 percent were between 21 and 23 years old, and the rest (0.6 percent) were between 24 and 26 years old. As for their educational backgrounds, the majority of respondents graduated from public high schools (71.1 percent) and the rest from private high schools (11.9 percent), public *madrasah* (10.6 percent), private *madrasah* (3.1 percent), and *pesantren* (3.3 percent). Following the quantitative survey, we conducted in-depth interviews with ten students from each campus, representing 70 informants in total. This qualitative data collection continued over three months in the seven different cities where the campuses are located. The entire research project was conducted over six months.

After completing data collection and analysis, we carried out similar mixed-methods research at twelve high schools in 2019 to explore and understand students' views of religious diversity. The twelve high schools are located in five cities across East Java: Surabaya, Malang, Kediri, Pasuruan, and Pamekasan (Madura). The East Java province was chosen because it is a prominent base of Islam, especially Nahdlatul Ulama, or NU (the largest Muslim organization in the country), and also has a significant number of Christians, both Protestant and Catholic. The twelve high schools chosen included public and private, non-religiously affiliated, and religiously affiliated schools (Christian and Muslim). From the twelve high schools, 500 students (grades 10–12) were selected as sample respondents, with 100 respondents from each city. Generally, public schools have students of various religions, and Christian schools often have Muslim students. However, there are usually no non-Muslim students in Muslim schools. Notably, public, private, non-religiously affiliated, and religiously affiliated schools use the national curriculum. As discussed earlier, what distinguishes private religious schools from others is the addition of religious courses, such as the Qur'an and hadith, Islamic history, jurisprudence (*fiqh*), and Arabic. In terms of religion, Muslim students were 79.6 percent of respondents, Catholics (11.8 percent), Protestants (8.4 percent), and Hindu (0.2 percent). In-depth interviews were conducted with 50 students from twelve schools across the five cities to evaluate how high school students perceived and practiced tolerance inside and outside school.

We conducted both the quantitative survey and the in-depth interviews face-to-face. Selected students answered questions verbally, and these answers were recorded, then transcribed, analyzed, and interpreted. One challenge stood in the way: creating an environment enabling young people to discuss religious issues that are often sensitive without their peers' influence. Therefore, we conducted these interviews not only in educational settings, but also at homes, in cafeterias, and even in mosques or churches in an attempt to minimize students' discomfort. We considered the ethical treatment of participants at all stages. To protect the privacy of respondents and informants, we use pseudonyms, and names of high schools are not identified. We conducted this study in compliance with the standards of ethical research established by Unair. Throughout this book, I employ various theories and insights that seem most appropriate to explain different complex issues. I also employ a strong element of a phenomenological approach in this book,[25] as it is intended to explore and understand the phenomenon of religious intolerance and radicalism among educated youth. However, my interpretive approach is also shaped by the grounded theory,[26] because the focus of this study is not only on discovering the nature of radicalization as it occurs but also on seeking a theory to explain it.

EDUCATION AND RADICALIZATION

The link between education and radicalization is not new. The involvement of educated individuals in militant activities is not a recent phenomenon, nor is it confined to Indonesia. There is a growing consensus among scholars that low levels of education and impoverished backgrounds are not characteristics of incarcerated extremists and terrorists.[27] Marc Sageman's study of members of extremist Islamist groups shows that lack of education is not a driving factor in radicalization. Of the levels of education of 132 terrorists examined in his study, he writes that "over 60% have had at least some college education, which makes them, as a group, more educated than the average person worldwide, and especially more educated than the vast majority of people in the third world."[28] Of the 17 terrorists from Southeast Asia, only two held just high school diplomas, and the rest had earned college diplomas or had even more education. Sageman concludes, "The data on the socioeconomic and educational background of the mujahedin in this sample empirically refute the widespread notion that terrorism results from poverty and lack of education. On the contrary, the global Salafi mujahedin came from relatively well-to-do families and were much better educated than the average population, both in their home countries and in the West."[29] Such findings undermine the view that Islamic extremism can be explained as resulting from ignorance, lack of education, or personal poverty and deprivation. Furthermore, at the time of joining radical networks, most extremists were in professional occupations or semi-skilled employment. A study by Diego Gambetta and Steffen Hertog, entitled *Engineers of Jihad: The Curious Connection between Violent Extremism and Education*, shows that graduates in engineering and medicine are enormously overrepresented in extremist groups across the Muslim world. Their study includes 497 members of violent groups active since the 1970s. In line with Sageman's conclusion, Gambetta and Hertog argue that university students and graduates are vastly overrepresented among Islamist radicals. They conclude that their findings "provide the first wide-ranging systematic confirmation that the core of the Islamist movement emerged from would-be elites, not from the poor and the dispossessed."[30]

The point here is simply to highlight that radicalization is no longer associated with lack of education or with poverty. Similar conclusions can be found in other studies, by Mitchell Silber and Arvin Bhatt,[31] or by Alan Krueger and Jitka Maleckova,[32] all of whom concluded that most radicalized people had completed secondary or some higher education. Of course, one may find among radicalized persons those without diplomas as well as those who are highly educated. This means that, as there is no causal connection between ignorance and radicalization, a negative relationship can also be established between higher education and radicalization. Radicals vary from low-skilled to highly educated. In countries like Nigeria and Sierra Leone, studies show that the majority of extremist groups consisted of young individuals who were homeless, unemployed, and had no education.[33] However, since many terrorists have higher educational degrees, which implies that they have spent a long time in school, people have asked this question: How could highly educated individuals join radical groups? This question continues to perplex both scholars and practitioners in Indonesia and around the globe as they encounter students and highly educated individuals who have become radicalized. Educational institutions are expected to produce citizens who uphold human dignity, not ones who stoke hatred. They are expected to produce citizens who pursue a peaceful world order, not a destructive one. The fact that educational institutions have become places for intolerance and hatred to spread is both baffling and contrary to the very purpose of education. Therefore, it is essential to pay attention to what makes educational environments susceptible to extremism and how to prevent radicalization. There is no robust evidence of an effective means to oppose extremism in education. Education systems are critical social institutions, and success in education is often seen as fundamental for future success in the broader society.

Research on radicalization shows that school-aged individuals are those most vulnerable to adopting extremist religious ideologies. Those young people are at a developmental age at which they seek to discover their identity, develop self-confidence, and search for meaning in their lives. While there is general agreement on the susceptibility of youth, no single factor can explain why one particular individual adopted an extremist viewpoint or joined a radical network, while another did not. There are at least five theories that have been posited to explain Muslim radicalization in the West. First, the socioeconomic deprivation theory suggests that the lack of social integration and unequal opportunities can drive someone toward radicalism. Second, some theorize that identity politics, alienation, discrimination, and humiliation explain why some well-off, educated young Muslims choose to construct a radical Muslim identity. Third, proponents of the social-affiliations theory suggest that radicalization occurs through social relationships like those of friendship, kinship, and discipleship. Fourth, others theorize that the marginalization of Muslim youth from mainstream politics and community, along with their inability to prevent this course of events, has driven many to seek representation through radical movements and groups. Fifth, still others theorize that the spread of Jihadi-Salafi rhetoric by preachers, texts, and media is responsible for radicalizing Muslim youth.[34] These theories were developed to account for the phenomenon of youth radicalization in the West. Yet they can also explain similar patterns and trends in the Muslim world and are not mutually exclusive.

Radicalization seems to be the result of not a single factor, but a combination of several interacting ones. Perhaps we need to problematize the very term "radicalization," as it is not clear what kind of transformation radicalized youth have undergone. "Radicalization" is a loaded and contested term. As I discuss in chapter 4, the concept is not universally understood in the same way. Despite a substantial increase in recent years in research on radicalization, many questions remain unanswered. For instance, we still do not know why radicalization flourishes in our society. Even what constitutes "radical views" as a category of religious radicalism seems to differ from one group to another or from one place to another, especially in the context of educated youth. A study by Diab Al-Badayneh on university students in Jordan revealed that 64.4 percent of respondents subscribed to radical beliefs, including martyrdom, jihad, hatred, and unity by force.[35] This category of "radical beliefs" may not be prevalent among radicalized students in Indonesia.

In light of this complex discourse on education and radicalization, in this book I discuss Muslim students' radicalization in contemporary Indonesia and the ways in which they developed intolerant and radical views and attitudes. In discussing and analyzing my findings, I benefit from insights that scholars in various fields have offered. This is a book that is truly built on diverse approaches and theories concerning religious intolerance and radicalization. There was a sound methodological imperative for my choice of Indonesia as the research focus. Indonesia is the largest Muslim-majority country that has had considerable success in deterring violent terrorism. Many observers have praised the country's successful transition to democracy. However, in the past few years Islam in Indonesia underwent what some scholars call a "conservative turn."[36] The growth of religious intolerance and youth radicalization in Indonesia is not unique, since the world seems to be increasingly violent and less free. Thus, while this study's focus is on Indonesian education institutions, the findings of this book have implications for the world well beyond Indonesia.

This book is divided into three parts. In the first I focus on the roots of religious intolerance among high school students. In the three chapters in that part I discuss various ways in which young Indonesians responded to and navigated diversity in the midst of the growing religious conservatism. I highlight questions such as these: What forces shaped their perception of others? What authorities did young people rely on when inquiring into alternate traditions? How did they balance their religious convictions with social realities? In the second part I explore how and why radicalization is a growing problem in universities. Because of the prevalence of higher education among individuals who have participated in radical groups and networks, a simple assumption has often been made: that the university is a significant hub or trigger of radicalization or its birthplace. In the next three chapters I problematize this assumption by exploring the ways in which radicalization tends to undergo a multitude of remarkable transformations from its inception, including self-deradicalization. In the two chapters of the last part of the book I compare the extent to which students of high schools and universities have been exposed to online radicalization and their engagement in hate speech. The Internet, and the use of social media in particular, has become a major tool in the radicalization of young people and the dissemination of hate speech, including antisemitic discourse. In the conclusion, I assert that educational institutions must ensure that students are safe from extremist materials both when accessing the Internet in schools and when interacting in their social networks.

PART ONE

Religious Intolerance at High Schools

ONE

Youth and Halfhearted Tolerance

Religious intolerance has become a global phenomenon. The Pew Research Center's Forum on Religion and Public Life has published surveys indicating an increase in prejudice and social hostility concerning religion in many countries, including Indonesia.[1] Myriad research institutions have reported cases of violence that threaten peaceful coexistence among different religious communities. Human Rights Watch (HRW), the International Crisis Group (ICG), the Setara Institute, and several other think tanks record various instances of violent action by radical groups in the country. For example, between 2010 and 2012, HRW confirmed a rise in violence targeting religious minorities. In its 2010 report, the Setara Institute recorded 216 acts of violence against minority groups. This increased to 244 cases in 2011 and 264 cases in 2012. Cases of majority pressure to restrict the practice of religious minorities, and even attacks on houses of worship, including vandalism and arson, have also increased each year.[2] These examples of religious intolerance are alarming. Some scholars contend that Indonesia is currently experiencing what some scholars call a "conservative turn,"[3] or "the end of innocence."[4] In the introduction to *Contemporary Developments in Indonesian Islam*, Martin van Bruinessen asserts that "the clearest expression of the conservative turn was perhaps given by a number of controversial fatwa (an Islamic verdict), authoritative opinions, issued by the Majelis Ulama Indonesia (MUI, Indonesian Council of Islamic Scholars)."[5] He refers to a fatwa issued by MUI in 2005 declaring secularism, pluralism, and liberalism prohibited (*haram*).[6] The more assertive role of Islam in public life, coupled with increasing intolerance toward religious others, has led scholars to argue that the conservative turn is a real issue. In an article published in *Pacific Affairs* (2014), political scientist Kikue Hamayotsu notes the increasing conservative trend in Indonesian Islam.[7] This shift toward conservatism affects the new generation, including high school students.

Large-scale research in secondary education, the focus of this chapter, has been conducted by several institutes, including the Setara Institute, Wahid Institute, and Center for the Study of Islam and Society (PPIM, Pusat Pengkajian Islam dan Masyarakat). In its 2016 survey of 171 private high schools (SMA, Sekolah Menengah Atas) in Jakarta and Bandung, the Setara Institute found that 5.8 percent of respondents favored replacing the state ideology of *Pancasila*, and 11.3 percent would support Indonesia's becoming an Islamic state. A 2017 survey by the Wahid Institute found that 40 percent of high school students who were involved in extracurricular Islamic activities, known as *Rohis* ("*Rohani Islam*," in English "Islamic spirituality"), admitted that they supported a cause to render Indonesia an Islamic state under the caliphate system. In the same year, PPIM released its extensive survey of 1,522 students from 34 provinces throughout Indonesia, which indicated that as many as 58.5 percent of students held religiously radical views. The survey also found that 34.3 percent of students had extremely intolerant views toward religions outside of Islam.[8] My research at twelve SMA involving 500 students in East Java, Indonesia, revealed a more nuanced picture. Although many students held intolerant attitudes toward certain issues, such as having non-Muslim leadership, giving Christians verbal Christmas greetings, or allowing interreligious marriage, almost all of them strongly supported the idea of tolerance. They expressed no problem with having friends from other religious traditions, in addition to vehemently rejecting the use of violence that has characterized radical groups.

This chapter discusses my findings regarding the views of young Indonesians about religious diversity. Indeed, the surveys of the Setara

Institute, the Wahid Institute, and PPIM have raised concerns about religious intolerance in Indonesia and how young Indonesians deal with interfaith issues. This discourse is undoubtedly crucial: it causes us to realize that the rise of conservatism and dogmatism affects youth, who are both targets and agents of this Islamic resurgence. The discovery of radicalization infiltrating campuses and schools also encourages teachers and policymakers to formulate strategies to address the growth of radicalization early in school. However, previous survey data fails to capture the dynamics of the views of young people on crucial issues that concern plural societies and the navigation of religious differences. My research combines quantitative and qualitative data, which allows us to better understand precisely how religious tolerance has been viewed and practiced in the daily lives of students. The goal of this study is to examine the views and practices of young Indonesians concerning religious diversity, and through this to explore not only their everyday practices,[9] but also the different ways in which they approach issues that concern them. As I argue in this chapter, without strong convictions and daily experience with interreligious relations, young people will embrace religious tolerance only halfheartedly. Therefore, my secondary goal in this chapter is to interrogate the utility of "contact theory" in reducing prejudice and fostering multicultural interaction among different religious communities in the modern context.[10]

RELIGIOUS DIVERSITY AND CONTACT THEORY

Indonesia is a multi-confessional state that recognizes six official religions: Islam, Protestantism, Catholicism, Hinduism, Buddhism, and Confucianism. Islam is the dominant religion, with 88 percent (around 220 million) of the population being Muslim. This makes Indonesia the largest Muslim-majority country in the world. It is not only religiously diverse; it is also a complex example of cultural diversity, with more than 375 ethnic groups, 700 languages, and the fourth-largest population on the planet, scattered across 6,000 inhabited islands. Administratively, it is divided into 34 provinces. Despite the extraordinary ethnic and religious diversity found across the archipelago, Indonesia has managed to maintain national unity.[11]

The Indonesian nation-state was built on the premise of its diversity, as articulated by the national motto, *Bhinneka Tunggal Ika* ("Unity in Diversity").[12] This motto is on the emblem of *Garuda Pancasila* ("Five Principles"),[13] the state ideology, which reflects its essential role in the country's social cohesion. It is studied in schools, is part of the public discourse, and is the primary guide for state policies. Since Indonesia achieved its independence on August 17, 1945, successive regimes have attempted to implement this motto to manage and maintain the peaceful coexistence of plural societies, mostly through imposing restrictive rules and regulations. To manage diversity, the first and second presidents (Sukarno and Suharto, respectively) adopted a centralized government with an emphasis on unity. The government often used military force to maintain the unity of Indonesia. Following more than three decades of authoritarian rule under Suharto, Indonesia has since 1998 undergone a successful democratic transition and consolidation to become the third-largest democracy in the world.[14] After Suharto Indonesia witnessed enthusiasm for democracy and the emergence of numerous political parties and diverse religious expressions, including radical ones.

In the late 1990s and early 2000s, outbreaks of sectarian and ethnoreligious violence in various regions across Indonesia placed national cohesion and management of diversity at the center of public debate, highlighting communal tensions and challenges for plural coexistence.[15] Although the frequency and severity of large-scale conflicts has decreased, a serious challenge facing Indonesian democracy and society is intolerance, which Sidney Jones says "is moving from the radical fringe into the mainstream."[16] To what extent religious radicalism has taken place in Indonesian Islam is a subject for discussion. As mentioned above, some scholars have shown an increase in evidence that mainstream Indonesian Islam has been undergoing a conservative turn, which has become more apparent in the past few years. The extent of the influence of the conservative turn can be observed in educational institutions, as a growing number of students exhibit intolerant attitudes toward other people of different religious backgrounds.

Therefore, it is understandable that much attention has been given in recent times to the role of multicultural education in promoting peace and tolerance in Indonesia. In particular, some scholars emphasize the importance of Islamic schools in designing curricula and teaching content that addresses religious pluralism, with religious education based on multicultural theology. Karen Bryner writes, "As levels of religious intolerance rise in Indonesia, it is important to look at Islamic schools that have developed within this revivalist period and ask how they shape their students' worldviews and subjectivities through intellectual and religious education."[17] Muhammad Zuhri argues:

> This is because, unlike public schools that are open to students of different religions, Islamic schools are religiously exclusive. Therefore, it is also necessary to broaden the meaning of religious education from only preserving certain religious beliefs and practices to include introducing the beliefs and practices of others. This, I believe, will lead future Muslim generations to not only preserve their religious faith and practices but also respect those of others. This will also lead the society to strengthen their national unity and have different religious communities live side by side peacefully.[18]

However, Zakiyuddin Baidhawy contends that exclusivist theology is not taught only in private Islamic schools. "Religious education in public and religious schools adopted an exclusive model," he writes, "teaching their own systems of religion or belief as the truth and the only path to salvation and regarding other religions as inferior."[19] According to Baidhawy, Indonesian schools during Suharto's time, both public and private, emphasized only the importance of harmony and unity and did not teach values that would lead to mutual respect, open-mindedness, interdependence, and peace. He writes, "When the state or schools teach about official religions, it means that education has failed to promote the values of democratic pluralism. By not teaching about the values of democracy, the state and the schools diminished the role of diversity and limited their pupils' and people's political freedom."[20] Both Zuhri's and Baidhawy's proposals are theoretical. The situation on the ground is more complicated than simply introducing interreligious content and values to students. Designing a curriculum of religious tolerance is one thing; the practice of tolerance is quite another. Erica Larson's ethnographic study of public and private religiously affiliated schools, both Catholic and Islamic, in North Sulawesi, Indonesia, shows the complex process of how high school students learn about and understand religious diversity as well as the impact on them of the public debate on how to respect and value differences within the national framework. Additionally, learning institutions often channel the national goals of education in their own ways through the formal curriculum and the daily reality of the schools. Describing how students negotiate the dynamic process of ethical deliberations, Erica Larson writes: "As young Indonesians navigate institutional policies and take classes in religious and civic education, they also make decisions about what to wear, whom to befriend, what to eat for lunch, whom to date, and in doing so engage in ethical deliberation about difference. Probing everyday interactions elucidates the types of moral registers in operation among Indonesian students, and allows for a delineation of the frameworks of coexistence that they undergird."[21] In many ways, my findings echo Larson's contention that educational institutions are not merely extensions of the state or mechanisms to reproduce a particular agency, ignoring the moment-to-moment contingency of education as a process. In this context, this chapter highlights how religious tolerance is navigated and practiced by students in their everyday lives. Admittedly, religious instruction is designed by the government to create a particular class of citizens. As a discursive apparatus of the state, education is also instrumentalized to form subjects who are loyal to the state. Therefore, according to Muhammad Zuhri, focusing on the role of a religious curriculum or a teacher "in shaping the religious perspective of Indonesian society,"[22] means following the "top-down" narrative and needs to be balanced with what Ben K. C. Laksana and Bronwyn E. Wood call "qualitative 'bottom-up' information about diverse religious Indonesian young people's everyday practices towards religious others and how they understand these encounters in the context of their lived religion, which is inseparable from their experiences of being a citizen of Indonesia."[23] Grounded in the notion of "lived religion" developed by such scholars as N. T. Ammerman, Meredith McGuire, and Daniel Levine,[24] Laksana and Wood have shown that many young people "draw on their everyday experiences of interacting with diverse religious peers and community members to establish their views on religious tolerance."[25] My findings tend to support this conclusion. Some students at Pamekasan High School in Madura admitted that they had never interacted with followers of other religions. Thus it was not surprising to find that they held prejudiced convictions toward others.

I argue that real encounters with religious others are essential in the realm of openness to religious diversity. Many scholars have found that contact between social groups is central to reducing prejudice and hostility among people of different religions and ethnicities.[26] Among young people, the importance of this intercultural and interfaith contact is even more apparent, as it is at their age that youths begin to show strong in-group preferences. Gordon Allport first introduced intergroup contact theory in his seminal work *The Nature of Prejudice*.[27] Allport developed contact theory based on the hypothesis that more frequent contact between different groups, including majority and minority, dominant and marginal groups, would abate prejudice and catalyze positive social outcomes. Allport's theory deserves to be quoted in its entirety:

> Prejudice (unless deeply rooted in the individual's character structure) may be reduced by equal status contact between majority and minority groups in pursuit of common goals. The effect is greatly enhanced by institutional supports (i.e., law, custom, or local atmosphere) and if such contact leads to the perception of common interest and common humanity between members of the two groups.[28]

Aside from equal contextual status, Allport added other conditions that ensure that the contact between various groupings might remove biases based on stereotyped views that contribute to prejudice. Those who meet these conditions must have good intentions and the ultimate goal of getting to know each other instead of finding fault with others. Therefore, contact must be intimate and authentic rather than superficial and impersonal. As mentioned in the quotation above, contact between groups must be sanctioned by the relevant authority. This last point is also emphasized by Thomas Pettigrew and Linda Tropp, who argue that institutional support is a critical condition for stereotype and prejudice reduction.[29] Therefore, social and institutional support must exist to help create a social climate in which tolerant norms can emerge.

Allport's contact theory has been widely used in relation to race, gender, disability, and ethnicity, with adults as well as with children.[30] Kaye adds that if students spend time together, they will learn more about each other and realize their similarities, while differences fade.[31] These sentiments are rarely found among the students examined in this book. It seems that there are obstacles to their meeting and associating with people of different religions. This is true in part because there are few to no non-Muslims in their schools or communities. It is also partly because parents prohibit such contact. Various studies have shown the positive impact of intergroup encounters. Marcus-Newhall and Heindl, for example, examined interracial school environments based on Allport's conditions of contact theory, revealing that children's self-esteem and self-reported academic performance were positively affected by contact with students of other races.[32] Michele Wittig and Sheila A. Grant-Thompson also used Allport's contact hypothesis and concluded that teachers likewise develop more positive attitudes toward the other when they teach students from different religions.[33]

For students to be wholeheartedly tolerant, convergence and interaction are necessary. Segregation and a lack of encounter are the origins of ignorance, and ignorance is the breeding ground for derogatory stereotypes and racial and religious hostilities. Biases based on stereotypes are lessened when members of two hostile groups meet, become accustomed to each other, and engage in some kind of cooperation. Over the past few decades, many scholars have revisited contact theory to examine the frequency and the various patterns of intercultural and interracial contacts at multicultural universities.[34] In the Indonesian context, Laksana and Wood have demonstrated that many students alter their perception of others after meeting and spending time with people they did not like before.[35] Of course, this does not discredit the importance of an inclusive understanding that supports coexistence.

The point to be stressed here is that tolerance requires interaction, encounter, and engagement, not segregation and isolation. Halfhearted tolerance emerges due to a lack of understanding of and acquaintance with others. However, the absence of encounter and interaction can also result in a reluctance to engage with others. Tolerance can be passive or active, and the notion of multicultural schooling needs to be concentrated toward active tolerance. Brian Leiter contends that tolerance is significant only when one group functionally engages with the other's existence, beliefs, and actions.[36] Indifference toward the other or members of a particular religion is not considered genuine tolerance in this framework, as it implies disfavor.[37] Tolerance (and intolerance) has been understood differently by different people. I will not delve into this debate, but suffice it to say that an authentic attitude of tolerance does not merely recognize diversity but also values it. It acknowledges differences and accepts them. However, as Torsten Knauth has argued correctly, there has to be some reason for passively or actively accepting (or even appreciating) the situation of difference.[38] My research findings, among other things, shed some light on these reasons.

ISSUES AND APPROACHES

Religious Tolerance

As mentioned above, the concept of tolerance and religious tolerance has been defined differently by different scholars. Some define it as the ability to exist with those of a religion with which one is in disagreement.[39] Others contend that the capacity to live alongside people of other religions is not sufficient. There has to be some acceptance of attitudes and actions that are different from those of one's own religion.[40] Despite these different conceptualizations, all have agreed on how important it is to develop tolerant attitudes toward the other, as no one today can live in isolation. Although the world has always been pluralistic, writes Walter Cardinal Kasper, "we experience this pluralism in a new way today; we are becoming more conscious of it than ever before, and we can no longer avoid the question of how to deal with it."[41] Thus, it is most likely that one will encounter people of other faiths or ethnicities in one's neighborhood or school and form friendships.

The present study involved 500 high school students who were asked about their perceptions of having friends from other religions, ethnicities, and political ideologies. The results can be seen in table 1.1.

TABLE 1.1. Students' responses to "Are you comfortable having friends from different religions/ethnicities/political ideologies?"

Categories	Comfortable	Indifferent	Uncomfortable
Different religions	59.6%	37.4%	3.0%
Different ethnicities	54.0%	44.2%	1.8%
Different political ideologies	33.4%	56.0%	10.6%

Note: n = 500; survey conducted in 2019.

TABLE 1.2. Students' responses to "Do you agree with the tolerant treatment of other students with different backgrounds?"

Attitudes	Percentage
Highly agree	57.8
Agree	29.2
Neutral/indifferent	7.0
Disagree	3.8
Strongly disagree	2.2

Note: n = 500; survey conducted in 2019.

It is apparent that the majority of students (59.6 percent) feel comfortable having friends from other religious traditions and that their discontent with peers of different religions is much less (3 percent) than it is with peers of different political beliefs (10.6 percent). This survey was conducted prior to the presidential election on April 17, 2019, so political tension was also felt among the students. It is interesting to note that the percentage of those who accept religious differences (59.6 percent) is also relatively higher than the percentage of those who accept different ethnicities (54 percent) and especially political differences (33.4 percent). When asked about the importance of tolerance toward other students with different backgrounds, the vast majority (87 percent) responded affirmatively, and only 6 percent of respondents disagreed (see table 1.2).

These results were confirmed by in-depth interviews with 50 students in which the students generally recognized the importance of tolerance in a plural society. Nuri (17 years old), from an SMA in Kediri, explained her views on the importance of tolerance as follows:

> In my opinion, tolerance is vital because we live with diversity. We have friends who are different from us. For instance, different religions, ethnicities, or tribes have different backgrounds that distinguish their views of life from us. Well, that difference, in my opinion, is not an obstacle or a threat to life. If we combine the same compassion among friends and fellow humans with the idea of tolerance, we can sympathize with others' lives. We would be able to respect each other, understand each other, and have a sense of belonging.

The significance of tolerance is agreed upon by all students for different reasons. Arman (18 years old), from an SMA in Kediri, emphasized that "tolerance is the key to living side by side with one another peacefully because our country is not inhabited by just one group." Coming from a public Islamic high school (MAN, Madrasah Aliyah Negeri) in Kediri, Susi (17 years old) interpreted tolerance as "respecting, not condemning, and considering others." He referred to the fact that "humans were created with diversity, and that, in my opinion, is a blessing." The comments of students from Surabaya are very positive, perhaps because Surabaya is a metropolitan city with a varied population distribution and is the second-largest city after the capital city, Jakarta. Arisa (15 years old), for example, believes that "diversity should be considered beautiful."

Most respondents choose friends who they believe will be "easy to talk to and connect with." Santi (15 years old), from an SMAN in Malang, explained the reasons for friendship as follows: "So far, I've never been picky about choosing friends. I can be friends with anyone. The important thing is that they're easy to talk to and connect with. The personal background is never a problem, because in my opinion it doesn't change anything, and it's cool if you have friends of different religions or other ethnic groups. I can learn a lot by sharing experiences." Here we see that the experience of encountering different forms of faith became a powerful learning experience for her. The same notion was stressed by Surya (15 years old), from an SMAN in Surabaya, who opens up when making friends: "I'm comfortable being friends with anyone," he said, "as long as they don't bother each other and instead respect each other. I open my friendship up to anyone." Sally (17 years old), from a Catholic school in Surabaya, described having close friends who used to spend time together frequently. I interviewed Sally in a church, and she said that she did not question the religious upbringing of her friends: "The important thing is to have similar interests and ideas because that way we can connect easily when talking."

When interviewed, some students stated that they had friends of different religions, whereas others did not. Initially, from a private high school in Pasuruan, Mila (16 years old) admitted to having non-Muslim friends in her class. She said, "Well, we often hang out with them. They're in my class. Maybe because it's a non-religious school, there is some diversity here, including in religion. And we are used to being different from one another." In contrast to Mila, Kurma (17 years old), from SMA 1 in Malang, said that she once had non-Muslim friends, but not anymore because "in my high school there are no (non-Muslim) classmates. If I were asked whether I like it, I'd say I just accept it." In Pamekasan in Madura, the situation is somewhat different because the number of non-Muslims and non-Mudurese ethnic groups is very small. The situation was explained by Fuad (15 years old), from a private SMA in Pamekasan, as follows: "I live among the same family and friends, not many outsiders, because we are all Islamic, we are all Madurese, and few friends outside of school are not Muslim. And in *pesantren* [traditional Islamic boarding schools], we are all followers of Islam." Similarly, Dulla (17 years old), from the same high school, earnestly said that he did not know how to describe religious tolerance: "I never had friends of different religions or races, so I don't know what it feels like. But maybe it's acceptable, as long as they don't cause any trouble." Madurese people are known to be strict in religious matters. This was felt by Saleh (16 years old), who, despite coming from the best high school in Pamekasan, admitted to not being accustomed to differences: "In addition to the pious lifestyle of a very religious community, our parents and my extended family also have deeply embedded religious values." Therefore, it is not surprising that Saleh felt reluctant to be close friends with people of different religions: "If it's just someone you know, it's okay. But, if you are close friends or study together, then no, because later it could be problematic." The necessity of tolerant boundaries was also emphasized by Kadir (17 years old), from an MA (Madrasah Aliyah, or private Islamic high school) in Kediri, who has always studied at *madrasah* and has never associated with people of different religions. He argued that tolerance is about doing no harm to others; however, in theological matters there is no tolerance. That is the limit of tolerance, he said. When asked to give examples of limits to tolerance, he called it *haram* (forbidden) to say "Merry Christmas" to Christians. It is interesting to note that Kadir strongly rejects radical extremism, such as suicide bombing, destruction of churches, and other violent actions, but he supports the establishment of a caliphate state.

Radical Extremism

Concern about youth radicalization is growing because Indonesian society is increasingly fearful of homegrown terrorism. Young people are vulnerable to recruitment by extremist organizations seeking to establish their ideal vision of society. My research confirms that high school students often access the websites of radical factions, although the majority (75.8 percent) claim to access the sites unintentionally, and only 9.2 percent access them deliberately. The remaining 11 percent of students admitted to being influenced by school peers, and 4 percent are influenced by teachers. When asked how often they access websites with radical content, 91 percent of students answered rarely or very rarely. In general, students are familiar with online radical content.

The good news is that although students often consume radical content, most of them (94.6 percent) are not interested in being involved with radicalism, and only 1 percent are deliberately involved—for example, by sharing radical content. Some 3.4 percent of students admit to agreeing or strongly agreeing with the existence of the Islamic State of Iraq and Syria (ISIS) (see table 1.3). However, when asked about their opinions of radical groups in Indonesia, the number of those who sympathized was quite high. Some 16.4 percent of students were sympathetic to the actions of radical groups in Indonesia, such as raiding hotels and liquor stores, forcing owners to close their stores during Friday prayers, and so on. The level of support for a caliphate was also high. When asked if they would agree to Indonesia's becoming a caliphate state, 10.4 percent answered affirmatively, 66.6 percent expressed discomfort, and 23 percent were uncertain of their support. Their rejection of violent extremism can also be detected in their view of suicide bombing other people's places of worship (81.8 percent disagreed).

To understand these dynamics, I conducted in-depth interviews and found recurring themes. For example, in general, the rejection of radical groups was very strong. Nuri from an SMA in Kediri, firmly stated: "Radicalism is very threatening and very dangerous for the Indonesian people. Why? Because, in my opinion, Indonesia already has an acceptable ideology, *Pancasila*. Right now, other ideologies should not be growing. If an [unfamiliar] ideology grows, not to mention extremism, it

TABLE 1.3. Students' responses to "Do you agree with the following issues?"

Categories	Highly Agree	Agree	Not Sure	Disagree	Strongly Disagree
Existence of the Islamic State of Iraq and Syria (ISIS)	1.8%	1.6%	6.0%	20.8%	69.8%
Establishment of a caliphate state	5.8%	4.6%	23.0%	31.0%	35.6%
Suicide bombing of other religious places of worship	1.0%	2.4%	4.8%	22.0%	69.8%

Note: n = 500; survey conducted in 2019.

would threaten the existence of the *Pancasila*, which has been our sacred heritage that has been very compatible with Indonesia's conditions and its diverse citizens." Arman added that radical groups are too coercive and will even use violence. This violence is clearly meant to oppose the existing conditions. Because the main objective of radical groups is over-coming *Pancasila*, Arman (the 18-year old from an SMA in Kediri) con-tinued: "The government should ban them." Some students claimed to be intrigued by the actions of radical groups broadcast by the media, and they sought further information via the Internet. After understand-ing the motivation of radicals' attacks, they became unsympathetic and believed the violence committed is not part of their religion. Soni (15 years old), from an SMA in Malang, said: "Honestly, I don't sympathize with radical things because the existence of radical groups can cause divisions. Isn't it the case that religion never taught us to hate other people?" Other students feel uncomfortable with radicalism because it tarnishes the reputation of Islam, and all students condemn terrorist acts committed in the name of religion. Anton, a Christian student (17 years old), from an SMA in Surabaya, explains:

> Terrorists have no relation to religion. In my opinion, terrorists are a kind of people that does brainwashing so that whatever is ordered must be obeyed; sometimes, they are in the name of the teachings of the Qur'an or other religious books. So they (terrorists), in my opinion, are wrong to claim that their principles (teachings) are

from religion, even though the teachings are distorted, and in [true] religion it is not permissible. Because in religion, it is unfathomable to kill people. As religious people, we must understand that the opponent is not from religion but the [terrorist] community. From my perspective, those who act in the name of Islam are wrong because in Islam there is nothing like that. In my opinion, there are also many terrorists from other religions . . . so in my opinion, what's wrong is the people, not religion.

Although the rejection of radical groups and their actions is quite strong, students' opinions on using violence to defend religion are quite different. Fuad (from a private SMA in Pamekasan) supported the actions of radical groups claimed to be in defense of Islam because he believes that Islam is the true religion. Other students from an SMA in Pamekasan fully support jihad in defense of religion because they believe it is God's command. Dulla (from an SMA in Pamekasan), for instance, contended that the duty to implement jihad is incumbent on every Muslim. He even openly wanted to join the FPI (Front Pembela Islam, or Islamic Defenders Front) and idolized its leader, Muhammad Rizieq Shihab. Regarding jihad, he said: "I really support jihad. Yes, in the Qur'an, it is explained that those who die as martyrs striving to defend religion in the way of Allah are guaranteed to go to heaven. I actually would like to if I could fight. Yes, that is the form of God's call to His servants."

Some students distinguish between radical actions and jihad. Desi (17 years old), from an SMA in Pasuruan, for example, considers radicalism synonymous with violence, while "jihad is certainly good, but without using violence." For her, people committing acts of violence, including suicide bombings, are not following religious teachings. Some students, such as Rudi (16 years old), from an SMA in Pasuruan, view jihadist groups as deviating from Islamic teaching. Rudi described coming from a religious family and said he was often taught stories of Islamic history. "Suicide and bombing are unlike the jihad at the time of the Prophet," he said. He also explained that the current situation is different from that at the time of the Prophet, when war was required to survive, whereas now, war is no longer necessary. From the conversation, it was clear that the problem is how acts of violence are considered jihad and, therefore, are considered Islamic. Under what conditions can jihad in the sense of taking up arms be justified? This question, undoubtedly, is subject to disagreement among scholars.

What about the caliphate? Is it a fundamental part of Islam or merely an Islamic political institution? Nearly all students who responded to the question about the caliphate did not explicitly reject this political system originating from Islam. What they disagreed on is whether Indonesia needs to be changed into a caliphate country and if so, why. Caliphate supporters usually believe that a caliphate would be good for Indonesia. As mentioned above, Kadir (from an SMA in Kediri) rejects radicalism because it stigmatizes Islam. Kadir thinks that a caliphate government not only upholds diversity but also provides legal stability. He said, "Whoever is guilty must be punished, and that will have a deterrent effect." He believes that a caliphate system would bring positive change to Indonesia. A student from a high school in Pamekasan believes that if a caliphate is upheld, justice will be created. He agrees with a caliphate system "because back then in the Prophet's time, it was also like that. This is in line with what was exemplified by the Prophet Muhammad. In my opinion, the caliphate system upholds justice, too, because lives must be paid for with lives. So that's fair."

Most students consider a caliphate to be incompatible with a pluralistic Indonesian society, even though they interpret it to be part of Islam. The following is the statement of Salman (18 years old), from an SMAN in Kediri, who confessed that he had never studied at an Islamic boarding school: "The caliphate is indeed Islamic teaching. I'm also sure that the teachings of the caliphate are the most correct. But I don't support it because Indonesia is a diverse country." Other students from Kediri said that a caliphate would cause Indonesia to be divided because the Indonesian population is not exclusively Muslim. Some students doubt that a caliphate would bring justice because the livelihoods of minorities would be marginalized. They believe the diverse and multicultural character of the Indonesian nation can be nourished only with *Pancasila*, not with the caliphate. Some students openly expressed their disagreement with the transnational Islamic movement Hizbut Tahrir Indonesia (HTI) because the caliphate ideology that they promote is in conflict with *Pancasila*. The following statement of a Pamekasan high school student summarizes the reasons why a caliphate is not suitable for Indonesia: "*Pancasila* is good; it can be accepted by many communities, which is not easily done. So there is no need to take away from the *Pancasila*, which has existed for decades. I would disagree with a caliphate state. Indonesia is predominantly Muslim; that is how it is. But it also has other communities that have different religions. Be respectful, that's how tolerance can advance."

Non-Muslim Leadership

Students' rejection of a caliphate by embracing *Pancasila* reflects their understanding that Indonesia is a multi-religious society. This willingness to embrace diversity can also be seen in their response to whether they support the nation's motto, *Bhinneka Tunggal Ika* ("Unity in Diversity"). Some 96 percent of respondents said that they agreed or strongly agreed with the notion of unity in diversity and only 2.6 percent disagreed; the rest (1.4 percent) were not sure. Interestingly, while most high school students emphasize the importance of religious tolerance, they seem reluctant to recognize the civil rights of non-Muslims, including their political rights to become leaders in Muslim societies. Non-Muslim leadership is a controversial issue about which many people in Indonesia are concerned. This is an issue that often arises when the elections of the heads of local governments (e.g., governors and regents) involve non-Muslims. The peak of controversy was the governor's election in Jakarta in 2017, in which one candidate, the incumbent, was a Christian named Basuki Tjahaja Purnama, nicknamed "Ahok." The Ahok controversy was complicated because it involved blasphemy accusations regarding Ahok's remarks about Qur'an 5:51, which is often interpreted as a prohibition of Muslims' choosing Christians or Jews as leaders. The heated discourse about non-Muslim leadership dominated the media, especially social media.

My research findings revealed that 59.6 percent of the students I surveyed either strongly agreed or somewhat agreed that leaders should always be Muslim, and only 24.8 percent either somewhat agreed or strongly agreed that non-Muslims should be permitted to become leaders (see table 1.4).

The percentage of students who objected to non-Muslim leadership was slightly higher than that found in a survey of the general population conducted by the Indonesian Survey Circle (LSI, Lingkaran Survei Indonesia), the Lembaga Survei Indonesia, which was conducted on a

TABLE 1.4. Students' responses to "Do you agree with strict Muslim leadership?"

Stance	No. of Responses	Percentages
Highly agree	148	29.6
Agree	150	30.0
Uncertain	78	15.6
Disagree	61	12.2
Strongly disagree	63	12.6

Note: n = 500; survey conducted in 2019.

TABLE 1.5. Responses to "Do you object to non-Muslims becoming . . . ?"

Categories	Object	Do Not Object	Depends	Don't Know/Not Applicable
President	59.1%	31.3%	8.2%	1.4%
Vice President	56.1%	34.2%	8.8%	0.9%
Governor	52.0%	37.9%	8.3%	1.8%
Mayor	51.6%	38.3%	8.5%	1.6%

Source: Indonesian Survey Circle (LSI), Lingkaran Survei Indonesia, 2019.

national scale in 2019 (59.1 percent). Table 1.5 illustrates the percentage of those who objected to non-Muslim appointments as vice president (56.1 percent), governor (52 percent), and mayor (51.6 percent). This is an increase from surveys conducted by LSI in 2016 (48 percent), 2017 (53 percent), and 2018 (59 percent).[42]

The rejection of non-Muslim leadership among students, in general, is based on the belief that the Qur'an forbids Muslims to follow non-Muslim leaders. The statement of Imran (17 years old), from a private SMA in Pamekasan, is reasonably representative of the views of students who reject non-Muslim leadership based on the Qur'an: "On matters of leadership, it should be from the Muslims themselves because the leader must be from our own people. In the Qur'an, it has been explained that people must choose leaders from their group. Because I believe in the Qur'an, I refuse non-Muslims leaders." Some students consider non-Muslim leadership in Muslim-majority communities strange because only a Muslim leader would be knowledgeable about the lives of Muslims. Other students from Imran's school said that it would be more acceptable to choose a leader of the same religion. They asked a rhetorical question, "If Muslims aren't the leaders of Muslims, then who else?"

There is also discourse surrounding the psychology of the leaders themselves. Salma (16 years old), from an SMA in Malang, for example, asked: "What about regulations or policies that come from Islam? The non-Muslim leader may be rather uncomfortable if policies don't come from his religion but are [still] his responsibility." Here we see that some students use the majority-minority notion to reject the leadership of minority groups. Other students from the same school reinforced their arguments by looking at Muslim society's current status quo. Karim (16 years old), from an SMA in Malang, explained his agreement with strictly Muslim leadership as follows: "If I were to disagree, the problem would be that despite having an Islamic leader, Islam is still being trodden on. Now, what if the leader weren't Muslim?" This student claimed to dislike political matters, but at home often heard his mother and father discuss the Ahok controversy.

Among those who approve of non-Muslim leadership, it seems that none of them proposed a different interpretation of the Qur'anic verses used as a reference by those who disapprove. They provided reasons from outside of religious texts, referring, for instance, to the Indonesian constitution, which gives all citizens the right to vote and be elected. Arman (from an SMA in Kediri) stressed the importance of adhering to the principles of *Pancasila*. He said: "Well, if the leader is always supposed to be a Muslim, I don't like it because it could turn radical. Because our country adheres to *Pancasila*, anyone should be able to become a leader. If anyone says the leader should be a Muslim, then that is against *Pancasila*. They have a radical mentality." Many students emphasized that the criteria for choosing leaders should not be ethnicity, religion, race, or class, also known by the SARA acronym (Suku, Agama, Ras, and Antargolongan), but rather competence. Feni (from SMA 3 in Malang) declared that leaders could be Muslim if they are kind and charismatic, but "not all of them are. After all, if there is a non-Muslim who has a better character and can lead more effectively than a Muslim, then why not choose the non-Muslim?" Many students expressed concern about corruption of state officials. This can be better understood in light of the numerous state officials—from members of the House of Representatives (DPR, Dewan Perwakilan Rakyat) to officials in various ministries—who on many occasions have been arrested by the Corruption Eradication Commission (KPK, Komisi Pemberantasan Korupsi) due to their involvement in acts of corruption. Concern about corruption is directly tied to the qualifications of leaders. On this point, Rama (16 years old), from SMAN 1 in Pasuruan, commented:

> When looking at the current status quo, many Islamic leaders are actually doing corruption, and I dislike this. My opinion is that those who are non-Muslims are less likely to be corrupt and more likely to be disciplined. The evidence for this comes from many cases in ministries, parties, and institutions that have been dominated by Muslims. Also, there was this leader of an Islam-based party who was also caught [committing corruption]. So leaders don't have to be Islamic. The most important thing is being honest and competent.

Many students said that they were uncertain about whether they believed leadership should be in the hands of Muslims. In the quantitative data shown in table 1.4, it can be seen that the percentage of those who are uncertain is quite large (15.6 percent). Uncertainty can be attributed to suspicion regarding news circulating on social media or cases in which Muslim leaders' actions contradict their personal beliefs—after all, when Muslim leaders act corruptly, they seem thereby to discredit the narrative that Muslim leaders must always be fair and just. Rudi (from the SMA in Pasuruan), for example, agrees with the view that leadership should be Muslim. A Muslim population, he said, should be led by someone of the same religion because such a leader would undoubtedly know what is best for predominantly Muslim society. However, he also realizes that many Muslim leaders, both legislators and heads of regional governments, were involved in corruption cases and other violations of law. "What should I do," he asked doubtfully, "if it turns out that non-Muslims govern well without any corruption?" He closed the conversation about non-Muslim leadership with the words "I'll just choose what's best for the people."

HALFHEARTED TOLERANCE

In this chapter I have explored the various ways in which young Indonesians have understood and dealt with religious diversity in their daily lives. Indonesia is a good testing ground for research on the changing dynamics of civic plurality because of its diverse religions and cultures, with more than three hundred different ethnicities and languages and more than six thousand islands. In 2006, the Freedom House ranked Indonesia as a "free" country. However, since 2010 Indonesia's civil liberties rating has declined to "partly free" due to the increase in restrictions on religious freedom as well as an increase in social hostilities. In the last few years, several surveys have shown that intolerant ideologies have also infiltrated many universities and schools. These developments are undoubtedly setbacks for religious pluralism. However, it is not clear how and to what extent religious conservatism and intolerance have taken root among Indonesian youth. How are we to navigate the ways in which religious (in)tolerance has been understood and practiced?

My findings show that young Indonesians embrace religious tolerance halfheartedly. This was illustrated significantly by the combination of their strong support for religious tolerance and peaceful coexistence and their vehement rejection of radicalization, paired with a stubborn intolerance when it comes to sensitive issues of interreligious relations in society, such as giving verbal Christmas greetings and having non-Muslim leadership. Some youth are unable to respect or accept completely different beliefs and practices without prejudice.[43] What seems to be missing in halfhearted tolerance is care and hospitality. Care is usually rooted in a deep commitment to engage with diversity and a genuine acceptance of differences as they are. In this sense, according to Maitumeleng Albertina Ntho-Ntho and Jan F. Nieuwenthuis, "the presence of this element of caring signifies the absence of indifference."[44] At the same time, the concept of hospitality refers to pure and unconditional openness to welcoming the other. In theological terms, hospitality here is understood as the ability to recognize and integrate the truth of other religious traditions into one's own tradition. In Catherine Cornille's view, this recognition of truth in other religions "presupposes some humility about the truth of one's tradition, commitment to a tradition which exercises hospitality, a general sense of interconnectedness between religions, and genuine understanding of the other."[45] Based on my research, it seems clear that serious effort is needed to promote wholehearted tolerance, including the implementation of curricula that reflect a multicultural theological perspective, without neglecting the practical dimensions of care and hospitality. In other words, normative knowledge that becomes an obstacle to embracing religious tolerance wholeheartedly must be transformed. At the same time, there is also a need to intensify interreligious or intergroup encounters.

My study has also highlighted the relationship between accepting tolerance as a prerequisite for harmony in living with one another and rejecting the radicalism that threatens the pillars of the Indonesian nation's solidarity and unity. There seems to be a strong consensus among youth that living peacefully with others is a shared vision, while religious intolerance is part of the problem hindering the goal of creating a more peaceful world. Of course, it is imperative to nourish this consensus among youth by fostering friendships and interpersonal connections that reflect a diversity of ethnicities, cultures, races, and religions, because this will help erode prejudicial biases. In the context of racial problems, Christopher G. Ellison and Daniel A. Powers, for example, show that when interracial contact occurs early in life, it is more likely that Caucasians and people of color will be able to develop closer friendships.[46] This was affirmed by Anthony L. Antonio, who shows that the character of one's friendships "depends on previous socialization as well as the current social context, and can vary as a social construct linked to culture, social position, or intergroup relations."[47] The fact that the vast majority of high school students claim to have no problem with friends of different religions or races is a positive sign. Parallel to a positive view of religious tolerance, young Indonesians perceive radicalism and intolerant violence as bringing harm to all societies, creating divisions instead of unity.

The problem is that certain religious narratives followed by youth make it impossible for them to be wholeheartedly tolerant with care and hospitality. This is evident from the two cases discussed in detail in this chapter: those of giving verbal Christmas greetings and approving of non-Muslim leadership. The widespread intolerance in both cases springs out of religious instruction by conservative religious teachers in schools, as well as Qur'an teachers (*ustadh*s) and parents. Although religious authorities have diversified in the modern era, students still tend to

adhere to a one-sided conservative perspective. Through in-depth interviews, I found only one student who sought a more progressive outlook.
If Indonesia really wants to develop a multicultural education model,
as outlined by Baidhawy,[48] it should also provide spaces for different
voices, including those of people who follow alternate interpretations
of specific religious texts. Regarding Christmas greetings, for example,
students following the guidance and direction of their religious teachers
firmly conclude that such matters are forbidden in the Qur'an. In reality, no verse makes any explicit judgment regarding the issue, and both
classical and modern scholars have a spectrum of views. Likewise, the
question of non-Muslim leadership is still subject to discussion among
Muslim scholars. The controversy over Qur'an 5:51 that brought Ahok
to court was politically charged. This verse is likewise understood differently by different scholars. If we look at the history of non-Muslim
involvement in the early Islamic state, we find several cases in which
non-Muslims held strategic positions in the caliphate. It could be argued
that the appointment of non-Muslims to public office has already been a
long-established policy of the state.[49]

Of course, in a religious culture, it is difficult for the younger generation to respect and fully accept the views and political rights of
people of different religions if theological obstacles still limit tolerance.
Therefore, normative work that implements a multicultural theological
perspective, as proposed by Baidhawy, is quite relevant. However, the
lack of interreligious and intercultural contact is also a serious problem in some schools, including universities. Although Indonesia is
renowned as one of the world's most diverse countries, many schools
(mostly religious institutions) exclusively accept students from only one
religion. Some students have admitted to never having non-Muslim
friends because there were no non-Muslims in their schools or neighborhoods. According to several studies using Allport's framework, the
stigma associated with religious, racial, and ethnic others can hardly be
reduced without real encounters. It is not unusual that people's interactions with religious others, new ideas, or new ways of thinking can
cause them to question their own beliefs, values, and ways of seeing.
Nonetheless, there is no question that prejudice reduction and religious
tolerance are necessary goals for any multicultural society that aspires
to function harmoniously.

CONCLUDING REMARKS

This study concentrates on interventions aimed at high school students because evidence reveals that suspicions and hostilities intensify at this age, whether for the first time or due to the accumulation of previous prejudices.[50] At this stage of identity formation, adolescents experience insecurity about their individuality and beliefs. Consequently, they may adopt a mentality of intolerance as a defense against their identity confusion. My research has found that the experience of interacting with people of other religions has had a profound impact in promoting a culture of openness and an attitude of inclusiveness. Some young people are open to having non-Muslim friends not because they were introduced to an entirely inclusive view but because of their daily experiences with interreligious connections. For example, if their friends of other religions wish them a happy Eid, invite them to hang out, or help them with homework; if their neighbors attend both religious and non-religious events and they mutually offer food to each other, it is unlikely that they will continue to be exclusivist in their theological views. This means that views about the religious other are more complex than a mere epistemic issue. Through intergroup interactions, students can renegotiate their perspectives and intuitions.

In addition to educational environments (educational curricula and teacher roles), this study has explored the extent to which friendship influences the development of young people, whether in the moral-cognitive realm or in terms of social interaction. It should be noted that there has been extensive research on several aspects of adolescent friendship, including issues pertaining to well-being,[51] social competence,[52] parent-child attachment,[53] and gender differences in friendships.[54] These studies, primarily focusing on interracial, intergroup, or interethnic relations, reveal that youths' establishment of close friendships with people of different groups can promote positive attitudes and behavior.[55] The role of social networks in shaping high school students' views of others will be discussed in the next chapter. It suffices to say, with Laksana and Wood, that "relational interactions across religiously diverse people helped inform and establish young people's inclusive citizenship, actions, and identities."[56] Other scholars, like Bruce R. Norquist, come to a similar conclusion. In his research on the relationship between the engagement of students with otherness and faith development in evangelical higher education, Norquist found that "students who operated at a low level of faith development reported much fewer exposures to diverse ways of thinking and much less extensive multicultural exposure."[57] This reinforces Gay Holcomb's conclusion that interaction with otherness is a significant impetus in faith development.[58] In line with these findings, my study suggests that normative work and relational interaction must go hand in hand.

TWO

The Influence of Social Networks
on Religious Tolerance

As I concluded in the previous chapter, the Indonesian high school students I surveyed tended to embrace religious tolerance halfheartedly. Their views of the other cannot be traced back to a single factor since the formation of any attitude is a multidimensional process. In this chapter I examine what shapes the views of young people and their attitudes toward others who are different from them. What and who most influenced their views of the other? Obviously, to focus exclusively on one factor would result in misleading information. In this chapter I will identify a variety of factors that shape the openness or hostility of young people toward the other. More specifically, I will illuminate the role of various social networks in shaping religious tolerance and intolerance among high school students in Indonesia in their interactions with one another and in the way they develop either positive or negative attitudes toward people of different backgrounds. The main finding of this study suggests that social networks—in this case, networks of peers and friends—play a pivotal role in shaping the views and attitudes of Indonesian high school students. Compared to more fundamental questions of identity, such as ethnicity, religion, race, or ideology, common interests, hobbies, and social compatibility seem to be more important considerations in the social relationships of young people. Additionally, encounters with informal religious authorities outside of schools and social media also play important roles in shaping their openness or hostility toward others.

The intensification of interaction and intermingling between people of different groups, races, ethnicities, or religions is one of the essential characteristics of the modern age. Wherever we live and find ourselves, we will encounter people of varying cultural, ethnic, racial, and religious backgrounds. Whether it be at shopping centers, in housing complexes, workplaces, or schools, diversity is apparent. It is self-evident that increased intergroup relations and harmony are absolute necessities for multicultural societies. To realize social harmony in multicultural societies, it is indispensable to develop strategies to facilitate interpersonal relationships. Adolescence is the appropriate developmental stage for such intervention because diversity is learned and experienced from an early age. Several recent studies focused on high school students because evidence shows that prejudice becomes intensified at this age, whether it is occurring for the first time or represents the resurgence of earlier attitudes.[1] One of the recurring issues is the process of identity formation during adolescence and young adulthood,[2] including attitudes toward diversity in religions, cultures, and ethnicities, whether they are open or hostile. According to Eric H. Erikson's development theory, adolescents are prone to hostile attitudes because they feel insecure about who they are and what they believe, leading them to fall back on intolerance of differences as a defense against their confusion.[3] Consequently, strategies to facilitate interpersonal relationships, including peer-group interventions, are particularly significant.

Although the importance of promoting open attitudes in high school students has been recognized, research on adolescence and religious diversity has been dominated by findings from mainstream Christian youth in Western countries, particularly in the United States.[4] In this chapter I investigate what shapes young people's openness or hostility to others and how the social networks of high school students play a role in the ways they interact with one another and develop positive or negative attitudes toward the other. Some of the guiding questions of this chapter are these: How do Indonesian youths view religious tolerance? What forces shape their views and attitudes? What categories do they use to determine the boundaries of their and others' communities (i.e., how do they determine who is close and distant)? What authorities do they rely on when inquiring into other traditions, and how do they resolve competing claims to authority?

RELIGIOUS EDUCATION AND SOCIAL NETWORKS

While religious and ethnic diversity and the various threats to the two in Indonesia have been the subject of extensive discussion,[5] the role of schools in encouraging or inhibiting coexistence has received much less attention, despite the clear fact that the next generation plays a critical role in the future of the nation's livelihood. Several studies have honed in on the role of *pesantren* in preparing the next generation to adapt to the trials of modern life, including religious diversity.[6] For instance, Florian Pohl argues that the response of *pesantren* to modernity has been more nuanced and imaginative than is commonly assumed. According to the wisdom of secularization theory, traditional Islamic institutions like *pesantren* are poised to become irrelevant. In reality, instead of retreating into religious subculture, contemporary *pesantren* strategies are often marked by a creative accommodation of the social and educational demands with which they find themselves confronted. Many *pesantren* have reacted to these challenges by altering their educational structure. Some have introduced teaching methods with grading systems commonly applied at state schools but have retained the religious nature of their instruction. Others have gone a step further, taking up the teaching of secular subjects in addition to the religious curriculum. Moreover, the traditional *ulama* (Muslim scholars) have proven to be able to play a role in enhancing civility in a heterogenous society.[7] In a similar vein, Ronald Lukens-Bull has demonstrated the ability of *pesantren* to negotiate creatively between tradition and modernity.[8]

Another strand of scholarship focuses on civic and religious education in contemporary Indonesia.[9] These studies assess religious education as a positive contribution to the development of democracy and multiculturalism. The overarching concern of these studies is determining how multicultural education might best prevent and avert the conservatism and intolerant inclinations currently on the rise in Indonesia. In the past few years, religious intolerance has elevated globally, including in Indonesia, the third-largest democracy in the world. Surveys by the Institute of Peace and Islamic Studies (LAKIP 2012), the Setara Institute (2016), the Wahid Institute (2016), and the Center for the Study of Islam and Society (PPIM 2018) reveal that young Muslims have been implicated in holding extreme, intolerant views toward religions outside of Islam. These findings lead Ben K. C. Laksana and Bronwyn Wood to ask "how the younger generation will deal with inter-religious relations and issues of religious intolerance within Indonesia."[10] Looking closely at how young people have navigated religious diversity in their daily lives, Laksana and Wood conclude that "their everyday lived experiences of religious diversity significantly shaped and reinforced their citizenship values and actions" in such a way that some of them "were highly critical of the narrowness or rigidity of their religious and citizenship education experiences and were dissatisfied withholding these as the only frameworks for approaching religious tolerance in their daily lives."[11]

Teguh Wijaya Mulya and Anindito Aditomo identify three factors in religious education that have enabled students to develop tolerance of civic culture and other religions: the narrative of nationalism based on the Indonesian motto *Bhinneka Tunggal Ika* ("Unity in Diversity"), the development of civic pluralism based on tolerant theology, and tolerant interfaith practices.[12] While Künkler and Lerner emphasize the relationship between education and democracy,[13] Muhammad Zuhri examined the content of Islamic religious education and how teachers have presented it to students. While the content of Islamic curricula can be interpreted to support "both moderate and conservative understandings of Islam," Zuhri argues that "religious education teachers situate religion into the very complex structure of today's society."[14] For his part, Zakiyuddin Baidhawy, in his article "Building Harmony and Peace through Multiculturalist Theology-Based Religious Education," calls for the implementation of a multicultural theological perspective "that respects the diversity of others; it is a theological interpretation of the religious, cultural and ethnic identity of others."[15] Baidhawy strongly believes that multicultural theology provides an important framework for peaceful coexistence "supported by a spirit of equality and equity, mutual trust, mutual understanding and respect for the similarities and differences among religions, and a firm belief in the unique insight of each religion."[16] He writes, "Religious education is an important instrument in implementing the framework of the multiculturalist theological perspective. Religious education in a context where both the intensity and the acceleration of plurality are continuing has to assert the end of a dogmatic approach and the strategy of indoctrination in the teaching-learning process."[17] Here Baidhawy's emphasis is on normative work that enables religious doctrine to be interpreted in light of contemporary realities or "the interplay between sacred texts and changeable social context."[18]

The conviction that education can help in promoting more robust discourse surrounding multiculturalism and religious tolerance is also expressed by Lyn Parker. In her article "Religious Education for Peaceful Coexistence in Indonesia?" Parker contends that, because Indonesia is a religious state and religion is central to education in Indonesia, "it is reasonable to propose that Indonesia should address the growing problem of religious intolerance through the teaching and practice of religion in schools."[19] However, unlike Baidhawy, who proposes that an exclusivist theology remains a serious obstacle to interreligious relations in Indonesia, Parker is in favor of a "non-theological" or "non-confessional" paradigm in directing religious education in Indonesia for two reasons. First, nearly all Indonesians identify with a religion, and many are strongly religious. They do not lack religious knowledge. Therefore, religious education "must be practical and useful for young people who will operate in a social world."[20] Second, respect and active tolerance can be derived from the virtues deeply rooted in the Indonesian state's philosophy, namely *Pancasila* (Five Principles). "This is a model of good citizenship," Parker writes, "that uses the ideology of the nation-state, the *Pancasila*, rather than within-faith teachings."[21]

While the emphasis on the practice of religious diversity rather than theology is helpful, we should not underestimate the importance of what Baidhawy calls a "multicultural theological perspective." If someone considers devotees of other religions "heretics" and "infidels" and association with such people injurious to their faith, how can interfaith coexistence be promoted and taught on theological grounds? True, to live in harmony, the followers of a religion do not have to abandon the principles they possess. Tolerance does not necessitate that adherents to each religion consider other religions as truth; tolerance will be stable if it is built on the foundation of faith. As I will discuss later in detail, many young Indonesians who consider religious tolerance essential do not dare to say "Merry Christmas" to Christians, for example, because their teachers teach them that Christmas greetings are contrary to Islamic beliefs. Of course, we understand that religious formation is not enough. Here what is important is combining normative tolerance and practical tolerance so that adolescents might respond to religious diversity from their whole persons.

Without dismissing the role of schoolteachers, it can be argued that students' social networks have a profound impact on how they develop their attitudes—positive or negative, open or hostile—toward cultural diversity. Additionally, their ability (or lack thereof) to interact and intermingle may shape their views of the other. Keeping in mind the diversity of students' social networks, we understand that the identity, outlook, and behavior formation processes of youth occur in a highly complicated manner that involves more than teachers' commitment and school culture. The results of the research show that, aside from teachers at school, students also tended to refer to "teachers" outside their schools whom they perceived as role models and guides in living their personal and social lives. This phenomenon suggests that the religious authorities on whom students rely when they inquire into religious others are undergoing diversification.[22] As explicated by Gudrun Krämer and Sabine Schmidtke, "religious authority can assume several forms and functions: the ability (chance, power, or right) to define correct belief and practice, or orthodoxy and orthopraxy, respectively; to shape and influence the views of others accordingly."[23]

In addition to educational environments, some studies also investigated the extent to which friendship influences young people's development, whether in the moral-cognitive realm or that of social interaction. As discussed in the previous chapter, interracial, intergroup, or interethnic relations and the ability of young people to establish close friendships with those of different groups has proven influential in shaping positive attitudes and behaviors.[24] It is not possible for inquiries into social networks that affect youths' tolerance or lack thereof to ignore the factor of friendship, mainly because high school age is crucial to their figuring out how friendship networks are formed. Additionally, the earliest environment in which young people interact, namely that of their families, is another element of their social networks worth noting.

For this reason, rather than focusing on one singular factor that shapes open or hostile attitudes, in this chapter I draw on social network theory to illuminate how young people construct their perspectives and attitudes in a society that is diverse in religion, ethnicity, race, or culture. Social network theory analyzes how the social structure of a relationship between people impacts their beliefs and behaviors. Relations, links, and ties are the basic units of the analysis and are fundamental to the social network approach. Social network analysis assumes that people are interdependent rather than independent and that network structure provides opportunities for and constraints on individual action.[25] Stephen Borgatti and Brandon Ofem argue that relationships within social networks can constrain or provide opportunities for the people involved.[26] Borgatti and Ofem also hold that when looking at people's views and attitudes in a social network environment, network theorists observe the personal factors associated with these people and their relations that allow them to expand or confine such views and attitudes.

In this chapter I discuss how the views and attitudes of young people toward other groups do not emerge in isolation and are not caused by a singular factor, as in the school educational model. Rather, they are conditioned within and influenced by social networks and relationships. Drawing on empirical data, in this study I aim to explore how high school students see the crucial issues of the modern world, notably issues of tolerance and a positive attitude toward diversity and multiculturalism. Indeed, this study has a limitation, as it focuses only on high school youths, which prevents it from being applied to adult social networks in general. The methodological strength of this research is that I recorded what the respondents and informants themselves conveyed concerning not only their views and attitudes, but also what and who influenced and shaped their perspectives and attitudes. Based on a survey involving 500 students and in-depth interviews with 50 students, this chapter presents my research findings and conclusions.

WHAT SHAPES THE VIEWS OF YOUNG PEOPLE?

The views of young people on groups of different religions, ethnicities, or political ideologies—whether open or hostile, tolerant or prejudiced—are influenced by complex factors. Those factors can be individual or of a sociocultural nature. On the one hand, several studies on intergroup attitudes in adolescence point out the means by which adolescents acquire their views of others. Megan O'Bryan, Harold D. Fishbein, and D. Neal Ritche, for instance, acknowledge the role played by parents in transmitting prejudice and stereotypes.[27] On the other hand, other scholars emphasize concrete interactions and the choices of friendships as catalysts through which young people develop their attitudes.[28] However, others contend that intergroup friendship is not a crucial factor. Instead, they argue for "the need to focus on 'individual inclination' as variables that are capable of influencing the choice of friendships."[29] On the other hand, some scholars, including Colleen Ward, Anne-Marie Masgoret, and Michelle Gezentsvey, argue that intergroup attitudes "may be affected by broader contextual factors" such as "the characteristics of the groups in contact, the educational institutions in which they are enrolled, the community in which they reside, and even national-level economic and political circumstances."[30]

It seems safe to say that adolescents acquire and develop their views on and attitudes toward others in ways that cannot be attributed to isolated factors, either individual or sociocultural. It is worth noting that the literature on the relations and attitudes of people with one another focuses primarily on negative aspects of intergroup relations, such as causes of prejudice or social stereotyping. For example, several studies have examined the nature of threats members of majority groups fear that can cause hostility toward minority groups.[31] Reflecting on the current literature, Rebecca S. Bigler, John M. Rohrbach, and Kiara L. Sanchez write: "Such a focus is understandable given the enormous human costs associated with hostile intergroup relations and attitudes, including war and violence. Less attention has been directed at identifying the persons and contextual variables associated with positive intergroup relations (i.e., affectionate, trusting, supportive, and close relationships with outgroup individuals) and attitudes."[32] Even less attention has been given to how young people experience openness and hostility toward the other. It is intriguing to discuss how youths choose friends and what considerations affect those choices. For instance, is being of the same religion a central criterion for their friendships? How should they treat the other in a political context? What constitutes tolerance for them, and what is its limit? My research findings confirm the findings of previous studies that revealed that inter-group and interreligious friendships could promote positive attitudes and behaviors. Generally speaking, the high school students I studied under-stood tolerance positively, but they also drew boundaries of tolerance that could not be trespassed. We will discuss their rationales for interacting with the other and how they referred to particular sources of authority.

FRIENDSHIP AND RELIGIOUS TOLERANCE

As youth transition from childhood to adolescence, friendship increases in importance. As a result, they often seek and go to friends instead of parents for the confidence of feelings, companionship, intimacy, and even support.[33] In comparison to their younger counterparts, adolescents report expecting less support from their parents and more support from their friends.[34] They spend more than twice as much time with friends as with their parents.[35] According to Jeffrey Jensen Arnett, more than 70 percent of youth he studied conveyed that they learned about life more from their close friends than from adults and that their close friends understood them better than adults. In a nutshell, friendships play a vital role in healthy adolescent development.[36]

Among high school students, there is a tendency to choose friends based on specific considerations, which recalls what Wyndol Furman and Duane Buhrmester refer to as "friendship networks," that is, networks of friends that encompass confidential discussions and social support, in which young people usually exchange important and privileged infor-mation with each other.[37] According to Penelope Eckert, high school students are more likely to be in academic classes and extracurricular activities than their peers who share similar interests and values com-pared to them during elementary school.[38] As can be seen in table 2.1, my examination of 500 high school students revealed that sharing the same religion was not a dominant factor in choosing friends, and only 3.4 percent of respondents considered sharing the same religion when choosing close friends at school. Two predominant factors were "Fun to talk with" (36.8 percent) and "S/he is good-natured" (32.2 percent).

When asked about the boundaries they set in friendships with those of different faiths, the vast majority felt comfortable with having

TABLE 2.1. Students' responses to "What are your considerations when choosing close friends at school?"

Considerations	Percentage
Fun to talk with	36.8
Same religion	3.4
S/he is good-natured	32.2
No particular consideration	27.6

Note: n = 500; survey conducted in 2019.

TABLE 2.2. Students' responses to "How comfortable are you with having friends of other religions in the following manner?"

People of Other Religions as …	Comfortable	Indifferent	Uncomfortable
Close friends	57.2%	38.0%	4.8%
Boyfriends/girlfriends	10.4%	33.4%	56.0%
Deskmates	48.8%	45.8%	5.4%
Friends to study together at home	47.6%	48.4%	4.0%
Friends for sleepovers	27.0%	51.0%	22.0%
Friends for hanging out at shopping malls	45.8%	45.4%	8.8%

Note: n = 500; survey conducted in 2019.

people of other religions as friends in all types of relationships except for courtship (see table 2.2). For instance, 57.2 percent of respondents felt comfortable with having friends of other religions, and only 4.8 percent said they were uncomfortable. However, 56 percent of the respondents admitted that they were uncomfortable with having a boyfriend/girlfriend of a different religion. This finding is perhaps attributable to the firm belief among Muslims in Indonesia that both Islamic and positive laws disallow interreligious marriage. Following the introduction of Islamic law into Indonesian family law in 1991, interreligious marriage is no longer recognized by state law and cannot be registered with the state. However, the 1974 marriage law does not regulate interreligious marriage. Hence, a couple from different religions can register their marriage under civil law. In 1980, however, the Council of Indonesian Ulama (MUI) issued a fatwa banning Muslims from marrying non-Muslims. The "Muslim aspiration" urge forced Suharto's regime at the end of his term to promulgate a compilation of Islamic laws, including one that forbids interfaith marriages. It appeared that this reality affected the way the students in my study viewed interreligious courtship.

Our informant Rudi (16 years old), from SMA 1 in Pasuruan, shared why he did not have a girlfriend of a different religion. He revealed that he was from a religious family and had a belief that interreligious courtship is not allowed in Islam. "Let alone interreligious dating," he said. "My parents are even against me having a girlfriend of the same religion." Despite attending a general school not affiliated with Islam, Rudi said he never had any friends of different religions. He also described his family at home, who, in his opinion, were somewhat reserved in the sense of not interacting with neighbors with different religious backgrounds. "When I go out, usually, it is because I am told to attend Islamic study forums [*pengajian*] at the mosque," he went on saying.

One informant confessed to having had a non-Muslim boyfriend and opined that interreligious marriage should not be banned because in matters of love people do not regard religious or ethnic backgrounds. Santi (17 years old), from an SMA in Kediri, was fairly active at school. For instance, she participated in student organizations' activities, allowing her to be familiar with friends of different religions. "Knowing and meeting different people is fun," Santi said. She was very appreciative of her ex-boyfriend, who was kind and understanding. When they were in a romantic relationship, religious matters were never an issue to either of them. She stated:

> I had a boyfriend who was not of the same religion as mine, but I never thought of such a difference as something strange. We reminded one another to observe worship according to our religions. For example, when it was time for prayer, he would remind me, and on Sundays, when it was time for him to go to church, I would remind him. But it was only known to my circle; my parents had no idea about it. I did not dare to tell them because I wasn't allowed to have a boyfriend in the first place. We broke up for nonreligious reasons. Even now, we are still good friends.

In general, the informants had positive attitudes toward interreligious friendships. Many, when interviewed, admitted to having friends of different faiths, either at school or outside it. As said Arman (15 years old), from an SMA in Surabaya, he did not have any problem with differences in religions, ethnicities, economic classes, or genders when choosing a friend. To him, the most important consideration was that the friend was kind and fun to talk with. "Usually, I choose a friend because they are fun and relatable to talk with," he said, "especially when we share a hobby, in which case I would click with them in just one conversation. I also frequently share knowledge with my friends." Since he was young, Arman had been used to socializing with friends of various ethnicities and religions, so he was okay with such socialization. He went on, saying, "We have a relationship with the person, anyway, not with the ethnic group or religion." Unlike him, Ani (15 years old), from an SMA in Kediri, although she had never had a non-Muslim friend at school, interacted with friends of different religions in scouting activities. She said: "My friends are from different schools, and I am comfortable with them because, so far, they never interfere with my religious life. When we are hanging out or talking, we never talk about religion. I am also careful when it comes to *'aqīdah* [creed]. So our business is just worldly business." Avoiding talk of religious faith is not uncommon on that ground. The strategy of building harmony by establishing interaction, even cooperation, strengthens relationships between communities of different religions. This interaction model, which is often referred to as "life dialogue," seems to be effective in promoting solidarity and togetherness. People worry that discussing religions would create tensions instead. Probably "theological dialogue" works better when engaged in by religious elites or leaders. However, avoiding talk of religion does not necessarily mean abandoning everything related to religion. As mentioned earlier, Santi, for example, did not hesitate to remind her boyfriend to go to his church, and vice versa.

Religious holidays often become moments for gathering with people of different religions. Joni, a Christian (17 years old), from an SMAN in Surabaya, stated that he often participated in providing social services with the church's general community, especially on holidays. He said that the activities conducted at his church were not restricted to Christians. For instance, in the month of Ramadan he would participate in providing food for *iftār* (fast breaking) for Muslims. He shared his activities with his Muslim friends: "Oh yeah," he would say, "I often attend *iftār* gatherings. Usually, we would book a place at which we would have *iftār*. Although I do not fast, I can withstand [not eating] to appreciate [those who fast] because it is not polite to eat or drink ahead while waiting for *Maghrib* [sunset prayer]." He said he had witnessed practices of religious tolerance in his neighborhood and the city of Surabaya in general. Surabaya is one of Indonesia's most heterogeneous cities, with quite significant sizes of Christian and Buddhist communities. On Buddhist holidays, Joni would visit the *vihara* (Buddhist monastery) and participate in activities involving multiple religious communities.

There was a keen awareness among the informants that today's realities do not allow people to live isolated from different communities. Indeed, the world has never been homogeneous. However, today the heterogeneity and plurality of modern communities have come close to us to the point that we no longer can avoid responding to and maintaining them. Indonesia's being one of the most diverse countries in terms of religion, ethnicity, and culture did not escape the high school students' attention. To preserve the harmony of a multicultural community like Indonesia, Indonesian people must appreciate each other. Joni opined:

> Indonesia is a country with diverse religions, ethnicities, and cultures. That is why I befriend anyone. I even have a friend who belongs to a religious minority sect, and I appreciate differences. I also have a friend who wears a *niqāb* covering her face, and we often discuss many things, just we never talk about religion. With such socializing experiences, I do not hesitate to talk to and befriend those who wear a *niqāb* or have beards because they do so according to their beliefs. What matters is that we keep talking. I think nothing should be negative.

Experiences with diversity seemed to have shaped positive attitudes among youths, which ultimately encouraged their growing appreciation for tolerance. As can be seen in table 2.3, the numbers of respondents not in favor of the other (those of different religions, religious sects, ethnicities, political ideologies, and economic classes) were fairly low.

It is interesting to note that such numbers are much lower than those of intolerant Indonesian adults at the national level. In 2012, the Indonesian Survey Circle (LSI, Lingkaran Survei Indonesia) released its findings from a survey revealing that 15.1 percent of respondents objected

TABLE 2.3. Students' responses to "How do you view people who are different from you?"

Differences	Neutral	Slightly Not in Favor	Not in Favor	Extremely Not in Favor
Different religions	92.0%	6.2%	0.2%	1.4%
Same religion, different sects	86.8%	9.0%	4.2%	0.0%
Different ethnicities	90.2%	7.2%	2.4%	0.2%
Different ideologies	81.0%	14.6%	3.4%	1.0%
Different economic classes	90.4%	8.6%	1.0%	0.0%

Note: n = 500; survey conducted in 2019.

to having non-Muslims in their neighborhood, and more than 40 percent objected to having those practicing non-Sunni Islam, such as Shia and Ahmadiyya, as neighbors (see table 2.4). In his study on Nahdlatul Ulama (NU) and Muhammadiyah leaders' views, Jeremy Menchik came to a similar conclusion, that NU and Muhammadiyah are more tolerant of Christians than of Ahmadis. Some 75 percent of Muhammadiyah leaders and 59 percent of NU leaders said no Ahmadi should be allowed to become the mayor of Jakarta. Meanwhile, 80 percent of Muhammadiyah leaders and 67 percent of NU leaders said that Ahmadis should not be allowed to build a worship house in Jakarta. Another 88 percent of Muhammadiyah leaders and 82 percent of NU leaders said that Ahmadis should not teach Islamic studies in public schools.[39]

Therefore, it is a relief that youths had positive attitudes toward other groups, including religious minorities. Hesti (16 years old), from an SMA in Surabaya, experienced living for an extended time in Adelaide, Australia. Pursuing an elementary-school education gave her an understanding of forms of religious tolerance. At school she had good relationships with her peers, some of whom were of different religions

TABLE 2.4. Responses to "Do you accept/object to having . . . as your neighbors?"

Type of Neighbor	Accept	Object	DK/DA
Those of other religions	77.5%	15.1%	7.4%
Shiites	54.0%	41.8%	4.2%
Ahmadis	48.2%	46.6%	5.2%

Source: LSI (Lembaga Survei Circle), 2012.

than hers. Despite many differences, especially concerning religion, she was highly appreciative of such differences between her and her friends. She believes that humans are created to be unique. She argued that religious tolerance constitutes an important aspect of respectful treatment between different religious adherents. "Tolerance," she said, "is practiced by not offending friends who adhere to religions other than mine because differences are natural, and we need to appreciate one another."

The majority of the informants linked tolerance to their appreciation for difference. If the difference is addressed positively, it is understandable that tolerance holds some urgency. For some informants, diversity is a living reality, necessarily good, and has beauty. Perhaps the opinion of Sukri (17 years old), from an SMA in Kediri, represents the vast majority of the informants: "Tolerance is of much importance because we live in diversity. We have friends who are different from us in terms of both religion and ethnicity. We are from differing backgrounds and even outlooks. In my opinion, having different views is not a hindrance or threat to collective life if we put tolerance with friends and other human beings to the forefront. Mutual appreciation will lead to mutual understanding, which is key to solidarity between human beings on Earth."

Another informant from Kediri understood tolerance as "appreciating and respecting one another, not insulting each other. I believe that human beings are created with a wide diversity, and whether it becomes a blessing will depend on how we see the difference" (Salman, 16 years old), from an SMA in Surabaya. Referring to difference as a blessing means that we see it as God's will. The implication is that believers must positively respond to diversity as a religious obligation because God's provisions must be obeyed. This fact is echoed by Rahim (17 years old), from an SMA in Kediri: "Although I'm pursuing Islam-based education," he said, "it does not necessarily mean that we are not tolerant of differences. Instead, studying Islam allows me also to study how to live in harmony amid difference." Rahim acquired such a positive view of tolerance at school and encountered it in the community life of his place of residence, where people of differing religions, ethnicities, and cultures lived, and they did so in peace: "If a resident has a misfortune befalling them," he said, "we would not hesitate to lend a hand. So it can be concluded that tolerance between people in our village is still strong."

Nonetheless, some informants argued that tolerance is not without boundaries or limits, though there was no consensus among them about what constitutes the boundaries of religious tolerance. Ani (the 16-year-old from an SMA in Kediri), who interacted actively with non-Muslims due to her involvement in scouting activities, explained that the boundary for tolerance lies in fundamental beliefs (*'aqīdah*) or worship practices. She believes that tolerance should not be practiced to the extent of going to the places of worship of other faiths: "The limit of tolerance," she said, "is when we touch *'aqīdah*, that is, when it comes to worship practices. As Muslims, we must be tolerant of Christians. I have many Christian friends, but that does not mean I should go to church. What is the point? Moreover, conversely, they do not need to go to the mosque or perform *salat* [prayer]."

The same was stated by Aldi (17 years old), from a MAN (public Islamic high school) in Pasuruan, who asserted, "Tolerance is appreciating difference with sincerity, but when it comes to religion, there are boundaries. For instance, questions of worship vary religion to religion, and they come with limits." According to Aldi, one of the forms of tolerance is wishing "Merry Christmas" to the Christians but not participating in Christian worship activities or agreeing with Christian *'aqīdah*. However, here is the problem: Are Christmas celebrations part of Christian worship and *'aqīdah*? Some students responded affirmatively and thus regarded giving Christmas greetings as crossing the tolerance boundaries allowed by Islam. This issue is a frequent subject of debate in Indonesia ahead of Christmas Eve in December. Many hold that Christmas wishes are *haram* (unlawful), usually based on MUI's 1981 fatwa. The fatwa does not explicitly ban giving Christmas wishes but only prohibits participation in Christmas celebrations, because such celebrations are considered part of Christian worship. Among Indonesian *ulama*, there are still ongoing debates concerning whether or not Muslims may give Christmas greetings.

Some of the youths we surveyed stated that Christmas greetings are the limit of tolerance. A couple of informants from an SMA in Pamekasan said they never gave Christmas greetings because they had no Christian friends or did not interact with non-Muslims, but also because Christmas wishes are forbidden in Islam. Fuad (15 years old), from the SMA in Pamekasan, for example, expressed his attitude as follows:

Until now, I never gave Christmas greetings to a friend because my parents have been against me doing so since I was a child. And after going to school, I have a stronger conviction not to say Christmas greetings because, as my religious education teacher said, tolerance must be following the Qur'anic teaching, that is, "to you your religion, and to me my religion." So I think it is not a problem not to say "Merry Christmas" as long as we refrain from insulting the Christians. I firmly believe that [not] restraining myself from wishing them "Merry Christmas" would be regarded as an offense.

In our interview with Joni, the Christian student from Surabaya, we elicited his reaction to some Muslims' attitudes concerning Christmas greetings. He answered, "Some friends wish me 'Merry Christmas.' However, what matters more is that they have tolerance in daily life for us to be pleased with each other." From his perspective, it is not necessary for believers of other religions to give Christians Christmas wishes, and it is more critical to maintain tolerance than to give each other greetings on religious holidays.

DIVERSIFICATION OF AUTHORITIES

Fuad's reason for not wishing Christians "Merry Christmas," that his parents and religious education teachers forbade it, is quite widespread among young people.

The dilemma of being tolerant or violating religious beliefs, especially for Muslims, is illustrated by the reluctance of many to wish a Merry Christmas to Christians. As exemplified above, Karim views difference positively as a blessing, and tolerance, according to him, is "respecting, not condemning, and considering others." However, he stressed that tolerance must not exceed certain boundaries. He confessed that both teachers and parents forbade him from saying "Merry Christmas."

The controversy over Christmas greetings inevitably surfaces every December. Those who prohibit wishing Christians a Merry Christmas argue that Christmas is an inseparable part of Christians' faith in the divinity of Jesus. Therefore, saying "Merry Christmas" is the same as confessing Christian teachings contrary to Islam. Usually Muslims refer to the fatwa issued by the Council of Indonesian Ulama (MUI, Majelis Ulama Indonesia) in 1981 to support their narrative. The MUI's fatwa was a response to a specific context wherein Muslims were invited to attend formal Christmas celebrations. MUI expressed its concern about this phenomenon, saying that Muslims participated in Christmas celebrations because of their misconception that Christmas and the celebration of the birth of the Prophet Muhammad were the same (that is, without ritual value). Some Muslims even participated in organizing Christmas festivities, especially in workplaces and schools, or in neighborhoods rather than in churches. Therefore, the fatwa was aimed at guiding Muslims to the "right" religious path because "Muslims should not mix their faith and rituals with the faith and rituals of other religions."[40]

Responding to the controversy, MUI explained that what is prohibited is participation in Christmas celebrations, while the Christmas greeting itself has no fatwa issued. It is strange that for an issue as sensational as giving Christmas greetings, MUI did not issue a fatwa. When students were asked if they had ever said "Merry Christmas" and to whom, they responded as recorded in table 2.5.

It is apparent that the number of students who have never wished anyone a Merry Christmas is relatively high. When asked who taught them that Christmas greetings were forbidden by their religion, the most frequent answers were both religion teachers (63.2 percent) and teachers of nonreligious subjects (52.6 percent). See table 2.6. The number of parents who forbad it was also quite high (48.4 percent).

Table 2.6 suggests that the religious views of schoolteachers (both religious and secular) can be categorized as fairly conservative. This is

TABLE 2.5. Students' responses to "Did you wish 'Merry Christmas' to the following people?"

Recipients of Greeting	Yes	No
Teachers	25.6%	74.4%
Family	28.2%	71.8%
Relative	32.4%	67.6%
Close friends	40.2%	59.8%
School acquaintances	39.0%	61.0%

Note: n = 500; survey conducted in 2019.

TABLE 2.6. Students' responses to "How often did you hear the prohibition against saying 'Merry Christmas' from the following people?"

Groups	Frequently	Rarely	Never
Teachers (who do not teach religion)	18.2%	34.4%	47.4%
Principals	9.8%	19.0%	71.2%
Religion teachers	41.0%	22.2%	36.8%
Parents	22.6%	25.8%	51.6%
Grandparents	15.2%	18.8%	66.0%

Note: n = 500; survey conducted in 2019.

in line with PPIM research results released in December 2016, which revealed that many Islamic religious education teachers at elementary and secondary schools tended to practice exclusivism and adopt an intolerant attitude toward groups of different beliefs, both Islamic and non-Islamic. The research was conducted in five regions, namely, Aceh, West Java, Central Java, West Nusa Tenggara, and South Sulawesi, with roughly 500 teachers involved in the survey and in-depth interviews. The results show that the majority of religious education teachers opposed non-Muslim leadership: 89 percent opposed leadership of a non-Muslim head of their region, 87 percent a non-Muslim headmaster, and 80 percent a non-Muslim head of office. As many as 81 percent disapproved of the erection of houses of worship in the region, yet 77 percent were against the closure or abolishment of minority Muslim houses of worship. Their attitude toward minority Muslim groups was negative, with 80 percent unwilling to accommodate Shiites and Ahmadis as their neighbors.[41]

This phenomenon of intolerance among elementary and high school teachers is relentless and worth attention. They are supposed to be crucial instruments in propagating tolerance and strengthening the pillars of a harmonious life among members of younger generations. As cited by Dadi Darmadi, in its 2018 survey that included both schoolteachers and university lecturers, PPIM found that the level of teachers' and lecturers' intolerance of internal Muslim "sects" (in this case, Shi'ah and Ahmadiyyah) was higher than that of non-Muslims. The percentage for intolerance of non-Muslims was 45.3 percent, while that for the intolerance of internal groups was 54 percent. Teachers and lecturers were more tolerant of non-Muslims than of Muslims of different sects, whom

TABLE 2.7. Students' responses to "How often did your parents, teachers, or friends encourage intolerant attitudes?"

Parties	Often	Sometimes	Never
Parents	7.8%	41.0%	51.2%
Teachers	3.0%	36.8%	60.2%
Friends	5.2%	53.6%	41.2%

Note: n = 500; survey conducted in 2019.

they regarded as deviating from their faith or misguided. As many as 87.89 percent of teachers and lecturers nodded to the government for banning minority groups; they considered such groups as deviating from Islamic teachings.[42] These PPIM research results show us that radicalism and intolerance were pervasive among teachers and lecturers of Islamic religious education. However, it was also apparent from the results that teachers' and lecturers' support for the Unitary State of the Republic of Indonesia and democracy was still high.

In my research, students were asked about the roles of parents, teachers, and friends in encouraging intolerant attitudes toward others. Table 2.7 illustrates that each of the three groups (parents, teachers, and friends) played a role with a different intensity. Some 7.8 percent of respondents said their parents often condoned and allowed hostile or intolerant attitudes; those who said their parents did sometimes were 41 percent, and those who said their parents never allowed or encouraged such attitudes were 51.2 percent. The percentages of those who said that their teachers taught intolerant attitudes are as follows: often/frequently, 3 percent; sometimes, 36.8 percent; and never, 60.2 percent. In comparison, the percentages for friends are as follows: often (5.2 percent), sometimes (53.6 percent), and never (41.2 percent).

It came as no surprise then, that we found that high school students were still halfhearted in showing their attitudes toward tolerance. On the one hand, they believed that tolerance is important for social harmony. However, on the other hand, they restricted themselves from anything they perceived as violating Islamic *'aqīdah*, such as giving Christmas greetings. In the case of the latter, they heeded the conservative teachings relayed by their schoolteachers. A student from a state high school in Pamekasan, Khalid (16 years old), stated that his religious education teacher frequently advised against giving Christmas greetings and explained that Islam disallowed it. The teacher would present Qur'anic verses and hadiths that delegitimize Christmas greetings, stating that Islam was introduced as a refinement of earlier religions, including Christianity. It seemed that the schoolteachers did not provide diverse views on religious issues and only indoctrinated the students with a single opinion they held.

My in-depth interviews revealed even more detailed rationales from those who did or did not give Christmas greetings to Christians. One of the recurring themes was that Qur'an teachers, *ustadh*s (conservative Muslim teachers and preachers), or parents forbade giving Christmas greetings because they purportedly violate the teachings of Islam. In general, the *ustadh*s received traditional Islamic education and were usually active in *da'wah* [proselytizing] and preaching at various forums attended by members of the general public, including youths. Some informants openly stated that they did not dare say "Merry Christmas" because they had the *ustadh*'s proscription in mind. Imran (16 years old), from an MA in Pasuruan, for instance, who lived at a *pesantren*, said that after school he would attend the *pengajian* with his *ustadh* at his dormitory. He heard the ban against wishing Christians "Merry Christmas" from the *pondok*. "In the routine *pengajian*," he said, "the *ustadh* would explain about what is *halal* and what is *haram*, the lawful and the unlawful, with argumentations from the Qur'an and Hadith." Unlike Imran, Rini (15 years old), from an SMA in Surabaya, had formerly attended *pondok* a couple of years before high school but currently was living with her parents. She was among the students who were of the view that the exchange of Christmas greetings is beyond the tolerance limit validated by Islam. When asked about where she heard about the law against wishing Christmas greetings, she said: "I have never given any Christmas greetings to Christians because it is not right. I fear to sin. My *pondok* teacher would, in every lesson, explain the law of saying Christmas greetings with evidence from the Qur'an. So I do not want to cross the teachings of the Book. However, I often receive greetings from my non-Muslim friends, for example, during the Eid al-Fitr and other Islamic holidays." It must be noted that religious authorities continue to become more diverse. Other than the schoolteachers and *ustadh*, the students also found religious guidance from *guru ngaji* (Qur'anic recital teachers). Many of the informants based their views and attitudes of openness and hostility to people of other religions on what the Qur'anic recital teachers taught them. An informant from an SMA in Malang, Anton (15 years old), never said "Merry Christmas" and believed that non-Muslims should never be leaders of Muslim communities, as his Qur'anic recital teacher had taught. He said, "I never said any Christmas greetings to my Christian friends because my *ustadh* told me not to do so. I follow what my *guru ngaji* said because I trust him." Some informants felt that the religious knowledge shared by their *ustadh* was more convincing than that imparted by their schoolteachers. This is perhaps because Qur'anic recital teachers usually teach how to recite the Qur'an at students' homes in a relaxed, informal atmosphere in which it is comfortable for the students to present a variety of questions. A female student went with her mother to community Qur'anic recitals held in her housing complex.

However, not all students necessarily bought into what the *guru ngaji*, schoolteachers, and *ustadh* told them. Some informants found the explanations provided by the *guru ngaji* unsatisfactory and sought more reliable information. This proves that the influence of social networks on students' views of diversity is more complex than what is generally believed. As mentioned above, Ani (16 years old), a student from Kediri, opined that tolerance has a limit: not participating in the worship practices of other religions. However, to her, Christmas celebrations do not count as worship. In her view, the Qur'an does not prohibit anyone from saying "Merry Christmas," because in the Qur'an Jesus himself is described as giving greetings of peace on his birthday. Previously, she had often heard the opinion of traditional *ulama* outlawing Christmas greetings, but she decided to find out more by listening to the preaching of Quraish Shihab, an Indonesian Muslim scholar specializing in Qur'anic exegesis (*tafsīr*), who graduated from al-Azhar University and is renowned for his moderate perspectives. She said, "From the sermon of Quraish Shihab, it became known to me that saying 'Merry Christmas' means we are acknowledging the birth of Prophet Isa, who in Christianity is more known as Jesus Christ."

Ani has resolved to challenge competing religious authorities in her way. She drew a line between saying "Merry Christmas" and participating in Christian worship. Even though many *ustadh* and *guru ngaji* confused the two, thanks to Shihab's illumination, Ani realized that wishing somebody Christmas greetings will not harm her *'aqīdah*. Similarly, Aldi

(17 years old), from a MAN in Pasuruan, also distinguished giving Christmas greetings from participation in worship. Just like Ani, Aldi felt the competing claims to authority. He was fully aware that many parties forbade giving Christmas greetings, including, to his knowledge, teachers at and outside of school. However, he witnessed Christmas celebrations being held at the Ministry of Religious Affairs, and even the minister himself allowed the giving of Christmas greetings. "I have Christian friends, so I am okay with throwing them Christmas wishes. What is important is not getting involved in any Christian worship activities," he said.

As is presented in table 2.6, the immediate environment at home also significantly affected the shaping of the views of the students, whether they were open or hostile to interreligious relations. Adolescents might share their opinions and feelings with their close friends, but their parents would endlessly try to guide them. Based on what some informants conveyed, the role of their parents in the formation of their religious attitudes was often put side by side with the role of their religious education teachers. Many of them even singled their parents out as references. When an informant from a high school in Malang was asked why he did not say "Merry Christmas," he answered briefly, "Because my mother and father themselves taught me since I was a child that saying Christmas greetings is forbidden."

The family is the first social group a child typically encounters in life, so it is little wonder if family exerts a significant influence on whether children would adopt an open or a hostile attitude. William A. Costanza is correct when he writes that "it is within the context of parental belief systems that ways of discursive interaction are first learned by the child that help influence the development of the child's cognitive tools."[43] Remember Rudi (16 years old), from SMAN 1 in Pasuruan, who was not allowed by his very religious father to have a girlfriend and frequently goes to Islamic study forums? The religious climate in his family was evident in his views. With respect to giving Christmas greetings, he said, "My father forbids me from giving Christmas greetings even to my friends or teachers. He said this is the limit of tolerance. It is a must to appreciate religious differences, but it is not necessary to go to the extent of saying Christmas greetings." He said that if it came to religion, he was ready to defend it. In his opinion, jihad is obligatory, although this can be understood in different ways according to the context. In a normal situation, jihad can be manifested in hard work in a field one masters, but under threats or in war, jihad means taking up arms.

It is noteworthy that a religious family life does not necessarily reflect exclusivist and radical views. One who is open and tolerant does not necessarily treat religion lightly. An informant from an SMA in Pasuruan, Karim (15 years old), lived in a strict family in terms of religious worship practices. His parents gave him a traditional Islamic education. In our discussion, he looked excitedly open and spelled out religious arguments to support his opinions. At school, he was seated with a Christian class-mate. When asked about tolerance, he answered, "Human beings should be tolerant of each other. My parents tell me so, and Islam teaches peace so humans can live peacefully, and so there is no more war in the name of religion." When asked further whether there is a limit to tolerance, he replied firmly, "No particular limit according to my parents as long as we respect and appreciate each other." It is interesting to note the habits practiced by our informants. According to Layla (16 years old), whose family resides in Pasuruan, the interreligious and cooperative climate in her neighborhood had successfully made tolerance a prominent part of the surrounding people's life experiences. She said:

> In my neighborhood, when Muslims are celebrating their holidays after fasting in the month of Ramadan, my neighbors to the right and the left side of my house all were sent foods, including those who are non-Muslims. Similarly, on Christmas Eve, our Protestant and Catholic neighbors would hold celebrations with feasting, and all other neighbors would get to enjoy the meals, whether Muslims or non-Muslims. We visit each other. Through the endless interreligious interactions, we grow appreciative of each other because we experience tolerance firsthand. We understand what is okay or appropriate and what is not okay or inappropriate to do.

CONTENDING AUTHORITIES OF SOCIAL NETWORKS

In this chapter I have used the approach of examining social networks as a lens through which to explore the conditions and environments shaping the views and attitudes of young people toward religious diversity.

Social networks are defined as the social connections provided by the environment to an individual,[44] and these connections can be used to model social processes and analyze the effects of social processes on the individual.[45] Research on adolescent social networks often focuses on the environment of encounter, especially at school, such as how students create friendship networks. Rebecca S. Bigler, John M. Rohrbach, and Kiara L. Sanchez inferred that intergroup, interethnic, or interreligious friendship networks allow for the development of open and tolerant attitudes in students.[46] In their words, "The formation of close social bonds with cross-group others is a vital component of positive intergroup attitudes and crucial to creating and maintaining social equity and justice."[47] The problem now is that in order to establish cross-group friendships, positive attitudes toward other groups are needed. A person with a prejudiced or hostile view will not be able to befriend others in the first place. Only those who are comfortable having friends of different groups will be open to establishing friendships with different groups. We found that the influence within a friendship network is reciprocal. Those who are positively influenced by the friendships in their network will also positively influence other members of the social network.

In our research, the social networks of students were expanded through the environment of school friendships to enable us to better understand the entire environment that influenced and shaped their views and attitudes. The students received directions and guidance on which attitudes they should adopt from various parties within and outside their schools. This suggests that the religious authorities on which they relied were quite diverse. In this context, "religious authority" is to be understood, according to Muhammad Qasim Zaman, as "the aspiration, effort, and ability to shape people's belief and practice on recognizably 'religious grounds.'"[48] In developing their attitudes, some students referred to the teachings and instructions of their schoolteachers, especially those teaching religious subjects, but many others followed what their *ustadh* told them. The fact that the teachers to whom the students referred were practicing conservatism sheds light on why many students showed a halfhearted attitude toward religious tolerance. They considered religious tolerance vital in a multicultural community and diversity as needing to be addressed positively, but they kept themselves from activities conservative Muslim groups understood as going against

Islamic teachings. A prime example enlightening this point is that of giving Christmas greetings, which in the understanding of conservative Muslim groups were acknowledgments of Christian *'aqīdah* and thus given the *haram* status. Some students maintained that religious tolerance came with a limit, that is, not saying "Merry Christmas." In other words, Christmas greetings were perceived as a limit of tolerance for those practicing Islam.

In this context, the students should receive a more nuanced religious understanding and alternative exegeses to complement what has already been presented by conservative teachers and *ustadh*. Today it seems that religious authorities have been undergoing diversification, as marked by the proliferation of individual religious authorities.[49] Previously, sources of authority were more centered on religious institutions, such as Majelis Ulama Indonesia (MUI), Nahdlatul Ulama (NU), and Muhammadiyah, among other organizations. In the past, people would consult certain *ulama* considered authoritative—for example, those running *pesantren*, for opinions. Not only do *ustadh* go to neighborhoods, mosques, and *pengajian* to give religious guidance, but now the quantity of them is great, as if they were in marketplaces. In theory, the growing number of *pengajian* events and the ready access to the opinions of a great many *ulama* or *ustadh* will democratize views, as people now can choose among the views available. What is disturbing now is that the religious public space is dominated by conservative views, leaving seekers with the options only of picking one conservative opinion or picking yet another conservative one. We must reiterate that alternative views of exegesis and understanding diversity are urgently needed.

It is worth noting that one student, Ani, mentioned above, sought alternative interpretations on her own, for example, by accessing online sources (e.g., YouTube) to obtain explanations from more progressive *ulama*. This contestation of religious authority helps expand the horizons of young people's understanding that the interpretations of religious doctrine are not monolithic. About Christmas greetings, for example, Ani came across Quraish Shihab's explanation, which challenged the views of conservative groups. Indeed, religious authorities will never get rid of contestation. Zaman has rightly noted, "So far as claims to authority are concerned, the significance lies rather in reminding us that authority is not a stable endowment but one that is always exposed to implicit or explicit challenge and that it waxes and wanes in response to the pressure bearing upon it."[50]

Another aspect of the social networks of students shaping their openness and hostility is their families, the earliest and most intimate environments in which they interact. Both quantitative and qualitative data revealed that parents and grandparents played a significant role in shaping the trajectory of students' open or hostile attitudes. Children do tend to obey the directions and words of their parents. This is especially true when the parents appear devoutly religious, which is perceived by children as a sign of the parents' double authorities, making the children likely to heed their parents' words. The mechanism by which children acquire certain attitudes from their parents involves not only teaching and direction but also direct observations at home of whether the parents are open or hostile to other groups. However, our findings should not be construed as a basis for one to conclude that if parents are hostile, the children also will be. In order to prove such a correlation, a more specific investigation is required. Frances Aboud and Anna-Beth Doyle's study of parents' influence on children's racial behavior states that "children's attitudes were not similar to their mother's positive and negative attitudes toward Blacks."[51] This conclusion supports our hypothesis that parents are not the only sources of children's positive or negative behaviors; neither are teachers or friends. We propose that the scope of the social networks that affect young people be broadened. In some cases, as discussed above, young people often refer to more than one source of authority, for example, a combination of teachers and parents, sometimes with reinforcement from the Qur'an.

CONCLUDING REMARKS

In this chapter I have confirmed the resilience of the social networks that have shaped the attitudes of young people toward religious diversity. The advantage of expanding the scope of the social networks of students is demonstrated in our study by how young people often refer to a variety of sources to develop and support their views. We must realize that both openness and hostility, or tolerance and intolerance, can spread through social networks, broadly construed. My study also builds on earlier research on the diversification of religious authorities by suggesting that students should be introduced to various religious understandings in order to adopt a more flexible, open attitude toward different groups in terms of religion, ethnicity, race, or culture. Additionally, this study contributes to informing more complex notions of attitude construction in a multireligious (and often conflicted) society and how this religious diversity is lived and experienced by young people in their everyday lives.

The findings of this study show that the social networks of students can have both positive and negative impacts on them. Of course, the nature of social networks' influence is not straightforward, as is commonly assumed. As shown in this study, young people are surrounded by multiple social networks simultaneously, be they friends, parents, or religion teachers. Mutual influencing is a complex process in which each individual has a peculiar agency to assess which attitude fits his or her situation in a particular context. Some students expressed their satisfaction with the options that were at their disposal. Therefore, the question is not whether or to what extent one has been influenced by one's social networks but rather under what circumstances social networks can be influential. At any rate, in this formative period of their lives, young people are quite vulnerable to high-risk behaviors, including incivility, as will be discussed in the following chapter.

THREE

Fragile Civility in Schools

In the first two chapters of this book I have shown the fragility of the attitudes of young people toward religious diversity in Indonesia. I have also examined the role of social networks, both within and outside of educational environments, in shaping the views of students on religious tolerance. I will further discuss the fragility of their views of others in this chapter by broadening our understanding of diversity to include not only the diversity of religions but also that of ethnicities, political views, and socioeconomic statuses. Indonesia is a multiethnic society, with hundreds of ethnic groups. It is true that defining one's ethnicity is often complicated. However, in Indonesia ethnicity is defined by using a patriarchal system. It is worth noting that there is no official system of ethnic identification in Indonesia. Most ethnic groups are small, and only thirteen groups have more than a million each.[1] According to the 2000 census, the largest ethnic group is Javanese, comprising 41.71 percent of the population, followed by Sundanese with 15.41 percent and Malay with 3.45 percent. In terms of religion, Islam is the dominant religion at 88 percent, followed by Protestantism (6 percent), Catholicism (3 percent), Hinduism (2 percent), Buddhism (1 percent), and other religions. Socioeconomic status is a complicated construct to measure. According to the

Central Statistic Agency (BPS, Badan Pusat Statistik, 2020), the percentage of Indonesians living in poverty as of March 2020 was 9.78.[2] Socioeconomic status seems to have an impact on education especially, and there is a high correlation between poverty and school participation rate. As Ouda Teda Ena notes, "When the poverty rate of a province is low, the school participation rate in that province is high and vice versa."[3] In Jakarta, the province with the lowest poverty rate, the school participation rate is high for all school levels, 99.16 percent, 91.45 percent, and 61.99 percent for elementary, junior high, and senior high schools, respectively. In contrast, in the province with the highest poverty rate, West Papua, the school participation rate is low for all school levels (76.22 percent, 74.35 percent, and 48.28 percent for elementary, junior high, and senior high schools, respectively).[4]

Myths and stereotypes about socioeconomic status, ethnicity, religion, gender, or political orientation can influence students' attitudes regarding mutual respect and living with diversity. As I will discuss in this chapter, Chinese in Indonesia are stereotyped as stingy and greedy, which leads to Chinese students' suffering bullying and discrimination. Although bullying happens in Indonesian schools, not much research has been done to measure students' involvement in bullying and methods of preventing it. In 2007, Amy Huneck conducted fieldwork at one elementary school in Indonesia and compared it with another elementary school in the United States.[5] Huneck's survey of 51 respondents revealed that many Indonesian students became victims of bullying. For instance, 55 percent of respondents said they were teased by their friends in schools in an unpleasant way, called hurtful names (49 percent), threatened with harm (9 percent), kicked or pushed in a hurtful way (37 percent), or talked about behind their backs (24 percent).[6] Farah Aulia did similar research on 258 students in grades 4–5 in Yogyakarta, which revealed that 62.8 percent of respondents experienced bullying in a physical form.[7] Studies on high school students conducted by Irvan Usman in Gorontalo, Sugiariyanti in Semarang, and Kadek Ayu Erika, Dian Atma Pertiwi, and Tuti Seniwati in South Sulawesi, indicated that there was an alarmingly high rate of bullying.[8] Extensive research on bullying at the high school level was done by Lucy Bowes and colleagues at four schools in South Sulawesi (involving 2,075 students) and eight schools in Central Java (involving 5,517 students). The result was that 57.5 percent of the students in South Sulawesi reported being bullied at least once or twice in the past thirty days and 64.4 percent of the students in Central Java experienced bullying at least once or twice in the past thirty days.[9] While the prevalence of bullying varied per school, the overall rates of bullying were relatively high.

These studies are quantitative. The present chapter confirms the prevalence of bullying and other uncivil behaviors among high school students based on 50 quantitative and in-depth interviews. Unfortunately, bullying has not been viewed as a social problem in Indonesia. People often reacted to peer-to-peer bullying as if it were an acceptable social norm. "Of the adults that have been interviewed in Indonesia," Huneck writes, "most still believe that peer-on-peer aggression is typical child's play; just a part of growing up."[10] In most developed countries, bullying is considered a major threat to student-to-student relationships and to creating a positive and safe learning environment. Bullying can lead to low academic success and lack of motivation to attend school.[11] Moreover, this incivility can have lasting effects on an entire school community and cause a serious problem in society. Scholars have reported that a child's mental and physical health can be affected by bullying. Students who are habitually bullied by their peers are at high risk of developing mental illness, including depression, and this treatment can even lead to suicide.[12] Several studies have also shown the prevalence of bullying in many parts of the world and suggested that schools have a positive effect on reducing delinquency and aggression.[13] However, bullying is only one form of uncivil and intolerant behavior among students. In this chapter I will discuss other examples of incivility or uncivil behavior, which is understood here as an undesirable behavior displaying a lack of respectful intent toward peers or others. While most studies focus on curricula, I address students' incivility based on their views and narratives in order to better understand the barriers to civility and seek to dismantle beliefs and practices that inhibit civility.

BULLYING AND INCIVILITY: THEORETICAL CONSIDERATIONS

There is no term in the Indonesian language equivalent to the word "bullying." The overall concept of bullying known to Western societies is absent from Indonesian society. However, as mentioned earlier, Huneck's survey indicates that children do hit, kick, push, and tease others and call each other names, and they acknowledge that these behaviors do not feel okay. According to Rebecca Puhl, Jamie Lee Peterson, and Joerg Luedicke, bullying is a form of aggression that includes intentional and repeated attempts to physically, verbally, socially, or emotionally hurt another person.[14] For an act to be considered bullying, the three factors that need to be present are these: (1) the behavior is intended to harm, (2) the same act or a similar act is repeated over a period of time, and (3) there is an inequality of power between bully and victim.[15] These characteristics of bullying are drawn from the work of the Swedish scholar Dan Olweus, who is regarded as one of the first pioneers on bullying research at the global level.[16] His definition emphasizes the distinction between bullying and other aggressive behavior in that bullying is repetitious by nature and is always characterized by an asymmetrical power relationship between bully and victim. Olweus and other researchers have shown that bullying behavior in schools has increased significantly in the past few decades.

For instance, in the United States, approximately 10–20 percent of students are bullied regularly by their peers, and 75 percent of school-aged children report being bullied at least once during the school year.[17] The percentage of bullying at local levels varies. On average, however, 50 percent of U.S. students have been bullied at school.[18] Bullying has become an all-too-familiar problem among students in American middle and high schools. Increased awareness of school bullying has prompted state legislation to combat the problem. Many American states have enacted laws aimed at reducing the incidence of bullying. These laws focus on the responsibility of schools in handling bullying situations.[19] There is no doubt that the passing of anti-bullying legislation was instrumental in informing the public that bullying is a problem that affects students socially and emotionally.

The situation in Indonesia is different. Despite its severe consequences, bullying has not been addressed seriously. Indonesian schools and society have not yet defined the term. In fact, the things that in Western societies fall in the category of "bullying" may be accepted as social norms or part of growing up. It is hardly surprising that teachers often react to bullying with ease. According to Amy Huneck, Indonesian teachers habitually rely on the moral values of their religions to address hurtful behaviors.[20] Muslim teachers often referred to prophetic traditions that stress the importance of good manners (*makārim al-akhlāq*). When they have to intervene in incidents of bullying, "they simply talk to the individuals [involved in such incidents], usually at the same time and try to get them to be 'friends' again."[21] Huneck explains this different treatment of bullying between American society and Indonesian society in terms of "cultural beliefs within American society versus Indonesian society [which] account for significant differences in adult reactions to bullying issues in these two educational systems (not to mention the important cultural differences within groups of Americans and within groups of Indonesians)."[22]

Without denying the cultural differences Huneck refers to, I would argue that the severity of bullying has not yet become a public concern in Indonesia due to the lack of people's awareness of its dangerous effects on both the victim and the bully. We have so little information about bullying in Indonesia because not much research has been conducted on the subject, especially concerning both the short- and long-term adverse effects on the bully and the victim. In the West, many scholars have shown that bullying has various emotional, psychological, and educational effects. Often both the victim and the bully suffer psychologically, which can result in low self-esteem, feelings of loneliness, increased stress, and less satisfaction with life.[23] Some studies focus on the long-term effects of bullying on victims, which include depression, aggression, increased thoughts of suicide, and antisocial behavior in adulthood.[24] Other studies show the negative effects of bullying on the academic achievement of its victims. Bullying has been linked to disrupted concentration in the classroom, disciplinary problems, lower student achievement, and increased absenteeism.[25] Moreover, some scholars make a connection between bullying and criminal behavior in adulthood or between bullying and school violence, including school shootings.[26] No similar research on the possible negative effects of bullying has been done in the Indonesian context.

There is an urgent need to inform the Indonesian public about the seriousness of this matter. Despite the high frequency of bullying, which is sometimes violent, there is no systematic attempt to research and understand it in greater detail and find strategies to prevent it. The Indonesian Commission for Child Protection (KPAI, Komisi Perlindungan Anak Indonesia), which is supposed to be the vanguard of identifying and documenting incidents of bullying, tends to display passive attitudes in that it is not proactive in collecting data, but instead waits to receive reports on bullying. It comes as no surprise that the number of bullying incidences reported by KPAI remains low compared to bullying at the global level. In its 2014 report, for instance, KPAI recorded only 19 bullying incidents in schools.[27] Through the year 2016, according to KPAI, there were 81 victims of bullying and 40 bullies found.[28] This number continued to increase year by year to the extent that it reached 2,473 cases in 2019.[29] It should be noted that this number is not based on research on the ground but rather on incidents of bullying reported to KPAI. On the one hand, this indicates that more victims had the courage to speak up and reported the incidents they experienced to KPAI. On the other hand, there must have been numerous incidents reported to schools that did not reach KPAI, and even more cases that were simply not reported. Mass media, both print and electronic, often has no interest in reporting bullying unless it is of an extreme nature, such as a suicide caused by bullying or an incident of a female middle-school student who was beaten severely by a male student in the classroom, which was recorded and shared on social media.[30] The government, especially the ministry of education and KPAI, and the general public should pay serious attention to bullying, which has severe effects on students and education.

Bullying takes many forms, both physical and verbal. These forms of bullying are known as "traditional" because they occur in face-to-face situations in which the victims know the antagonists. Incidents of physical and verbal bullying involve physical contact, verbal abuse, or mean facial expressions.[31] This direct bullying can easily be recognized; it includes (1) hitting and pushing, (2) name-calling and taunting, (3) threatening gestures, (4) stealing or hiding others' property, and (5) any other physically or verbally overt act of intimidation or oppression. Contrasting with direct bullying is indirect bullying, which is more subtle but at least as severe as direct bullying, if not more so. Indirect bullying is hidden and repeated aggression to spread malicious rumors and isolate others from social situations.[32] In other words, indirect bullying can be more covert and specifically designed to create uncomfortable social situations for victims. With the widespread use of the Internet and other forms of technology, cyberbullying has become an increasingly common phenomenon. This type of bullying can include texting, emailing, or instant messaging to communicate hostile, aggressive, inappropriate, or humiliating messages that have the intention of harming others.[33]

Review and analysis of the literature reveals how much research has been conducted on bullying and educational environments. Such research is absent in the Indonesian context. More research needs to be done to increase public awareness of bullying as a serious problem in schools. It is important to emphasize that academic success is heightened in learning environments that are supportive and safe. Students learn and understand caring and civility when they are being accepted and respected. However, bullying is not solely connected to the student who bullies or the victim. Just as the way that students view the other, in either a tolerant or a hostile manner, is shaped by complex social networks, as discussed in the previous chapter, so does bullying evolve in the social context: the actions of peers and teachers, school and family factors, and societal influences maintain bullying and allow it to thrive. Several studies have explored the effect of the cultural environment on caring and concern for others and its opposite.[34] The question is this: How can we foster civil and prosocial behaviors among youths, both within and beyond the school environment, that can reduce their delinquency and promote their constructive civic engagement?

Most efforts to address bullying in schools have focused on supporting the victims or providing counseling or punishment for the bullies. A more recent approach focuses substantial attention on the community of bystanders who, although not actively engaged, may cheer the bully on or at least allow his or her behavior through their silence. This approach is based on the idea that having a sense of community in school can help reduce bullying and other delinquent behaviors.[35] Key to this approach is the development of what Nancy Eisenberg and Richard A. Fabes refer to as "prosocial behavior," which they understand as "voluntary behavior intended to benefit another."[36] Thus, there is a strong connection between prosocial behavior and concern for others. This approach makes sense, as both bullying and incivility are forms of aggression and should be treated in the same way. Increased reporting of school bullying and violence gives the impression of incivility in the educational system.

Incivility is the opposite of civility. In his *In Search of Civility: Confronting Incivility on the College Campus*, Kent Weeks describes civility as "a combination of considerate conduct toward others embodied in the

Golden Rule and a notion of civic duty and responsibility to the community."[37] Weeks makes it clear that civility includes a personal responsibility
to a community and points out how civility is "usually demonstrated
through manners, courtesy, politeness, and a general awareness of the
rights, wishes, concerns, and feelings of others."[38] The opposite of this virtue is incivility, which refers to behavior that is contrary to the well-being
of the community, including behaviors that distract, disrupt, stereotype,
or discourage others. Some scholars, including Jennifer L. Aranda, distinguish between bullying and incivility, saying that "bullying takes incivility
to a higher level of intimidation."[39] Other scholars, such as Lynne M.
Andersson and Christine M. Pearson in the context of adults in the
workplace, offer a definition similar to that of bullying, such as "behaviors with ambiguous intent to harm the target, in violation of workplace
norms for mutual respect."[40] Although most studies have been focused on
incivility in the workplace, scholars generally agree that, as Pier M. Forni
writes, "incivility is on prominent display: in the schools, where bullying is pervasive; in the workplace, where an increasing number is more
stressed out by coworkers than their jobs; on the roads, where road rage
maims and kills; in politics, where strident intolerance takes the place of
earnest dialogue; and on the web, where many check their inhibitions at
the digital door."[41]

There are many ideas about what underlies civility and incivility and
their impacts on youth in Indonesia today. Indonesia is a complex case
of cultural diversity. Intricate social constructs and the interplay among
them inform civility and incivility. As Amy Huneck has shown, American
society regards certain things as bullying that are viewed by Indonesian
society as acceptable, as they are parts of growing up. Ruth Braunstein has
rightly noted that the very act of defining civility and incivility is a contest
in which individuals or groups compete to draw boundaries between civil
and uncivil behavior and to define how those boundaries apply to individuals and groups.[42] Therefore, when drawing the boundaries between
civil and uncivil behaviors, one must consider the influence of cultural
perceptions, including stereotypes and biases, as one's understanding of
civility and incivility is often influenced by social constructs such as religion, ethnicity, gender, and socioeconomic status. In any diverse society,
the dynamics of majority-minority issues often play a crucial role in how
civility and incivility (and even bullying) are constructed, promoted, and

contested. Minority groups and families of low socioeconomic status often become the targets of aggressive behaviors. As the definitions of bullying and incivility suggest, there is an imbalance of power between the bully and the victim. This imbalance can be in socioeconomic status, gender, religion, ethnicity, physical size, ability, or any number of other attributes. Within each of these categories, there is a group that is dominant and therefore systemically privileged and a group that is considered subordinate and therefore systemically oppressed and often the target of incivility and bullying in its many forms.

With religious conservatism and intolerance on the rise in Indonesia today, hostility and uncivil attitudes toward disadvantaged individuals and groups tend to color intergroup relations, including among youth. As my findings below illustrate, a significant number of high school students showed hostile attitudes toward individuals, groups, or beliefs that are different from their own. Bullying and uncivil behaviors were also on prominent display among Indonesian youth. My study confirms prior research indicating that individuals from underrepresented and marginalized groups face bias and discrimination.

FRAGILE CIVILITY AMONG YOUTH

Suppose civility in its essence is about respecting the other. In that case, a person is called "civil" when he or she is willing to embrace diversity and respect individuals with differing backgrounds, values, and beliefs. Of the 500 students who participated in my research, only 6 percent said that respecting other students with different backgrounds is not crucial for social cohesion. The vast majority of respondents (87 percent) agreed about the importance of respecting others, and the rest (7 percent) expressed their indifference. It seems clear that students value respect for others highly. Respect can be viewed as a public virtue and is often ranked above other societal values. However, respect for others did not manifest when students were asked about groups they hated the most. As table 3.1 illustrates, a significant number of respondents (43.4 percent) claimed that they hated corrupt politicians and businessmen. This is quite understandable, as corruption continues to plague Indonesia. According to Gallup: "More than 8 in 10 Indonesians say

TABLE 3.1. Students' responses to "What groups do you hate or dislike the most?"

Group	Percentages
Corrupt politicians and businessmen	43.4
Israelis	24.2
The Islamic State of Iraq and Syria (ISIS)	20.4
People of other religions	4.6
Chinese	4.4
Americans/Westerners	2.2
Wealthy people/conglomerates	0.8

Note: n = 500; survey conducted in 2019.

that corruption is widespread throughout the nation's government and businesses. Compared with citizens in other Southeast Asian countries, Indonesians are much more likely to say that corruption is prevalent in both the government and business sectors."[43] The second-most hated people are Israelis (24.2 percent), followed by the Islamic State of Iraq and Syria (ISIS) (20.4 percent), people of other religions (4.6 percent), Chinese (4.4 percent), Americans/Westerners (2.2 percent), and wealthy people with multi-industrial companies (0.8 percent). The Israeli–Palestinian conflict is a sensitive issue in Indonesia, and it often becomes a political commodity. While many Muslim-majority countries, including those in in the Middle East, have established diplomatic relations with Israel, the Indonesian government still does not recognize Israel because of Israel's occupation of Palestine. Most Muslim leaders and organizations appealed to the Indonesian government not to open diplomatic relations with Israel because it would be a violation of the Indonesian National Constitution of 1945, which, among other things, opposes any kind of colonialism. It seems that this sentiment against Israel remains strong among young people, who do not distinguish between the state's foreign policy and its people. Fuad (15 years old), from an SMA in Pamekasan, Madura, said: "I learned from news media about the brutality of Israelis against Palestinians. What they did there is unjustified. Although that doesn't happen here in Indonesia, we Indonesian Muslims should feel the pains." We will come back to this issue in the final chapter of this book.

Another significant indication of fragile civility among Indonesian youth is their negative attitudes toward people of other religions and

Chinese. Through in-depth interviews with 50 students, nuanced explanations were discovered. Since their responses to religious issues have been discussed in chapters 1 and 2, now we will analyze other dimensions of cultural diversity, including ethnicity and socioeconomic status. Among people of various ethnicities, Chinese people were singled out by respondents as among those they disliked. Although many informants thought it would be inappropriate to treat people differently based on their ethnicities, some associated Chinese with negative attributes, such as stinginess. Nila (16 years old), from an SMA in Surabaya, said that she lived within a community that respects differences; however, "sentiment against an ethnic Chinese can be found. For instance, [members of my community] called a Chinese group stingy or arrogant." Fuad, the 15-year-old from Pamekasan mentioned above, admitted that he rarely encountered an American or Westerner in his city, but he saw many Chinese with high economic status: "I don't know much about Western people, like Americans, because I rarely saw them here in my city.... With regard to the Chinese, yes, there are many Chinese people in this country and they are mostly rich, while Indonesian people remain poor."

In the city of Pasuruan, many Chinese owned businesses in markets, malls, and other shopping centers. There is no secret that Chinese companies have dominated Indonesia's private sector. Even in a small city like Pasuruan, Chinese-owned businesses are quite visible. Heti (16 years old), from an MAN in Pasuruan, admitted that she bullied her Chinese peer by making fun of her ethnicity. She said:

> When I was at middle school [SMP, Sekolah Menengah Pertama], I had a Chinese friend who in my opinion followed a different kind of ethics of friendship, at least compared to my other friends from Java. According to Javanese ethics of friendship, we don't recognize stinginess for friends. However, that person [Heti mentioned her name] showed her stinginess to me and to other people who wanted to borrow her power-bank [to charge phones]. I was used to that kind of treatment, so I reacted by making fun of her, hoping that she could change her stingy attitude. Many of us used what seemed to be racist language, such as "Hey, Chinese girl." She used to hear this type of thing as a joke.

Heti argued that she teased her Chinese friend not because of her different religion and ethnicity, but due to different friendship ethics (*etika berteman*) between them. "Because she is a heartless miser," Heti said, "I bullied her by calling her by her ethnicity. If she was stingy but not Chinese, I might still refer to whatever her ethnicity is."

Bullying is a serious problem among Indonesian youth. During my interviews, I found many students who admitted to being either bullies or victims of bullying. However, before I elaborate on the incidences of bullying on the basis of their stories, it is worth noting that their intolerant behaviors included various forms of bullying. From table 3.2 we learn that 22.6 percent of respondents admitted that they spread gossip and rumors about other persons' religious beliefs either frequently or occasionally. When asked whether they have ever derided or isolated others because of religious differences, those who derided others were 21.4 percent and those who isolated others were 10.4 percent. Moreover, 19 percent of respondents claimed that they tried to limit their friendships with students of different religions, while 8.2 percent took physical actions against others.

When asked about forms of bullying they have committed, whether against students of the same backgrounds or not, they tended to distinguish between bullying and other forms of mean behavior. As shown in table 3.3, some 33 percent of respondents said that they used harsh language or were rude, 11.4 percent spread untrue rumors, 14.4 percent bullied, and 6.4 percent physically abused others. All of these behaviors can fall in the category of bullying.

TABLE 3.2. Students' responses to "How often did you exhibit the following intolerant behaviors against other students of different religions?"

Categories	Frequently	Occasionally	Never
Gossiped	6.4%	16.2%	77.4%
Limited friendship	3.8%	15.2%	81.0%
Isolated	1.8%	8.6%	89.6%
Derided	4.4%	17.0%	78.6%
Did physical harm	1.8%	6.4%	91.8%

Note: n = 500; survey conducted in 2019.

TABLE 3.3. Students' responses to "Did you treat other students in the following manners?"

Categories	Yes	No
Used rude/harsh language	33.0%	67.0%
Spread untrue rumors	11.4%	88.6%
Bullied	14.4%	85.6%
Did physical harm	6.4%	93.6%

Note: n = 500; survey conducted in 2019.

From the literature review and analysis above, it is apparent that bullying takes many forms, including verbal abuse (e.g., taunting, teasing, making threats, and spreading rumors) and physical abuse (e.g., pushing, hitting, and coercing others), as well as one of the newest forms of bullying, cyberbullying, or the use of technology to cause harm to peers and/or socially isolate them. It seems that, from the perspective of Indonesian youth, bullying is a specific kind of persecution that is more abstract than being rude or physically abusing someone. During my in-depth interviews, I found that students defined "bullying" in various ways and that there is no consistency in their use of the term. Some students equated the verb bully with the word *menganiaya* in Indonesian, which can be translated into English using various terms, such as "mistreat," "molest," "manhandle," or even "persecute." Regardless of different understandings of bullying, this term was used frequently by high school students, mostly referring to verbal bullying. Dela (16 years old), from an SMA in Pasuruan, defines "tolerance" as showing respect for others and not bullying them: "Tolerance is about having friends from other religions. When I establish a friendship with others, the key is respecting one another. I respect them, and they respect me. So there is mutual respect. One should not bully others or something like that. My environment [at school] is far more tolerant than in other places." The incidence of bullying is often regarded as an obstacle to tolerance at schools. "The reality," said Karim (17 years old), from an SMA in Pasuruan, "is that intolerance is there at schools because not all students realize how important respecting differences is." Karim saw friends being bullied with sarcastic words due to different skin colors. He offered the following explanation:

Intolerant actions can be found in many places. There is no doubt about that. The reason is that not all people are conscious of the reality of differences around us. What I see as ironic is that some students make fun of differences. I often saw in classrooms where some students apologized because their skin colors are dark, and do you know what happened? They were bullied. There was a student who shouted, "You look like Ambonese" or "You look like black Chinese." So, they used differences to tease others.

Differences of ethnicity, skin color, or body size have often made young people the targets of bullying. As Dula (16 years old), from an SMA in Malang, said, he witnessed his friend being bullied because of his skin color, which was darker than that of others. In Dula's view, it is hard to measure the level of tolerance at schools because "there are those who are tolerant toward others, while others are intolerant and hateful." Dula told the following story: "One of my close friends was bullied because he was the smallest in class. However, other students stood up to defend us. That means that there is a real tolerance among us." Regardless of Dula's understanding of tolerance as simply the fact that the victim of bullying was protected, the reality is that bullying seems to be prevalent everywhere at schools. Susi (17 years old), from an SMA in Kediri, recounted various forms of bullying taking place at schools as follows:

> Of course, I saw bullying happening in this school. My female friend was bullied because her body size is big. She is also the youngest among us. I cannot believe she is often targeted for bullying. Sometimes, she was teased by making fun of her size. On other occasions, her stuff was taken and hidden without her consent, such as her books, or shoes, or bag. Bullying can be physical, such as pushing or kicking someone. I saw a female student from other grades was harassed. I knew it because she cried while others laughed at her.

Another student from the same town, Nora (15 years old), confirmed that bullying happened at school. Although she never experienced bullying herself, she heard about other students' being bullied. Her school was quite pluralistic in terms of student demographics. Some students who attended the school came from different religions, ethnicities, or socioeconomic statuses. Nora claimed that she had Christian friends both at school and outside school, and they respected one another. However, she witnessed discriminatory attitudes and bullying occurring at school. "While bullying is happening," she said, "it does not take the form of persecuting or harming others. That is a violation of human rights. Every human being is free, and his or her rights should not be infringed. Our religion also teaches us to respect and regard others with high esteem," she said.

Although bullying is happening both within and outside of educational environments, it has not been viewed as a serious problem. Several students contended that bullying was regarded as a kind of joke, as seen above in Susi's testimony and those of other students. Arman (16 years old), from an SMA in Surabaya, felt that religious tolerance at his school was quite strong, including toward people of other ethnicities. "However," he said, "you will find people who make fun of others with the intention of bullying." Similar testimonies were given by many other students during my interviews, namely, speaking of bullying others as if it were simply joking. The following testimony by Yasmin (17 years old), from an MAN in Kediri, reflects precisely that attitude: He claimed that he never bullied others; however, he jested by making fun of other students:

> I myself have never been involved in bullying, either as a perpetrator or victim. What I did was merely making fun of and teasing other students. That is something that many other friends have done the same. When we met, I joked about his or her appearance, outfit, or something of that nature. I also have not isolated others. When there was something between us, like uneasy relations, I simply stopped talking with him or her for a few days, but then we were fine. We got together again as usual.

It is worth noting that those who were victimized also tended to regard what happened to them as jokes, although they did not feel okay with such ridicule. Rama (16 years old), from an SMA in Pasuruan, said: "I did experience being a victim of bullying on more than one occasion. I am a playful type of person, I like making jokes. So when other people made fun of me a bit, I considered it a joke. I have been used to loving jokes with my friends when we get together. Therefore, I did not take their bullying seriously. I just laughed when I encountered people making fun of me as long as they did not attack me personally on sensitive issues." Some students did not distinguish between bullying and joking, or they did not feel bullied even when they encountered unpleasant behaviors that they disliked. A female student of Arab ethnicity, Maryam (17 years old), from an SMA in Surabaya, admitted that she did not experience bullying. "However," she said, "it happened that I was teased by my friends calling me 'an Arab girl,' which I do not like. At first, it was okay, but when they repeated it over and over again, I felt irritated."

From interviews it is also clear that the perpetrators of bullying generally wanted to show their power and privilege, including their socioeconomic status, or how tough they were. Nisa (15 years old), from an SMA in Malang, recounted her experience of being bullied when she was a middle-school student (at SMP, Sekolah Menengah Pertama). The perpetrator, according to her, was her own friend, whose parent was of high economic status. Being the granddaughter of a mayor in the city, the bully had a gang consisting of three other students who also were daughters of members of the District Representative Assembly (DPRD, Dewan Perwakilan Rakyat Daerah). Nisa said that she was not very close with them; however, one day they shouted at her, calling her "*cewek wek wek*" ("*cewek*" means "girl"). "I ignored them because they wanted to make fun of me," said Nisa, "but then they poured Coca-Cola on my pants." It seems clear that these bullies acted aggressively toward a female student when their mockery was ignored; they felt powerful and demanded to be treated differently. This understanding of bullying as a stratagem to exert domination over others was confirmed by perpetrators themselves, who admitted to what they had done. Born into a well-off family, Dulmatin (17 years old), from an SMA in Surabaya, came to school riding his own motorcycle. He said that he had a gang outside school, whose members met regularly and biked together. When asked whether he ever bullied others that he disliked, he responded as follows:

Yes, I mocked my own friend who followed a different understanding of religion. I was irritated when I saw her wearing a weird dress, such as a black jilbab covering all her face. It is so strange that she lived in this country with that kind of outfit. So I mocked her in this way: "You dress all black like a demon. Don't you feel stifled with that dress?" I was not comfortable seeing her dressed like that. I admit that I often talked rudely to my friends and bullied them, because I have my own gang who can understand me.

From the above testimony, it appears that the student bullied by Dulmatin was a female who was powerless to respond to his bullying. When asked why he did what he did, he responded, saying: "I felt happy expressing my distaste and reprimanding others in my own way to show who I am. Others should regard members of my gang with high esteem."

From my quantitative research, it seems clear that the rate of occurrence of uncivil behaviors was quite high. Tables 3.2 and 3.3 above illustrate two types of uncivil behaviors: intolerance and persecution, or *menganiaya*. Although there can be overlaps between the two categories, the former is defined as "not tolerating others whom one dislikes," and the latter refers to forms of expressions that can harm others. How frequently they exhibited uncivil behaviors to others can be seen in table 3.4. While it is true that uncivil behaviors were not exhibited frequently (intolerance by 3.2 percent of students and persecution by 5.8 percent), the percentage of incivility remained high, with 29.2 percent occasionally exhibiting intolerance and 36.2 percent persecution.

In addition, the number of bystanders (those who have witnessed incidences of uncivil behaviors) is high. The percentage of those who frequently saw intolerant actions was 5.2 percent, while 53.6 percent of respondents saw incidents of incivility occasionally, and 41.2 percent said that they have never seen intolerance in schools. This means that there is a need for an approach that pays attention to the community of bystanders, as discussed above, to overcome and prevent bullying and violence in schools.

TABLE 3.4. Students' responses to "How frequently did you exhibit the following uncivil behaviors to others?"

Categories	Frequently	Occasionally	Never
Intolerance	3.2%	29.2%	67.6%
Persecution	5.8%	36.2%	58.0%

Note: n = 500; survey conducted in 2019.

TABLE 3.5. Students' responses to "What would you do if students of other religions, ethnicities, or political ideologies were badly treated by other students?"

What I would do	Percentage
Would sympathize, but have no courage to defend them	29.2
Would defend and protect them only if they were close friends	16.4
Would defend and protect them even if they were not close friends	54.4

Note: n = 500; survey conducted in 2019.

The vast majority of respondents (80.6 percent) believed that intolerant attitudes toward others are not appropriate, and only 19.4 percent considered them appropriate. My research also explored the views of bystanders concerning what they would do if they saw uncivil behaviors toward others in their schools. Table 3.5 shows that the majority of respondents (54.4 percent) said that they would defend and protect the victims even if they were not their close friends. Moreover, 16.4 percent said they would defend them only if they were their friends, and the rest of the respondents (29.2 percent) expressed sympathy but said they have no courage to defend them.

Sympathy and the willingness to help others who suffer from oppression and discrimination are civic values that must be taught to students. The spirit of helping each other remains strong among the students that I interviewed. Some students contended that helping the weak is a religious obligation, while others related it to the principle of *gotong-royong*, a term used to refer to working together to achieve common goals, which many Indonesians uphold in the family and social life. Moreover, students narrated their experiences of being victims of discrimination and violence, and they aspired to prevent what happened to them from happening to others. Fuad, for instance, was born to a low-income family in Pamekasan as mentioned earlier, and he told his story as follows: "When my friends realized that my family was kicked out of our rented house, I was mocked and humiliated for being homeless. This happened just recently, so I still feel the pain and remember their mockery very well. My socioeconomic status is different from theirs. I wish I can intermingle with them, but they don't welcome me, what can I do? It is painful, but I have to be realistic about my situation. So I decided to befriend others who can accept me." Fuad did not want any kind of intolerance to be exhibited to him and other people, especially those he knew well. Therefore, he strove to help others who suffered from unfair treatment. He said, "I don't want other people to experience my sufferings, as I don't want this to happen again. I am committed to help and protect others who become the victims of mockery and humiliation. I hate being bullied. I feel the pain in here [he pointed to his chest]. That kind of behavior cannot be tolerated. Being different is okay and should not be the target of humiliation." The problem is that whenever intolerance and persecution occur, the incidents have not been settled by addressing the root causes. For instance, there is a lack of forums and initiatives that will enable students from different backgrounds to interact, intermingle, and get to know each other better. In many cases, tensions and conflicts among students were resolved among themselves. The following is the testimony of Nirma (17 years old), from an SMA in Surabaya: "In this school, there is no forum [wadah] for students of different religious backgrounds; however, students are all nice here. There can be some tensions between them, such as debates or misunderstandings, but there are no serious issues. I would intervene and help if I saw any of my friends were being treated unjustly, even if they were not close to me. I would protect them as far as I can." When students were asked about activities that can be used to enable them to interact, such as sports, hobbies, or academic and social activities, most students said that such activities were simply not there. Those who said that such activities were still available were small in number, and others said that activities that had been designed as forums for students with diverse backgrounds were no longer active, as can be seen in table 3.6.

TABLE 3.6. Students' responses to "Are activities available at your school that allow students from different religions, ethnicities, and political ideologies to interact with one another?"

Types of forum	There are, and they are still active	There have been, but are no longer active	Not available
Sports	40.2%	8.2%	51.6%
Hobbies	39.2%	8.6%	52.2%
Academic activities	45.0%	8.4%	46.6%
Social activities	36.4%	10.8%	52.8%

Note: n = 500; survey conducted in 2019.

WHY CIVILITY MATTERS

The findings presented above demonstrate a civility deficit in Indonesia, and we have reasons to be pessimistic about a civil future in the country. Of particular concern is peer bullying, which seems to be quite prevalent both in and outside of educational environments. Bullying by peers has become a significant problem in many schools worldwide, often resulting in severe consequences for the bully and the victim. In a cross-cultural study of several countries, bullying was found to be a universal phenomenon.[44] In Indonesia, according to the Global School Health Survey in its 2015 report, more than 20 percent of Indonesian children in grades 7–12 reported having experienced bullying in the last month.[45] This number is quite conservative compared to the findings of Lucy Bowes, mentioned above. According to the UNICEF Annual Report for 2015, as many as 40 percent of adolescents have been bullied in school, and 32 percent have reported that they have been victims of physical violence.[46] At any rate, Indonesia is a country with a high rate of aggressive behavior, such as bullying among adolescents. However, there is a lack of comprehensive data.

This is alarming, especially because of the negative effects of bullying on victims, perpetrators, bystanders, and society. Victimization in childhood has been related to unhappiness, poor social adaptation, behavioral problems at school, and anxiety and social phobias in adulthood. Studies show that the causes of several cases of school shootings in the United States have been rooted in bullying. Researchers found that the perpetrators of many such violent crimes were youths who acted to avenge long-term bullying, victimization, and social isolation.[47] While studies need to be done to allow us to better understand the contextual variables that allow and encourage bullying to thrive in schools, it is equally important for the Indonesian public to see this as a social problem that needs to be addressed. Schools have to play a more assertive role in teaching and nourishing civic values in students. Schools should have climates conducive to the daily practice of civility. Tolerance and respect for others must be presented as public virtues to counter egocentrism and ethnocentrism. As discussed in my research finding above, bullying can be seen as one way adolescents manage peer relationships and exert dominance as they transition into new social groups. My interviews with bullies show that bullying is a way of achieving dominance and demonstrating their socioeconomic position.

Findings from this study indicate that the range of what constitutes bullying and incivility is wide, thus confirming the literature that has catalogued types of bullying and incivility. While bullying and other uncivil behaviors can have significant and devastating impacts, such as contributing to school shootings, they can also be experienced in small nuisances and inconveniences, such as people's cutting in line. Civility in the lives of students has always been understood and experienced positively through interactions with friends and family and exchanges with strangers. Schools and other public entities have the responsibility to promote civility among their constituents and to encourage and promote civility both in and outside of educational environments. In a society with diverse ethnicities, religions, races, and groups, civility plays an important role. Research on civility has described it as a virtue and explains it as behavior to reduce intergroup conflicts and guide social interactions. In this context, civility should not be confused with etiquette or being nice. It is also about showing respect and dignity for oneself and others.[48] Giovinella Gonthier refers to civility as being consciously aware of human dignity and the value of human life at all times. She argues that civility is a way of life, evident in how we live and how we treat others.[49] In other words, the mutual exchange of rights, responsibilities, and respects is indispensable.

Living in pluralistic societies, we cannot avoid differences. According to Stephanie Oppel, "Civility that is based on respect, including respect for difference in terms of identity, culture, custom, and experience, will do more for people and, in turn, society, than civility that is based on a set of behaviors that is drawn from the dominant culture and applied as if it were universal."[50] Schools should teach students how to negotiate and settle their differences peacefully. Thus, tolerance for others is the standard of civility that will allow those with conflicting views to live peacefully. There is a close relationship between tolerance and civility, although civility goes beyond tolerance to include progressive civilization, modernity, and the notion of order. Civility must be taught and learned. Drawing on the multiculturalism of Canada, Daniel Coleman writes, "Education in civility shepherds people onto the path of progress because it names a future ideal as if it were a present norm. It projects an ideal of social interaction (all members of society should be freely included and accorded equal respect) as something to which individuals should aspire: if you wish to join the egalitarian progressive company, you must be willing to improve yourself, to become worthy of the respect that characterizes the civil group."[51]

Unfortunately, children spend an inordinate amount of time learning from television and social media, which seem to perpetuate violence and endorse rudeness. It is also important to note that civility is not just a concept to be written on walls or taught in classes. It is, first and foremost, about the daily lives of people. Just as being bullied can lead the victims to bully others, writes Oppel, "being treated with civility [can impact] their lives in a positive way, sometimes even impact them to be even more civil in their relations with others."[52] Practices that honor differences promote civility, and practices that demonstrate inequities because of differences promote incivility. Thus, civility must be employed for good: to improve outcomes, to make people feel welcome, included, and heard. Civility should bring people together to go further and do better.

The question is this: How do we cultivate a climate of civility in schools' daily routines? As discussed in my findings above, educational environments do not seem to be conducive to enhancing civic engagement among students with diverse backgrounds or to helping them overcome barriers to civility and develop mutual trust, respect, and equality. For instance, the schools of students I studied tended to be indifferent to student gang activity, which has caused serious concerns about students, especially those who were vulnerable to becoming victims of uncivil behaviors. Members of dominant groups engaged in bullying and other uncivil behaviors to obtain a socially dominant position. From the literature review, we learn that bullying exists when a student with more social or physical power deliberately dominates and harasses another with less power. In this chapter I have discussed examples of uncivil behavior by those who demanded to be treated differently due to their perceived power vis-à-vis the weak and marginalized students whom they victimized. This coincides with Robert Sutton's research on incivility in the context of the workplace, which concluded that acts of incivility are usually focused on those who are less powerful.[53]

This hierarchal inequality begets another barrier: fear. This may include fear of being different in terms of skin color or body size, fear due to being of a different ethnicity or religious minority, or fear to react against oppressive and discriminatory treatment. On the one hand, there is fear on the part of specific individuals or groups, and on the other hand, there is indifference and ignorance from others. Fear and ignorance can cause mistrust, which is also a barrier to civility. If schools provide no forums that enable students to interact with one another on an equal footing, it is challenging to overcome self-importance and a lack of empathy among individuals. As discussed in chapter 1, intergroup contacts can reduce prejudice and enhance trust. Harriette Scott writes, "Trust engenders respect, respect shows the value, and each of these traits demonstrates civility in relationships and discourse."[54] Therefore, schools must be deliberate about creating a culture of civility, because the existence of an open environment where people can see each other and interact can promote civility.

CONCLUDING REMARKS

Civility and incivility are different yet closely connected concepts that are manifested in a complex manner inside and outside of educational environments. In this chapter I have highlighted different forms of uncivil behaviors among students, including bullying, reflecting the fragility of civility among Indonesian youth. Anecdotal evidence of incivility among young people in Indonesia is present in various forums, including social media and news media. These anecdotal reports are supported by this research, which has found that bullying, including intolerant and aggressive behaviors, is prevalent both in and outside of educational environments. As discussed in this chapter, incivility in education is not only a problem in Indonesia but is also on the rise throughout the world. Concern about behavioral issues is not limited to any particular demographic group or socioeconomic status. Students are experiencing uncivil behavior at both lower and higher levels of education. However, these uncivil behaviors are often not addressed with a sense of urgency in Indonesia. The issue of civility in schools is part of what Rudy H. Fichtenbaum calls a "broader concern about civility in the workplace and a perceived lack of civility in society in general."[55]

My findings raise a critical concern about the future of Indonesia if this fragile civility among youth is not taken seriously. In developed countries, like the United States, the rise of incivility among young people has caused increasing attention to be given to the issue. Literature on civility is published with increasing frequency, and there are increasing calls for civility in the national conversation. In general, civility is considered a good thing, as it provides the basis for and supports the continued existence of a civil society in which individuals and groups live well together. In their review of the literature, Keenly Wilkins, Paul Caldarella, Rachel Crook-Lyon, and Richard Young argue that "young people are the leading citizens of tomorrow; if they can be taught to realize the values and resist the threats to civility, a more civil society may be encouraged."[56] There is a trend toward using schools as one of the primary sites for teaching civility to children. The Indonesian public must begin to pay serious attention to this critical issue by implementing civility curricula as a mechanism for reinforcing character development and moral formation, creating initiatives to enhance civility in schools, and establishing policies and procedures that advance civility. If these measures are not taken, students will continue to suffer from incivility in their primary and secondary education environments. The next step is to promote civility in higher education, where behavioral issues continue, as will be discussed in the following chapter.

PART TWO

Radicalization in Higher Education

FOUR

Religious Radicalism in the Making

The involvement of young people in radical groups remains a concern in the West, where there is an increased fear of homegrown terrorism. The threat of domestic terrorism and the involvement of youth in violence continues to attract global attention, from the presence of the Taliban—which literally means "students"—in Afghanistan to Boko Haram in Nigeria, as well as the young jihadists who have joined the Islamic State of Iraq and Syria (ISIS). It is no surprise that within a few years, the radicalization of youth has become a prominent topic of discussion among policymakers and those in intelligence agencies, as well as in the academic world.[1] In Indonesia, the largest Muslim-majority country in the world, the involvement of young people in radical groups has become alarmingly widespread. In 2016, researchers from the Indonesian Institute of Sciences (LIPI, Lembaga Ilmu Pengetahuan Indonesia) indicated that radical movements had infiltrated campuses, resulting in a recruitment program whereby students became involved with radical study circles and student activist groups.[2] A senior LIPI researcher, Anas Saidi, contends that "Indonesian youths are experiencing radicalization and increasingly intolerant, while hardliners and radical groups have infiltrated many universities."[3] A 2017 survey by the Alvara Research

Center indicated a trend of radical and intolerant attitudes in the university student community. It revealed that 29.5 percent of university students did not support any appointment of non-Muslim leaders, 23.4 percent of students supported Indonesia's becoming an Islamic state under a caliphate, and 23.5 percent of them agreed with ISIS.[4] The survey was carried out at 25 universities throughout Indonesia and included 1,800 respondents.

Perhaps most shocking were the findings published in 2018 by the National Agency for Combating Terrorism (BNPT, Badan Nasional Penanggulangan Terorisme), which showed that seven leading state universities—the University of Indonesia (UI), Bandung Institute of Technology (ITB), Bogor Institute of Agriculture (IPB), University of Diponegoro (Undip), Institute of Technology Sepuluh Nopember (ITS), University of Airlangga (Unair), and University of Brawijaya (UB)—had been infiltrated by radical groups and that a significant proportion of their student populations were sympathetic to radicalism.[5] Andi Intang Dulung, the head of the Sub-Directorate for Community Empowerment of the BNPT, reported that 39 percent of students in 15 provinces expressed an interest in radicalism: "These results reinforce the notion that the younger generation is the target audience of the propagation of radicalism, and that the university campus is vulnerable to this propagation."[6] All of the findings above indicate that the threat of radicalization among educated youth in Indonesia is real and concerning. As a response, the government has involved various levels of civil society, implementing numerous efforts to confront the threat of radicalism, such as the shutting down of radical organizations that are believed to have infiltrated educational institutions, both high schools and universities. In 2017, through the implementation of new legislation, President Joko Widodo (Jokowi), shut down the transnational Islamic movement Hizbut Tahrir Indonesia (HTI) because it propagates a pro-caliphate ideology that contradicts *Pancasila*.[7] Education leaders introduced policies for dealing with the spread of radical thinking on campuses. However, not only has the effectiveness of state and university policies been questioned, but also such policies have often been proven to be counterproductive. For example, the policy of some campuses of forbidding students to wear the *cadar* (a full-face covering) instigated a violent reaction from the students and the communities in general, which caused the universities' leadership to be pressured into withdrawing this policy. Thus it is evident that state and university policies have not been based on careful and detailed research.

There is little doubt that the response of the state and the universities to the infiltration of radical ideologies into educational institutions was out of touch with the complex issues on the ground. It should be noted that the LIPI, the Alvara Research Center, and the BNPT surveys are quantitative; as such, they cannot illustrate precisely how young people become radicalized. In this chapter I discuss my findings, both quantitative and qualitative, to allow us to better understand how the radicalization of youth occurs. My research, which involved 70 in-depth interviews, was conducted with 700 students from the seven universities that the BNPT found were exposed to radicalism. Specific pathways of youth radicalization and their patterns will be analyzed. It should be noted that various forms of the "pathways" approach have been used by different scholars who have described various stages, including a detailed discussion of each stage's characteristics.[8] While my findings do not discredit the notion of stages, I do show that the patterns of the pathways are not uniform or linear. On the basis of in-depth interviews, I highlight patterns of radicalization that are more diverse and complex than have commonly been assumed. Unlike previous studies that have proposed various models to conceptualize the path of radicalization toward Islamist terrorism, in the present chapter I focus on how educated youth become radicalized in the first place. The analysis and findings are drawn from quantitative surveys and in-depth interviews with university students who have been exposed to radical ideologies. How are individuals drawn into the process of radicalization? What forces shape their radical views and attitudes? In this chapter we will follow the pathways toward youth radicalization with insights from conversion theory.

RADICALIZATION AND CONVERSION THEORY

Along with the rise of religious intolerance in Indonesia, the involvement of youth in radical groups has become alarmingly widespread. Of particular concern is radicalization leading to acts of violence, especially against minority groups. It is the scholarly consensus that radicalization does not happen overnight. The widely accepted definition, as will be discussed later, describes radicalization as a process that is dynamic and not conditional.[9] This means that people become radicals or act violently not because of mental illness or sudden abnormalities. In most cases, they develop their radical ideas or become radicals gradually.[10]

Among academics, diverse radicalization theories have been influenced by social science disciplines such as sociology, anthropology, criminology, law, political theory, policy studies, as well as religious and cultural studies.[11] Unlike governments that often use a definition of radicalization that emphasizes its "endpoints" (violence or terrorism), a number of scholars have analyzed the connection between ideas and actions. For example, Brian Jenkins differentiates between "internalizing a set of beliefs" and "transforming oneself into a weapon of jihad."[12] John Horgan follows a similar argument. At the START symposium in Washington, DC, he argued that academics overemphasize cognitive radicalization, assuming that extreme beliefs represent the precursors to violent action, describing this as "the inevitable logic."[13] These critics of cognitive radicalization do not aim to neglect the danger of extreme ideas and beliefs. They only mean to encourage a more holistic understanding of radicalization so that other associated issues, such as group dynamics, social networks, suffering, personal crises, and so on, might also be brought to public attention.

The concept of radicalization is connected not only to what Asta Maskaliunaite refers to as "what goes on before the bomb goes off."[14] In his study of the radicalization literature, Alex Schmid begins with discussions of radicalism at the micro, meso, and macro levels and then explains that radicalization studies should "approach the field of extremism and terrorism by focusing on the processes through which individuals become socialized into engaging in political violence without moral restraints."[15] This approach does not neglect religious knowledge, because a belief system is also susceptible to being politicized. It is relevant to mention some definitions of radicalization that reflect the recent scholarship. Tim Stevens and Peter Neumann note that "most of the definitions currently in circulation describe radicalisation as the process (or processes) whereby individuals or groups come to approve of and (ultimately) participate in the use of violence for political aims. Some authors refer to 'violent radicalisation' to emphasize the violent outcome and distinguish the process from non-violent forms of 'radical' thinking."[16] Chuck Crossett and Jason Spitaletta offer a broad viewpoint when they define radicalization as follows: "The process by which an individual, group, or mass of people undergo a transformation from participating in the political process via legal means to the use or support of violence for political purposes."[17] In their discussion of homegrown extremism, Alex Wilner and Claire-Jehanne Dubouloz write: "Radicalization is a personal process in which individuals adopt extreme political, social, and/or religious ideals and aspirations, and where the attainment of particular goals justifies the use of indiscriminate violence. It is both a mental and emotional process that prepares and motivates an individual to pursue violent behaviour."[18] Maskaliunaite describes radicalization as "a process by which a person adopts belief systems which justify the use of violence to effect social change and comes to actively support as well as employ violent means for political purposes."[19]

A number of the definitions above consider radicalization to be a process, often gradual and in stages, while the end result is social change. This means that radicalization does not occur instantly or in a vacuum. There is a context—or, at a minimum, a social component. Can a person be self-radicalized? Several theories suggest that this is possible. Nevertheless, self-radicalization also requires a context, with interaction either virtual (online) or real (recruitment). Although the two stages of radicalization can be identified—*support through religious beliefs* and *implementation*—the first stage does not necessarily give birth to the second. In other words, Maskaliunaite writes, "One can adopt radical beliefs and not act upon them, and vice versa, one could act without even holding some deep and inalterable beliefs."[20] At the same time, these definitions can accommodate variations within radicalism, including different pathways toward becoming radicalized.

One of the most well-known radicalization models is the four-phase framework proposed by Mitchell Silber and Arvin Bhatt.[21] This framework identifies four phases, namely, "pre-radicalization," "self-identification," "indoctrination," and "jihadization." It was developed on the basis of the authors' analysis of five prominent homegrown cases of Islamic terrorism in North America and Western Europe. The first phase refers to individuals' world before their exposure to Jihadi-Salafi ideology, followed by their exploration and embracing of the ideology, with which they begin to identify themselves. In this second phase, self-identification, Silber and Bhatt emphasize a personal crisis as the key impetus for turning to a more assertive form of Islam. The third phase, indoctrination, marks the intensification of belief in Jihadi-Salafi ideology, which for adherents justifies the use of violence against anything considered un-Islamic. In the final phase, jihadization, members of a cluster are committed to violent jihad to achieve their goals.

Similar models of sequential stages have been introduced by other scholars, including Thomas Precht, Quintan Wiktorowicz, and Randy Borum.[22] Precht's four stages include (1) pre-radicalization, (2) conversion to and identification with radical Islam, (3) indoctrination and increased group bonding, and (4) either plotting or committing actual acts of terrorism.[23] Wiktorowicz's framework, which is based on social movement theory, theorizes that an individual who joins an extremist religious group will undergo (1) "cognitive opening" as a result of a personal crisis that renders a person receptive to extremist ideas, (2) "religious seeking," in which the person's sensibility is directed toward religious faith, (3) "frame alignment," whereby the person regards extremist worldviews as coinciding with his or her own, and (4) "socialization," which is achieved when he or she embraces the ideology and officially joins the group. Borum's theory, unlike Wiktorowicz's, is psychological in that it describes the psychology of an individual who adopts an ideology that justifies violent actions. However, like the other three scholars mentioned above, he also develops a four-phase process of radicalization, starting with (1) an individual's feeling of being in unfavorable conditions, then (2) comparing these conditions with those of others and (3) considering this inequality unfair, and finally (4) developing hatred toward others who are viewed as responsible for the existing unfavorable conditions. Eventually, this negative stereotype of the other legitimizes violence.

It seems clear that not only do the models presented by Silber and Bhatt, Precht, Wiktorowicz, and Borum share an important commonality in their stepwise understanding radicalization, but they also reflect a linear progression. This linear progression has been challenged in more recent scholarship. For instance, Mohammad Hafez and Creighton Mullins contend that "we do not find evidence in the vast empirical literature on radicalization to justify this orderly image of a process."[24] Hafez and Mullins caution radicalization specialists not to fall into the trap of "radicalization models with seemingly neat categories and check-lists of predictive indicators based on overt attitudes, outward appear-ances, and manifest behaviors."[25] To resist this temptation, some scholars address conditions and contexts in which radicalization can take place instead of depicting a sequential order of stages. Marc Sageman, for ex-ample, refers to radicalization as a result of the interplay of four factors, the first three of which can be considered cognitive, while the fourth is situational.[26] One cognitive aspect leading to radicalization is a percep-tion of particular circumstances that result in anger, for example, arbi-trary acts against Muslims, ill treatment of the Palestinian people, or the U.S. invasion of Iraq. Another cognitive factor is the mentality used to understand international relations, such as the ostensible rift between the "West" and Islam. The perception that the West is fighting against Islam can encourage the development of radicalization. Personal experiences, such as discrimination or unemployment, are also highlighted by Sage-man as triggers. These three cognitive factors can reinforce one another, resulting in a powerful impulse toward radicalization. In addition to the cognitive factors, "mobilization through networks" or interactions with like-minded people serve as crucial catalysts for radicalization.

Other non-linear explanations have been proposed by scholars such as Max Taylor and John Horgan, Arie Kruglanski and Shira Fishman, and Clark McCauley and Sophia Moskalenko.[27] They offer broad expla-nations that capture the complexity of radicalization, but are perhaps too general to describe pathways to radicalization.[28] These theories, both specific models and general frameworks, are useful for considering the complex issues involved in the process of radicalization. They allow us to think critically about factors leading to radicalization, what Hafez and Mullins refer to as "grievances, networks, ideologies, and enabling environments and support structures."[29] These models also suggest that there needs to be a multi-level analysis of phases and stages. However, at the center of this analysis is the link between radicalization and violent extremism, which has recently been called into question. Schmid is cor-rect in saying that radicalization studies "approach the field of extrem-ism and terrorism by focusing on the process through which individuals become socialized into engaging in political violence without moral restraints."[30] This connection between radicalism and violent extremism has recently been viewed as problematic. As Tinka Velddhuis and Jorgen

Staun believe, the fact of the matter is that "although every terrorist is a radical, not every radical is a terrorist."[31] As Maskaliunaite has rightly noted, "An individual who adopts quite radical political/religious beliefs does not necessarily act on those beliefs and does not necessarily move from a legal, political action to an illegal one."[32]

My own findings support this view. Most students who can be categorized as radical are not committed to violent acts, as will be discussed later. On the basis of his analysis of three historical instances of radicalization in Palestine, Ireland, and Cyprus, Chares Demetriou contends that the use of violent tactics needs to be distinguished from the radicalization of one's political ideas, although the two may develop together and even reinforce one another.[33] The purpose of the present chapter is not to develop new models for understanding radicalization as a process leading to violent extremism, but simply to decipher how and why individuals become radicalized in the first place.

In this regard, conversion theory can help highlight interrelated factors in the process of radicalization. Conversion is a concept that is rarely considered by scholars when researching radicalization, even when radicalized people have changed their religions. Neil Ferguson and Eva Blinks argue that radicalization has similarities to religious conversion and emphasizes that the use of conversion theory can help explain the process.[34] In a similar vein, Jose Vargas contends that conversion theory provides "insights into a better understanding of how individual factors, experiences and dynamics relate to the religious, social and cultural environment of individuals."[35] The very term "conversion" is a contested concept for social scientists, and it has become the subject of much discussion.[36] As David Snow and Richard Machalek argue, "Conversion concerns not only a change in values, beliefs, and identities, but more fundamentally and significantly, it entails the displacement of one universe of discourse by another, or the ascendance of a formerly peripheral universe of discourse to the status of a primary authority."[37] Perhaps the most advanced conversion theory is the one developed by Lewis Rambo in his *Understanding Religious Conversion*.[38] To frame the different approaches toward conversion, Rambo employs the stages of "context," "quest," "crisis," "advocates," "interaction," "commitments," and "consequences." In the context of radicalization, Vargas envisions the following analogous stages:

The individuals' environment (context), their loss of emotional or moral balance resulting from a traumatic episode (crisis), their desire to regain the lost balance (quest), and the emergence of a guide or advocate to assist in the quest for balance (encounter). The strengthening of the relationship with the advocate or guide and the introduction of a new ideology (interaction) leads to the individual's conscious decision to embrace the new ideology (commitment). The final stage concerns the outcomes of this commitment (consequences).[39]

Vargas admits that the sequential stages from "context" to "consequences" do not have to follow a specific order. However, he concludes that "the stages of radicalization that the model provides help visualize the progression towards extremism."[40] The problem is that the data used by Vargas was obtained from interviews with local and state law enforcement agents, military antiterrorism officers, and security personnel from military installations in North Carolina, not from people who were actually radicalized. My findings not only do not support the assumption that radicalization proceeds in a linear fashion, but they also reveal that not all stages envisioned by Rambo will always be present in each individual, nor will any one factor always be more dominant than another. Vargas did admit that conversion theory has limitations when applied to the data he collected. Like Vargas, this chapter takes insights from Rambo's conversion theory as a starting point for understanding the interplay between various factors in converting to radicalism.

BACKGROUND NOTES ON RADICALIZED YOUTH

The question of why young people have become so vulnerable to the infiltration of radicalism and also targets of recruiting terrorist groups has been the subject of many studies.[41] Of course, there is no single, definitive explanation because the problems faced by young people in each region are different. Muslim immigrant children in the West face the challenge of negotiating multiple identities across ethnic, social, and religious dimensions, which complicates how they situate themselves in their particular societies. In other parts of the world, the problem of radicalization is more closely related to the marginalization of disenfranchised youth disillusioned by the lack of economic and political opportunities available to them. In areas affected by prolonged conflict, young people come to trust radical groups due to their suspicion of the parties trying to solve the conflict. Thus, radical groups provide them with sources of safety and security. Some young people live in family and community environments that support radical ideologies. In some Islamic schools (*madrasah*s), radical doctrines and intolerant attitudes are integral parts of their curricula. A common thread running through these various cultural scenarios is that susceptible youth encounter the temptation to become radicalized in ways distinctive to their particular environments.

My study on students at seven state universities identified by BNPT as having been infiltrated by religious radicalism revealed their diverse backgrounds. In terms of economic background, most of my respondents (75.4 percent) came from well-off families. As many as 80.2 percent lived in boardinghouses and had motorbikes to use to get to school. The seven state universities that I studied are public campuses, not religious educational institutions. Thus, it is not surprising that 83 percent of respondents were graduates of general secondary schools, not traditional Islamic educational institutions such as *madrasah* or *pesantren*. Only 3.3 percent had graduated from *pesantren* and 13.7 percent from *madrasah*, both public and private.

When asked whether they have been involved in radical activities and networks, a significant number of students (30.4 percent) claimed that they have been and are still (as of 2018) actively involved in radical networks, while 29.7 percent of respondents said that they no longer participated in radical activities (see table 4.1). The rest (39.9 percent) have never been involved in and were not attracted to radical ideologies.

TABLE 4.1. Students' responses to "Since college, have you ever participated in radical activities?"

Response	Percentage
Yes, and I am still active currently	30.4
Yes, but I no longer participate	29.7
Never participated	39.9

Note: n = 700; survey conducted in 2018.

TABLE 4.2. Students' responses to "Who or what encouraged you to become radicalized?"

Party	Percentage
Friends in religious study forums (*teman pengajian*)	48.3
Senior mentors or *musrif*	8.3
Professors	1.3
Parents	1.0
My own understanding of the Qur'an	6.0
No response	35.1

Note: n = 700; survey conducted in 2018.

It is worth noting that the process of recruitment into radical groups was often carried out by other students who were already involved in radical networks. As table 4.2 shows, among those who have been involved in radical groups, either still active or no longer active, 48.3 percent admitted that they were attracted to radical ideologies because their friends or peers on campus persuaded them. The influence of older mentors (*mushrif*) was 8.3 percent, professors/lecturers 1.3 percent, and parents 1 percent. As many as 6 percent of respondents claimed that they got involved in radical groups because of their own understanding of the Qur'an. The rest of the respondents did not answer.

Other interesting observations from the respondents concerned the role of social media platforms. While it is true that a significant number of respondents were exposed to radicalism through joining a religious study forum (*pengajian*), at 47.5 percent, respondents actively interacted with the Internet, including online radical content. As illustrated in table 4.3,

TABLE 4.3. Students' responses to "How were you first exposed to radicalism?"

Source	Yes	No
Reading from social media	53.3%	46.7%
Reading from an Internet website	49.3%	50.7%
Watching a video on YouTube	32.6%	67.4%
Reading a brochure or pamphlet	25.1%	74.9%
Joining religious study forums (*pengajian*)	47.5%	52.5%

Note: n = 700; survey conducted in 2018.

TABLE 4.4. Students' responses to "What activities did you participate in to help spread radical ideologies?"

Actions/Behaviors Respondents Participated in	Frequently	Rarely	Never
Preaching doctrines to other friends	29.0%	37.0%	34.4%
Distributing brochures and leaflets	4.7%	16.4%	78.8%
Inviting friends to a religious study group	28.4%	36.7%	34.9%
Writing an article for the purpose of sharing	3.0%	6.6%	90.4%

Note: n = 700; survey conducted in 2018.

respondents accessed various online sources, from websites to social media (Twitter, Facebook, Instagram, Line, Snapchat, and chatrooms) to movies or videos on YouTube.

When respondents were asked how they felt after participating in radical religious study groups, as many as 31.4 percent said they felt they were on the right path, and 12.4 percent felt purified. Interestingly, the number of those who felt wrong entering or participating in the religious study groups was not small, 24.9 percent, and 6 percent wanted to leave. Among the changes that took place in them after being involved in radical groups were an increase in their disdain for the United States (40.2 percent) and more active involvement in religious study forums (61.4 percent). The activities of respondents in spreading radical ideas are illustrated in table 4.4.

To find out the respondents' commitment to "Muslim aspirations," I asked for their levels of support for the motives behind radical groups (see table 4.5). The number of respondents who wanted the implementation of Islamic law or *Shari'ah* was very high at 60.6 percent, while 20.4 percent were undecided and 19 percent did not support it. I inquired in more detail about their support for laws regarding cutting off the hands of thieves, stoning adulterers, and replacing commercial banks with *Shari'ah* banks. It turned out that the number of those who supported these niche issues was lower than that of those who favored the general implementation of *Shari'ah*. I also asked for respondents' views on the establishment of an Islamic state, a caliphate state, and the Jakarta Charter. The latter is an old issue in Indonesian history; in the Jakarta Charter the initial formulation of the state ideology of *Pancasila* included the phrase "with obligation for Muslims to implement their religious teachings."

TABLE 4.5. Students' responses to "Do you support the following aspirations?"

Muslim aspirations	Support	Undecided	No support
Implementation of Islamic *Shari'ah*	60.6%	20.4%	19.0%
Implementation of a ruling or law on cutting off the hands of thieves	27.3%	42.9%	29.9%
Calling for stoning for adulterers	35.0%	33.6%	31.4%
Replacement of commercial banks by Islamic banks	46.6%	29.1%	19.0%
Making Islam the state religion	38.1%	40.1%	21.7%
Creation of a caliphate state	25.9%	28.9%	45.3%
Establishment of the Jakarta Charter	41.0%	42.0%	17.0%

Note: n = 700; survey conducted in 2018.

NARRATIVES OF RADICALIZATION CONVERSION

To better understand the process of radicalization among young people, I conducted in-depth interviews with 70 students at seven state universities (see table 4.1). In these interviews, specific patterns were found in how young people described their conversion to radicalism. Based on their own testimonies, I classify conversion narratives according to the driving forces in students' becoming radicalized.

Conversion through Influence and Pressure from Peers

As seen in the quantitative data presented above, radicalization typically occurs due to the influence of those involved firsthand in radical groups. Almost all state universities in Indonesia have student Islamic organizations, and these student organizations are usually managed by students who are radical in their understanding of and support for the ideology of Islamist groups such as Hizbut Tahrir Indonesia (HTI). Students who are members of Islamic organizations are active and militant in spreading their radical agendas and recruit members as widely as possible by inviting other students to partake in *pengajian*, which they call "*liqā*" (literally: meetings). Invitations come in many forms, starting with small things like group work, studying, or helping with school assignments and moving on to offering financial rewards, such as purchasing basic necessities like clothes or books or offering scholarships.

The following is the story of Rina (22 years old), from Unair in Surabaya:

> At first, I was invited to know radicalism because of someone I met when studying at the Faculty of Economics and Business (FEB). She is our senior. After getting to know her, we continued to chat. I was invited to study. She would always invite me to go out, and this made our friendship really close. Even though at first I refused [to join HTI], she remained persistent until she arrived at my house, offered to pay my tuition, offered to help my studies by paying me, and gave me *shar'i* clothes. She also once waited until late at night, until it rained. She was just relentless.

Recruitment through study groups is found on many other campuses. For instance, in UB in Malang, the spread of radical ideology is dominated by study activities carried out by organizational cadres suspected of being radical. After organizations such as HTI were banned, they infiltrated intracampus organizations, such as the Spiritual Unit of the Faculty of Agriculture (MT Funa). One of the informants shared his experience of being invited to participate in a religious gathering, which involved indoctrination concerning the caliphate: "It was the first time I was invited so kindly." He continued, "Because I felt obligated due to their kindness, I felt that I had to join. In the session that I attended, we were immediately led to opinions about the superiority of the caliphate system and how the tyranny of this country will continue to occur if the caliphate system is not implemented." The informant also explained that he was told to bring friends to the second meeting and to spread the idea of the caliphate system.

The banning of HTI did not automatically stop the movement of its young followers. Knowing that the campus had been infiltrated by radical groups, the leaders of Undip in Semarang conducted strict supervision of radical organizations' activities on campus. One professor who was also an HTI activist was dismissed from his position as the director of the graduate program of the Faculty of Law. Professor Suteki used his social media to defend HTI. According to the official letter signed by the rector of Undip, Suteki was fired because he was under investigation by the Ethics Committee due to his involvement in the radical group.[42] Suteki served as an HTI expert witness during the court hearing. The court rejected HTI's defense of its being banned unconstitutionally. Salman (24 years old), from Undip, explained his early joining of a radical organization on his campus: "I was invited by friends to join," he said. With the supervision of radical activities getting tighter, he admitted that his peers had changed their invitation strategy to make it lower profile: "After the unfortunate ban of our chairman, we no longer preach openly to uphold the caliphate and the idea of Islam as a comprehensive way of life (*kāffah*), but privately." If not the caliphate or the Islamic state, then what is the recruiting agenda? He answered simply: "We have our own way."

The informant at ITB in Bandung, Ina (23 years old), admitted that, at first, she did not expect to join the women's wing of HTI. Initially, she was invited to a study group focused on the theme of the future of Islam and its youth. The ideological orientation of the movement that hosted the study group was hidden. "If I objectively study religion, I really like it," she said. However, as the study group progressed, the focus shifted to politics and the necessity of establishing an Islamic state. Susi (21 years old), a student at UB, recounted an instance in which her boyfriend was almost coerced to join a radical group: "At that time, my boyfriend was invited by his peers from the radical group to learn *liqā'* every Friday night," she said, "however, when my boyfriend became aware of their agenda of promoting the caliphate and Islamic law enforcement, he didn't want to participate anymore."

Conversion through Mandatory Conditioning

Radical groups often use student housing to entice followers. The issue that surfaced in my interviews on every campus was the existence of dormitories or boardinghouses that require residents, who are generally students, to take part in a group study or *liqā'*. The informant at ITB described how, around campus, "a lot of rented housing is used as their basecamps." These boardinghouses are explicitly intended for Muslim students. This housing is quite attractive to students because the rent is generally cheaper than for other places and provides a variety of religious activities. For students who have had no previous religious education, a hostel like this is considered appropriate for acquiring such knowledge. It should be added that students who receive scholarships provided by radical groups are forced to live in Islamic housing. Here is the story of Sasa (19 years old), from Undip: "I live in the Sofiyah dorm. At Undip, the residents of Islamic housing are all Muslims. It is mandatory to participate in religious studies forums. After dawn prayer, there is a compulsory study, and after is a morning assembly. At night there is one also. Usually, the lecturers are seniors or religious teachers from outside. The material is taken from books. The dorm coordinator has provided the book. I don't know where they got it from; the book has been passed down and used as religious study material for some time." The same scenario was found in Unair, where students who received financial aid from radical groups were placed in certain houses that had sufficiently complete facilities for religious learning activities. The boardinghouses in the Keputih area provide various books, such as the works of Sayyid Qutb and Maududi, that must be read by residents of the houses according to the length of their residence. There is also mentoring conducted by the management of the Etos scholarship foundation. Mega (20 years old), from Unair, was offered a rented house to live in, an offer that required her to join a religious study group. "*Al-hamdulillah* [Praise be to God], the housing, is indeed suited for studying religion," she said. The informant at ITS, in Gama (22 years old), felt the religious guidance he received in his dorm opened his eyes to the necessity of upholding the truth of Islam at all costs. He claimed that he had found his Islamic identity by living in the hostel. Some informants initially felt forced to live in a dormitory or pressured to attend a study or *liqā'*. Because there was no other choice, they stuck with it and focused on the positive aspects. Faza (21 years old), from UB, added, "Now I am in an environment that fully supports me to do good." Faza and other residents of Islamic housing felt obliged to disseminate the religious teachings taught to them because, according to him, preaching is the duty of every Muslim.

It seems that what is achieved in the student housing reinforces Islamic activities held in campus mosques. As is well known, mosque activities at various state universities are central in shaping Muslim students' religious lives. For example, Salman Mosque at ITB has several religious units that influence student organizations. The same is the case at IPB, in Bogor, which is sometimes mocked as the "Bogor Pesantren Institute" instead of the "Bogor Institute of Agriculture" (both are abbreviated "IPB"). It is worth noting that, in the few years before the disbanding of HTI, campus mosques were controlled by radical groups who were pro-caliphate. In such places, it appears that students were in a situation in which they had no choice but to participate in radical circles.

Conversion through Family Ties

Youths' home environments certainly have a significant impact on their radicalization. The family is the first social group that a child normally encounters in life, so it is not surprising that family ties provide a pattern for the child's development. The study of the relationship between radicalization and family issues usually highlights the deterioration of the family as a significant factor in a person's adopting radical behavior. Vargas argues that the lack of a family structure and poor parental involvement "might lead individuals to embrace associations to fill that void, a situation that could favor the introduction of external influences."[43] This is undoubtedly true, but there are also situations in which young people become radicalized due to living in a radical family environment. Family is the closest social environment to children and can influence their cognitive development and shape their worldviews. In this context, William Costanza writes, "A child is subjected to a learning style to inculcate a specific set of unchallengeable beliefs in order to establish a personal commitment to a narrow interpretation of an ideology that can be translated into disciplined action."[44]

We found two scenarios among my informants who had become radicalized: an environment of a "broken home" with deeply rooted family problems, and an environment in which there was indifference toward the children's development. Both led informants to adopt a desire to gain religious knowledge with radical doctrines. The following is testimony from Sultan (23 years old), of Unair:

> Initially, I did *hijrah* [literally: migration] because I was sad living with my family. The thing is that my family is riddled with problems, so maybe through *hijrah* I can improve the conditions of my family. I realized at that time that I was disobedient and behaved poorly, so maybe at that time God reprimanded me in that way. I first repaired myself and then I repaired my family. My father and my mother were far from religion and have been said to have sinned

often in their past. They both were alcoholic, and my mother also smoked. It was recklessness done in vain. It was both sin and not seeing what is right, but thank God after I did *hijrah*, my father and mother slowly began to recognize religious teachings. Even though they are no longer together anymore, they are on good terms.

The term *hijrah* is often used in Indonesia to signify a shift or conversion to a strict Islamic model. Another informant mentioned a similar reason for joining radical activities: he wanted to save his family from the fires of hell. Karim (24 years old), from IPB, quoted the Qur'an 66:6: "O you who believe, protect yourself and your family from a Fire." He believed that by being a pious child, he could bring salvation to his family. For him, routinely taking part in *pengajian* and participating in *da'wah* (preaching) brings merit.

However, extremist beliefs and values can also be introduced to an individual through indoctrination in a radical family environment. Costanza rightly notes that "youths around the world grow up in cultural environments where family and community narratives support beliefs that might be considered radical."[45] Khalid (22 years old), from Unair, claimed to accept pro-caliphate ideology, which was propagated by HTI cadres on campus, because it did not conflict with the religious doctrines that he received at home: "Honestly, my family and I have already joined HTI, and we have never questioned it because we believe they are right. . . . I went to boarding school and then college. In the boarding school, we had to read religious books and read the Qur'an. We were so busy that we don't join religious organizations on campus. We didn't have time." Some informants confirmed the fact that students accepted radical ideologies and even joined *liqā'* and intolerant groups because they came from family environments and/or educational backgrounds that supported radicalism.

Conversion through Searching for Radical Beliefs

Notably, a lack of religious knowledge also makes one vulnerable to radicalization. The fact that the seven universities suspected of being infiltrated by radical groups are public universities indicates that a lack of religious knowledge can be a significant factor contributing to youths' susceptibility to extremist ideologies. A recurring theme that emerged from my research is the absence of alternative viewpoints to those taught by radical groups. According to an informant from Unair, many of his friends agreed with the radical understanding instilled by the cadres of radical groups on campus because there were no other religious perspectives with which to compare it. Here are the words of Sherly (21 years old), who was involved in the Islamic Spirituality Section (SKI) of the Faculty of Economics and Business at Unair:

> I used to seek mentorship from seniors, including HTI members, deliberately. I often felt uncomfortable because their teachings contradicted the teachings of Nahdlatul Ulama (NU). So I just participated a few times and didn't continue again. SKI FEB itself is still dominated by HTI, it's just not as much and not as visible as before. But those who dare to oppose it openly are not many, at most only a few. Others tend to accept it. Sometimes, friends who actually join HTI don't have a strong religious basis and don't have a strong grasp [of their religion], so it's easy to be influenced [by radicalism]. In Unair, as far as I know, there are still many SKIs dominated by HTI, such as at FEB, the Faculty of Medicine, and the Faculty of Science and Technology. In fact, many of them are science faculty students.

Some informants who became radical claimed that their purpose in engaging with these groups was to strengthen their knowledge of Islam. Entering a network of religious peers facilitates the study of religion, which many perceive to be a way to improve oneself. There are also those who decided to convert to radicalism after reading brochures or bulletins in order to learn more about religion. Mega (22 years old), from IPB, said: "I have read the Islamic bulletin and the *da'wah* bulletin. I have moved afterward. From the media, I learned about the dress code in accordance with *Shari'ah*. That is, we as Muslim women must cover the genitals with baggy and loose garments, unlike men. From that, I consulted further with seniors who understood more about Islam. After being taught, I became aware of my obligations as a Muslim. I must obey what Islam says." Additionally, the doors to radical doctrines are opened wide through online platforms like websites and social media. Many informants search for radical beliefs by accessing radical-content websites to address their personal religious inquiries. Rini (20 years old), from ITS, for example, claimed, "I started to *hijrah* initially because I learned about it from social media, especially through *da'wah* accounts. Actually, I enjoyed it. Studying religion is our duty as Muslims, and indeed after reading a lot, I finally committed to *hijrah* to feel more spiritually complete." After radical indoctrination through social media, spiritual experiences have a substantial impact on young readers who feel they have little initial understanding of Islam. Some informants said they felt that they had now "found the right path" or had become "purified" after entering a radical circle. Searching for the meaning of life effectively influences the thoughts and attitudes of those who feel that they need to upgrade their religious commitment.

Conversion through Personal Depression

This category includes a wide range of incidents, from personal frustration because of failed love to deep disenchantment over life's unpredictability. Many studies have identified certain unfavorable situations as key triggers in the process of radicalization, including grievances due to "economic marginalization and cultural alienation, deeply held sense of victimization, or strong disagreements regarding the foreign policies of states . . . personal disaffection, loss, or crisis that leads one to seek a new path in life," as Hafez and Mullins state.[46] At this level, my research found that personal tragedy, from a breakup to an acute identity crisis, can lead to depression, which acts as a starting point influencing informants to look for ways to get closer to God and eventually perform *hijrah*. Depression can make it easy to sympathize with radicals. Salma (23 years old), from ITB, described her journey to join a radical group. She did not describe what caused her depression because she felt that it was too personal. She did say this:

> The main thing is I felt so embarrassed and felt so worthless; I felt that my life had no meaning at all. When I was alone, I was contemplating suicide. But on the other hand, I felt that I still had God. Finally, I realized that I had to get closer to God. I began to attend *pengajian* often and hear religious talks. From there, I began to vent to one of my friends who had done *hijrah* before me. She already

wore a veil. From her I had more enthusiasm to improve myself, for example, by wearing long robes and hijabs. Then she often joined the grand *tablīgh* (preaching) assembly, and I was invited there. Yes, that's how it was, I felt saved by joining my current circle of friends.

Personal anxiety among students, on the one hand, and the availability of assistance from radical groups, on the other hand, can be an impetus toward involvement in a radical environment. Finda (23 years old), from ITB, had joined HTI for only two weeks. She admitted that she was still in the phase of strengthening her *'aqīdah*; she had very few responsibilities as a group member. She recounted her experience as follows:

> At first, I joined HTI because I was often stressed. I always worried about my thesis revision. Then I met with a senior student involved [with HTI], and she was very kind. She was also an alumna. She told me that there is no reason to feel excess stress because she could help motivate me and help me with my thesis. Anyway, she was very nice, and she told me that I had to wear long robes. Because I didn't have one, I was given a robe and clothes from her, but I felt that I burdened her. I told her that I should buy it myself. I'm no stranger to running out of money, and she's helped me so much anyway. I was so persistent with her [about money] until she helped me find a job. I'm grateful to have met her. After this interview, I plan to study with my group.

Another informant from Unair told us how he felt stressed when completing his undergraduate paper and said that "after praying at the mosque, someone suddenly came to me, inviting me to join a religious discussion." He admitted that, at that time, he had not yet become an official member of HTI and was still trying to learn more about its ideology. He rejected allegations that HTI was a radical organization. "I feel there is nothing in common between the allegations and HTI's teachings," he said. "All of the accusations are slander because HTI's teachings are nothing out of the ordinary." Although HTI has indeed been formally banned by the government, the groups still find no difficulty recruiting new members, including students with strained personal lives.

Conversion through God's Guidance

Some radicalized youths believed that their conversion was due to God's grace and guidance (*hidāyah*). They believed that the radicalization process was unexplainable and unforeseeable and that their development of radical sympathies was possible only due to God's help and providence. Understood in this way, all types of conversion are instances of the divine will, whether they involve physical self-discipline or not. However, only a few informants explicitly experienced their journeys to radicalization as a divine pull toward truth. The following is the account of Anne (20 years old), from Unair:

> Well, when I'm asked about why I committed to the *hijrah* process, which many see as unreasonable and irrational, I tell them it's because it happened because of the will of God. If people ask, 'How come you've changed so much?,' the only answer is "Fate." Of course, there are those who say that they were fortunate to receive spiritual guidance. That is correct, but if God did not allow us to accept guidance and show us the way, it would not be possible. Personally, I committed to *hijrah* because there was someone who gave me motivation, someone who opened my eyes and my mind. I was initially blind in various ways, and then I became conscious and alive.

The person referred to by Anne contacted her through the Internet; they had never met in person. He is a man from Nigeria, and she remembers him as an "angel" who changed her life. They became acquainted and eventually fell in love. The man suddenly cut ties with her, however, simply because he did not want to date. Anne did not know what was happening. However, the incident made her realize that she should not be concerned with anything other than God. "Ordinary people would think it is impossible not to care about the world around them," said Anne, "but God can make the impossible possible. For the time being, I do *hijrah* because of Allah and Islam, not because of His creatures."

Included in the category of conversion through God's guidance is a narrative that describes the challenges faced by someone in the process of becoming radical. Most think that the conversion to radicalism is easy because it is facilitated and fulfilled by recruiters. However, this is not the case, because radicalized individuals face obstacles that are perceived to be challenging to overcome without God's help. This was testified by Icha (22 years old), from Unair:

> I used to experience social shunning and rejections; it wasn't just once, but it happened frequently. When I was suggested to do *hijrah* and turned into a pious Muslim committed to upholding the law of God like I am right now, I experienced objections from myself and friends around me. They accused me of being radical and joining the movement of terrorists. But with guidance from Allah, I found a way to answer the doubts in myself and others. *Al-hamdulillah*, all my questions were answered by my senior recruiter, who changed me for the better and became my *ustadhah* [female religious teacher].

Perhaps radicalized youth feel that the struggle against misconceptions about and injustices toward Islam will never end because of the conflict between internal and external temptations. Therefore, as Muslims, they must not remain silent. Ridwan (21 years old), from ITB, said: "I still wish to enter HTI, but the organization has been disbanded. I will not remain silent." What was conveyed by Sabto (23 years old), from ITS, was the commitment of radical youth who claimed they joined the radical group because they received guidance from God: "It has already [been] described [in religious teachings] that the fighters of the Islamic religion at the end of times were holding embers [an Indonesian idiom meaning to complete a difficult task]. It is tempting to give up. However, God has promised heaven. So it is better to hold the embers than to feel the heat of hellfire."

RADICALIZATION: BEFORE AND AFTER

The above narratives of radicalization are created retrospectively, that is, they are told after someone has joined a radical group or become radicalized. Past events are reconstructed in light of current convictions. This reconstruction process takes place at the individual as well as the group level. Radicalized youths shared their radicalization experiences with one another, and they often narrativized it for the sake of spreading the *da'wah* and recruiting new followers. Radicalized youth also include elements of their satisfaction or dissatisfaction with their new environment in their narratives. As a result, their radicalization is often described in such a dramatic way as to contrast their well-being before radicalization and that after. We need to consider radicalization narratives as part of a larger pattern of "proselytizing" as well as "teaching" an ethical model of faithful Muslims. This means that the narratives are important sources for studying the way radicalization is understood and expressed by radicalized youths. However, they do not always give us direct access to the original motives and rationales for radicalization.

Whatever the reason for radicalization, one can see that there has always been a particular context influencing radicalized youth that served as a turning point in the conversion process. As Rambo has noted, "This context encompasses a vast panorama of conflicting, influential, and dialectal factors that both facilitate and repress the process of conversion,"[47] which includes "cultural, historical, political, social—operating throughout the conversion process that may accelerate or impede its development."[48] In the case of radicalization among educated youth, the context for radicalization comprises a wide range of environmental factors, such as circles of friends, living situations, family relationships, and new religious knowledge, as well as personal tragedies or other related situations, which, according to the informants, cannot be explained rationally. Other elements in the conversion process, such as personal crises, quests, encounters, interactions, commitments, and consequences, can be identified, even though they are not sequential or linear. Each element might play a different role because one factor can appear more prominent than another. For example, crises caused by personal or social disruption appear to be prominent in conversion narratives involving depression or broken homes, but it is not so prominent in those involving the influence of a friend's invitation or a dormitory environment. This does not mean there is no crisis in every case of radicalization, but the magnitude of the crisis is different in each instance. Likewise, informants who feel radicalized because of divine guidance tend to be more robust and active than those initially forced into radicalism due to housing and accommodations offered.

The characterization of the radicalization of Muslim youth as the result of alienation dominates the literature.[49] This notion is not very apparent in my findings. The problems of radicalism and terrorism related to integration, segregation, and multiculturalism seem to be typical in Western countries. Moreover, the issue of identity crisis and belonging that is central in terrorism literature did not appear to be a significant factor contributing to the vulnerability of Indonesian youth to radicalization in my research. A recurrent theme in literature on terrorism is that an identity crisis is often associated with the process of radicalization. For instance, youth often face the dilemma of whether their identity is oriented toward Western states and cultures or toward transnational organizations originating from Muslim countries, especially in the Middle East. As Orla Lynch has rightly argued, "These concerns with transnationalism confuse notions of integration and loyalty with issues of radicalization and terrorism,"[50] as if young people have to choose between loyalty to a national structure and loyalty to a transnational structure. "This binary construction," Lynch argues, "in no way captures the complexity of the multiple locations of identity for Muslims."[51] Arguably, the presumed relationship between identity confusion and vulnerability to radicalization is vague and neglects, in some significant way, the complexity of identity theory from psychology and sociology. Furthermore, the scholarly debate on this issue is exploratory rather than explanatory, as it is mostly not based on evidence. As Lynch concludes, what is lacking is "the perspectives derived from Muslim youths' own experiences."[52]

Based on the narratives and testimonies of young people I studied who were exposed to radical ideas, my findings show that there is no problem being Muslim and Indonesian at the same time and that emphasizing one's Muslim identity does not mean reducing one's Indonesian identity. When radicalized youth contrast two times in their lives (before and after "*hijrah*"), it does not need to be read as a binary construction between Islamic and Indonesian identity. Instead, it is a process of becoming a good Muslim. Some radicalized often refer to a prophet hadith, "Those whose day is better than yesterday are prosperous." Every Muslim, radical or not, holds this kind of understanding. What distinguishes radicalized youths from "ordinary Muslims" is the understanding that becoming more pious Muslims is manifested through following a particular version of Islam exclusively, adopting stricter ideologies, fighting for the application of Islamic *Shari'ah*, and establishing an Islamic or caliphate state. In this context, deradicalization efforts must offer alternative narratives that expose students to various interpretations of Islam. As some of my informants complained, when radical ideas are introduced on public campuses, not many people can reject the arguments based on authoritative religious sources because there is a lack of religious knowledge among students. This fact also explains why radical groups often target public campuses as centers for spreading radical ideology. HTI, for example, was initially developed at IPB and, on the same campus, support for the caliphate was first declared.

The purpose of this chapter is not to challenge the characterization of Muslim youth in the literature, but primarily to contribute to our knowledge about the process of youth radicalization. Both quantitative and qualitative data suggest that we need to consider a broader conceptualization of the radicalization process rather than confining it to a form of recruitment. My research findings support Quintan Wiktorowicz's contention that, when exploring the radical Islamic movement, we need to pay attention to the role of mobilizers in drawing individuals to the process of radicalization, for instance, how mobilizers were able to influence individuals and convince them to do things that are not in their own interests, such as participating in high-risk behaviors that could lead to their arrest or death, as well as how mobilizers capitalize on or create "cognitive openings," defined as periods in which individuals are willing to question their own previously held personal beliefs and consider new, radical ideas.[53] Most of the informants surveyed and interviewed were converted to radical ideologies through friendships and mentorships. Although the techniques used by Islamist militants to influence people to adopt their point of view are not denied, youth involvement in radical social networks seems to be a dominant driving force in the pathway to radicalization.

Radicalization is a process involving choices that influence the way of thinking among educated youth. As discussed earlier, conversion is a complex phenomenon. From a sociological perspective, it is important to understand the various factors involved before and after radicalization. Based on my research, it is apparent that not all students at the seven state universities included in my study acknowledged that their daily behavior and activities changed after they had exposure to radical ideology. In fact, in this study's findings, a significant number of students did not change their internal beliefs after exposure to radical information. Because of their embarrassment around newfound mentors, some students chose to act more radical than they really were. For instance, they did not want to be seen as immoral and secular individuals, and thus they chose to take on the appearance of being radical. Interviews with a student from UB revealed that one of the instruments often used by radical groups to convince students of the relevance of the caliphate was the phrase "shaking off sinfulness." This means that as students and educated youth, it was hoped that they would not live lifestyles of consumerism and worldliness, but instead would embrace the calling of the community of faith to take on the religious struggle in which the youths believe.

A number of students interviewed acknowledged that when they gathered together with those categorized as radical, the new students were pressured to adapt and adjust, which they did so that they would not be rebuked or viewed negatively by the group. The easiest thing for students to do when they were involved with radical groups was to embrace physical changes, such as changes in their clothing to match that of their mentors. The students acknowledged that these most elementary adjustments, the changes of their clothing and appearance, became parts of their daily lives. As they became more involved with radical groups, female students would normally change the types of head coverings they wore in accordance with Islamic law and would no longer wear trousers (particularly jeans). Male students would begin to wear long-sleeved shirts, grow their beards, and often become involved in activities at the mosque as well as religious campus activities. The physical appearance of these groups was usually marked by conservative religious clothing. However, this indicator of radicalized youth can be deceiving, because they often did not embrace radical ideologies wholeheartedly.

Many radicalized students acknowledged feelings of shame if they rejected the invitations of senior students and friends to join their religious study groups. However, as revealed in the interviews, many students who were involved with radical study groups did not exhibit a wholehearted commitment. As many of the newer students engaged in study activities, it was clear that their involvement was not because of a religious need or a deepened belief but was more closely related to the need to socialize and build a broader network of relationships. A significant number of students joined radical networks simply because they did not want to have a difference of opinion with their seniors, and therefore felt obligated to be involved when senior students invited them. Those students who appeared radical, when observed more closely, were not necessarily radical in their personal beliefs.

CONCLUDING REMARKS

In this chapter I have examined the nature of student conversions to radicalism at seven state universities in Indonesia by identifying common patterns in their own testimonies about their conversion experiences. In addition to identifying circumstances that have led Indonesian youth to become radicalized in the first place, this chapter has also addressed the question of how individuals came to accept and adopt radical Islam as their own worldview. The trajectories of university students who adopted radical viewpoints or joined radical groups are quite diverse. The faith networks allow them to be exposed to radical teachings, not necessarily uniformly. It is interesting to note that changing dynamics occur when there is a shift from a pre-radicalization phase to a self-identification phase and when one is already involved in a radical group. The struggle of students who are involved in radical groups was revealed during the in-depth interviews. While some radicalized youth felt that they indeed discovered "the true path" and became more Islamic, a significant number of students struggled to make sense of what was going on with the numerous new rules in their lives and the new leadership in their adopted groups, together with the "standards of godliness" to which these radical groups adhered.

My findings urge us to pay serious attention to moral and religious vulnerabilities that allow young people to embark on the path of radicalization. The number of adolescents who joined radical groups due to their interest in defending Islam as the solution to all problems turns out to be quite significant (see table 4.1). Among this group, the level of susceptibility to radicalization is high. Thus, there is a need for continued normative work to convince them that radical ideologies should not form the basis of their personal, communal, or state lives. Instead, they should be offered an alternative of inclusivity and interreligious understanding. This is not to suggest that religious understanding is the only driving force for radicalization. As the narratives of students' conversion to radical ideologies show, there are many different factors that trigger the radicalization of educated youth. These triggers for radicalization will be discussed in the next chapter. While it is important to prevent youth from falling victim to simplistic views of the public role of religion, attention must also be given to the root causes of youth radicalization.

FIVE

Reluctant Radicals and Violent Extremism

While in the previous chapter I addressed the prevalence of religious radicalism among educated youth in Indonesia, in this one I will further analyze the nature of religious radicalism adopted by Indonesian students. The radicalization of youth is no longer related only to a lack of education or poverty. The university has now become a significant environment for the spreading of radical ideology. In Indonesia, for example, students at seven prominent public universities have been significantly exposed to radical groups. As discussed before, the National Agency for Combating Terrorism (BNPT, Badan Nasional Penanggulangan Terorisme) has recently published its research findings pointing to seven leading state universities, namely Universitas Indonesia (UI), Institut Teknologi Bandung (ITB), Institut Pertanian Bogor (IPB), Universitas Diponegoro (Undip), Institut Teknologi Sepuluh Nopember (ITS), Universitas Airlangga (Unair), and Universitas Brawijaya (UB), as having been infiltrated by radical groups. In this chapter I identify those students who have been attracted to extremist ideologies as "reluctant radicals" because they were uncommitted supporters of violent extremism and could easily leave radical networks, as will be discussed in the next chapter. These reluctant radicals recently embraced a radical viewpoint, and they were not firmly attached to an exclusive and extreme religious viewpoint that justifies militant attitudes and violent actions.

The involvement of youth in jihad and extremist groups such as the Islamic State of Iraq and Syria (ISIS), the Taliban, Boko Haram, or al-Shabaab has attracted global attention. As Charles Kurzman notes, "Terrorists are grimly successful at attracting public attention. Of the thousands of violent incidents that occur around the globe each day, the world media efficiently sifts for hints of terrorist motivations, then feeds these incidents over the wire services and satellite networks to news consumers who may not realize how rare terrorism really is."[1] It is no surprise that within a short period, the discourse surrounding youth radicalization has become a major topic of discussion among policymakers, intelligence agencies, and those in the academic world.[2] However, the tendency to directly connect religious radicalism with violent terrorism is based on a false premise, that is, that the result of radicalization is necessarily violence.

My field research findings in Indonesia and other recent studies do not support a direct line of cause and effect between religious radicalism and violent terrorism. The premise of the connection between religious radicalism and terrorism has its source in an epistemic confusion: why does a person carry out violent, inhumane actions? Scholars have proposed complex theories about the psychological roots of inhumane acts. Some argue that people with mental illness generally do not commit violence; such acts are more usually committed by people without mental illness who are thinking in a calculated and systematic manner.[3] In a review of the social psychology of a wide range of terrorist groups, Clark McCauley and Mary Segal conclude that "terrorists do not show any striking psychopathology."[4] Other scholars are convinced that there is a correlation between terrorism and mental illness, which causes individuals to carry out violent actions like suicide bombings.[5] In this view, antisocial attitudes in the terrorist community are the products of zealotry infused with mental illness. Still other scholars attribute terrorist acts committed by white perpetrators to mental illness while attributing the same behavior by non-whites to ideological motivations.[6]

The empirical data do not support the connection between religious radicalism and violent terrorism; radicalism does not necessarily entail carrying out acts of terror. Many acts of terror are not the results of religious radicalism.[7] In this chapter I call into question the assumption that religious radicalism is necessarily connected to terrorism and challenges state-led rehabilitation approaches that aim to replace radical religious belief with an ideology that is more compatible with the state's moral principles. I aim to capture and explore the characteristics of what I call "the reluctant radicals" that will help us understand the nature of religious radicalism on campus. The findings in this chapter are drawn from a quantitative survey and qualitative, in-depth interviews with university students who had been exposed to radical ideologies. Some of the questions here are these: How did they come to be radicalized in the first place? What forces shaped their radical views and attitudes? How did they view religious violence? What is generally absent from youths' radicalized discourses in Indonesia is precisely an extremist ideology that would legitimize violence.

RADICALIZATION AND VIOLENT TERRORISM

Literature concerning religious radicalism often connects the phenomenon of radicalization with extremism and terrorism. This is understandable because the "radicalization" concept emerges as an instrument that allows policymakers to explore the process whereby an individual or groups become terrorists and, at the same time, analyze methods and strategies to prevent extremist and terrorist threats.[8] Indeed, prior to the debate about terrorism at the beginning of the twenty-first century, "radicalization" was usually used to refer to "actual use of violence, with escalation in terms of forms and intensity,"[9] according to Donatella Della Porta and Gary Lafree. These authors emphasized how the understanding of radicalism was used in the 1970s in the study of political violence as "the interactive (social movements/state) and processual (gradual escalation) dynamics in the formation of violent, often clandestine groups."[10] Peter Neumann contends that, until the early 2000s, there was hardly any reference to the term "radicalization" in books about terrorism and political extremism. Possibly the terrorist attacks on American soil on September 11, 2001, became the turning point at which "radicalization" became the new buzzword surrounding terrorism, especially in the media.[11]

The concept of radicalization has been widely discussed since 2005 in conjunction with concern about the growth of homegrown terrorism in many Western countries. This has particularly been true in the United States and Europe, resulting in their governments' developing diverse counter-radicalization and deradicalization programs. Indeed, after 9/11, public discussion of the causes of terrorism was often limited to simplistic explanations, for instance, that terrorism was being carried out by fanatics inspired by a simplistic and evil ideology. Because this explanation is simplistic, it does not need to be analyzed any further. Many questions were asked, such as "Why do [the terrorists] hate us?," with the answers always tied only to religious belief. The answers might include "Islam is strongly grounded in its traditions and cannot be reformed, and even political and economic change is not able to transform Islam's hatred." After 2004, following the American "victory" in the war with Iraq, there emerged a realization that military victory was not enough. It was also necessary to touch the hearts and minds of Muslim peoples. It was realized that violence would not win the war on terror. Because of that, there was a need for a new discourse to direct the West in its efforts to oppose terrorism. At this point, the concepts of "radicalization" and "deradicalization" became central points of the discussion concerning terrorism.

Many scholars have started to realize the complexity of the study of radicalization, with a new understanding that the connection between radicalism and terrorism is not as straightforward as commonly believed. For instance, Randy Borum argues that some of those exposed to radical thinking have not been involved in terrorist acts and that some terrorists do not have an ideology and/or exhibit radical thinking in the traditional sense.[12] Borum writes, "Different pathways and mechanisms operate in different ways for different people at different points in time and perhaps in different contexts."[13] To become "radical" by developing or adopting extreme beliefs that justify violence is only one of several paths that an individual might take to become involved in terrorism. Because of that, explains Borum, a broader question needs to be asked: How do people become involved and stay involved in terrorism, and, sometimes, disengage from it? This type of question allows the unveiling of a complex problem rather than letting us merely assume that we know the reason for the connection between radical religious belief and violent extremism. Much evidence has shown that the radicalized are not alone in carrying out or being involved with terrorist acts. Surveys performed by Pew and Gallup revealed that 17 percent of Muslims were sympathetic to radicalism, even though a substantial proportion of them had no desire to carry out violent acts.[14]

In this chapter I affirm the Pew and Gallup findings about the prevalence of radicalization in Indonesia. However, I takes a further step by looking at a variation that I refer to as "reluctant radicalism," which contributes to the complex profile of the radical community that has been developed by a number of scholars. Before discussing the conceptual framework of reluctant radicalism in existing typology, it is best that we first understand the complex phenomenon of radicalism and radicalization, which has numerous variations that demand multi-disciplinary approaches. Indeed, the term "radicalism" is often used; nevertheless, it is not often defined or well understood. A narrow focus on radical ideologies often risks providing the understanding that religious radicalism is a proxy for terrorism. This type of viewpoint is still quite dominant in policy documents. The U.S. Department of Homeland Security, for example, defines radicalism as "the process of adopting an extremist belief system, including the willingness to use, support, or facilitate violence, as a method to effect social change."[15] The British government's Prevent strategy refers to radicalization as "the process by which a person comes to support terrorism and forms of extremism leading to terrorism."[16]

The tendency to connect radicalization with "extremist belief systems" as a pathway to "terrorism" has received an adverse reaction from some scholars. For example, Andrew Hoskins and Ben O'Loughlin consider radicalization as a type of "myth" promoted by the media and Western intelligence agencies with the purpose of "anchoring news agendas ... and legitimizing policy response."[17] Frank Furedi refers to radicalization and the response of the British government as "always having a fantasy-like character" and being deliberately designed to alienate Muslim teenagers so that radicalization appears to be a "psychological virus," with everything done to redirect attention from "the real cultural divisions that afflict British communities today."[18] Hoskins, O'Loughlin, and Furedi appear to exaggerate the issues, even supporting conspiracy theories. It is clear that radicalization is not a myth, even though its meaning is ambiguous. "This ambiguity," Neumann asserts, "explains the differences between definitions of radicalization; it has driven the scholarly debate; and it provides the backdrop for strikingly different policy approaches."[19]

What is a myth is the cause-and-effect relationship between radicalization and violent actions. My field research does not confirm the assumption that radicalized youth embrace an extreme ideology as a stepping stone toward terrorist actions. In this chapter I refer to radicalized students as reluctant radicals because of their lack of commitment to supporting extremist actions. These reluctant radicals are newcomers who have just begun experimenting with what it means to be radical. In associating with radical groups, they have had an opportunity to study religious beliefs more deeply. Interestingly, most students attracted to radical ideas are generally from secular universities with no religious affiliations. In other words, these students do not have a profound religious educational background, and the campus itself, which has been exposed to radicalism, offers limited religious teaching. On the other hand, among Islamic educational institutions, such as State Islamic Universities (UIN, Universitas Islam Negeri), and the networks of religious campuses run under the auspices of the Department of Religion, the concern about radicalized students is minimal. One factor that might explain the absence of radicalism on Islamic campuses is that students there are introduced to a variety of religious opinions; thus, when radical Islamic propaganda is presented, it is much easier for the students to draw upon alternative counter-arguments.

It is likely that reluctant radicals on state university campuses have been encouraged by a global religious revival. Young people desire to appear more religious by displaying religious symbols to show the world that they are godly and committed to religious teaching. Reluctant radicals are interested in becoming involved in religious discussion forums that have been prepared by the mentors of radical groups. In his research on the Salafi-jihadi ideology in Europe, Peter Nesser identifies several personal roles in radical jihadist groups. According to Nesser, the leader usually is someone who is charismatic and idealistic, having an interest in politics. His subordinate is a protégé, an energetic youth who is educated, skilled, and clever, with an enthusiasm for activism much like that of the leader. Other types include "the misfit"—that is, a subordinate who often simply receives commands—and "the drifts," who connect through the social ties of someone who is already established in the radical group.[20] In a study concerning a Muslim who became a radical in Amsterdam, Marieke Slootman and Jean Tillie documented the profiles, roles, and motives of many members of radical groups. Interestingly, although members of a radical group did not seem to have much conviction or a strong radical viewpoint, they gradually separated and isolated themselves from their previous communities. Additionally, a number of them were not allowed to go to the mosque because those in the mosque were concerned that they would spread radical ideas. The result of this severance from their communities was a radicalization process whereby they came to consider the communities around them to be corrupt and broken.[21]

My research confirms the tendency among educated youth who became radicalized to distance themselves from non-radicals and make outward displays of piety. However, it is difficult to ascertain the level of their commitment and involvement in radical groups regarding "an extremist belief system, which allows violence, although it is not unavoidable," write Mohammed Hafez and Creighton Mullins.[22] How long have youths been connected to the radical group? What is the extent of their involvement? How strong is their commitment to an extremist belief system? Are they extremely committed, or are they just trying something new? How convinced are they of this extreme understanding? The same questions can be presented concerning the final element of extremism, violence. The level of commitment, seriousness, and involvement will vary from person to person. The research that was completed by Angel Rabasa, Stacie L. Pettyjohn, Jeremy J. Ghez, and Christopher Boucek concerning some Muslim extremists indicates that "there is an inverse relationship between the degree of commitment and the likelihood of disengagement or deradicalization."[23] Certainly, the issue of commitment cannot be decided simply by determining how long the radicalized person has been a member of the group. In other words, prolonged membership to a radical group does not necessarily mean that an individual is more committed to or even actively involved with that group. Commitment can be normative, affective, or pragmatic.

Now, how do we situate "reluctant radicalism"? It is difficult to confirm a specific place that can be categorized as the location of reluctant radicalism in the framework of radicalization pathways for two reasons. First, radical groups themselves are very diverse and dynamic, in relation to both their management structures and their membership hierarchies.

Second, reluctant radicalism does not have a specific level of commitment, origin, degree of involvement, or standard participation. In the student context that I researched, the students did not become parts of radical groups as full-time activists. Additionally, their introductions to and knowledge of radical ideas were very different from one to another. Some became aware of radical ideas during high school, while others were exposed to such ideas after arriving at the university. Moreover, the religious backgrounds of their families were quite diverse: some were from families who were very committed to an understanding of an exclusive Islam, while other students were in fact opposed by their families when they expressed radical views and were forbidden to associate with radical groups by their parents. What is clear is that the community of reluctant radicals is not structured in its leadership, nor are there activist ranks or a leadership and protégés. They tend to be spread among the categories of newcomers, supporters, sympathizers, drifters, and misfits.

EDUCATED YOUTHS' EXPOSURE TO RADICALISM

A consensus has formed among scholars that religious radicalism does not occur instantly, and several explanations have been offered of the stages that individuals move through as they become involved in a radical network. Although there are varying opinions about the phases and the process by which an individual becomes radicalized and whether those phases are linear, it is possible that there are significant turning points at which an individual is converted to radicalism. This research focuses on youth who have recently been exposed to radical thinking. Students who are categorized as radicals are often youth who have been exposed to radical ideas and have intolerant attitudes and exclusive mindsets in viewing their own social network. Radical youth even choose the path of violence and carry out jihad to defend the fate of their "brothers," those who have been oppressed for the sake of their beliefs. This study, which was carried out at the seven prominent state universities, revealed that some radicalized youth actively participated in study groups sympathetic to the caliphate system and expressed their support for those who departed for Syria and joined ISIS. At the Bogor Agricultural Institute (IPB or Institut Pertanian Bogor), a number of informants revealed that at the local mosque where they prayed on Fridays, prayers were often given for their friends who had left to join ISIS. Not only were the students who had departed to carry out jihad viewed as brave and honored, but also those on campus would offer routine prayers for them, just in case later those who had departed were to lose their lives in their efforts.

At these state universities, it should not be understood that students used their time only to study and to work on assignments provided by their lecturers. The activities carried out by the students were not limited to their studies in classrooms or works on academic tasks. Many students were also involved in numerous social and political activities, such as participating in demonstrations or discussions. Nevertheless, many students were also involved with numerous activities that would be classified as radical. After becoming new students, many became the targets of seniors who followed a militant ideology. From the first time they set foot on the campus, some of the new students would be invited by seniors to be involved with religious study activities. They would discuss the validity of the caliphate as a way out of numerous problems confronted by the nation, with many others developing intolerant thinking, keeping a distance from other social groups, and taking the path of radicalism.

Of the 700 students who participated in my research, as many as 85 percent acknowledged that they were first exposed to radical thinking while in college, with only 15 percent saying they were exposed to radicalism in high school (see table 5.1). Thus, radicalized students can be referred to as "reluctant" because they supported radicalism reluctantly and their involvement with radical groups is not based on extremist religious belief. The vast majority of respondents said that they were exposed

TABLE 5.1. Students' responses to questions about their involvement in radical activities

Question	Response	Percentage
When was the respondent first introduced to radical thinking?	At university	85.0
	At high school	15.0
Since enrolling in university, has the respondent been involved in or invited to radical activities?	Yes, active until now	30.4
	Yes, but no longer active	29.7
	Never been involved	39.9

Note: n = 700; survey conducted in 2018.

to radical ideology during their time at the university. When asked whether they were involved in radical groups, 39.9 percent responded that they had never been, while 30.4 said that they had joined the radical networks and were still active, and 29.7 percent indicated that they were no longer involved in the radical networks.

Some students involved in radical group activities generally did not take steps toward the groups on their own, out of a personal interest in being actively involved in study groups that support the caliphate. What generally happened was that a new student was approached first, being motivated and invited by a senior who was already a part of the radical movement on the campus. We can imagine how a new student, with few friends and having difficulty adjusting, would feel when suddenly approached by a senior student and offered assistance and help with new challenges. The assistance is not only in the form of friendship but also in that of financial help, which students often need. In this type of situation, usually the student who is assisted has a sense of being indebted, is sympathetic, and later is open to learning from the senior student through discussions and studies carried out by the campus's radical groups.

Finda (22 years old), a student of ITB, said:

> I don't follow any other organizations, I only follow the HTI (Hizbut Tahrir Indonesia) community. I recently joined it, two weeks ago. I wasn't involved in any other activities, and the problem was I wanted to get stronger in my moral character. Initially, I joined the HTI group because I was often confused, including the direction of my thesis writing. It was at that time that I met my mentor, who was very good to me. She was a graduate, and she provided motivation for me and helped me in my thesis. She also provided me with a long robe, although I didn't feel comfortable borrowing this, so I bought one myself. She often helped to pay for small expenses for me and helped me to look for work. In fact, after our prayers today, we will meet together.

The sources of this radical knowledge are relatively diverse. The 70 interviews I conducted revealed that the sources were as follows: reading materials (53.3 percent), websites (49.3 percent), YouTube videos (32.6 percent), brochures and leaflets (25.1 percent), information from friends

(47.6 percent), and group studies (35.1 percent). We can observe that the online sources are quite dominant, even though in reality the students were not accessing radical Internet content very frequently. When asked how often they accessed the Internet for radical information, 60.9 percent of respondents said that they rarely (at the most, once a month) viewed radical content online, 15.1 percent accessed radical content every day, and 24 percent accessed radical content once a week. Those who had accessed radical information for the first time in the past year totaled 42.7 percent, with 25.1 percent accessing radical information for the first time in the past two years and 22.2 percent more than two years ago. All of this strengthens the hypothesis that radicalized students at public universities are beginners with regard to their exposure.

Although the sources of radical information are both online and offline, the fact of the matter is that many respondents acknowledged that they were first introduced to radical Internet content through their offline friends. According to the data, 21.7 percent of respondents had actively looked for radical websites, 36.4 percent got to know these websites through friends, 15.6 percent were informed through the recruitment process of radical groups, and the remaining 26.3 percent said that they had accidentally come across radical content online. An individual who initially gets to know radical content on the Internet may later seek out friends who have been exposed to similar material to justify his or her journey. My research showed that this phenomenon usually occurs among those who feel that the religious instruction they have received from their teachers or parents is inadequate and want to deepen their religious knowledge through the Internet. Sometimes a student has personal issues, such as depression or dysfunctional family situations in which minimal attention has been given to the individual's development, as discussed in chapter 4. In such a case, the individual may be more likely than other students to embrace radical teachings and become integrated into the radical network.

It is evident that there are many pathways to radicalization for those who are disappointed with their current life situations. It is not a coincidence that recruiters to radical groups, especially HTI, target secular campuses to propagate their radical ideology. Generally, on these campuses students do not have enough background knowledge of Islam to oppose the onslaught of radical teachings presented to them.

Interestingly, at secular universities such as IPB, many students first declared their support for a caliphate. Before the government officially disbanded HTI in 2017 in a decision supported by the High Court in 2018, mosques and student organizations on campuses were infiltrated and mentored by HTI personnel who were pro-caliphate.

Additionally, campus leadership was often sympathetic to a version of Islamic ideology promoted by hardline Islamic groups. This infiltration of campuses by radical network shows how vulnerable university students are to radical ideas. Roidatus (19 years old), from Unair, revealed her experience with being exposed to radical groups:

> From the first time I entered the campus, I was introduced to and assisted by older students in the class, who were very good to me. I was assisted in finding a cheap yet comfortable dormitory. I later shifted to a dormitory together with friends who did religious recitations together. I was very happy to be invited to these religious meetings; I felt rather than being a stranger, it is better to be involved in religious activity. In my home, I was often invited to recite the Qur'an, including by my mother.

Thus, student social networks have been dominated by an environment that supports the circulation of radical information and is intolerant toward other religions. One informant, Erna (23 years old), from Unair, a state university in Surabaya, explained her involvement in student organizations in the Faculty of Economics and Business (FEB), which was dominated by HTI cadres. "From the beginning, I was not at peace with their activities," said Erna, "because they would slander government policies and propagate the caliphate political system as a solution for Indonesia." Interviews with informants indicated that, in this mentoring network, there was a strong tendency to promote the caliphate system as the solution to all problems, including moral degradation, corruption, poverty, and even the destruction of forests in Indonesia, and that all these convictions were framed in religious language. For example, radicalized youth would mention that the obligation to embrace the caliphate system had its foundation in the Qur'an and hadith, as well as in Islamic political history. Erna observed that no students refuted or contested the propaganda of the HTI leaders, partly because they did not have enough religious knowledge to provide counter-arguments. Erna recalled, "There was very little bold opposition to this propaganda. Basically, everyone just accepted it because no one could offer an alternative."

What happened at FEB has also occurred at other institutions, such as the Faculty of Medicine, Technology, Agriculture. In other public universities, such as UI, the Faculty of Medicine is regarded as a breeding ground for radicalization and the dissemination of radical ideologies. At ITB, Salman Mosque activists are very prominent. The Salman Mosque has a long history as the source of Muslim activists at a national level, and the network from the Salman Mosque is extensive, impacting students far beyond ITB. One of the informants, who is known as a radical, said that his introduction to radicalism began at a meeting with students from the Education University of Indonesia (UPI). This informant was first invited to discuss religious issues with groups of students and to join study groups. In the interview, he openly acknowledged that he was a member of HTI but did not consider it a radical organization because he felt that it did not promote or encourage violent actions. He acknowledged that the activists of the Salman Mosque had successfully infiltrated student organizations across the campus, but claimed they did not turn them into extremist networks.

That a social network informed and shaped the radicalized knowledge and attitudes of students is also reflected in the quantitative data shown in the previous chapter. A significant number of respondents (36.4 percent) had been exposed to radical websites by others (friends or recruiters). There was also a large percentage of students (48.3 percent) who were encouraged to go one step further by joining a radical group, and the rest (8.3 percent) were directly influenced by a senior recruiter. In this connection, the respondents who became radicalized through radical interpretations of the Qur'an were only 6 percent; even smaller numbers were influenced by lecturers (1.3 percent) or parents (1 percent). The remainder did not answer questions relating to who their primary influencers had been.

When asked what had given rise to their attraction to radical activities, the students' primary responses were a friend's invitation and the conditions in dormitories (pressure to attend Islamic studies circles); nearly 49 percent said they were attracted in these ways. It is clear that the radical recruiters and mentors were very persistent in finding and persuading new followers. They used numerous approaches, such as studying with the new students, assisting them in their academic studies, and financially helping students meet their dormitory costs. Several informants, such as Rudy (22 years old), a student from Undip, Semarang, acknowledged that they were lured in by various forms of help promised if they joined the radical groups. "When I felt distressed with my thesis, a senior came and offered assistance," said Rudy. Students such as Rudy found it very difficult to reject this sort of offer, not only because of their need for support but also because of the persistence of radical leaders. Rudy explained that some seniors were willing to befriend him and even waited for him for hours if he had to remain behind with his class. Later they would pick him up so that they could study together.

Another respondent, Shelfi (23 years old), a student from UB, acknowledged that she was offered assistance with her studies, such as being loaned books. She was even provided with a more conservative head covering to comply with a specific interpretation of *Shari'ah*. In daily activities, Shelfi already wore the *jilbāb*, but this was not adequate, according to the radicals, which led her to wear loose-fitting clothing. Another respondent, named Kadar (21 years old), a student from Undip, lived in a dormitory that was overseen by an HTI leader because the leader had obtained a scholarship from Etos (an organization also involving radicals). In the dormitory courtyard, there was a sign reading "This dormitory is only for Muslims." According to Kadar, besides the fact that it was cheaper to rent a room in this dormitory than in others, there were numerous Islamic activities, especially Islamic study forums, which were obligatory for anyone living there. For those students who did not come from educated religious backgrounds, attending these discussion forums was a way to enhance their religious knowledge, but it was through these types of study groups that a radical ideology was disseminated.

Other respondents offered interesting observations concerning their motivations to get involved in radical activities, including the belief that Islam is the solution to all problems (27.6 percent), a commitment to defend the suffering of Muslims (10.9 percent), the belief that Islam is superior to other religions (8.9 percent), and the belief that this is the way to enter heaven (3.6 percent) (see table 5.2).

It is noteworthy that motivation by a desire to enter heaven is relatively low (3.6 percent), which can be explained in a number of possible

TABLE 5.2. Students' responses to "What motivates you to become involved in radical activities?"

Response	Percentage
Invitations from friends and pressure to attend Islamic studies circles	49.0
A belief that religion is the way to overcome problems	27.6
A commitment to defend the suffering of Muslims	10.9
A desire for the supremacy of Islam	8.9
In order to enter heaven	3.6

Note: n = 700; survey conducted in 2018.

ways. First, the view of the struggle for the "aspiration of Muslim peoples" (proclaiming Islam as true, defending the suffering of Muslims, and struggling for Islam to be seen as the one true religion) may, in itself, be seen as the path to entering heaven. These radicalized youth tend to believe that the kind of jihad that can be carried out in the modern era is the effort to help Muslims "onto Allah's straight path" (*fī sabīl Allāh*). Second, the radical movement among youth is not based on apocalyptic beliefs, such as those held by ISIS, who portray their organization as a "salvation movement" for the last days. ISIS propagates a mission and a struggle based on an end-time vision derived from hadith and a particular interpretation of specific Qur'anic verses. This apocalyptic model has not yet taken hold in Indonesia. When the respondents were asked whom they hated most, they said ISIS (23.1 percent), as well as those practicing corruption (36.6 percent) (see chapter 8). Therefore, the radical movement among youth reflects a desire to be godly Muslims, which is expressed in religious symbols such as clothing, use of the Arabic language, and an exclusive attitude toward other groups, including other Muslims. Third, generally speaking, the struggle of radicalized youth is not aimed at ending their life in martyrdom. They realize that they are young and have their whole lives ahead of them; they desire to see heaven on earth and are not dreaming of the last days. This is possibly one of the most distinctive traits of the reluctant radicals when they have a taste of what it means to be radical. If they are not comfortable with this taste, they simply return to their previous lives.

There was a strong sense among the respondents that Muslims in general do not adequately understand and practice what they understand as "true Islam." In other words, they believe that the adversity experienced in the Muslim world is not caused by Islam, but by the fact that the Islam that is practiced there is not Islamic enough. According to the radicals, the true Islam for which they struggle would bring a revival for Muslims, similar to what was seen in the early "Golden Age" of Islam. This view placed an emphasis on the purification of an individual's faith as the basis for a commitment to devote one's energy and possessions, and even one's life. In other words, there is a strong feeling that Islam is under threat and facing external pressures. In the minds of radicalized youth, Muslim suffering at the national and global levels is evidenced by the way the "enemies of Islam" have aspired to destroy the religion. Thus, as young people became connected with these radical groups, they felt the urge to do two things: to fight for the benefit of all Muslims by, for example, freeing Palestine from the Israeli occupation and to show the superiority of Islam over all other religions.

For young reluctant radicals, defending Islam in the face of external threats is a religious responsibility. Neglect of this obligation is understood as indicating a lack of commitment to living up to Islam's true teachings. One of the questions that confronts young radicals is whether joining radical groups turned them into radicals in their religious understanding. Perhaps their views of the caliphate illustrate their ease with this system. As mentioned in the previous chapter, 25.9 percent of respondents supported the establishment of a caliphate state, and 45.3 percent rejected it. However, when it came to how they would react toward anyone who was reluctant to uphold the caliphate, the majority of respondents (81.7 percent) said they would feel fine because everyone can follow his or her own view (see table 5.3). Only 8.3 percent

TABLE 5.3. Students' responses to "What do you think of people who oppose the caliphate system?"

Response	Percentage
It's fine, because everyone can have different views	81.7
It's a sin	8.3
They need to be invited to work together	7.3
They are cowards	2.4
They are enemies	0.3

Note: n = 700; survey conducted in 2018.

of respondents thought that such a person was a sinner because of his or her rejection of the religious duty, and 7.3 percent said that they strove to invite him or her to work together.

In broad terms, university students who have been involved with the activities of radical groups on campus generally can be divided into two categories. The first category is a group of students who choose to follow a pathway toward becoming increasingly radical. The second group is that of the reluctant radicals, who do not hold to radical viewpoints. However, they participate in the activities of radical groups and adopt their style of dress because of a desire to be a part of a social network. The first category is generally made up of those who have a militant attitude and a tendency toward an exclusive and intolerant mindset. In a number of the educational institutions, although these student groups do not necessarily carry out extremist actions with their peers, they have a commitment to defend their beliefs. Beyond this, there is a tendency to segregate themselves, limiting their social interactions to those who have a shared belief system. On a number of campuses, militant student groups such as these are actively involved in religious study activities, as well as preaching, with the goal of seeking out new recruits. Militant students, who may become leaders of religious organizations on campus, are often involved in activities that produce radical content. This content is disseminated and forwarded through social networks, primarily through social media.

Regarding the reluctant radicals, this group may not necessarily be significantly different from the first group in their physical appearance. As table 5.4 shows, their viewpoints also started to become radicalized. However, in their daily activities, generally they are quite fluid, reflecting the mindsets of urban youth, who spend a significant amount of time in activities undertaken for personal pleasure.

Table 5.4 shows that after exposure to radicalism, some students acknowledged that they started to change their behavior and activities. As many as 32 percent of the respondents acknowledged that they were increasingly diligent in following religious studies, and 18.4 percent followed preaching that propagated radical viewpoints. As many as 20.5 percent of the respondents said that they started to limit their social interactions with other religious groups, while 26.9 percent of the respondents said that they had an increased dislike of America, which in their minds represented the nations that were the enemies of Islam.

TABLE 5.4. Students' responses to "What changes did you exhibit after your exposure to extremist viewpoints?"

Behavior Change	Yes	Sometimes	No Change
Diligently attend religious study groups	32.0%	29.4%	38.6%
Attend preaching meetings	18.4%	30.4%	51.2%
Limit meeting other ethnic groups	0.4%	17.9%	81.7%
Limit meeting other religious groups	20.5%	19.6%	59.9%
Limit meeting the upper economic classes	4.3%	3.7%	80.0%
Do not like America	26.9%	13.3%	59.8%

Note: n = 700; survey conducted in 2018.

Indonesian students who have followed the route of becoming increasingly radical generally believe that there is something wrong with how their country and community are operating and that the errors can be overcome only through embracing the caliphate system. Rahmah (20 years old), from Unair, for instance, said: "Indonesia must implement Islamic law; the global caliphate will surely be restored, and we need to prepare ourselves now to welcome this era." After joining the radical group, Zulfa (20 years old), from ITB, no longer listened to music. She said: "I no longer go to the cinema. There are some books and papers I still read; however, most things we are commanded to avoid, as these things contain material that breaks Allah's law. Besides the films, which contain a lot of sexually graphic content. At the campus there are many boyfriend and girlfriend relationships, those sitting down together with the opposite sex."

Beliefs such as these have developed rapidly among the students of the seven higher education institutions that I have researched. The so-called supremacy of America, as understood by these students, reflects a superior and arrogant attitude of an economically developed nation. These tertiary students consider America as involving itself in other nations' internal affairs and acting as the "global policeman."

Becoming radical is a process involving choices that influence the way educated youth think. Nevertheless, not all students at the seven state universities acknowledged that their everyday behavior changed after exposure to radical ideology. In fact, in the findings of this study, there were a significant number of students who did not change their internal beliefs after exposure to radicalism. Because they felt embarrassed to be themselves in front of their newfound mentors and friends, who had invited them to various activities of the radical groups, and because they did not want to be seen as immoral and secular individuals, some of these students chose to take on the appearance of being radical, but in reality, they were not. A student from UB in Malang stated that one of the instruments often used by radical groups to entice students concerning the relevance of the caliphate was the phrase "shaking off sinfulness." This means that it was hoped that they, as students as well as educated youth, would not merely live lifestyles of consumerism and worldliness. They should also embrace the calling of the community of faith to take on the religious struggle that that community believes in.

Several students who were interviewed acknowledged that when they gathered together as students with those categorized as radical, the new students were pressured to adapt and adjust. They did so in order to not be rebuked or viewed in a negative light within the group. The easiest thing for students to do when they were involved with radical groups was to embrace physical changes, such as changing their clothing or growing long beards so as to be the same as their mentors. The students acknowledged that these most elementary adjustments became parts of their daily lives. As they became involved in the activities of radical groups, female students would typically change the types of head coverings they wore to ones more strictly in accordance with Islamic law. Additionally, they no longer wore trousers, in particular jeans. Male students would begin to wear long-sleeved shirts, grow their beards, and often become involved in activities at the mosque and religious campus activities.

Many students acknowledged feeling shame in their daily lives if they rejected the invitations of senior students and friends in order to follow their religious studies. However, as revealed in the interviews, it seems clear that the involvement of many students in radical study groups was often not something to which they made a wholehearted commitment. While newer students joined study groups, it was not because of a religious need or a deepening of their beliefs, but was more related to their need to socialize and build broader networks of relationships. A significant number of students did not want to have a difference of opinion with the seniors and felt obligated to get involved when the senior students invited them. Karim (21 years old), a student of political sciences at Unair, offered the following testimony:

I was [embarrassed] if I continually rejected the invitation to attend the studies. If I didn't have any prior commitments or immediate assignments, I usually just went along with them. At the gathering places, I met many new friends and saw their environment. I was just happy to sit and observe their discussions. I got to know who were more radical, and who was just following along. Very soon after I started attending, I realized that this was an extremist group. I had read about this in the mass media and was reminded about these groups by my campus friends. However, if I suddenly stopped attending, I didn't feel good about that, as I had received some scholarships and other assistance from them. I tried not to be late to their meetings, and despite realizing it was an extremist group, there was nothing really negative that entered my thoughts about them.

The physical appearance of these groups was conservative; they usually wore standard religious clothing. This is a clear indication that the students in these groups were *not* homogenous. Those students who appeared radical, when observed more closely, were not necessarily radical internally in their beliefs. For a long time, student groups who had been introduced to radical activities included some who quietly sought opportunities to withdraw from the groups, as will be discussed in the next chapter. There were even those who made public statements that they no longer wanted to be involved with religious activity that was considered extremist. When it came to their support for violence to promote their religious convictions, the vast majority of educated youth rejected any extremist actions. For instance, as table 5.5 illustrates, 96.6 percent of respondents disagreed with the destruction of other people's places of worship; only 0.6 percent claimed to actively support such violence, and just

TABLE 5.5. Students' responses to "Do you support the following activities?"

Types of Violence	Actively Support	Passively Support	Do Not Support
Destruction of places of worship of other religions	0.6%	2.8%	96.6%
Suicide bombing of Islam's enemies	1.0%	3.4%	95.6%
Jihad in defense of religion	5.7%	32.1%	62.1%

Note: n = 700; survey conducted in 2018.

2.8 percent passively supported it. This is a significant finding because, according to the national survey, the majority of Muslims in Indonesia objected to having non-Muslim houses of worship in their neighborhoods.[24] Similarly, when the students in my survey were asked whether they supported the suicide bombing of Islam's enemies, 95.6 percent said that they didn't like it, and only 1 percent said they would actively support it. Regarding the use of violent jihad to "defend religion," only 5.7 percent of respondents claimed to actively support it, and 62.1 percent opposed violent actions in the name of religion.

HOMEGROWN RADICALISM WITHOUT EXTREMIST VIOLENCE

The findings of my study concerning the development of radical ideology in Indonesian higher education are quite alarming, as discussed above. Logically, educated youth should be more open to diverse viewpoints, think critically concerning their beliefs, and follow a path that at least does not violate fundamental human rights. However, in reality, a large segment of students have been exposed to and are interested in radicalism. Although the influence of radical transnational ideology cannot be neglected, the development and dissemination of radical viewpoints among university students is generally a domestic issue, with local networks using a recruitment model, resulting in what can be referred to as "homegrown radicalization." It is worth noting that the stages of radicalization among students are not uniform, just as the students who become involved in radical groups are also quite diverse.

It is both easy and challenging to become radical. It is easy because youth are the targets of a vast recruitment program that makes it as easy as possible for individuals to join radical groups. As was discussed above, the recruitment paradigm is focused on persuading students through a variety of means, one of which involves having senior students contribute time, tutoring, and material assistance (such as scholarships, provision of dormitories, etc.) to new students. The persistence and militancy of the radical mentors in pursuing new recruits is evident. Nevertheless, becoming a radical is also tricky, as it requires a high level of commitment and patience to progress through the various stages that are considered necessary parts of the radical program. Besides introducing the principles and mission as formulated in a book written by Taqī al-Dīn al-Nabhānī, the founder of Hizbut Tahrir, entitled *Niẓām al-Islām* (The system of Islam), reluctant radicals are also expected to have a "true character," in line with the Islamic paradigm as the recruiters see it.

Most radicalization experts do not discuss the stages that radicalized individuals must progress through after their involvement in the radical networks. Instead, they focus on the pathways toward radicalization. There are two bodies of literature on this issue. On the one hand, some scholars refer to linear stages, although they disagree on how many steps are involved.[25] The model most often quoted is that of "four pathway stages," developed by Mitchell Silber and Arvin Bhatt: "pre-radicalization," "self-identification," "indoctrination," and "jihadization."[26] Fathali Moghaddam prefers the image of a "staircase to terrorism" with five steps: "psychological interpretation of material conditions," "perceived options to fight unfair treatment," "displacement of aggression," "moral engagement," "solidification of categorical thinking," and "the terrorist act."[27] On the other hand, other scholars suggest that radicalization emerges from an interplay among a number of non-linear factors. Marc Sageman, for example, mentions four factors, including three that are cognitive and behavioral in nature (a sense of moral outrage, a frame used to interpret the world, and resonance with personal experience) and one that is situational (mobilization through networks).[28] All models agree that radicalization does not happen overnight.

It seems clear that the process of radicalization includes different stages; even after becoming radicalized, there are certain stages that reinforce converts' commitment and faith, and these require self-discipline regarding the mission and the principles of radical values. What is absent from the discussion of radicalized youth and the case studies from Indonesia is the assumption that the result of radicalization must be violent terrorism. This is understandable, as the pathway models to radicalization noted above are mostly theoretical or based on case studies of violent terrorists who have been captured and studied.

Contrary to the findings of other research that mentions how extremist groups go through a radicalization process that is somewhat predictable,[29] in this study I discovered that the radicalization trajectories are more dynamic. Not only is there no linear connection between radicalization and extremism, but the process of transition to radicalism is also quite diverse and unpredictable. Indeed, there are students who are exposed to radicalism because they are in search of a religious model that they consider the true path or they feel their lives are not fulfilling their religious understanding about God. However, others join radical groups simply because of the influence of their friends, or enter into radical groups unintentionally, or even become radical because they are disillusioned with their academic studies.

The literature on radicalism and radicalization also emphasizes that radicalization is the result of a process of increased commitment or, in the words of Brian Michael Jenkins, "the process of adopting for oneself or inculcating in others a commitment not only to a system of beliefs, but to their imposition on the rest of society."[30] Because of that, social scientists often argue that radicalization is a lengthy process. Once again, my research tends to dispute this type of conclusion because the trajectory of radicalizing is not uniform. This means that there is no fixed means of measuring and confirming the timeline of an increased commitment to radicalization. Likewise, the assumption that radicalization is always linked to a radical ideology is not necessarily the case. Certainly, there are many types of radical behaviors that can be characterized as ideological, for example, being influenced by HTI ideology, especially related to the caliphate. However, social and demographic characteristics (e.g., age and gender) are also significant influences that form a radical student's behavior. Thus, there are many diverging variables between radical student groups, significant differences of radicalization paradigms, and diverse types of social networks.

Nevertheless, these empirical findings are not intended to deconsolidate theories that have been developed by experts related to radicalization models. This study affirms that homegrown radicalization trajectories are much more dynamic and diverse than is generally understood. I hope these findings concerning reluctant radicalism among students who have been exposed to radical viewpoints make us realize that becoming a radical is not necessarily based on a particular religious commitment that supports violent actions. The extent of the role of religion in radicalization is still debated among members of the scholarly community.[31] My findings are somewhat similar to the conclusions of Anne Aly and Jason-Leigh Striegher, that "religion plays a far lesser role in radicalization toward extremism" than previously thought,[32] and that theories that see religion, "especially Islam," as a key factor in the process of radicalization "are often conceptualized without any reference to actual empirical evidence."[33]

As discussed earlier, there are at least two scholarly viewpoints about pathways to radicalization. On the one hand, a number of scholars have argued that the radicalization process *cannot* be scrutinized in terms of a fixed series of stages. On the other hand, other scholars are convinced that radicalization *does* follow a fixed pathway and process, with terrorism the peak manifestation of radicalization. One of the oft-quoted radicalization models is that of the four radicalization phases developed by Mitchell Silber and Arvin Bhatt, described above.[34] The "pre-radicalization" phase is the initial period of the radicalization process before individuals are exposed to a Salafi viewpoint. During the phase of "self-identification," individuals are exposed to internal and external triggers, such as trauma, social alienation, discrimination, or marginalization, that encourage them to pursue a drastic change in their lives, including their religious beliefs. The "indoctrination" phase occurs when the individuals are increasingly focused on adopting a Salafi-Jihadist ideology and viewpoints that justify militant actions. Finally, the "jihadization" phase occurs when the individuals position themselves as "warriors of a holy war" and consider jihad as their religious obligation.

Based on my findings, Silber and Bhatt's theory can be analyzed as follows. First, they assumed that radicalization is a problem related only to Islamic terrorism and neglected other extremist groups. Second, they implied that Salafism is the primary vehicle for radicalization, although Salafism is not necessarily a violent version of Islam. As discussed earlier, not all Muslim extremists embrace a radical form of Islam, and not all Muslim radicals carry out extremist and violent actions. Third, Silber and Bhatt also failed to understand the complex factors that trigger radicalization, both religious and non-religious factors. Through my findings I have provided evidence that many students joined radical networks not merely because of religious factors. Other factors played a significant role, such as a sense of pressure to accept the offers of senior students or a sense of obligation to follow members of the radical group who had previously provided them with various forms of assistance. Fourth, Silber and Bhatt tended to confuse the motivations and historical context of the individuals involved in radical actions. In her book *Terrorism and Global Security: Historical and Contemporary Perspectives*, Anne Aly differentiates between religious and secular factors, the latter of which include such aspects as politics, economics, and social contexts.[35]

My findings also demonstrate that many students who were involved in radical groups actually did not necessarily change their religious beliefs in any substantial way. They may have changed their physical appearance, especially their clothing; however, this does not mean that they embraced religious beliefs that justified jihadist violence. Many students I interviewed concluded that militant jihadist actions are not relevant in Indonesia because the situation and the conditions do not require the "Holy War doctrine." This is in line with the views of some scholars who have recently questioned the assumed link between radicalization and terrorism, arguing that endorsing beliefs is one thing and acting on them is another.[36]

CONCLUDING REMARKS

In this chapter I have highlighted a number of important issues related to the radicalization of youth and offered insights into the complex factors involved in the process of radicalization. On the basis of both qualitative and quantitative data, I have attempted to show how some Indonesian universities have been exposed to radical viewpoints. My purpose is to emphasize the importance of understanding local contexts through empirical research in order to better understand the variables involved and the diverse paths to radicalization. The trajectory of university students who convert to radical ideologies or join radical groups is not monolithic. The networks that allow them to be exposed to radical teachings are also diverse. It is worth noting that they continued struggling as members of radical groups not only during their change from the "pre-radicalization" phase to the "self-identification" phase (to borrow Silber and Bhatt's terminology), but also when they were already involved in the radical groups.

My study confirmed the conclusions of Aly and Striegher that "there is no single pathway to radicalization and no distinct pattern to profile an individual throughout any of the stages of radicalization."[37] As pathways toward radicalization are not monolithic, it is also important to nuance the connection between radicalization and violent terrorism. Examining these diverse pathways to radicalization can help us understand the complexity of factors driving students to become radicalized and facilitating the process. In sociological terms, the dynamics of the involvement of new students in radical groups and their struggle are interesting to observe because these students are self-determining agents capable of challenging and resisting the structures of domination. As will be discussed in the next chapter, some chose the path of deradicalization, removing themselves from the environment of radicalism. Students have to assess the impact of their involvement in the radical networks on themselves, their families, and others. Besides those who felt they had discovered "the true path" and had become more "Islamic" through radical groups, there was a significant number of students who questioned the relevance of absolutist radical ideology, as well as the "standards of godliness" promoted by the radical groups.

SIX

Self-Deradicalization of Educated Youth

In chapter 4 I demonstrated that pathways to radicalization are neither uniform nor linear. I will argue in this chapter that radicalization is not an irreversible process, either. If people can adopt radical beliefs and attitudes and decide to join particular radical groups, then they can also abandon and leave those groups by changing their beliefs and attitudes. Attempts can be made either to prevent the radicalization process from happening in the first place or to deradicalize those who are already radicalized. In the previous two chapters we discussed the ways in which young people converted to radical ideologies and joined radical networks, as well as what shaped their views and attitudes. In this chapter I focus on how radicalized youth give up their radical views, with particular attention to the triggers for deradicalization. There are at least three recurring themes in the scholarly discussion on why people leave radical networks. First, disillusionment with leaders and fellow members, followed by physical and/or psychological burnout, is the most common reason for leaving.[1] Second, an inability to tolerate the brutality and pressure involved, as well as negative intragroup dynamics, can prompt radicalized people to weigh their membership and affiliation.[2] The third most common reason for leaving radical networks is a desire to return to a normal life.[3] In their study of disengaged jihadists in Indonesia, Julie Chernov-Hwang, Rizal Panggabean, and Ihsan Ali-Fauzi identify four themes among those who had decided to leave extremist activities: disillusionment with leadership; an awareness that the costs of action outweighed the personal or movement-wide benefits; developing new friendships away from extremist groups; and changes to their personal ambitions, such as pursuing education, having children, or providing for a family.[4]

In recent years, a number of studies have addressed what may be done to promote and encourage radicalized individuals to return to mainstream society and normal life. What intervention strategies can effectively facilitate deradicalization? There is a general agreement among scholars and practitioners that no single model of deradicalization is universally applicable. Indeed, any effort to understand the factors that drive deradicalization for each individual will necessarily be based on, or derived from, a particular context. The prominent deradicalization expert Daniel Koehler mentions variant models of deradicalization that have been developed in different parts of the world and says that such interventions cannot simply be transplanted from one country to another, even to countries in the same region. According to Koehler, Western deradicalization programs are mostly focused on offering economic assistance and counseling, and they place little emphasis on ideological concerns linked to deradicalization. In comparison, state-run Middle Eastern programs "heavily rely on a theological component."[5] Koehler argues that the most effective method of countering the threat of extremism from subject participants is to walk them through ideological reform, along with applying practical rehabilitation methods like skills training and social integration.[6]

In Indonesia, deradicalization and rehabilitation programs have mostly been orchestrated by the state through repressive measures. Following the 2002 Bali bombings, on the pretext of waging "the war against terrorism," the government passed the 2003 Law on the Eradication of Terrorism Crimes and set up the special taskforce, known as Detasemen Khusus 88, or "Densus 88," as an elite counter-terrorism unit. Hundreds of militants involved in acts of terrorism have been captured and put in jail.[7] Masdar Hilmy notes that "most of the security operation carried out by the Densus 88 is in the forms of ambushing and killing."[8] Cameron Sumpter is correct when saying that "the National Police (Polri) had been highly effective in thwarting attacks and dismantling terrorist networks, particularly through the work of its elite counterterrorism unit, known as Densus 88 (Special Detachment)."[9] However, the implementation of the 2003 anti-terrorism law through Densus 88 sparked criticism and controversies, particularly among Islamic activists. They rejected the harsh methods used by the government to deter terrorism as being excessive and against human rights. Most of the suspected perpetrators of terrorist acts were shot dead. Islamist groups accused Densus 88 of being funded by the U.S. government and under the direction of the CIA, FBI, and other American intelligence agencies.[10]

In addition to forming Densus 88, the government also established the National Agency for Combating Terrorism (BNPT, Badan Nasional Penanggulangan Terorisme) in 2010, following the 2009 hotel bombings in Jakarta. The main task of the BNPT is threefold: (1) prevention, protection, and deradicalization, (2) operations and enforcement, and (3) international cooperation. Part of the BNPT's deradicalization program is the creation of several prevention forums, known as *Forum Koordinasi Pencegahan Terorisme* (Coordinating Forums for Counterterrorism), in thirty-two of Indonesia's thirty-four provinces since 2012, with the main task of preventing the spread of radical ideology.[11] The state-run deradicalization programs in Indonesia have been criticized for their emphasis on a security approach. For instance, on December 18, 2011, five Muslim organizations, namely, Jamaat Anshorut Tauhid (JAT), Gerakan Reformasi Islam (Garis), Front Pembela Islam (FPI), Forum Ummat Islam (FUI), and Majlis Mujahidin Indonesia (MMI), held a meeting in Cipanas, West Java, rejecting the government's deradicalization programs, especially those policies and measures introduced by the BNPT. The Indonesian Council of Ulama (MUI) issued a mixed reaction. While the central MUI sided with the government on waging the war against terrorism, the MUI branch in Surakarta, Central Java, challenged state-run deradicalization and accused it of weakening the unity of the Muslim community (*ummah*) and undermining *Shari'ah*.[12]

The government also launched a deradicalization program targeting those who have been arrested and imprisoned, including "re-education" intervention. In 2013, the BNPT invited three clerics from the Middle East to visit the Cipinang Prison in Jakarta and Pasir Putih Prison in

Nusakambangan Islam to persuade Muslim terrorists to abandon their radical beliefs.[13] Former terrorists were also used to influence other inmates to relinquish their views based on the assumption that jihadists only listen to other jihadists. The purpose of this re-education component is to engage with detainees on religious grounds and attempt to convince them that their religious justification for violence was based on a corrupted understanding of Islam. The British counter-terrorism expert Nick O'Brien contends that the Indonesian program is able to exploit the radical group Jemaah Islamiyah based on the internal split within the group of those who have adopted violent tactics against Western targets and others who oppose these tactics.[14] However, many jihadists have a distrust of police. In his study of seventy Indonesian jihadists, Ian Chalmers concludes that "most (but not all) 'committed jihadists' retain an almost visceral hatred of the state apparatus and its kufr prison system. Until such time as their antipathy towards the authorities as agents of a global enemy has waned, the prospects for rehabilitation are remote."[15] Even former jihadists may quickly lose their credibility because of their cooperation with police.

At any rate, the Indonesian model of deradicalization, like those of other countries, emphasizes the application of external pressures by the state apparatus and other stakeholders, including civil society. Furthermore, most studies that identify triggers or factors that facilitate deradicalization focus on assessments of rehabilitation programs for prisoners, along with personal narratives of those who have themselves been deradicalized, specifically among detainees. In the present chapter we discuss the ability of radicalized youth to deradicalize themselves without state-run deradicalization and rehabilitation programs. Those exposed to radical viewpoints were categorized in the previous chapter as "reluctant radicals" because they are not strongly grounded in an exclusive and extreme religious viewpoint that justifies violent actions to them. They might identify themselves as "the defenders of Islam" who opposed the threat of a "secular culture," created a clear dividing line between Islam and "others," and demanded the implementation of Islamic law. Nevertheless, their way of thinking remains similar to that of urban youth who embrace a cosmopolitan lifestyle. This explains why they can easily leave radical ideologies if they no longer feel comfortable without being pressured from outside. This model of "self-deradicalization" or "deradicalization from within" has not been much discussed. There is a tendency among scholars to view radicalism as inherently involving religious beliefs that justify violent actions and terrorism to them, as if radicalization is irreversible.

SELF-DERADICALIZATION: THEORETICAL CONSIDERATIONS

Simply stated, deradicalization is the opposite of radicalization. While radicalization, according to Angel Rabasa, Stacie L. Pettyjohn, Jeremy J. Ghez, and Christopher Boucek, is "the process of adopting an extreme belief system, including the willingness to use, support, or facilitate violence, as a method to effect societal change,"[16] deradicalization as defined by the same authors, is "the process of abandoning an extremist worldview and concluding that it is not acceptable to use violence to effect social change."[17] The literature on deradicalization, similar to that on radicalization, is quite diverse and reveals conceptual diversity, especially regarding the dichotomy between the cognitive variables and behavior, that is, *ideas* and *actions*. For example, John Horgan argues that scholars fail to differentiate between the cognitive and behavioral dimensions of deradicalization. There is a tendency to mix up these two, resulting in the understanding that deradicalization means "armed Islamist groups leaving their pathway of violence." According to Horgan, this is not *deradicalization*, but rather *disengagement* because it relates to behavioral change. Horgan defines deradicalization as the "social/psychological process whereby an individual's commitment to, and involvement in, violent radicalization is reduced to the extent that they are no longer at risk of involvement and engagement in violent activity."[18] Disengagement, on the other hand, is a process involving a "a change in role or function that is usually associated with a reduction of violent participation."[19] In other words, while deradicalization is ideological, disengagement is behavioral. Unlike deradicalization, disengagement does not demand a change in ideas or viewpoints but only rejects the use of physical violence. With this, disengagement refers to "a behavioral change, such as leaving a group or changing one's role within it. It does not necessitate a change in values or ideals, but requires relinquishing the objective of achieving change through violence," write Naureen C. Fink and Ellie B. Hearne.[20]

The relationship between deradicalization and disengagement has been the subject of discussion among scholars. Alex P. Schmid argues that disengagement may take place without deradicalization.[21] Disengagement remains a prerequisite for deradicalization. Even though disengagement often precedes deradicalization, the former is not sufficient to guarantee the latter. Horgan points out that disengaged terrorists may not be deradicalized or repentant at all. However, he continues that contributing factors for disengagement are likely to aid the process and be some of the tools required to eventually lead to deradicalization.[22] Because of this, along with Tore Bjorgo he maintains that the primary challenge for deradicalization is the false assumption that "radical views predict radical behavior,"[23] which fails to make a distinction between the cognitive and behavioral dimensions. Other scholars, like Bjorgo, identify "push" and "pull" factors that determine an individual's decision to leave radical activities. "Push factors," Bjorgo writes, lead an individual to weigh the decision to join a radical network, while "pull factors" help the person make the final decision to quit through alternate options.[24]

Another leading deradicalization expert, Omar Ashour, concurs with Horgan and Bjorgo that a distinction needs to be made between deradicalization and disengagement. He defines deradicalization as "a process that leads an individual or group to change his attitude about violence—specifically about the appropriateness of violence against civilians."[25] While disengagement requires the abandonment of violence, he argues that deradicalization seeks to delegitimize ideologies that violate social norms. More specifically, in disengagement the individual has left the radical group but has not necessarily altered or renounced his ideology. Ashour believes that deradicalization has three types: (1) *Comprehensive deradicalization* refers to "a successful de-radicalization process on the three levels (ideological, behavioral and organizational)"; (2) *substantive deradicalization* represents "a successful process of de-radicalization on both the ideological and behavioral levels, but not on the organizational level (usually a failure on that level is followed by splits, factionalization and internal organizational conflict, and/or the marginalization of the de-radicalized leadership)"; and (3) *pragmatic deradicalization* includes "a successful behavioral and organizational de-radicalization process, but without an ideological de-legitimization of violence."[26] The typology of Ashour is interesting because it reveals changing patterns in deradicalization from one type to another, which means that an important aspect of a specific type is not necessarily central to another. Pragmatic deradicalization, for example, does not view the change of ideas and views as necessary. Ashour refers explicitly to the process of deradicalization among members of the jihadist community in Egypt where they reject violence but hold on to "misogynist, homophobic, xenophobic, and anti-democratic views."[27] Thus, according to Froukje Demant, Marieke Slootman, Frank Buijs, and Jean Tillie, cognitive change does not necessarily mean the adoption of liberal views or norms associated with "de-radicalized views" in the West.[28] This means that deradicalization needs to pay attention to local needs. Rabasa, Pettyjohn, Ghez, and Boucek explain the following: "The best-designed plans leverage local cultural patterns to achieve their objectives. One implication of this observation is that deradicalisation programs cannot simply be translated from one country to another, even within the same region. They have to develop organically in a specific country and culture."[29]

To observe local aspects is crucial since it is agreed that deradicalization takes many forms. Deradicalization is similar to radicalization in that a change takes place within the individual or group. As there are diverse pathways toward radicalization, so, too, is this the case with deradicalization. Building on this understanding, scholars and practitioners developed deradicalization initiatives that involve various stakeholders, including the state, community, and family. Vivienne Chin argues that community-based initiatives have the ability to enhance the capacity of the community to promote alternative activities to radicalization.[30] Education has also been touted as having an impact on deradicalization. All of these approaches suggest that everyone should play a role in the deradicalization of those who have been exposed to radical ideologies.

My findings reveal that a significant number of reluctant radicals tend to deradicalize themselves without external pressure. This deradicalization from within does not mean that an individual will suddenly change his or her viewpoint; on the contrary, certain factors involved in such deradicalization are internal struggles, incompatibility, and personal disappointment. It is evident that complex factors that surround an individual influence a personal decision to depart from a radical community. In this context, the deradicalization of reluctant radicals can be understood in light of what Mohammed Elshimi identifies as "de-radicalization as a technology of the self."[31] Elshimi developed a theoretical framework based on the conceptual lens of Michel Foucault's "technologies of the self," defined as "[that which] which permit[s] individuals to effect by their own means or with the help of others a certain number of operations on their bodies and souls, thoughts, conduct, and the way of being, so as to transform themselves."[32]

Technologies of the self posits the self as an agent of change; nevertheless, the subjectivity of the self is to be shaped by, or to become the result of, what Nikolas Rose refers to as "a range of human technologies, technologies that take modes of being human as their object."[33] The early work of Foucault was largely criticized because it appeared that he neglected the role of subjectivity;[34] nevertheless, in later works Foucault revealed a different approach. Although he did not abandon his previous viewpoint, Foucault at least later provided greater room for the subject within his or her environment. He wrote: "I would say that if now I am interested, in fact, in the way in which the subject constitutes himself in an active fashion, by the practices of self, these practices are nevertheless not something that the individual invents by himself. They are patterns that he finds in his culture and which are proposed, suggested and imposed on him by his culture, his society and his social group."[35]

Foucault's concept of "technologies of the self" has important implications for understanding self-deradicalization, as explored in this chapter. Although reluctant radicals have the capacity to make choices and take actions themselves, governments, those who are in positions of power, and civil society cannot stay silent and neglect designing a deradicalization program so that those in the radical community have the capacity to remove themselves from the trap of radicalism. The "technologies of the self" that were initiated by Foucault included analysis of self-formation techniques, "specific techniques that human beings use to understand themselves,"[36] which allow for "self-determining agents capable of challenging and resisting the structures of domination in modern society."[37] However, this does not mean that Foucault made the subject free of self-responsibility. He believed that self-formation requires involvement, encouragement, and conducive conditions "that he finds in his culture and which are proposed, suggested and imposed on him by his culture, his society and his social group."[38] In other words, deradicalization never occurs suddenly. The capacity of the self in the concept of self-deradicalization refers to the individual's having the capacity to remove himself from radicalism; however, this does not mean to deny the role of community power structures. "Through the technology of the self," Elshimi argues, "de-radicalisation is not only situated within governmentality but also brings to the fore the capacity of subjects to make choices and act."[39] In other words, the responsibility of deradicalization rests upon the shoulders of all communities that desire peace: the government, the campus, and civil society. Intervention is even more crucial in youth, who often become the targets of radicalization.

YOUTH'S "STRUGGLES" IN RADICAL NETWORKS

In Indonesia, numerous efforts have been made to implement the process of deradicalization. For example, Schmid studied how the community connected to online activity opposed radicalism by using social media, making memes, hashtags, comics, or even videos of their choice.[40] These deradicalization efforts have also been implemented by involving former combatants, former terrorists, and other such people to develop and implement efforts to reconstruct radicals' attitude toward radical groups. Among students, the efforts toward deradicalization usually are carried out by a campus leader by contesting radical ideology and presenting an alternative that can compete with, and eventually oppose, it. At the University of Diponegoro (Undip) in Semarang, for example, the rector issued a policy to limit the activities of students who had been exposed to radical viewpoints. On numerous campuses, similar efforts have been implemented with various levels of success. At the Bogor Agriculture Institute (IPB, Institut Pertanian Bogor), the leader of the spiritual activities unit for students, who was considered radical, was asked to resign and replaced with a new leader. This type of structural intervention was intended as a specific measure to suppress the attraction of students to radical ideologies.

Repressive measures and policies developed by some higher education institutions to regulate and limit the activities of radical ideology appear not to have been effective. It is true that radical student movements and activities seem to have disappeared from public view. Nevertheless, radicalism among students does not cease to exist. Radical networks manage to maintain their existence and propagate their messages underground.

TABLE 6.1. Students' responses to "How do you feel after joining religious study forums?"

Responses	Percentage
Found the true path	31.4
Became more pious	12.4
It was a wrong decision to join them	24.9
Want to leave	6.0
No response	25.3

Note: n = 700; survey conducted in 2018.

The findings of this study suggest that among many students the process of deradicalization cannot be implemented effectively by repressive regulations and policies issued by the leadership of higher education institutions. Numerous students interviewed for this study said that they left religious activism that was categorized as radical primarily because of personal reasons rather than due to institutional restrictions.

In chapter 4 I highlighted the diverse backgrounds of radicalized youth and the nature of their conversion. From a sociological perspective, it is interesting to examine what happened after they joined radical networks. Among the 700 students at seven prominent state universities who were asked what their feelings were after joining and participating in radical groups' activities, such as religious study circles (*kegiatan pengajian*), 31.4 percent said that they found "the right path," and 12.4 percent felt that they became more pious, as shown in table 6.1. Interestingly, 24.9 percent of respondents admitted that it was a wrong decision to join the radical groups, and 6 percent said they wanted to leave the groups.

Those radicalized youth who felt that they had discovered the right path and become more pious in their lives were increasingly committed to a radical ideology. As we can see in table 6.2, some 45 percent of respondents had no intention of leaving radical activities. Besides visible outward signs, such as wearing particular clothing or long beards, certain exclusive attitudes tended to limit their social connections with other radical groups. A number of respondents used the term *hijrah* (literally "migration") to refer to a change in their lives after their conversion to radical ideas. In Islamic tradition, the word "*hijrah*" is used to describe the emigration of the Prophet Muhammad and the early Muslims from Mecca to Medina. The significance of the *hijrah* is reflected in the fact

TABLE 6.2. Students' responses to "Have you taken steps to leave the radical networks and activities?"

Responses	Percentage
Yes	27.7
Yes, but have returned	14.0
Never	45.0
Never, because I have never joined a radical group	13.3

Note: n = 700; survey conducted in 2018.

that it is commemorated as the beginning of the Muslim calendar year. In Indonesia today, *hijrah* is used by radical groups as a sign of leaving behind a past that was full of darkness and moving toward a future full of light. The problem is that this understanding of *hijrah* has often led them to display intolerant attitudes toward others who do not share their views, which causes some concerns.

Both the government and university leadership have implemented specific measures to prevent the spread of radical groups. The networks of the transnational Hizbut Tahrir Indonesia (HTI) on campus, for instance, have faced serious obstacles since the government officially disbanded HTI and university administrators began to limit their activities. Especially since the publication of the BNPT research findings, which connected the seven state universities with radicalism, university leaders have taken steps to implement policies concerning radical groups, such as removing them from student organizations and supervising mosque activities to eliminate radical elements on campus. Even invitations to Islamic clerics to visit campus mosques were under the control of the university. In Undip, for example, Professor Suteki, who held a position as the director of the graduate program in law and was the head of the senate of the Law Faculty, was removed from his post on November 28, 2018, because of his affiliation with HTI. He served as an expert witness against the banning of HTI during the judicial review in the High Court in October 2017. Besides losing the court case, Suteki suffered significant financial loss, given that he lost his jobs on campus, too.

HTI followers viewed Suteki's dismissal as a setback for the pro-caliphate movement. Several informants acknowledged that they needed to adjust their strategy for propagating their message, from being open to going underground. Karin (24 years old), a student from Undip, said that the treatment of Suteki was not just, and the leadership of HTI at that time were confused because of the harsh policies of Undip's administration toward HTI's pro-caliphate network. Although all of the campuses introduced strict policies for the surveillance of radical movements, Undip was one of the strictest in their application. The Undip leadership has recently issued regulations to prevent the circulation of radical ideologies. A campus committee selects the Muslim clerics who are allowed to preach on campus and monitors the topics they can address. Repressive measures have been received with mixed reactions among students. Some have applauded the administrators' policy to limit the radical activities on the campus firmly. They have argued that the presence of radical groups became an obstacle to harmonious relationships, as they often created boundaries between their groups and others. Others expressed disagreement with the repressive policies, arguing that such hostile measures tended to violate the freedom of expression. Among radicalized students, the repressive campus regulations led them to change tactics in the ways they disseminated their ideology. Interestingly, almost no one admitted that they decided to leave the radical networks because of the university's pressure. This study shows that some of the respondents deradicalized for a variety of other reasons. The various factors that led to students' moving toward deradicalization and how this was achieved reflect the ability of youth to self-deradicalize after being involved in radical networks. As many as 27.7 percent of respondents had taken steps to remove themselves from radical activities, and 14 percent acknowledged that they had removed themselves but later returned, while 13.3 percent had never joined a radical group in the first place, despite being exposed to radical ideology (see table 6.2).

When the respondents were asked what made it difficult to remove themselves from religious radicalism, 29 percent said that they believed in the mission of the radical groups, 13.7 percent acknowledged that they were intimidated by the leaders of the groups, and 1.9 percent of the respondents wanted to learn more, while 45 percent did not want to disclose their reasons. Perhaps, they were unsure whether they would leave the group or not. As for the reasons given by respondents for deciding to leave the activities of radical groups, 25 percent said that they had begun to realize the errors of the teachings and were not comfortable with them, 14.1 percent were forbidden by their families from

TABLE 6.3. Students' responses to "What was your reason for stopping attending radical activities?"

Responses	Percentage
Feared it affected my salvation	4.6
Forbidden by family	14.1
Incorrect teachings/not at peace	25.0
Advice from a friend	5.9
No answer	50.4

Note: n = 700; survey conducted in 2018.

associating with the groups, 5.9 percent left because of advice from their friends, and 4.6 percent were fearful that the radical groups would affect their salvation (see table 6.3).

In the in-depth interviews, informants gave diverse reasons for why they had decided not to stay involved in radical activities. As we can see in table 6.3, the answers "not at peace" or "became aware of incorrect teaching" were the most frequently cited, by 25 percent of respondents. Those who said they were not at peace expressed it in various ways. One recurring theme was that they felt that the radical teachings were not compatible with the understanding of Islam that they had had before. Some informants from the University of Airlangga (Unair) in Surabaya, for example, explained that the ideology of HTI was different from the understanding of Islam that they had received from their families, communities, and schools, which were affiliated with Nahdlatul Ulama (NU), the largest Muslim organization in Indonesia. Karim (23 years old), a student from Unair, graduated from a *pesantren* in East Java and joined the HTI group on his college campus. Karim had been active in student organizations since his time in the *pesantren*, so it was not surprising for him to be involved in discussion groups initiated by the HTI leaders. According to Karim, he initially enjoyed religious discussions because he was a graduate of a religious school. However, after a few meetings, the theme of the discussions transitioned to establishing an Islamic state to fulfill the aspirations of the Islamic community, which were oppressed globally. The idea of the caliphate system was presented as the solution to all the problems confronted by the Muslim community. From there, Karim began to feel that the ideology of HTI was incompatible with the Islam he understood from his upbringing at the *pesantren.* "NU itself recognizes four schools of law, while HTI considered only the ideology of the caliphate as the true version of Islam, and [taught] that it must be defended," explained Karim. From that time, he wanted to limit his involvement with HTI, meeting instead with his friends from a *pesantren* organization, who encouraged him to reconnect with a more moderate version of Islam. After a lengthy evaluation, he disconnected from the radical community, although it was difficult to avoid the HTI meetings on the campus.

The religious intolerance of radical groups came to the attention of many students who experienced deradicalization. Sarah (21 years old), a student from the University of Brawijaya (UB) in Malang, acknowledged that she did not enjoy the pressure that she experienced as part of a radical group. Sarah is a graduate of a public high school and is from a family without an educated religious background. Therefore, she was initially interested in joining the studies of the religious group because she felt she needed to learn more about Islam. For one semester, Sarah felt somewhat comfortable, despite wearing a different *jilbab* from the other girls at school and being required to have more loose-fitting clothing. Over time, some of those leading the studies enforced what they considered proper *Shar'iah* clothing, which was considered more compatible with their interpretation of *Shari'ah*. "If you continue to wear your clothing and your perfume, you will be categorized with those who are trying to attract attention to themselves," said those leading the study. Sarah's friends in the study group made it clear that girls who wear perfume are "harlots" and, from that moment, Sarah did not want to be involved in the study group.

Self-deradicalization can occur when an individual does not feel comfortable in a radicalized community. Any sense of being watched and restricted in one's actions, or forced to follow the radicals' standards, can cause an individual to feel uncomfortable in that environment. The radical group wants its members to have an internal cohesion, displaying as one conspicuous differences from the outside world. However, this exclusive attitude can cause its followers to feel ostracized from their more secular social networks. This was a typical response from various reluctant radicals, although some considered this situation a natural consequence that they had to face. They look at the example of how the Prophet Muhammad started preaching accompanied by a small group of companions, and how he overcame significant challenges. Their ostracization shows that they are on the right path and need to overcome challenges, as the Prophet did in Mecca. However, for other reluctant radicals, this situation gave them an incentive to rethink the path they had taken and question whether it was true. Darman (20 years old), a student from Sepuluh Nopember Institute of Technology (ITS), had been active in study groups since high school and continued while at the Faculty of Technology. He spoke about his difficulties in finding friends to help him with his assignments:

> I was previously involved in a radical group because, since high school, my teacher taught me to hold onto the teaching of the Qur'an and the hadith, both in my personal life, in my family, and in the community and nation. When I went to university, I was interested in the activities organized by the HTI leaders and became a part of their network. However, in the second year of my university studies, I took a class that required a group of people to work together on a project. It was in that situation that I faced challenges in finding friends to work with me, as I was a part of the exclusive HTI network. I thought if I continued my connections with HTI, I would fail my studies! Because of that, I am no longer connected to HTI; however, I continue to try to be obedient in my understanding of Islam. I want to live according to *Shar'iah* law, but at the same time, I want to be able to connect with the old friends I had before I joined HTI.

One important characteristic of the deradicalization of educated youth in Indonesia is that they easily decided to distance themselves from radical groups. In a number of higher education institutions, this study had found that a number of students removed themselves from radical activities, such as the study groups, preaching activities, and so on, when the students had romantic relationships that were forbidden by the radicals. They often felt prevented from "enjoying their youth," not being able to participate in dating, online games, watching films, or listening to music. In Unair, for example, this study has found that students who were known to ride around with their girlfriends felt that they became the targets of bullying when senior students harassed them, declaring that they were not being good Muslims. According to these younger students, when they were riding with their friends of the opposite sex, they were simply platonic friendships, without any romance. For some students, this activity was simply allowing a female to get a lift home to save money. Of course, radical groups were attractive to students for a variety of reasons. The strict rules the reluctant radicals have to follow and implement in their lives, including certain limitations on their daily activities, caused them to rethink their involvement in the networks and even led some to leave the groups and their radical activities.

Santi (20 years old), a student from Bandung Institute of Technology (ITB, Institut Teknologi Bandung), acknowledged that her senior mentors had warned her that she would have to leave behind all of the worldly attractions that were parts of her life before the *hijrah*. The issue of dating was a frequent theme mentioned in the study groups she belonged to. She confessed that she was close to a boy whom she considered her boyfriend, even though their relationship was limited to text messaging and was not physical. Nevertheless, the study groups did not allow it. Fearing that her mentor would judge her, Santi avoided the radical meetings. She spoke about the content of the meetings, where they often referred to youth who wasted their time, not living according to the path of Allah, but playing games instead. Another individual, Kadar, felt uncomfortable with the excessive rules and chose not to attend the gatherings anymore: "I am quite resentful; why am I not even allowed to play games? If the games had porn in them, fair enough, but they said that the games were a product of the West, deliberately made so the Muslim world would become lazy, resulting in a gloomy future."

Besides this, others felt frustrated when they could not follow popular culture, such as movies and pop music. In particular, students were passionate fans of K-pop (Korean pop music). Although involved with HTI, many informants confessed that they continued to listen to the latest K-pop music via social media, as well as watching the latest music videos and Korean dramas. A student who claimed to be a member of the HTI movement admitted that she has an Instagram account in order to follow stories of her K-pop idols. While some radicalized youth expressed a debt of gratitude to their HTI mentors who had guided them to "the true path" of life, others considered the restrictions of the true path the driving force that led them to withdraw from the radical networks. For example, a student at UB admitted that, after having been involved in numerous radical group activities for nearly two years, he suddenly decided to leave when his mentor stated that the K-pop that he liked was forbidden. This student had disclosed in the interview that he had been a fan of K-pop since junior high school. Usually, before going to bed, he would listen to Korean music or watch a Korean television series. With his enjoyment of Korean popular culture, when it was suddenly declared forbidden because of religious standards, he straight away chose to stop being active in the radical study groups. He chose to remain a fan of K-pop.

Apparently, some students who had been fans of K-pop since high school, for example, experienced a dilemma when they were forced to choose a path to the future. Even though, at the starting point, they acknowledged interest in radical activities, when they were advised by their mentors that K-pop was a product of the global popular culture that was religiously forbidden, the choice for them was not easy. A number of students who were K-pop fans expressed that it was difficult for them to receive criticism from their senior student mentors for their interest in K-pop. When confronted with this situation, some students decided to leave the radical path and maintain their old interest in K-pop and other popular culture that they considered enjoyable. The following is the testimony of Febi (23 years old), a student from UB:

> I liked K-pop, actually, I loved it; I am a fan of the boy group Exo, and the girl group Blackpink. I have followed them since I was in junior high. I didn't like it when the religious teacher kept preaching about everything I couldn't do. I couldn't like K-pop because of this or that. I know that I need to have a deeper religious understanding, and I know that I can't be excessive about it if I like something. Previously I tried to stop doing certain things, but it was difficult. The problem was whenever I explored Instagram, new things would keep appearing. I try to avoid it, but it was difficult because there were always new things that I couldn't stop myself from looking at. Beyond this, my friends all like the same things and they are the community I hang around with. So, I decided to stop being active in the religious study groups because I couldn't leave my hobbies of K-pop.

Informants such as Febi found it challenging to follow the stages of being integrated into the radical group. Another student, Bila (18 years old), from the same university, said: "You can't watch these, according to my mentor and senior students. 'Don't watch these films, or listen to the worldly songs,' they would say. But what was I supposed to do when they were really good, especially if dramas came out like 'Goblin' or 'The Legend of the Blue Sea'? Who can reject that? Therefore, in the end, I quietly went along and watched these films, which were my hobbies."

A number of students interviewed for this study stated that senior students and mentors from the radical groups often declared that the younger students needed to be more serious about the faith. They were told that they needed to give up their time for spiritual struggle and follow the true religious path they believed in. The students were asked to regularly give up two or three hours to be a part of studies and discussions about the caliphate system as an alternative government. This sacrifice was presented as evidence of their solidarity and effort in their religious struggle for what they believed. Regarding this time commitment and attitude, many students generally did not consider it a problem. However, when there was a demand that they apply these teachings in their everyday lives and sacrifice their personal interests and lifestyles, those newly radicalized youth often changed directions. Some of them were devout fans of popular youth culture.

At this point, for students who chose the route of going deeper in radical activities, they generally committed long-term. They chose to distance themselves from "worldly ways" and commit their lives to religion and honor the beliefs to which they held. However, even some students who had been committed to this movement for a long time became disoriented and confused about the radical viewpoints when they came to later and more critical points in their lives. Following an increasingly radical route was their path, but sometimes a later critical point caused them to turn in an opposite direction. Coming from the typical background of urban youth while maintaining exposure to global popular youth culture, despite being a member of a radical group, was a factor that caused some students to change directions from the increasingly radical groups. Radical groups usually have certain books that are obligatory reading for their followers. The Gema Pembebasan network at Undip uses *Niẓām al-Islām* (The System of Islam), written by Taqī al-Dīn Nabhānī, the founder of Hizbut Tahrir in Palestine. It contains a list of laws and principles that must be fulfilled to create an Islamic state. According to one informant, the Muslim dormitory usually provides various books that are mandatory reading for the students and other activities such as meeting with mentors and routinely seeking counsel from the leaders of the religious foundation, an organization that provides student scholarships. Some students acknowledged that they could not abandon their enjoyment of K-pop and were unable to complete the study of *Niẓām al-Islām*, which runs to several volumes. At Unair, it was used by HTI for their followers to study systematically. Studying the first and largest volume of *Niẓām al-Islām* was required of all candidates for membership in HTI. However, to be able to continue to the next volumes required a long period of study. Many informants explained that they had been studying these books for five years but were still not allowed to progress to the next volumes because they were considered imperfect in their character and faith. Some had to repeat the study of *Niẓām al-Islām* three times, which resulted in a sense of inferiority that caused them to withdraw from the group. Fatimah (23 years old), a student from Unair, explained, "Every time I changed mentors, I was required to start from the beginning again. This was repeated three times. They explained that I was not ready to continue to the next volume."

Some students acknowledged that it was not easy to remove themselves from radical activities. Their mentors were generally trained and persistent in persuading the students and making them realize that it was vitally important for them to return to the struggle of defending their beliefs. When choosing the route of deradicalization, reluctant radicals usually experienced a phase of moving back and forth in their beliefs. A number of students said that when they were confronted by this challenge, the possibility of returning to radical activities was very real. However, when experiencing the new freedom of everyday life and having enjoyable hobbies, their interest in global popular culture generally was greater than the urge to return.

This study found that the mechanism that was developed by students to avoid being involved with the activities of the radical groups varied from one student to another. As many as 29.8 percent of the respondents acknowledged that they avoided involvement with radical religious groups through stopping contact with the senior students who had

TABLE 6.4. Students' responses to "What did you do to avoid involvement in radical activities?"

Mechanisms Developed by Students	Yes	No
Avoided contact with those who invited me	29.8%	70.2%
Got involved in other activities	58.4%	41.6%
Did not want to be involved	39.7%	60.3%

Note: n = 700; survey conducted in 2018.

previously been their mentors or friends and had invited them to various activities (see table 6.4). As many as 58.4 percent tried to avoid contact through deliberately being busy in alternative activities. Another group of about 39.7 percent of respondents stated that they avoided the radical groups by clearly verbalizing their rejection of the radical activities.

Whatever their choice and route, this did not mean that these students' problems immediately disappeared. The persistence of their mentors in inviting the students to return and become active once again in the study groups and other activities would often continue. However, it was usually serious personal reasons that determined the choices of the students. For the students who had easily engaged in becoming involved with the radicals' study activities, they also often easily disengaged from the radicals' activities as well.

DERADICALIZATION AND STATE INTERVENTION

The above findings show that youth involvement in radical activities is not as straightforward as is often assumed. It can also be inferred that radicalization is not irreversible. Entering into radical groups opens the minds of students to Islam and a political agenda for which they can fight, as well as providing them with an opportunity to be personally involved in its cause. As they became aware of the version of Islam presented by radical groups such as HTI, the students increasingly asked themselves whether this was the type of Islam that would contribute to a global civilization in which they can live.

My findings also call into question the commonly held assumption that presents deradicalization methods as part of counter-terrorism strategies,[41] with the primary goal of reducing the appeal of extremism in the Muslim world.[42] Daniel Koehler writes, "Deradicalization programmes are the cornerstone of counter-terrorism strategies in many countries."[43] Such deradicalization programs focus on the role of the state and civil society "to challenge and break the psychological or ideological commitment of members of terrorist and violent extremist organizations."[44] Although there is much evidence to show that an ideology or the religion of Islam is not the primary factor in radicalization,[45] a large portion of government intervention with the goal of deradicalization is based on the belief that radical Muslims have extreme religious beliefs, which, in their view, justify their violence. Therefore, in the deradicalization programs there is a need to carry out the task of rehabilitating, correcting, and changing the mindsets of radicals.[46] In Saudi Arabia, for instance, terrorist detainees are seen as victims of false interpretation of Islam; therefore, the Saudi rehabilitation programs use psychological counseling, vocational training, and religious education to convince terrorists to give up their violent ideology.[47] In Indonesia, too, religious clerics and former terrorists have been co-opted by the state to change the views of prisoners on religion and the state. Sumpter rightly notes that "with the military in charge of prevention and de-radicalization, it is somewhat unsurprising that Indonesia's founding state ideology of *Pancasila* (belief in one God, nationalism, humanitarianism, social justice, and democracy) features prominently in BNPT-led CVE [Countering Violent Extremism] initiatives."[48]

In this chapter I challenge state-led rehabilitation approaches that aim to replace radical religious beliefs with an ideology that is more compatible with the state's moral principles. This is in line with Chalmers's conclusion that "a more efficient and more powerful security apparatus is, however, unlikely to lead to the rehabilitation of large numbers of former jihadists if not accompanied by broader social and cultural changes."[49] Some deradicalization scholars, including Koehler himself, have questioned the effectiveness of deradicalization programs that emphasize that "either religious authorities should be tasked with debating extremists into submission using theological arguments, or psychologists should determine and treat the underlying mental health issues of the radicalization process to extinguish the bond between the individual programme participant and the extremist ideology or group."[50] I would argue that too much focus on state-sponsored deradicalization programs tends to ignore the ability of youth to deradicalize themselves. As discussed, some students have deradicalized themselves due to their rejection of the dogmatic ideologies and practices of absolutist Islamic groups. Through their involvement in radical networks, those radicalized youth have an opportunity to question the impact of their involvement in the radical networks on themselves and others. As a result, they can deradicalize themselves without necessarily subscribing to the kind of religious understanding promoted by the state.

However, the emphasis on violence as the necessary outcome of radicalization has shaped the mindsets of many scholars on deradicalization. In relation to Islamist movements, for instance, Omar Ashour defines deradicalization as "a process of relative change within Islamist movements, one in which a radical group reverses its ideology and delegitimizes the use of violent methods to achieve political goals, while also moving towards an acceptance of gradual social, political and economic changes within a pluralistic context."[51] Along this line, Stefanie Mitchell refers to deradicalization as "the process of breaking with radical belief systems as well as the violent behaviors associated with them."[52] The emphasis on "breaking" with past belief systems is underpinned by the generalized assumption that radicalized individuals are driven by extremist religious beliefs that justify, and inevitably lead to, violence. Thus, this religious belief system must be demolished by replacing it with a more secular one that better fits with our pluralistic society.

This approach to deradicalization not only neglects the fact that the deradicalization process can follow many models,[53] but also does not take account of the internal radicalization dynamics, both within a particular radical group and between the diverse radical ideologies themselves. Drawing on her ethnographic engagement with a group of twenty-eight young Salafis in Tunisia, Aitimed Muhanna-Matar shows that deradicalized Salafis did not totally abandon "the whole Salafi ideology"; instead, they adopted "a reformist interpretation of Salafism that denounces violence and supports political engagement."[54] This does not mean, however, that they then embraced a secular ideology or the version of Islam that was promoted and enforced by the state. In a similar vein, deradicalized students in Indonesia expressed their appreciation of the religious belief they had gained and practiced when joining radical groups, but, at the same time, they rejected the radical agendas of the groups.

Within the critical framework provided by Muhanna-Matar, I argue that more attention must be given to the ability of youth to self-deradicalize instead of maintaining the one-sided focus on external interventions particularly prevalent in security studies. Muhanna-Matar rightly notes, "It is through individuals' experience of engagement with an absolutist ideology and interaction with the structure of power which establishes that radical people may have the chance to question the effects of their radical identity, the particular discourse of truth it presents about the existing system of power, and the effect of power on discourses of truth."[55] The dialectical dynamics of this radical identity are not fully appreciated by the state-led approach to deradicalization, which positions "radical youth as docile and unknowing subjects who are incapable of thinking and acting rationally."[56] What becomes the focus of state-led rehabilitation programs is how to destroy this toxic extremist Islamic ideology, which it is assumed necessarily creates hatred and terrorist violence. As discussed above, many radicalized youths have renounced their radical ideologies even without external intervention and pressure.

Drawing on Michel Foucault's theoretical frameworks, Muhanna-Matar has convincingly demonstrated an individual's ability rationally to choose available options within surrounding conditions. She defines "self-deradicalization" as "individuals' capacity to be critical of their radical Islamic identity and to deradicalise themselves without necessarily following a government's authorized version of Islam compliant with the state value system, or without abandoning their Islamic identity."[57] Muhanna-Matar develops this concept based on Foucault's theory of critique and experience,[58] arguing that, as a critique of self in relation to others, self-deradicalization "does not mean complete destruction and denial of the radical identity and its normative categories."[59]

In this chapter I confirm Muhanna-Matar's conceptual framework of self-deradicalization, as some informants expressed appreciation for the religious educations they had received when they connected with the radical networks. At the same time, however, they had a more critical understanding of radical ideologies that reflected their experiences of being radicalized. Muhanna-Matar admits that "self-deradicalization is not a linear process leading to determined progressive outcomes," and it "happens with different accelerations and contingent outcomes due to the particularity, as well as the intensity, of experience of each person."[60]

Conceptualizing deradicalization as a technology of the self (to use Foucault's term) allows us to debunk the prevalent notion that deradicalization aims only at preventing the use of violence. This means, Elshimi writes, that deradicalization is not only "about the mitigation of violence, [but rather] about making of a particular subjectivity—political, social, and ethical—in our contemporary historical place and time."[61] In this context, the capacity of the self in self-deradicalization refers to the individual's having the capacity to remove himself or herself from radical networks. This understanding of the capacity of young people for self-inspection, self-examination, and self-regulation allows us to debunk the prevalent notion that deradicalization is concerned only with mitigating the possibility of violence. The self-deradicalization process can result in the formation of subjects that are different from the dominant, state-sanctioned forms of Islamic subjectivity. The preoccupation of state-sponsored deradicalization interventions with the threat posed by ideology, Elshimi argues, has "placed deradicalization as merely an instrument of counterterrorism."[62] Therefore, it is imperative to give serious attention to how the self-deradicalization of educated youth takes place.

CONCLUDING REMARKS

This study on radicalized youth who have undergone self-deradicalization reveals that they developed a critique of the dogmatic mindset when they experienced a radical absolutist ideology. This critique takes many forms, including a rejection of being compelled or coerced to follow a radical way of life and to wear particular clothing. Some deradicalized youth challenged a rigid understanding of religion in the context of the pluralist Indonesian community and questioned the version of Islam presented by radical groups, which is understood as being contradictory to that of mainstream Islamic groups such as NU. Some deradicalized students also criticized the "rules of the game" and the painful process required to become part of the exclusive radical community. Nevertheless, the criticisms made by these deradicalized youth do not diminish their appreciation of the more positive aspects of their experiences, in which they acquired a more profound knowledge of religion and, in certain respects, felt they had become more godly. However, the deradicalized students called into question why the depth of one's religion and godliness should be measured by accepting radical ideologies such as the pursuit of establishing an Islamic state or restoring the caliphate. They acknowledged the benefit of their time in the radical community, namely, acquiring a solid foundation for their faith and concrete facts, which actually enabled them to question the viability of the radical ideology itself and its relevance to life in the modern world.

The self-deradicalization of educated youth offers many valuable lessons, not only in explaining how to implement effective deradicalization programs, but also in understanding the issues confronting an educated individual who becomes radicalized. The pressing issue is how to prevent Muslim youth from becoming targets of radical extremist groups in the first place, through informed public education, publications, support and caring, and alternative (and more nuanced) approaches to religious beliefs. Teaching methods at the university need to emphasize critical thinking and rigorous engagement with various subjects, including religion. Nevertheless, deradicalization is not only the task of the government and the university; it is also a challenge for social networks that shape the views and attitudes of youth. As shown in table 6.3, the roles of family and friends are very significant in the decisions of radicalized youth to depart from their radical ideologies. However, above all else, the self-awareness of the individuals and their intention to deradicalize themselves are the major factors, though sadly, this has not attracted more attention from scholars and others in authority. It is this self-deradicalization that needs to be taken more seriously in studies on deradicalization.

THREE

From Cyber-Radicalization to Hate Speech

SEVEN

Student Vulnerability to
Online Radicalization

In the final two chapters of this book I will explore two case studies of the use of the internet to attract young people to involvement in radical networks and of the prominence of radical discourse. Despite efforts to stop the tide of radicalism on social media in Indonesia, radical groups continue to emerge on digital platforms, sowing seeds of intolerance and violence. The increasing visibility of radical materials on the internet has drawn the attention of scholars and policymakers to the issue of online radicalization. Online radicalization has been defined by Till Baaken and Linda Schlegel as "the process of adopting beliefs justifying and/or compelling violence primarily through online media consumption."[1] A 2017 study by the Center for the Study of Islam and Society (PPIM, Pusat Pengkajian Islam dan Masyarakat), in collaboration with the United Nations Development Program (UNDP), showed that 84.94 percent of students from hundreds of schools and universities across the country had internet access and 96.2 percent of them accessed it using mobile phones, while 61.05 percent reported daily use of the internet in order to search for religious information.[2] The study also found that younger Indonesians, who are internet savvy, are more vulnerable to radical ideas than non-active users. They tend to be more intolerant of other religions and believe that violence should be used to protect Islam. More than 49 percent believed that the government should ban religious minority groups, while 10 percent favored a theocratic Islamic state.[3] The lead researcher of the study, Jamhari Makruf, admitted that religious websites students often visited "are dominated by exclusive and intolerant views."[4]

Incidents of terrorist attacks revealed that their perpetrators had visited these radical sites. For instance, the suicide bomber attacking the Bethel Injil Sepenuh Kapunton church in Solo, Central Java, on September 25, 2011, had visited extremist websites before conducting the attack.[5] Shortly after the incident, the Ministry of Communication and Information of Indonesia announced that it had, since August 2010, blocked three hundred of nine hundred "radical online sites," defined by Nur Azlin Mohamed Yasin as those containing materials inciting hatred and intolerance.[6] In 2015, the Indonesian government shut down twenty-two websites for displaying extremist propaganda but reconsidered its decision amid public outcry over the act's violation of free speech.[7] In the face of cyber-radicalization, the government has taken several steps to counter radicalization, including the enactment of laws and regulations to keep track of offensive and extremist materials on the internet. On May 25, 2018, the Indonesian parliament passed the amended Eradication of Criminal Acts of Terrorism Law following a suicide attack on churches in Surabaya, East Java, on May 13, 2018, which killed thirteen churchgoers and a security officer and took place days before the start of Ramadan. This anti-terror law, which amends the 2003 law, expands the power of the police and military to take action against potential terrorists and those spreading radical ideology. Under the law, the Indonesian National Police can conduct preemptive arrests and detain people for being members of a group declared a terrorist organization. The law empowers authorities to "open, examine, and confiscate mail and package by post or other means of delivery . . . and intercept any conversation by telephone and other means of communication,"[8] including social media.

Serious concerns were raised that these measures could facilitate the violation of civil rights by the state. On the one hand, responding to Islamic extremism with a more heavy-handed approach may increase the degree of repression that can be used to silence opposition. On the other hand, the danger of religious radicalism, especially through the internet and social media, requires the state to be firm. Of particular concern here is the use of social media by radical groups to disseminate their extremist propaganda and target Muslim youth for radicalization. This chapter is neither interested in tracing Indonesia's counter-terrorism measures nor discussing the controversy surrounding them. Its purpose is to examine the way in which students of both high schools and universities have been exposed to radicalism through the internet and social media in con- temporary Indonesia. To what extent have the internet and social media become catalysts for radicalization among educated youth? How were youth exposed to online radical content? What did they do with such content? To put it simply: How did online radicalization occur? Does online radicalization entirely transform the process of youths' conversion to radicalism, or do face-to-face interactions still play a role in this digital age? To answer these and similar questions, this chapter relies on both quantitative data and in-depth interviews with students of high schools and universities who have been exposed to radicalism. It is intended to uncover specific mechanisms by which the internet and other online plat- forms, as well as in-person interactions, facilitate processes of radicaliza- tion into radical networks.

ONLINE RADICALIZATION IN PERSPECTIVE

In the previous decade, the internet and social media became omnipres- ent features of Indonesian life, especially among youth. Indonesians are some of the most active internet and social media users in the world. As of January 2020, there were more than 175 million internet users and 160 million social media users in the country.[9] Unsurprisingly, not only did the internet transform daily life, but also radical groups sought to use this new connectedness to disseminate extremist ideology. The role of the internet in promoting radicalization has been the subject of much discussion among both scholars and policymakers. However, most studies on online radicalization have focused on the use of the internet by Muslim terrorist groups in their recruitment of jihadis beyond the confines of geographical barriers. Indeed, the reach of the internet has blurred the geographical barriers and connected distant individuals in the virtual world. Several studies have shown that the internet allows terrorists to reach those individuals who would not have been accessible in any other way.[10]

Several studies have explored how terrorist groups benefit from social media in spreading their propaganda-messages and in recruitment. Likewise, some experts have identified how terrorists use online media, including how they disseminate their ideology, appeal for support, propagate fear of attack among their foes, provide instruction in tactics and weapons, and gather intelligence about potential targets to support terrorist operations. Luke Bertram calls their terrorist activity "operational digital actions, which includes digital activities of terrorist organizations that are intended to spread terror."[11] The most significant benefit of the internet and social media to terrorist groups has been the capability of those who use them to recruit others by reaching out to potential radicals, creating virtual communities of like-minded extremists, and coordinating organizational activity.[12] The internet allows terrorist organizations to expand their reach and capture a larger and more diverse population because it allows radicalization to occur without physical contact, removing geographical barriers. Terrorist groups have benefited from social media to radicalize and recruit introverted individuals without being detected, as it offers a platform for secret communication.[13] This aspect of the benefit that terrorist groups receive from the internet and social media is summed up effectively by Bertram, who writes, "The manner in which social media has affected terrorist organization recruiting practices is broad. These technologies have provided the ability to cross borders unseen digitally and have shown these organizations into the home of any potential radical. Organizational recruiting can be viewed from two points: being the overcoming of distance and sovereign boundaries."[14]

Another set of studies focuses on both terrorist websites and social media used to attract and recruit new members. The use of websites to spread the message of terrorists continues to increase as the number of websites continues to grow. In its 2009 report, the U.S. Homeland Security Institute recorded that in 1998 there were only a total of twelve terrorist-related websites active. By 2003, there were approximately 2,630 terrorist-related websites, and in January 2009, 6,940 terrorist-related websites were active on the internet.[15] In 2019, the Indonesian

Ministry of Communication and Information blocked 1,500 websites and social media accounts with radical content. Since 2009, the Ministry has claimed to have blocked more than 11,000 online radical contents.[16] Terrorist websites include official sites of terrorist organizations and websites of supporters, sympathizers, and fans. For example, al-Qaeda in the Arabian Peninsula has created an enticing and modern English web magazine called *Inspire*. This online terrorist magazine is easily accessible as a downloadable file from various websites. Topics covered include how to make bombs and encrypt messages, what to expect in jihad, the jihad experience, and schooling.[17] Scholars also note that some radical websites have no formal terrorist affiliation, making it difficult to monitor them.[18] The growth of terrorist websites has raised two major concerns among researchers and practitioners. First, the ease of website development has led to the vast presence of extremist groups online. Second, these websites are accessible with limited regulation. Once a website is operational, the content is available to Internet users around the globe. In the Indonesian context, Merlyna Lim extensively discusses the role of the internet in fostering Islamic radicalism and anti-Americanism, showing that these radical groups use the internet to "disseminate the messages of Islamic radicalism, anti-Americanism, and other sentiments from local to global scales."[19]

Other studies examine the extent to which terrorist groups have used social media to spread their ideology quickly and efficiently. Tanja Dramac Jiries argues that "social media has proven to be a very powerful communication tool and community medium, perhaps ever more powerful than the local imam or any local mosque one could go to for gaining knowledge and information."[20] Because of the popularity of social media platforms, especially among youth, it comes as no surprise that terrorist groups weaponize them to proliferate propaganda, support virtual networks of aspirants and supporters, and radicalize and recruit new members. Aaron Smith and Monica Anderson have reported that more than 90 percent of American young adults are active YouTube users, 80 percent have Facebook accounts, 70 percent are on Instagram and Snapchat, and 45 percent are on Twitter.[21] Terrorist groups have maintained their strong presence on these social media platforms. Several researchers have conducted content analyses of YouTube extremist video contents to identify the production features of those most used, including their modus operandi and intended effects.[22] Their studies show the multifaceted strategies used to attract a sympathetic audience. Moreover, unlike other social media platforms, Facebook is typically not used for direct recruitment, but rather is used as a decentralized center for distributing information and videos, perhaps to find like-minded supporters and show support rather than to direct sympathizers.[23] Both YouTube and Facebook have codified strategic policies aimed at preventing and removing terrorism-related materials from their platforms. Studies by Christina Schori Liang and James P. Farwell revealed that Twitter had been the primary social media platform of choice for members and supporters of the Islamic State of Iraq and Syria (ISIS).[24] Recognizing these ISIS supporters on their platform, Twitter reported suspending thousands of users, as a result of either government requests or through its own "internal, proprietary spam-fighting tools," according to Selena Larson.[25]

It seems clear that the internet and social media have become breeding grounds that help extremism to thrive and grow. A recent surge in research has examined the relationship between radicalization and the so-called "dark web." In 2013, Ines von Behr and colleagues examined 150 articles that describe the impact of the internet on the process of radicalization in terms of "facilitating," "reinforcing," "accelerating," or serving as the "primary or sole driving force of radicalization."[26] Von Behr and associates write: "Almost *all studies ascribe a role to the internet* in promoting radicalisation. Most studies suggest that the internet serves as a reinforcing agent or an accelerant and has the ability to break down the traditional barriers for individuals wanting to recruit new members and sympathizers. A handful of studies suggest that the internet is a driver of radicalization."[27] Of course, there are some observers who doubt that the internet plays a significant role in violent extremism. It can play a role in fund-raising, recruitment, or information dissemination, but Hanna Rogan insists that "physical contact, in addition to online communication and propaganda, is essential."[28] In other words, most jihadists need more than online instructions to be convinced to perform violent actions. Joanne Hinds and Adam Joinson argue that "while there is clear evidence for the power of social media to fuel and support social unrest (and hence similar situations that may lead to violent extremist activity), none of these examples provide ample evidence that the people participating were radicalized."[29] Hinds and Joinson further contend that "online activities, therefore, provide little insight for online radicalization, as those that may appear to hold strong beliefs and even encourage or threaten violent extremism online may have no intention of taking offline action."[30] According to Maura Conway, the skeptical argument focuses on two issues. First, "most, although not all, contemporary violent online extremists are dilettantes, in the sense that they restrict themselves to using the Internet to support and encourage violent extremism, but pose no 'real world' threat."[31] The argument is that those exposed to radical content might desire violence but have no real commitment to engage in it. The second argument is that "claiming violent online content violently radicalizes individuals is senseless given that other consumers of the same content are not similarly affected."[32] For instance, *Inspire* magazine was read by a large number of Muslims, but there is no evidence of a causal effect. While extremist online content can buttress an already sympathetic individual's resolve to engage in violence, it is not generally the original cause of such a commitment.

In my view, these two arguments are entirely sound. As discussed in this book, there is no credible correlation between a person's being radicalized and his or her determination to engage in violent actions, as there is no direct causality between exposure to extremist online content and conversion to radicalism. While I agree that the internet provides material that can enable, strengthen, or accelerate the process of radicalization, I believe that it cannot be regarded as a causal factor. Individuals exposed to radical contents are not passive "receivers" who simply adopted a radical way in an isolated context. As Anne Aly has rightly noted, the audience of online radical narratives are "not just receivers but also active interpreters of media messages that may carry certain embedded meanings and attributing individuals with the capacity to accept, negotiate, or reject these meanings."[33] While von Behr and colleagues write that "there is *no clear attribution of causality* to the increasing number of web sites leading to an increase in radicalisation online,"[34] this is not to suggest that the role the internet plays in the radicalization process is limited. As mentioned earlier, scholars have identified unique advantages of the internet in overcoming geographical barriers and reaching otherwise unreachable spaces. With its ability to break down some of the barriers that exist in the physical world, the internet opens opportunities to radicalize a broader range of people than it would otherwise. What makes the internet and social media platforms so effective in radicalizing people is their ability to transfer information and messages at a relatively low cost. Additionally, the internet provides radical individuals and groups with a safe environment suited to clandestine activities, as it provides a potential measure of secrecy and anonymity. In other words, as Daniel Koehler writes, "The Internet provides a perceived constraint-free space and anonymity."[35] Tom Holt and associates capture the breadth of online radicalization nicely as follows:

> The internet has tremendous value as a communication vehicle for extremist and terrorist groups. Easy and immediate access to technology, coupled with anonymity and scale afforded by computers and the internet, make email, forums, instant messaging, and virtually all other forms of computer-mediated communications ideal for interpersonal communications. Even developing nations now have substantial forms of internet connectivity, whether through cellular service providers, high-speed fiber-optic connectivity, or even dial-up Internet access. Groups can maintain contact and reach out to others, no matter where they may be located, through plain text messaging, email, and forums.[36]

Despite the recent surge in the literature on the relationship between the internet and radicalization, little attention has been given to the interaction between online and offline behaviors, which is a key area of focus in this chapter. From the 150 articles examined by von Behr and colleagues, "only three studies dealt with the interplay of online and offline factors in radicalisation in an empirically robust manner."[37] A major issue in this online-offline interplay is which means of radicalization is most significant. On the one hand, some observers, such as Marc Sageman, assert that "face-to-face radicalization has been replaced by online radicalization."[38] As discussed earlier, scholars ascribe to the internet roles such as "facilitator," "accelerator," "primary driver," and so forth. On the other hand, observers such as Jason Burke contend that social media cannot be a substitute for grassroots activism and offers little help for terrorist groups to reach their goals.[39] They argue that it is in-person contact that ultimately leads to a successful radicalization process characterized by violent actions. Those who support this line of argument emphasize the role of local contexts that shape radicalized individuals.

More recent studies tend to call into question this one-sided approach to the radicalization process. Radicalization is a complex phenomenon that involves various contributing factors. Both online and offline exposure to radical ideas are equally important causal factors. As von Behr and associates rightly note, "The Internet is one aspect of radicalization, and it is essential for future research to look both online and offline to be able to understand the process as a whole."[40] My own research supports this approach, as both online and offline factors play an interconnected role in the radicalization process of educated youth in Indonesia. "The Internet is not a structure separated from the 'real world,'" Daniel Koehler argues, "but dynamically connected with it. It has therefore been argued that this relationship between offline and online networks allows activists and potential recruits to assure themselves of the strength of the movement, commit to the cause and specialize in the ideology."[41]

The second major issue concerns the primary driving force of online radicalization: structure or agency, or the importance of organizations as opposed to individual socialization. Till Baaken and Linda Schlegel refer to this as "a top-down or bottom-up process."[42] Bruce Hoffman and Marc Sageman, two seminal figures in terrorism and radicalization studies, offer conflicting approaches to the directionality of terrorist recruitment, whether it is top-down (hierarchical) or bottom-up (via a network). Hoffman contends that the driving forces of extremism are the top-down organizational structure of terrorist groups.[43] In contrast, Sageman argues that social group processes facilitate extremism in a bottom-up manner.[44] However, neither Hoffman nor Sageman develops his theory on the basis of empirical research. The former examines the role of the organizational structures of terrorist groups such as al-Qaeda and ISIS to argue that jihadist organizations maintain strong and strategic control over the individuals who choose to engage in terrorism. The latter emphasizes the networks of "a bunch of guys" who have the same ideas and mindsets, which facilitated and influenced individuals' pathways toward radicalization. In practice, however, Hoffman's and Sageman's approaches are not mutually exclusive. In this context, Baaken and Schlegel note:

The internet facilitates radicalization by enabling bottom-up and top-down processes; it essentially empowers organizations and social movement dynamics alike. Bottom-up processes are facilitated through the creation of echo chambers, which constantly repeat and thereby normalize violent narratives.... On the other side of the debate, the internet empowers organizations to increase their reach and effectiveness in spreading propaganda. Organizations can control the development and dissemination of content through their social media branches and the use of specialized "staff" as content managers on websites used for radicalization purposes.[45]

My research findings confirm the conclusion of Baaken and Schlegel and their colleagues. These authors criticized Hoffman and Sageman for "the lack of empirical data";[46] however, the conclusion of Hoffman and Sageman was also based on literature review and analysis. In fact, most of the literature on the relationship between the internet and radicalization is theoretical. Whenever empirical data are included, most studies are small-scale and rely on limited data sets. In their 2017 article titled "Terrorist Use of the Internet by the Numbers," Paul Gill and associates write that "an exhaustive search using a dedicated academic research database produced only three data-driven studies about how convicted terrorists made use of the Internet."[47] Von Behr and colleagues examined 15 radicalized individuals, and two studies by Gill and associates analyzed 119 individuals. In addition to their 2017 article, which used a larger data set (223 individuals), I would add three other studies, one by Scott Kleinmann with a sample of 124 American radicalized people,[48] one by Mehmet Bastug, Aziz Douai, and Davud Akca with 51 Canadian individuals, and another by Koehler with 8 German former right-wing extremists.[49] The latter author admits that his "study only used a small empirical basis to find indicators for the importance of further research about the relationship between the Internet and individual radicalization."[50]

In what follows, I will discuss findings from a 2018 study of 700 students from seven prominent public universities in Indonesia that have been infiltrated by radical networks and 500 high school students from five cities in East Java. In addition to qualitative data, this chapter also includes reports of in-depth interviews with more than 100 students from both universities and high schools.

RESEARCH FINDINGS

Youths' Vulnerability to Online Radicalization

Research on the reception of radical information over the internet and its influence on youth is limited. While we have witnessed a recent surge in scholarly research, most of it focuses on the reception of such information by self-styled users from violent Islamist terrorist groups, and very little examines the effects of such propaganda on young people at large. Global mapping of research conducted by UNESCO shows that the current research on the links among the internet, social media, and youth radicalization is minimal:

> We found two empirical studies on online influence on youth. Bou-zar, Caupenne, and Sulayman (2014) present the results of interviews with 160 French families with radicalized (though not violent) children aged mainly between 15 and 21. The vast majority of the young people claimed to have been radicalized through the internet, regardless of their family characteristics. The vast majority of the families (80%) did not follow any specific religious beliefs or practices, and only 16% belonged to the working class (Bouzar, Caupenne & Sulayman, 2014). At the same time, it is unclear how such broad findings compare to offline and online peer-group communications, which the surveyed youth may have sought to conceal.[51]

One of my key findings is that while youth are vulnerable to online radicalization, in reality, the radicalization of youth is nuanced and far from a linear process that occurs exclusively online. Of 500 high school students, 5.4 percent joined the radical networks; however, only 1 percent of respondents claimed to be active members. Among university students examined in this study, 45.8 percent said they were involved in radical social media. This is an exciting finding, as it shows university students were more susceptible to radical ideas than were younger students in high school. What accounts for this phenomenon? First, university-aged adults tended to surf online more intensively and extensively than high school students, which is evident from my quantitative research that shows university students accessing online radical content

TABLE 7.1. Students' responses to "How often did you visit radical websites?"

Frequency/Intensity	High School Students	University Students
Very often (every day)	0.3%	15.1%
Often (at least once a week)	7.8%	24.0%
Rare (once a month)	25.0%	25.9%
Very rare (once in more than a month)	66.0%	35.0%

Note: n = 700 college students and 500 high school students; surveys conducted in 2018 and 2019.

more frequently. Table 7.1 illustrates the frequency or intensity of youths' access to radical websites. The percentage of university students who frequently accessed online radical contents was very high (39.1 percent), while only 8.1 percent of high school students claimed that they often or very often visited radical websites. A striking difference can also be seen in the number of those who "very rarely" visited radical websites, namely, with high school students at 66 percent and university students at 35 percent.

The second explanation for the difference in the consumption of radical internet content by the high school students versus the college students concerns the knowledge of higher education students about global affairs. As they had already passed through the secondary education phase and taken a wider variety of courses, it is understandable that they became knowledgeable about the world. On the one hand, the campus environment allowed students to learn more things, including about issues beyond campus. On the other hand, education at high schools tended to focus on skill development and basic knowledge and less on broader issues. This is evident from my interviews with high school students, who seemed less knowledgeable than college students about global terrorist groups except for ISIS, whose coverage was widespread in the media. When asked about the practice of intolerance, some high school informants referred to the media coverage of ISIS beheading non-Muslims and their enemies. Even when asked whether they followed the news about various radical groups in Indonesia, only 3.4 percent of 500 respondents said they closely followed the news. In comparison, most respondents (56.6 percent) rarely read the news, and 40 percent of them never knew about the radical groups. It is apparent that high school students were not much interested in searching for religious information on the internet. Concerning the type of information frequently accessed by high school students on the internet, quantitative data indicated the following: infotainment (51.2 percent), hobbies (18.1 percent), general knowledge (14.2 percent), religion (7.6 percent), political news (4.6 percent), and other information (3.8 percent).

In contrast to high school students, the interest of university students in online radical content was greater, including their interest in religious information. They surfed the internet in search of a wide range of information. For instance, 22.1 percent of respondents claimed that they frequently visited websites to learn about the status of Muslims worldwide, 57.6 percent said they rarely accessed them, and only 20.3 percent said they never accessed the internet. Concerning news about the caliphate movement, 41.4 percent of respondents admitted that they never accessed the internet to research the caliphate movement, whereas the majority said that they did visit the internet to research the caliphate movement, either frequently (22.3 percent) or rarely (57.6 percent). My quantitative research also showed that many university students accessed online radical content to find information about how to make a bomb frequently (32.1 percent), rarely (36.9 percent), or never (31 percent). All of this explains why university students tended to be more vulnerable to radicalism than high school students. This level of vulnerability is also evident from their motives for accessing websites that published radical content (see table 7.2).

From table 7.2 it seems clear that the percentage of university students who accessed radical websites in order to gain deeper knowledge was greater (31 percent) than that of high school students (4.8 percent). The vast majority of high school students visited radical websites due to

TABLE 7.2. Students' responses to "What is your motive for visiting radical websites?"

Motive	High School Students	University Students
Just curious without a particular purpose	80.4%	51.0%
Interested in knowing more/deeper	4.8%	31.0%
To understand radical groups' goals	12.8%	10.3%
To look for materials to share	2.0%	7.7%

Note: n = 700 college students and 500 high school students; surveys conducted in 2018 and 2019.

their curiosity, without a particular purpose (80.4 percent), compared to 51 percent of university students. However, when it came to their motives for wanting to understand the goals of radical groups, the student groups were nearly even. The phrase "just curious without a particular purpose" is a translation of the Indonesian word *iseng-iseng*, which is difficult to translate into English. While in other contexts *iseng* can have a different meaning, here it means doing something not intended to achieve a specific result. The term is sometimes used as an excuse for doing something ridiculous. Another striking difference between high school and college students was that university students were more active in sharing radical content (7.7 percent) than were high school students (2 percent), a result that will be discussed in more detail later.

Perhaps the high number of university students involved in radical networks also reflects the fact that they became the primary targets of radical groups compared to high school students. As discussed in this book, radical groups have been actively infiltrating campuses to spread their radical ideology. For instance, the National Agency for Combating Terrorism (BNPT, Badan Nasional Penanggulangan Terorisme) identified seven prominent state universities (IPB, ITB, ITS, UB, UI, Unair, and Undip) as having been infiltrated by religious radicalism. Not only have campus mosques been under the control of radical groups, but they have also dominated student government bodies. This is not the case in high schools, despite their being influenced by intolerant ideologies as well. The PPIM research findings showed that a significant percentage of high school teachers embraced intolerant and radical ideas.

Nonetheless, the infiltration of college campuses by radical networks has no parallel in high schools. Radical groups have likely been successfully designing online radical content appealing to university students. This impression, for instance, can be gathered from my interview with Amalia (21 years old), from Unair:

> The delivery of Islamic *da'wah* today must be designed in such a way that it attracts young generations. If Islamic study sessions (*pengajian*) target old people, how can Islam be fully embraced by the younger generation like us? Today, we know many types of media for *da'wah*. Social media such as YouTube, Instagram, and Facebook made me aware that many young people take part in *da'wah* today.

Some time ago, a video of Hawariyun was quite viral because of their *da'wah* activities. I am sure that they will inspire many young people, including girls, hehehe.

Dennis (22 years old), from ITB, admitted that online content suits his needs. He was born to an irreligious family, and he felt that his religious knowledge was minimal, so he needed religious information that fit his situation. He testified:

Learning about Islam can be done in various ways. Islam is a vast subject; you can begin learning about it from reading materials available on social media or any *da'wah* accounts, which are abundant today. My experience was that I started reading something that I felt so close [to in] my own life first, some basic things, for instance, about human relations in Islam, like how permissible male and female relationships should look. I then came to know that males and females must be segregated and cannot mix unless there is another person among them, either in markets, clinics, or classrooms. Dating is prohibited, and there is no such thing as an Islamic way of dating. From online materials, I learned how to interact with people of other religions. Now I realized that Islam encompasses all aspects of life, not just about personal rituals such as prayer, almsgiving, or fasting. Eventually, I became more interested in learning more about my religion.

Another informant, Tenti (18 years old), from UB, admitted that online radical content has convinced her to convert to radical ideology. "I started my *hijrah* after reading da'wah accounts on social media," she said. As discussed previously in this book, the word *hijrah* is often used by radicalized youth in Indonesia to describe a change in their religious conviction toward a version of Islam that they deem *kāffah* (comprehensive). This is the kind of maximalist approach to religion in following Islamic law formulated by medieval Muslim scholars to be incorporated as wholly as possible into their everyday lives. Tenti went on to say, "The study of religions is a religious obligation for the Muslim *ummah*, and in fact, after reading materials available online and learning more, I decided to declare *hijrah* in my heart in order to feel tranquil and happy."

Online and Offline Dynamics

Tenti joined the radical networks because of her religious convictions after having accessed radical content online. She was among 45 percent of radicalized youth who have been exposed to radical ideologies through the internet and social media. However, the internet is not the only factor that drove students to become radicalized. It is worth noting that, as revealed by the PPIM mentioned above, the number of students of high schools and universities who accessed the internet was relatively high, about 85 percent of all students in Indonesia. Of course, radicalization can be triggered by online sources as well as personal offline relationships, or a combination of both. The preceding chapters have explored the extent to which social networks have shaped young people's views and attitudes. The role of a mentor (*mushrif/mushrifah*) in the process of youth radicalization should not be overlooked. Nonetheless, as discussed in chapter 4, radicalized youth admitted that most of them were influenced by their fellow students.

Again, comparing the sources of the knowledge of students of radical websites reveals an exciting result. When asked about how they came to know and access radical websites, the majority of high school students (75.8 percent) said that they incidentally found the sites, and only 9.2 percent of them admitted that they searched for the sites by themselves. However, among university students, the percentage of those who incidentally came across radical sites was much smaller (26.3 percent), while that of students who searched for such sites by themselves was high (21.7 percent). As table 7.3 shows, the role of fellow students or friends in radicalization is significant. In the case of high school students, 11 percent claimed to have been told of radical sites by their friends, while the number of university students being told by their friends was much higher (36.4 percent). Additionally, radicalized mentors or senior students who served as recruiters tended to play a significant role among university students (15.6 percent).

My interviews with both high school and university students confirmed this dynamic relationship between the internet and the radicalization processes. I found some high school students who accessed online radical content. Either they came across it incidentally, searched for it by themselves, or were told about it by their friends. They were

TABLE 7.3. Students' responses to "How did you know about radical websites?"

Sources	High School Students	University Students
Searching by themselves	9.2%	21.7%
Friends	11.0%	36.4%
Senior recruiters	0.0%	15.6%
Teachers/Professors	4.0%	0.0%
Coming across incidentally	75.8%	26.3%

Note: n = 700 college students and 500 high school students; surveys conducted in 2018 and 2019.

generally aware of those websites or radical content because the materials were widespread on Instagram or other social media platforms. For instance, the news about a celebrity who declared *hijrah*, and left behind his glamourous world, and instead promoted the idea of a caliphate was viral on social media. From my interviews, it appears that not many students were interested in knowing why someone decided to declare *hijrah* or act violently. The testimony of Marwan (16 years old), from SMA in Kediri, for instance, represents the view of some students who have accessed radical content: "When I looked at radical content, it was not to follow the ideology. There is nothing [wrong] with having some knowledge about these radical movements. For me, through reading the media coverage about them, I wanted to know what these groups were all about and what their main goals were. So, when someone acted according to these radical groups, I could anticipate." Another student, Aldi (16 years old also), from SMA Malang, was among those who happened to search for news about radical groups on the internet. His intention, he said, was to understand the goals of radical groups so that he could avoid them. Aldi said: "I happened to search for news about radical groups. My purpose was to simply know what radicalism is, what the movement is about, as well as its goal. Besides, I wanted to know what forms radicalism might take so that I could turn myself away from it. Well, I looked to that news a long time ago, about a year ago when there were incidents of suicides in some parts of Indonesia."

The link between the internet and student radicalization is more nuanced among university students interviewed in this study. Some students "consumed" radical content to help them grow in their religious knowledge. It is worth noting that the seven prominent state universities infiltrated by radicalism were non-religiously affiliated institutions of higher education, and the majority of students in them do not have educated religious backgrounds. Having access to radical content does not mean that they would automatically sympathize with radical groups, let alone join them. They argued that numerous radical websites published useful religious information that they could learn from. When asked what radical Indonesian-language websites they had visited, their responses were as follows: EraMuslim.com (20.7 percent), VOA-Islam .com (13.6 percent), NahiMunkar.com (2.9 percent), Hidayatullah.com (2.6 percent), Arrahmah.com (1.1 percent), or others (3.2 percent), and more than half gave no response (55.9 percent). While accessing radical websites, they claimed that they gained religious "enlightenment" they needed to understand their religion better. Therefore, as discussed in chapter 6, when radicalized youth deradicalized themselves, they continued to appreciate what they had learned in the radical networks and did not necessarily change their religious outlooks for more secular ones. Feri (19 years old), from ITS, recast his experience accessing online radical content on the Internet and social media platforms: "I am now trying to be a better person," he said: "I start learning religion, accessing religious information available online and on social media platforms as I realize that we live in this world shortly and death and the day of judgment is near. So it is better to start learning and reading religious content on the internet, *da'wah* sites, and watching sermons on YouTube."

Several students confirmed that they accessed websites and social media to follow Islamic study sessions as they felt that face-to-face learning was insufficient or limited. "I have been overwhelmingly active in accessing religious information through websites," said Dila (19 years old), from IPB, "not only because such knowledge is abundantly available, but also you can do it any time, unlike *pengajian*, which requires physical presence and often [has] a time constraint." Concerning religious sermons on YouTube, Azhar (21 years old), from Unair, gave his testimony as follows:

Those *ustadh*s whose religious sermons are uploaded on YouTube and other social media platforms are really great, so why should I go far away if I need *pengajian*? The subjects of their talks are quite diverse. Those who have less religious knowledge like myself are in good spirits wherever I listen to their videos, especially when the *ustadh*s themselves encouraged us to keep us in good spirits. *Da'wah* should utilize these modern platforms to attract younger generations. I personally like *Ustadh* Khalid Basalamah, whose sermons are straightforward. If "A" must be stated as "A," there are no grey areas. I know some of my friends also like watching *pengajian* on YouTube, as it is flexible. *Inshallah* [if God wills] those *ustadh*s are genuine and responsible people, not like those who wanted to become famous.

I also found students who combined both online content and face-to-face interactions. Lista (23 years old), from UB, said that the radical group that she followed provided online groups for its members and sympathizers. A number of different issues were taught in the online group; however, the group usually decided to discuss difficult issues face-to-face. Mutiara (18 years old), from ITB, acknowledged that her *ustadh* chose websites or content for her to access. She followed her *ustadh* because there are many hoaxes on the internet, so she had to choose the correct sources of knowledge. Mutiara said:

> I was not allowed to visit other websites, fearing that such sources may include *bid'ah* [unlawful innovations]. It is better to utilize the correct websites [as directed by *ustadh*s], or we can find the suggested sites in our group. We have a WhatsApp group as well as LINE OA "tarbiyahsunnah." As for websites, there are many [suggested websites], such as rumaysho.com, muslim.or.id, and muslimafiyah.com. Those websites provide online consultations. So [information about religion] is easily accessible for us.

While it is true that peer relationships played an important role in radicalization processes, Mutiara's testimony points to top-down interventions in the sense that charismatic figures from radical organizations decided and managed what could or could not be done by those who became the targets of radicalization. Thus, as this study does not confirm the online and offline dichotomy, top-down and bottom-up radicalization do not seem mutually exclusive. It is worth noting that the percentage of students who believed that the radical content was intended to influence youth who accessed it was higher (47.7 percent) than that of those who cast doubt about its intentions (16 percent), and the rest claimed uncertainty (36.3 percent). This means that the students were aware of being targeted for radicalization, yet they continued to access the information they got online.

Between Consumers and Producers

What happened to youth after they had accessed websites or social media with radical content? Did they react passively, or did they help promote and disseminate the content? Again, on this question my findings show a significant difference of attitudes between high school students and university students. In general, university students tended to get more involved in sharing and circulating radical online content than did high school students. This is in line with the findings discussed above that most high school students came across radical websites or radical content unintentionally and viewed them with no specific purpose or *iseng*. They surfed online mostly to find infotainment or hobbies rather than to search for religious information.

Meanwhile, many university students accessed radical content to learn and better understand their religion, as they believed that the internet and social media provided religious sources they needed. Therefore, it comes as no surprise that they were more actively involved in circulating information or media coverage that they considered useful for the enhancement of religious knowledge. They believed that learning about religion is obligatory and sharing it with others is virtuous.

Table 7.4 shows that youths' participation in sharing radical content took many forms. This included sharing it on their social media timelines, forwarding it to other groups, or circulating it through other social media platforms. When asked what respondents did when they received radical content on social media, more than 70 percent of them (both high school and university students) said that they simply read it, while the percentage of those who commented among high school students was higher (7.8 percent) than that of university students (4.6 percent). However, when it came to their activity in sharing and circulating such content, the percentage of university students who shared on their timelines was higher (13.9 percent) than that of high school students (3 percent). Some high school and university students shared the content they received with

TABLE 7.4. Students' responses to "What did you do with radical content on social media platforms?"

Activity	High School Students	University Students
Just read	72.2%	75.9%
Offered comments	7.8%	4.6%
Shared in timeline	3.0%	13.9%
Shared to groups	0.6%	3.7%
Disseminated through other social media platforms	0.0%	1.9%
Didn't read, but quickly deleted	16.4%	0.0%

Note: n = 700 college students and 500 high school students; surveys conducted in 2018 and 2019.

groups, namely 0.6 percent and 3.7 percent, respectively. University students also shared radical content they received through other social media (1.9 percent), compared to high school students (0.0 percent).

Table 7.4 shows that university students were more active in dealing with radical content on social media than were high school students. My in-depth interviews revealed that many high school students tended to ignore the radical content that they received. Ani (17 years old), from SMA Kediri, said that she "often received [radical content], and I glanced at them quickly." Ani went on to say, "If the content is not good, I just ignore it, because if I offer a comment, it may turn viral." Karni (17 years old), from SMA Pasuruan, recast his experience of receiving radical content from his friend as follows: "Friends often shared with me radical content such as ISIS or suicide bombing. Usually, they shared that content with WhatsApp groups. When the shooting at a mosque in New Zealand took place, I received a lot of news about it from friends, including videos. People whom I followed on Instagram also shared similar content at that time." Moreover, Karni expressed his disagreement with radical groups in Indonesia: "I myself disagreed with the bombing of churches because the reality is that there are many different religions in Indonesia. I fear that such violent actions will cause non-Muslims in Indonesia to hate Muslims. In fact, Islam is not like that, and only certain Islamic organizations don't want to have non-Muslims live in this country."

Among university students, involvement in radical networks is greater. In turn, their participation in circulating information about radical ideology is also greater. Several students who have joined radical groups said that their networks managed their own online groups to strengthen members' faith and encourage them to practice religion more fully. Usually, online groups were differentiated according to gender, so they could engage in conversations in ways that fit members' needs. For instance, groups with female members mostly address women's issues, such as how to become virtuous *Muslimah*s. When the government banned the HTI in 2017, its online group remained active as usual. As said Novi (22 years old), from Undip: "When our movement [HTI] was restricted on campus, I only shared online content with internal groups to avoid being arrested [by police]."

There is a strong feeling among university students that what they did in sharing information provided by radical groups was to counter hoaxes on social media that continued to discredit their groups. "I have been active in sharing information about HTI and wrote about the truth of this organization because our society needed this information," said Nada (22 years old), from UB. She continued, saying, "I feel dismayed by the wide spread of wrong information on social media; therefore, I write to tell the truth through our own social media." Mega (20 years old), from Unair, argued that her sharing and writing activity is a form of *jihad*. She said:

> The concept of *jihad* can take many forms; one of them is *jihad* through social media. For instance, by sharing the correct information about our organization and *da'wah*. If we are not able to write, we can simply share what is available online. Now everything is easy. What we need to do is just to share it. We should not use social media for worthless things. Usually, youth used social media to access unavailing things or followed a futile account. We have to change our habits to become better persons and get closer to God."

When asked how they shared or circulated radical content, 22.5 percent of respondents said that they often shared and 35.2 percent said they sometimes shared, while 41.3 percent admitted that they only consumed the news. Besides sharing online content, some students served as administrators or moderators on social media–managed radical groups. Table 7.5 shows that 13.4 percent of respondents were involved as admins/

TABLE 7.5. Students' responses to "Have you ever become an administrator/moderator for social media with radical content?"

Platform	Percentage
WhatsApp	13.4
Instagram	2.6
Twitter	2.6
Facebook	0.3
Telegram	0.1
Pinterest	0.0
YouTube	0.0
Not answered	80.7

Note: n = 700 college students; survey conducted in 2018.

moderators on WhatsApp groups and other social media platforms, such as Instagram (2.6 percent), Twitter (2.6 percent), Facebook (0.3 percent), and Telegram (0.1 percent). However, 80.7 percent of students didn't respond when asked about their involvement in social media in this role.

When asked how they described themselves in dealing with online radical content, either as consumers or producers or prosumers (producers and consumers), 83 percent thought of themselves as consumers, 0.7 percent as producers, and 16.3 percent as prosumers. The radical content produced included posters, memes, heroic stories, news, invitation letters, videos, and sermons.

COUNTERING RADICAL CONTENT WITH ALTERNATIVE NARRATIVES

Indonesian youths are particularly vulnerable to cyber-radicalization. All over the world, the young generation is tech savvy, but their lack of deep religious understanding coupled with a high level of religious sentiment has been exploited by radical groups. There is no single factor that drives youths' vulnerability to recruitment by radical groups. It is important not to generalize the phenomenon of youth radicalization without paying sufficient attention to specific contexts. In a certain context, identity crisis can be the trigger, and in another context, it can be high levels of unemployment among youth. The political situation and prolonged conflicts may create space for radical groups to target youths. Perhaps the common factor is the rapid development of communication technology, which allows transnational movements to influence and recruit youths beyond geographical constraints, and in a way that is hard to detect. The case of youth radicalization in Indonesia is unique in that it is not triggered by the above factors. For instance, just as socioeconomic factors do not seem to play any role in the conversion of youth to radical ideology, neither is violent conflict the dominant factor. The seven prominent state universities that have been identified as having been infiltrated by radical networks are located in big cities in Java, which are relatively free from deadly conflicts like the one in Maluku, which has almost torn apart the region. The radical groups actively engaged in the recruitment of Indonesian youth are homegrown radical movements, not transnational organizations. What seems unique is that these homegrown radical groups preyed on youth from state institutions of learning, particularly non–religiously affiliated universities.

The fact that many educated youths have been exposed to radical ideologies shows that a lack of education in and of itself is not a driver of radicalization. Nonetheless, the Indonesian experience shows that education is one of the most essential tools for reaching young people. Therefore, it can be used to address some of the "push and pull factors" that may drive young people toward radicalism. Youth radicalization in school and university environments is not due to religious indoctrination such as that experienced in the madrasas of Pakistan or Afghanistan, but is rather accomplished through the infiltration of ideology coordinated by off-campus radical groups. It is of note that those radicalized students, generally speaking, do not have educated religious backgrounds; however, those studied showed an enthusiasm for religion that they had not had before. They expressed an intensified and religious focus on morality. Such enthusiasm can be seen, for instance, in the intensity of their search for religious knowledge available on the internet, in addition to offline *pengajian*. It is hardly surprising that radical groups used the rapid development of communication technology to recruit new members and sympathizers among youth, particularly students, who are major consumers or prosumers of social media.

The radical Indonesian groups appear to be active on the internet and social media, particularly Instagram, Twitter, Facebook, YouTube, LINE, Snapchat, WhatsApp, and other online platforms mostly used by young people. In the age of technology, the battle for hearts and minds has been transformed from pamphleteering to posting. Radical groups have used the internet to expand their enterprise to learning institutions, with the ability to remain anonymous and transcend boundaries. The radicalization process that occurs through the internet can speed up the time of conversion and allows sympathizers to transition from passive supporters to active promoters. My findings have shown that a significant number of university students did not receive online radical content only passively; they also were active in sharing it on their timelines and in online groups.

The involvement of educated youth in radical networks and organizations should be disconcerting to all societies around the world. Youth are the foundation of any country and provide for the continuation of society. The Indonesian government has implemented several plans and strategies to counter online radicalization. However, the state's focus on repressive measures, such as shutting down or censoring a few websites or online radical content, does not seem adequate, because radical groups can reach youth in innovative ways. As mentioned earlier, the government has enacted some legislation to ensure cybersecurity. However, that legislation raised some concerns among the general public about the risk of its being abused to violate civil rights.

As Ghaffar Hussain and Erin Marie Saltman report, the literature on countering violent extremism (CVE) refers to curbing or filtering radical content as "negative strategies," as opposed to positive strategies that "seek to challenge extremist narratives and propaganda by producing counter-content."[52] The authors argue that negative measures are designed to "block, filter, take-down or censor extremist content."[53] The Indonesian government, like most governments, tended to be more concerned with negative strategies, combating cyber-radicalization by monitoring extremist websites and blocking radical content. It should be acknowledged that the Indonesian government has been quite successful in pressuring and preventing offline terrorism by dismantling terrorist cells and capturing suspects before they committed violence. The Counterterrorism Special Detachment 88, known as Densus 88, was established in 2003, following the Bali bombing in 2002, has drawn praise for stemming a wave of bloody attacks in the sprawling Muslim-majority nation. However, when it comes to the government's strategies to contain online radicalization, its repressive and negative measures seem less effective in combating cybercrimes. According to Hussain and Saltman, several studies have shown that "the potential effectiveness of such [negative] measures is subject to a number of practical and political limitations."[54] For instance, "There is simply too much content on the internet to try to sift through it all," Garth Davies and colleagues write, "it is too difficult and expensive to clock, filter, or censor content; and even if it were possible, there are issues surrounding what properly constitutes 'extremist content' that has thus far remained resistant to resolution."[55] Additionally, the problem with monitoring and filtering cyberspace at universities is that such a measure violates academic freedom and freedom of speech. It is crucial that any positive or negative measures taken must uphold civil rights.

While governments continue to implement negative measures that hinder intellectual curiosity and freedom of speech in a progressive democratic society, attention has increasingly turned to trying more positive CVE strategies. In addition to developing measures to restrict and reduce the supply of radical content, the government should reduce the demand for radical content on the internet. Tim Stevens and Peter T. Neumann suggest that the appeal of extremist content can be reduced by increasing media literacy through schools and other stakeholders.[56] The Indonesian government needs to focus its efforts on defeating radical ideas by positive measures and peaceful means. Related to this last point, the government can play a positive role by orchestrating public awareness of online threats and developing social resiliency against them. People from all levels of society should be involved in preventing radicalization, since it is a social problem. The experience of a successful counter-extremist program, like that of the United States, suggests that investing in and empowering communities is crucial in developing and implementing locally tailored prevention and intervention. The resiliency of civil society seems to be more effective than negative measures.

One of the keys to developing social resiliency against online radicalization is to challenge extremist ideas with alternative narratives. While it is hard to assess the effectiveness of this mode of intervention, some recent research suggests that the use of alternative narratives could be a promising strategy in prevention, as it undermines the appeal of radical ideas by offering credible alternatives.[57] This strategy aims to confront and discredit radical propaganda and opinions, delegitimizing the core of extremist arguments and reducing the impact of radical messages on audiences. Davies and associates sum up the scope of alternative narratives as follows: "Counter-narratives highlight what is wrong with extremist ideologies, challenge assumptions, expose fallacies, and dismantle associated conspiracy theories. It involves creating and promoting narratives that stand in opposition to those presented by extremists and is intended to undermine extremist ideologies and compete for potential recruits' 'hearts and minds.'"[58]

During the past decade, the American government has set up counter-narrative programs to win the "war of ideas." Studies show that these programs, in the United States and other Western countries, have serious credibility.[59] Although campaigns presenting alternative narratives show promising results, there are still fundamental challenges to address, such as the need to scale up campaigns dramatically to address the volume of information released by radical groups. In this context, strategies using alternative narratives must involve both government and civil society activists and groups to construct and deliver the chosen narratives. The Indonesian government has recently been trying to promote "Islamic moderation" through the Ministry of Religion; however, it has not been successful in its efforts to integrate the Council of Ulama (MUI, Majelis Ulama Indonesia), as the Council tends to be inclined toward Islamic conservatism. This is in contrast to Singapore's Islamic Religious Council (MUIS, Majlis Ugama Islam Singapura), which joined the efforts of the Singaporean government to counter online radicalization. For instance, MUIS developed websites for youth, including a site that responds to religious queries and a site devoted to rebutting extremist ideologies.

Unlike MUIS, members of the Indonesian Council of Ulama (MUI) often exhibit critical attitudes toward the "Islamic moderation" project, even though they do not explicitly support radical Islamic ideologies. Fortunately, the two largest Muslim organizations in Indonesia, namely Nahdlatul Ulama (NU) and Muhammadiyah, have been quite active in countering online radical content. With its networks of Islamic scholars and *pesantren*, NU has been actively stemming the tide of religious radicalism, either through offline or online strategies. In July 2003, NU Online was first introduced to provide information about NU networks with Islamic content. However, as radicalization has increasingly posed a threat in the past few years, the NU has also established a social media division to promote its vision of moderate Islam to the millennial generations. NU members and sympathizers, especially the younger generation, have been actively challenging Islamic radical groups with their own narratives. According to a research report published in 2017 by the Center of Cultural Study and Social Change at the University of Muhammadiyah Surakarta, NU Online was visited more than two million times per month, which reflects its popularity.[60] Muhammadiyah manages an official website as well as around 550 websites it manages at local branches. The Muhammadiyah websites seem less centralized than those of NU. Its online magazine, *Suara Muhammadiyah*, has been actively promoting *wasaṭiyah* ("moderation"). In addition, there are several sites managed by youth cadres of both NU and Muhammadiyah.

NU and Muhammadiyah have played a significant role in challenging radical groups in Indonesia, which has over time reduced the demand for radical content among the general public. What makes the narrative of "Islamic moderation" promoted by the NU and Muhammadiyah so appealing is that the two organizations can speak about Islam authoritatively. They represent the largest segments of the Muslim community in the country. The government cannot counter radical narratives with its own narrative, as it does not have religious authority like that of NU and Muhammadiyah. While the Ministry of Religion has launched a campaign of "moderate Islam" to challenge radical Islam, its effectiveness seems to depend on support from the members of NU and Muhammadiyah. At any rate, according to Bharath Ganesh and Jonathan Bright, the content moderation promoted by NU, Muhammadiyah, and the Ministry of Religion represents alternative narratives on the internet that can have an important impact because such a strategy involves "decisions about decreasing the presence of extremist narratives or suspending exponents of extremist viewpoints on a platform, thereby reducing the potential that audiences might be exposed to extremist narratives."[61] If reducing the supply of radical content through repressive and negative measures can create short-term results, reducing the demand for radical content through positive strategies such as alternative narratives creates an enduring social resiliency to radicalization.

Schools and universities, as academic institutions, need new strategies to engage in a campaign similar to those of government and civil society. The most reasonable means to protect the academic environment from the infiltration of radical networks is to engage its communities with rigorous scholarship and critical thinking. This is the form of the alternative narratives that academic institutions should endeavor to spread in order to win the "war of ideas." Liam Sandford argues that "through the use of education the application of critical thinking could help individuals build resilience to negative influences, including both misinformation and radicalization."[62] Students should be educated to think critically and to have the ability to challenge narratives that will affect them and the community at large. Sandford identifies three important points that schools and universities should address to enhance their capabilities for addressing radicalization, as follows:

> First, engaging students in discussions on challenging issues and developing a greater understanding of drivers to becoming involved in undesirable activities. Second, by producing counter-narratives, students will be creating products that will showcase their skills, and therefore enhance their employability as a result. Third, by understanding the issues, students can begin to develop greater resilience to negative influences and better challenge information.[63]

CONCLUDING REMARKS

In this chapter I have highlighted how high school and university students have been exposed to radical ideologies through the internet and social media. There is little doubt that online radicalization poses a serious threat to Indonesian institutions of learning, as the internet and social media penetrate their environments in a way that is hard to detect. The literature on the relationship between the internet and radicalization has increased in the past two decades, reflecting the ubiquitous nature of the internet and social media in relation to contemporary life, as well as the extensive use of online platforms by radical extremist groups. Reported reasons for the popularity of the internet and social media have been identified as follows: (1) anonymity and lack of censorship, (2) ease and speed of access, (3) low costs, (4) large audience size, (5) affordances of Web 2.0, and (6) provision of identity for marginalized individuals.[64] It should also be noted that recent research has paid attention to the vulnerability of youth. Based on both quantitative data and in-depth interviews, it can be concluded that student radicalization involves both top-down and bottom-up processes, as discussed above.

My research found that university students were more likely to become radicalized by online extremist content than were high school students. The reasons for this finding have been discussed in great detail. In addition to these students' media savviness, this research explored the motivations with which users visited radical websites and found that university students tended to be more curiosity-driven, often searching for religious information available on the internet. It has also been argued that using the internet to transmit factual information to combat radical extremist propaganda can be the quickest way to reach youth. In combatting online radicalization, the fight needs to be waged online, on the same battleground as that occupied by the antagonist, as would a traditional war. Cyberspace is the online battleground. The injection of alternative narratives causes an upstream of positive information to combat radical ideologies and gives youth options, rather than giving them a monolithic and rigid view of Islam. Therefore, in this chapter I argue that education should be incorporated into preventive, not reactive and repressive, measures to make students resilient citizens. Religious radicalism is a social problem, and all elements of society, including institutions of learning, should play their roles to educate the public about the importance of critical digital literacy. Most important, students must see the relevance of what they learn and develop a critical understanding of the world. This literacy will preempt some of the triggers that push and pull them onto the dangerous path toward radicalization.

EIGHT

Religious Intolerance and Antisemitic Discourse

Thus far I have demonstrated that religious intolerance among youths has recently been on the rise in Indonesia and that a significant proportion of university and high school students are sympathetic to radicalism. In the previous chapter I examined the extent to which internet and social media platforms have been used by radical groups to recruit followers among youths and to disseminate their ideology to wider circles. With the internet, online radical content from all over the globe can easily be consulted by students. Our research has found substantial evidence of radicalization among young Indonesian Muslims connecting to radical networks via the internet. This internet-based radicalization and recruitment has posed particular challenges, as the digital world has no boundaries. This is also the case with the use of social media to spread hate speech, including antisemitic propaganda and prejudice. Referring to the spreading of antisemitism in the West, Florette Cohen-Abady, Daniel Kaplin, Lee Jussim, and associate write: "Antisemitism was also promoted throughout much of Europe through internet and other media connected to Middle Eastern and other Muslim countries that promoted hatred of Jews as a part of a political message intended to delegitimize Israel."[1] While hatred against Jews on online platforms has become a major concern, and so too the high level of antisemitism in the Muslim world, it is wrong to suggest that antisemitism is merely an Islamic issue, since it is still a serious problem in many parts of the Western world. Günther Jikeli is correct when he says that "antisemitism is still widespread in the general, largely non-Muslim society."[2] Muslim antisemitic discourse, in both the Arab world and the West, has been influenced partly by Islamic sources and partly by historical Christian antisemitism.

The focus of this chapter is not on comparing antisemitism in the West to that in the Muslim world. Nor do I attempt to prove or disprove the importation of Middle Eastern disputes into the West. Rather, in this chapter I will discuss the nature of antisemitic expressions among students in both high schools and universities in Indonesia. Although the focus of my research is on how these students were attracted to radical ideologies and their involvement in radical networks, I asked them about their most hated groups, and Jews appeared to be one of them. Since my research on their views of Jews is limited, as it was not the main issue addressed in my research, I will discuss the question of antisemitism in Indonesia more broadly by looking at other research findings on religious intolerance, especially how Jews have been viewed in the country. As I will demonstrate, the widespread antisemitism among Indonesian students reflects a bigger picture, illustrating what scholars call the "conservative turn."[3] Of course, the growth of antisemitism and youth radicalization in Indonesia is not unique, as several campuses in the West have also been wrestling with a similar issue. In 2008, for instance, an independent task force investigating patterns of antisemitic intimidation at the University of California at Irvine concluded that "acts of antisemitism are real and well documented" and that "Jewish students have been harassed."[4] According to the Anti-Defamation League (ADL),[5] in 2005 alone there were nearly a hundred antisemitic incidents on American college campuses,[6] and many acts of harassment and intimidation remain unreported because of fear of further escalation. The internet plays a significant role in the spread of antisemitism. Talking about the nature of internet-based antisemitism in Britain, Andre Oboler writes, "Today there is a nexus between antisemitism on the campus and on the internet."[7]

In Britain, as in many other countries in the West, antisemitic expressions often take the form of anti-Zionist sentiments or hostility toward the Jewish state of Israel. There is a complex and controversial question here as to whether some anti-Israel sentiments ought to be considered variants of antisemitism. It is, of course, the case that not all criticism of Israel and/or anti-Zionism can be considered antisemitic.[8] In Britain, however, as Robert Wistrich notes, "Such criticism frequently leaves the bounds of civilized debate and engages in demonization, flagrant double standards, and the implicit denial of Israel's right to defend itself—thereby appropriating more traditional modes of antisemitism."[9] I will come back to this issue later. Suffice it to say at this moment that antisemitic discourse among educated Indonesian youths tends to take a similar form, namely, virulent and disproportionate hostility toward the Jewish state. For this study, I adopt Theodor Adorno's widely recognized classic definition of antisemitism as "stereotyped negative opinions describing the Jews as threatening, immoral, and categorically different from non-Jews, and of hostile attitudes urging various forms of restriction, exclusion, and suppression as a means of solving 'the Jewish problem.'"[10] What I am going to show in the first part of this chapter is how hostility toward and prejudice against Jewish people is constructed gradually. In the second part I will present students' negative perceptions of Jews in light of the increasing religious intolerance in Indonesia. In the final part I will offer possible explanations for the rise of antisemitism in the country.

IMAGINED AND REAL JEWS IN INDONESIA

Scholars like James T. Siegel often refer to antisemitic discourse in Indonesia using the term "antisemitism without Jews."[11] That is to say that, while antisemitism has gained popularity among Indonesians, most of them are not aware of the presence of the small Jewish community in the country and cannot conceptualize Judaism as a religion. Judaism is not among the country's six officially recognized religions, which are Islam, Protestantism, Catholicism, Hinduism, Buddhism, and Confucianism. In addition to the fact that the number of Jews in Indonesia is small, the fact that Judaism is not recognized in Indonesian law has contributed to its limited visibility in the public space. Interestingly, despite the unfamiliarity of the public with Judaism and Jews, common tropes of allegations against and conspicuous antagonism toward Jews are widespread in the country. Indonesian Jews suffer the age-old prejudice, stereotyping, and hostility, which fits with Bernard Glassman's view that antisemitism can flourish in places where Jews are not present.[12]

The flourishing of antisemitic discourse is evident from popular publications that can easily be found in bookstores, both online and offline. To mention but a few, antisemitic publications bear such titles as *Gerakan Zionis Berwajah Melayu* (A Zionist Movement with a Malay Face), by Sidik Jatmika (2001); *Zionisme: Gerakan Menaklukkan Dunia* (Zionism: A Movement to Subjugate the World), by Zaini Azhar Maulani (2002); *Rahasia Kekayaan Yahudi* (The Secret of Jewish Wealth), by Sakri Faisal (2008); *Rahasia Kecerdasan Yahudi* (The Secret of Jewish Intelligence), by A. Maheswara, 3rd ed. (2008); *Kemenangan Yahudi: Makanan Mengepung Dunia* (Jewish Victory: Food Encircles the World), by Fathony Arsyad (2008). As the titles indicate, these books entertain the idea of a global Jewish conspiracy. Jews are seen as controlling all aspects of public life. The authors of these books develop the idea that the world economy, politics, and culture have been manipulated and controlled by Jews in order to gain global hegemony and suppress non-Jews, especially Muslims. Sidik Jatmika, for instance, contends that the Jews control the world through American military power and media. Not only does Jatmika see the US-Israeli alliance as the cause of instability in the Arab Middle East; he also refers to Indonesia's former Dutch colonizers as being Jewish. Today, he says, Jewish control over Indonesia continues through the domination of multinational companies and the influence of foreign governments in Indonesia.[13]

Most of the titles mentioned above were reprinted several times, which reflects their popularity among Indonesian readers. An example is the work of a popular author from Jakarta, Ridwan Saidi, titled *Fakta & Data Yahudi di Indonesia* (Facts & Data about Jews in Indonesia), which was first published in 1992. Fourteen years later, in 2006, this book was republished with additional data provided by Rizki Ridyasmara under a new title, *Fakta & Data Yahudi di Indonesia: Dulu dan Sekarang* (Facts & Data about Jews in Indonesia: Past and Present). This book has been reprinted five times since. Some of the Indonesian antisemitic literature is translated from Arabic. For instance, *Yahudi Sang Penghancur Dunia* (Jews: The Destroyers of the World), by Dr. Abdullah Al-Thail, is a translation of the author's dissertation presented to al-Azhar University. Muhammad Thalib and Mustafa Mahdamy compiled a volume titled *Dendam Barat dan Yahudi terhadap Islam* (Western and Jewish Revenge to Islam), which is a translation of three separate articles written in Arabic, namely, "Qādat al-gharb yaqūlūna ḍammirū al-islām 'abīdu ahlahu" (Western Leaders Declaring the Demolition of Islam and Its Adherents), by Jalāl 'Ālam; "Qiṣaṣ min al-tārīkh" (Stories from History), by Shaykh 'Alī Ṭanṭāwī; and "Ḥaqīqat al-yahūd wa al-maṭāmi' al-yahūdiyyah" (The Truth about Jews and Jewish Aspirations), by Namīr al-Khaṭīb.[14]

In her discussion of sixteen Indonesian antisemitic publications, Eva Mirela Suciu points to the complexity embedded in antisemitism, anti-Zionism, and anti-Israelism as overlapping social realities and categories in Indonesia. Most antisemite authors in Indonesia tend to focus on the international perspective of a Jewish conspiracy by looking at Israel as the epitome of evil, from which Jews aim to subjugate the world, Muslims in particular. "The perception of Israel as the tangible evidence of a Jewish attempt to destroy Muslim unity," Suciu writes, "is a recurrent theme throughout most of the books studied."[15] It is also worth noting that some Indonesian authors associate the Indonesian state ideology of *Pancasila* with the work of Zionists. Dr. Muhammad Thalib and Irfan Awwas, for instance, put together a volume under the title *Doktrin Zionisme dan Ideologi Pancasila* (The Doctrine of Zionism and the Ideology of Pancasila) (1999) arguing that, since its birth and throughout Indonesian history, *Pancasila* has been shaped by Zionist interests. Moreover, some authors even accuse Muslim leaders such as Abdurrahman Wahid (Gus Dur), the NU leader and former president of Indonesia, of being Jewish agents.[16]

In fact, several prominent Muslim intellectuals who are associated with "liberal Islam" have been accused of promoting the Jewish agenda to destroy Islam. The prominent Muslim scholar Nurcholish Madjid, for instance, was labeled "a Zionist agent" for his efforts to reform Islam and promote religious tolerance. His critic Daud Rasyid writes, "It is hard to understand that Nurcholish who claims to be rendering a service to Islam in Indonesia in fact actually damages Islamic thinking. The most difficult thing to say is that Nurcholish is a Zionist agent who ruins Islam from within."[17] Accusing leading Muslim thinkers of being Zionists and agents of Judaism is not uncommon in Islamic media, such as

Media Dakwah, Sabili, or *Suara Hidayatullah.* The cover of one of *Media Dakwah's* issues, headed "Where Nurcholish Madjid's Thought Comes From," has a design showing someone entering a maze. At the end of the maze is a Star of David.[18] The message to be conveyed is quite clear: Nurcholish's progressive ideas originated from or can be traced back to Jewish propaganda. Martin van Bruinessen rightly notes:

> It is hardly surprising that we recently witnessed in Indonesia some Muslim thinkers with cosmopolitan views who have been labelled "Jews" and "Zionists." Islamic reform movements that question orthodox views and offer new interpretive paradigms and promote tolerant attitudes toward others have been put under scrutiny by those who uphold religious orthodoxy. Throughout history, reformers have often been accused of attempting to undermine religion (while they themselves claimed to restore religious essence to its central place). With the increasing popularity of Jewish conspiracy, and following the logic that everything that threatens Islam or any establishment is perceived as a Jewish or Zionist agenda, Islamic reform will easily be suspected as part and parcel of a Jewish conspiracy.[19]

To further illustrate this point, when I got a Fulbright scholarship to pursue my graduate studies in an American institution, one of my former teachers at my *Pesantren* (traditional Islamic boarding school) was upset because he thought I would study with Orientalists and, in his view, eventually end up being a Jewish Zionist agent. There are, at least, two dimensions of Jewish labeling given to Muslim thinkers. First, their progressive ideas are thought to be influenced by Orientalists who purport to serve a Jewish agenda to destroy Islam. How is Orientalism associated with Jews? *Media Dakwah,* an Islamist magazine, for instance, presents Islam as a real threat to the West. Due to its failure to physically colonize the Muslim world, the West, under the control of Jews, seeks to influence Muslim thinkers. "For *Media Dakwah,*" Burhanuddin writes, "the fact that gifted liberal Muslim thinkers have the opportunity to learn from a number of Orientalists at Western universities is due to the Jewish conspiracy."[20] The second dimension, perhaps more relevant to this chapter, is not only about the association of Orientalism with Jewish conspiracy, but also about the fact that even the terms "Jew," "Zionism," "the West," and "foreign power" are often used interchangeably. This shows the irrelevance of the actual terms in blaming powerful others as the reasons for one's own deteriorated situation. According to Martin van Bruinessen, "[Many Indonesian] Muslims, and not just the radicals, believe in the existence of an international conspiracy, involving the assorted enemies of Islam—Zionists, Christian missionaries, imperialist politicians, and their various local allies—aiming to destroy or weaken Islam in Indonesia."[21] They tend to blame an imagined outsider as the cause of all problems, both historical and current. It is hardly surprising that antisemitism might even be linked to social, economic, and political tensions between Muslims and the other, thereby making the Chinese into what Anthony Reid calls "the Jews-in-the East."[22]

Before discussing possible reasons for the popularity of antisemitism in Indonesia and the conceptualization of "imagined Jews" as an invisible threat that is attractive to Indonesians, a few observations about "real Jews" are in order. Rabbi Benjamin Meijer Verbrugge from Lampung, Sumatra, estimates that some 140 Indonesian Jews are now living in the country scattered in big cities such as Jakarta and its surrounding areas, Surabaya, and Manado.[23] However, it is almost impossible to ascertain the exact number of Jews in Indonesia today. in part because Jews cannot identify themselves as such on their ID cards since Judaism is not an officially recognized religion. Some have to register as Christians or members of other recognized religions on their ID cards. To have a national ID card that lists an unrecognized religion or leaves the space for religion blank will cause administrative problems, making it challenging to register marriages or births or to enroll children in schools.[24] In addition, in an atmosphere of an increasing threat of antisemitic rhetoric, families of Jewish ancestry would think twice about declaring their faith or practicing it openly. An Indonesian Jew who used to identify himself on his ID card as "Hebrani" (perhaps a combination of "Hebrew" and "*Ibrani*"), for instance, decided to change to the approved "Hindu" category when nationwide riots occurred in 1998 that led to the collapse of the authoritarian Suharto regime. Of course, he did not convert to Hinduism but simply changed his ID card for security reasons. As Jeffrey Hadler notes, "He was proud, at least, to keep the letter 'H.'"[25]

The history of early Jewish settlement in Indonesia has not been discussed much by scholars. A few studies about Jews' arrival in the region focus on the Dutch colonial period. While there is no conclusive evidence, it seems likely that Jews might have been in Indonesia much earlier. In the tenth century, for instance, the Persian traveler Buzurgh ibn Shahriyar, in his book *Kitāb 'Ajā'ib al-Hind* (The Book of the Marvels of India), mentions the story of a Jewish merchant, Isḥāq al-Yahūdī, who made a stop at Sarira or Sribuza on his way from Oman to China.[26] Sarira or Sribuza may have been a reference to Sriwijaya, the oldest Buddhist kingdom on the island of Sumatra. At least in the thirteenth century, some Jewish merchants were reported to have actively engaged in trading camphor in Fansur, the common Arabic name for the camphor-producing region of Barus in Sumatra.[27] Later, with the arrival of Europeans in South Asia, especially Spanish and Portuguese, a Jewish community was discovered. The sixteenth-century Jesuit missionary Francis Xavier (d. 1552) reported that during his visit to Malacca in 1547 he met with Sephardic Jews who already had their own synagogue.[28] It is not clear whether they were traders or they resided in Indonesia to escape the Inquisition.

We find more evidence of Jewish settlement during the Dutch colonial period, from the seventeenth century onward. When the Dutch government established the VOC (Vereenigde Oost-Indische Compagnie) to merge various competing trading companies in the East Indies, several Jewish merchants were involved as investors.[29] The increasing presence of the VOC in Indonesia paved the way for Jewish migration, though the influence of Jews on the VOC should not be exaggerated. The VOC only employed Christians to serve as clerks and officers, which made it difficult for Jews to play any role in the company. It is no wonder that in the seventeenth century some Jews requested to be baptized as Christians so they might be able to travel to the East Indies. The situation changed in 1782 when the VOC began to recruit Jews due to a lack of sufficient employees. There is good reason to believe that Jews came to the peninsula not only because of their employment in the VOC. Some sources indicate that they were also employed by the British East India Company (EIC) as translators. When John Jourdain from the EIC traveled to Ambon, the eastern part of Indonesia, he employed a Jew from al-Mukha in Yemen named David who mastered Arabic, Portuguese, and other languages.[30] In 1762, British captain Thomas Forrest is reported to have met with a Jewish translator named Abraham at the palace of the Sultan in Aceh.[31]

In the nineteenth century the presence of the Jewish community was more visible, though the Jews were not yet organized. The Dutch colonial government took over the East Indies from the VOC. Under the colonial administration, some Jews obtained important positions. In addition to having important positions in trading in Surabaya, Makassar, and Kuta Raja (Aceh), some of them were appointed to public office, including as a mayor in Makassar in the 1920s and as Resident in Surabaya. Interestingly, not all East Indies institutions were willing to accept Jews. Bank Java and the East Indies Commercial Bank, for instance, continued to reject Jews from their organizational structures.[32] Moreover, when Singapore was founded as a British colony by Stamford Raffles in 1819, Baghdadi Jews were able to develop their community and commercial networks to the extent that one of them, David Saul Marshall ben Farha (d. 1995), was appointed the Chief Minister of the Malay Federation at the time.[33] Their condition continued to improve until the Second World War.

The flourishing of Jews is evident from a report made by the Zionist fundraiser Israel Cohen in 1921. The Jews of the Indies described by Cohen were active and, though still lacking state support, thrived relatively. Speaking in the Theosophical Hall in Batavia, he said, "I learned that there were several hundred Jews—perhaps as many as 2,000—scattered about from Batavia to Soerabaya, but as most of them concealed or denied their Jewish origin it was impossible to form an approximate estimate of their number."[34] Cohen expressed his fear that the Dutch Jews were on the verge of losing their Jewish identity, also observing a few Jews with native wives. During his four-day tour of the Jewish centers of Java, Cohen was introduced to congregations of Indies Judaism that included Dutch, Austrian, Russian, Romanian, and Baghdadi congregants. When visited Semarang, he attended a performance of a Yiddish-Russian opera. Cohen published his *Journal of a Jewish Traveler* in 1925, and one year later the first Jewish newspaper, *Erets Israel* (*Het Joods Land*), was published in Padang, West Sumatra. In its first issue of September 9, 1926, the journal announced proudly that it would be Zionist in conception and distributed free to the Jews of the Indies. According to Jeffrey Hadler, in 1928 Zionist fundraising offices could be found in Batavia, Surabaya, Bandung, Semarang, Malang, Yogyakarta, Medan, and Padang. "In the late 1920s," Hadler notes, "both the *Nederlands Indie*

Zionistenbond [The Netherland-Indies Union of Zionists] and the *Vereenging van Joodsche Belangen* [Association of Jewish Affairs] were established, making Jews an officially visible colonial category."[35]

When Japanese forces defeated the Dutch and occupied the Indies in 1942, things did not change in favor of the Jewish community. The Japanese policy to erase the Dutch influence in the Indies led them to distinguish people according to their races, including a distinction between Ashkenazi (European) Jews such as Dutch, German, Russian, and Romanian Jews, on the one hand; Sephardic Jews; and Mizrahi Jews such as Baghdadi and Armenian Jews.[36] During the first year of the Japanese occupation, Jews were still mostly left to travel and trade freely until the time when the Japanese colonizers were under pressure from the Nazis to arrest all the Jews, both European and Asian. Antisemitism was propagated by the Japanese forces and later spread among local peoples.[37] The perception of a global Jewish conspiracy was spread in the local Japanese-language newspaper, *Java Shimbun*. It is not surprising that some Indonesian leaders recapitulated antisemitic propaganda by developing conspiracy theories about the role of Jews in Dutch colonialism. Perhaps as a reaction to the Japanese anti-Jewish propaganda, some Jews participated in armed resistance against the Japanese forces.[38]

Japan surrendered a few days after the U.S. atomic bombings of Hiroshima and Nagasaki, on August 14, 1945, and, as a consequence, Indonesian Jews were released from prison. After the end of the Indonesian National Revolution (1945–49), all Dutch soldiers withdrew from Indonesia. Most Jews left the former Dutch East Indies, returning to Europe or migrating to the United States, Australia, or Israel. In 1956–57, the first president of Indonesia, Sukarno, ousted the remaining Dutch and nationalized Dutch corporate assets. Eventually, all Jews with Dutch passports had to leave the country. After the enactment of Sukarno's nationalization policies, the number of Jews in the country decreased significantly.[39] In 1957, the World Jewish Congress (WJC) found only thirty Jewish families remaining in Jakarta and reported that "some Oriental Jews of the older generation still keep Jewish traditions alive" in Surabaya.[40] Until recently, a Jewish community of Iraqi origin maintained a small synagogue in Surabaya with distinct Sephardic characteristics. However, in 2007 and 2009 a number of anti-Israel protests were staged in front of it as a reaction to the Israeli blockade of the Gaza Strip. At the same time, it was designated a national heritage site, Islamic hard-liners sealed the building. Four years later, in 2013, this only remaining synagogue in the country was demolished.[41] A handful of unofficial syna-gogues exist in Indonesia, including the one in Tondano, North Sulawesi.

Thus, for most of Indonesian history after it achieved independence, "real Jews" were not really visible due to their insignificant number, but antisemitism was widespread and continues to flourish. The lack of an actual Jewish presence in Indonesia raises questions of perceptions and knowledge about antisemitism, as it appears to be directed against forces other than Jews themselves. Again, the question is this: Why do Indo-nesians blame Jews when confronted with acute problems, be they eco-nomic, political, or cultural? What has influenced their perception of the Jews? Given that Indonesia has no sizeable Jewish community, how can we explain its long history of antisemitism?

HOSTILITY TOWARD JEWS AND THE "ISRAELI FACTOR"

Antisemitism in Indonesia has not attracted much scholarly attention, despite the fact that an alleged global Jewish conspiracy is one of the most talked-about topics in the country. With the tidal wave of religious intolerance in the past few years, hostility toward an imagined outsider, especially "the Jew," seems to be on the rise as well. Most surveys reveal that the level of antisemitism in Indonesia is quite high. According to the ADL survey conducted in 2014, some 48 percent of Indonesians have negative attitudes toward Jews, a percentage much higher than the global average (26 percent). The anti-Jewish sentiment in Indonesia is the second-highest in Southeast Asia, under that in Malaysia (61 percent). In the Middle East and North Africa, the index score of antisemitism is 74 percent. The ADL survey includes such questions as whether the Jews have too much power in the business world and control over media and global affairs. Some 59 percent of Indonesians think that the Jews have too much control over the American government, and they hate them because of the way Jews behave (67 percent).[42] A report of the Pew Research Center published in 2010 suggests that 74 percent of Indone-sian Muslims expressed unfavorable views of Jews, compared to only 43 percent expressing unfavorable views of Christians.[43]

TABLE 8.1. Ten Least Disliked Groups According to the Wahid Institute/Indonesian
Survey Institute Survey

March–April 2016		October 2017	
Groups/Categories	Percentage	Groups/Categories	Percentage
LGBT persons	26.1	Communists	21.9
Communists	16.7	LGBT persons	17.8
Jews	10.6	Jews	7.1
Christians	2.2	Christians	3.0
Shi'ites	1.3	Atheists	2.5
Chinese	0.4	Shi'ites	1.2
Wahhabis	0.5	Chinese	0.7
Catholics	0.4	Wahhabis	0.6
Buddhists	0.4	Catholics	0.5
Confucianists	0.1	Buddhists	0.5

Source: Wahid Institute and Indonesian Survey Institute (LSI, Lembaga Survei Indonesia),
Laporan Survei Nasional Tren Toleransi Sosial-Keagamaan di Kalangan Perempuan Muslim
Indonesia, Wahid Foundation 2018.
Note: n = 1,520.

No Indonesian think tanks have ever conducted surveys focusing
on antisemitism. However, a few surveys that showed the level of hostility toward Jews among Indonesians were conducted to investigate
the phenomenon of religious intolerance. In 2016 the Wahid Institute
in collaboration with the Indonesian Survey Institute (LSI, Lembaga
Survei Indonesia) conducted a nationwide survey that indicated that
the three most hated groups of people in Indonesia are LGBT persons
(26.1 percent), Communists (16.7 percent), and Jews (10.6 percent). In
this survey participants were simply asked which group from a given
list they disliked the most. According to this survey, about one of ten
selected Jews as the most disliked group. A year later, as table 8.1 illustrates, a survey by the same institutions revealed that those who disliked
Jews had decreased slightly, from 10.6 percent in 2016 to 7.1 percent in
2017.[44] Of 1,520 respondents, 59.9 percent said that they did not like
certain groups, and about 92.2 percent of the people reportedly did not
want those hated people to serve in any governmental offices. Moreover,
82 percent objected to having those hated people as their neighbors.

In 2016, Saiful Mujani Research and Consulting (SMRC) conducted
a similar survey with different groups of disliked persons mentioned;

TABLE 8.2. Students' responses to "Which of the following groups do you dislike the most?"

Groups/Categories	Percentage	Groups/Categories	Percentage
ISIS members	23.0	Catholics	0.4
LGBT persons	15.3	Hindus	0.4
Communists	14.0	Buddhists	0.4
Atheists	11.5	Ahmadis	0.3
Jews	6.4	Muslims	0.2
Christians	2.0	Confucians	0.2
FPI (Islamic Defender		Javanese	0.1
Front) members	1.8	Arabs	0.0
Shi'ites	1.2	Other groups/categories	0.8
HTI (Hizbut Tahrir)		No disliked groups	19.5
members	1.0		
Chinese	1.0		
Wahhabis	0.5		

Source: The Saiful Mujani Research and Consulting (SMRC), "Sikap Publik atas Isu Kebangkitan PKI," Temuan Survei Nasional, updated September 23–26, 2020, https://saifulmujani.com/sikap-publik-atas-isu-kebangkitan-pki/, slides page 32.

while it included members of ISIS, it did not mention the category "Jews." The results were as follows: ISIS members (25.5 percent) were at the top, followed by LGBT persons (16.6 percent), Communists (11.8 percent), Christians (2.6 percent), and Chinese (0.8 percent). According to Saiful Mujani, the purpose of the survey was to investigate people's attitudes toward ethnic Chinese in Indonesia, and it concluded that Indonesians are quite tolerant of Chinese. "Almost throughout history following the *Reformasi* [political reform after the collapse of the authoritarian Suharto regime]," he contends, "the trend that considers Christians, Catholics and Chinese as the least liked social groups is relatively small."[45] In its 2019 survey, which includes a longer list of social groups, including Jews, SMRC reports that the Jews were ranked number 5, with ISIS members at 23 percent, LGBT persons 15.3 percent, Communists 14 percent, Atheists 11.5 percent, and Jews 6.4 percent.[46] The complete list can be seen in table 8.2.

From the above findings we can infer that the level of dislike or hostility toward Jews among Indonesians ranges from 6 percent to 10 percent, which is much less than that recorded in the ADL findings (48 percent). How can we explain the big gap between the findings of the ADL survey and the reports of Indonesian think tanks? First of all, the ADL and Indonesian research think tanks aim to understand two different phenomena. On the one hand, the ADL index score is based on several questions used to assess antisemitic views. The eleven questions included in the ADL survey served as instruments to measure whether people believed in various stereotypes commonly attributed to Jews. The Indonesian researchers, on the other hand, attempted to examine the level of tolerance and the lack thereof in plural societies. Tolerance, understood as "willingness to 'put up with' those things one rejects or opposes,"[47] as John L. Sullivan, James Piereson, and George E. Marcus put it, is viewed as an essential component of a political culture for democratic stability, since, according to Mujani, "the presence of a large intolerant mass may contribute to repressive regime behavior which in turn can weaken democracy."[48] Therefore, it is understandable that, in addition to identifying the disliked groups, the Indonesian researchers developed a general measure of tolerance, namely: How many social groups does a respondent reject as neighbors?

In its most recent survey (in May 2022), SMRC found that more than half of the Indonesian population objected to having Jews as their neighbors (an average of 51 percent), as teachers at public schools (57 percent), and as government officials (61 percent). As elaborated in other parts of the report, there was a significant difference between their views of Jews and of Christians/Catholics as their neighbors (13 percent objected), as teachers at public schools (19 percent), and as government officials (26 percent). While there was no noticeable difference between male and female respondents, between rural and urban ones, or between different ages of respondents, Muslims tended to be more hostile to Jews compared with members of other religious communities. Table 8.3 shows that 56 percent of Muslims objected to having Jews as their neighbors, and only 14 percent of non-Muslims (others) expressed objections. Concerning Jews as teachers and government officials, over 60 percent of Muslims said that they objected.[49] According to Saiful Mujani, the negative views of Jews in Indonesia can best be explained in relation to the state's discriminatory approach toward Judaism. As mentioned earlier, Judaism is not recognized as an official religion despite the fact that there are Jews in the country. Nor does the Indonesian state have diplomatic relations with the Jewish state of Israel. Mujani contends that

TABLE 8.3. Percentages of Indonesians with various attitudes toward Jews according to respondents' demographies

	Base	*As neighbors*			*As schoolteachers*			*As government officials*		
		Objected	*No Objection*	*No idea/ no response*		*No objection*	*No idea/ no response*	*Objected*	*No objection*	*No idea/ no response*
Gender										
Male	50.5	50	43	7	58	35	7	60	33	7
Female	49.5	51	39	10	56	34	10	63	27	10
Area of Residence										
Rural	50.1	51	41	8	57	35	8	62	31	8
Urban	49.9	50	41	9	57	34	9	62	29	9
Age										
<=25 years	23.1	53	43	5	62	34	5	69	26	5
26–40 years	36.6	49	43	8	56	36	8	51	32	8
41–55 years	25.1	57	34	9	62	30	8	64	27	9
>56 years	15.2	42	44	14	44	40	16	48	36	15
Religion										
Islam	88.0	56	37	7	61	32	7	66	27	7
Other religions	12.0	14	70	16	27	56	16	29	55	17

Source: The Saiful Mujani Research and Consulting (SMRC) research findings were presented by Saiful Mujani during his talk show, "Bedah Politik Bersama Saiful Mujani," on the SMRC YouTube Channel from June to August 2022. See the SMRC YouTube channel, https://www.youtube.com/c/SMRCTV/videos.

the state's lack of recognition of Jews and Israel has had legal implications in that adherents to recognized religions are protected under the constitution. Thus, the lack of the state's recognition of Judaism and Israel contributes to people's intolerant views and attitudes toward Jews.[50]

Up to this point, it has seemed clear that the methods employed by the Indonesian researchers and the ADL were quite different. While the ADL asked people about their views of several common stereotypes and allegations attributed to Jews, the Indonesian think tanks used open-ended questionnaires with a list of categories for respondents to use to compare Jews with others. The latter also tended to focus on measuring the level of tolerance and the lack thereof as indicators of respondents' support for democracy. My own research on high school and university students can provide another possible explanation of the gap between the ADL findings and those reported in the Indonesian surveys. Sympathizers with the kind of antisemitic discourses propagated by Islamist media such as *Media Dakwah* tend to increase in number when the hostility toward Jews is conflated with anti-Israel sentiments. For reasons that will be discussed later, the level of anti-Israel sentiment in Indonesia is relatively high. As in other parts of the world, hostility toward Jews in Indonesia is a conjunction of animosity toward Israel for its conflict with Palestine and the Middle East in general, cemented by antisemitic literature and anti-Israeli media as well as the perceived threat from external powers.

This "Israeli factor" is evident in my research, which shows that when the category "Jews" is changed to "Israelis," the negative perception of Jews by Indonesians increases significantly. Of 500 students from 12 high schools in five cities in East Java, the survey found that 24.2 percent of respondents did not like Israelis, the second-highest category after corruptors (43.4 percent). As shown in table 8.4, the rest of their answers were as follows: they did not like members of ISIS (20.4 percent), people of other religions (4.6 percent), Chinese (4.4 percent), Americans/Westerners (2.2 percent), and wealthy people with multiple companies (0.8 percent). Among the students of seven public universities identified by the National Agency for Combating Terrorism (BNPT,

TABLE 8.4. Students' responses to "Which of the following groups do you dislike the most?"

High school students (n = 500)		University students (n = 700)	
Groups	Percentage	Groups	Percentage
Corruptors	43.4	Corruptors	36.6
Israelis	24.2	ISIS	23.1
ISIS members	20.4	Israelis	19.7
People of other religions	4.6	Americans/Westerners	18.4
Chinese	4.4	Chinese	1.6
Americans/Westerners	2.2	People of other religions	0.4
Wealthy people with multiple companies	0.8	Wealthy people with multiple companies	0.2

Note: Surveys conducted in 2018 and 2019.

Badan Nasional Penanggulangan Terorisme) as having been infiltrated by radical ideologies, 700 of whom I surveyed, those who disliked Israelis were 19.7 percent, the third-highest after "corruptors" (36.6 percent) and members of ISIS (23.1 percent). It is worth noting that among students of universities that have been infiltrated by radical ideologies, the number of those who disliked Americans is quite high (18.4 percent).

On the basis of the above findings, I would like to highlight two things. First, while there is no significant correlation between education and hatred of Jews, university students tended to be more hostile to Americans/Westerners (18.4 percent) than high school students (2.2 percent). As for their views of Jews, our survey confirms the SMRC findings that the level of education does not play a significant role in shaping people's views of Jews, either positively or negatively: People with university degrees are not necessarily more tolerant than those without degrees. According to the SMRC findings, the range between those with elementary school certificates and those with university degrees was 5 percent when it came to objecting to having Jews as their neighbors: from elementary school (53 percent) to middle school (51 percent), high school (49 percent), and university (48 percent). My findings reveal that the difference between high school students and university students was 4.5 percent. However, when it came to their views of Americans/Westerners, university students were significantly more hostile than high school students, perhaps due to their exposure to anti-American media and literature.

Secondly, the fact that respondents' negative view of Israelis (in my findings) is significantly higher than their negative view of Jews (in the SMRC and Wahid Institute's findings) sheds important light on the unfavorable impression of Israel in the Arab-Israeli conflict. Even in the United States, where hostility toward Jews has tended to decline in the past few years, anti-Israel sentiments remain high.[51] Although, as the editors of *Antisemitism in North America* note, "when asked to choose sides in the Arab-Israeli dispute, most Americans and Canadians who are willing to do so side with Israel."[52] It is true that criticism of the Israeli state is not necessarily antisemitic and that a distinction can be made between legitimate and illegitimate criticisms. However, as Judit Bokser Liwerant and Yael Siman write, "Criticism of Israel is often expressed by using rhetoric or images that resonate as antisemitism: holding Israel to higher standards than other states, and for no

good reason; articulating conspiracy theories; using demonizing categories; casting Jews in the role of oppressors; formulating criticism in such
a way as to pick a fight with the vast majority of Jews; using the word
criticism but meaning discriminatory practices against Israelis or against
Jews."[53] In this sense, anti-Israel sentiments and antisemitic attitudes
are linked. Perhaps, as illustrated in my interviews with students discussed below, we now can talk about "old" and "new" antisemitisms: As
Liwerant and Siman conclude, while "[the old antisemitism] involved
discrimination against the personhood of Jews, the new antisemitism
involves discrimination against the statehood of Jews."[54]

MAJOR THEMES OF ANTISEMITIC DISCOURSE

Unlike other surveys, my research includes in-depth interviews with 50
high school students and 70 university students. The lack of data on
antisemitism among Indonesian youth requires an explorative approach
and a qualitative description of common tropes before addressing possible causes of widespread antisemitic discourse. Through my in-depth
interviews we can understand how young people argue to support their
negative views of Jews and Israelis and the way they express their arguments. Such an approach also allows the researcher to take seriously the
ways of thinking of the informants and the environments and social
networks that may have shaped their views and attitudes. What arguments do they use to justify hostility against Jews and/or Israelis? Are
there patters of antisemitic argumentation that emerge from their articu-
lation? Indeed, from these interviews we can identify a variety of reasons for their dislike or hostility toward Israeli, which, for the most part,
reflect major themes of antisemitism.

At least three recurring themes emerged from my interviews, all of
which reflect profound concerns among Indonesian youths with regard
to the dominant power of the state of Israel and its treatment of Palestinians. First, Israelis have too much power, and their main ambition
is simply to control the world and use the United States as their agent.
From the ADL survey we learn that almost half of the Indonesian population thinks that Jews have too much power in the world and 42 percent
claim that Jews have too much control over global affairs and don't care

about anyone other than their own kind (55 percent). One student from ITB (Bandung) contended that the United States is powerless when it comes to defending itself from Israeli political interests, particularly in the context of the Israeli-Palestinian conflict. He said:

> The United States is the agent of Israel. When Donald Trump moved the U.S. Embassy to Jerusalem, it became evident that the U.S. has nothing to do but to appease Israelis. Even with the existence of the United Nations, no one can confront Israelis. The UN Congress does not function. Can you imagine if the Israel-Palestine conflict is brought to the UN? The members of the UN Security Council will vote for the benefit of Israel. Even if many states opposed Israel, those superpowers will act solely for the interest of Israelis. So nothing can be done. Ideally, all Arab countries are united and work together to defeat the state of Israel, the most arrogant nation.

Obviously this student employed tropes of modern antisemitism that have become "classic," with an emphasis on "Jewish influence" and "Jewish power" in politics, economics, and media. The most common modern tropes involve Jews conspiring with other superpowers, such as the United States, the American government, the American president, or the American people. Many students think that Israel and the United States are collaborating closely. This type of conspiracy theory is intended to make the point that even an institution as powerful as the UN has no courage to resist Jewish pressure. Interestingly, the above student not only blames the powerful Jewish state, but also the inability of the Arab countries to forge a unity to challenge Israel. This is typical of arguments put forth by proponents of conspiracy theories, namely, seeking a simplistic explanation of complicated issues.

Among Indonesian university students, anti-Americanism seems to be quite strong. A student from Unair (Surabaya) reiterated the above point concerning a world conspiracy, especially involving the Americans, not only to control natural resources in Indonesia, but also to prevent the awakening and flourishing of Islam. "We do not govern ourselves," she said, "but rather the world system controls us and slowly kills us." She continued arguing that what happened in Indonesia was nothing more than American subversion:

Our government is no different. Since last time and up until now, we have been messed up by the U.S. Their intention is merely to control our natural resources, but also to prevent the unity of the Muslim *ummah* from awakening. They know very well that Indonesia is the largest Muslim country and, therefore, the Muslim community is divided so we cannot attain our strength as one *ummah*. Do you know that Jokowi [the current president] is driven by foreign power? So Pak SBY [the previous president], too, won the presidential election because of the role of Americans. Indeed, one of their strategies to prevent the Muslim community from unity is by spreading the *fitnah* (false propaganda). My HTI friends have never been trying to sabotage the state, but we were accused of being a radical organization.

HTI (Hizbut Tahrir Indonesia) is a branch of an international pan-Islamist political movement that aspires to establish the caliphate system to unite the Muslim community (*ummah*). In 2017 the Jokowi government banned the HTI to contain the spread of caliphate ideology, particularly its infiltration into governmental institutions, including public universities. Salsa, a sympathizer of HTI, believes that both President Jokowi and the previous president SBY (Susilo Bambang Yudhoyono) were controlled by the United States. A few other students from various high schools expressed similar concerns about the Israeli-U.S. alliance becoming the dominant power and controlling the world. One high school student claimed that she had heard information that "the U.S. is the superpower with a specific mission to rule over the world, and their plan is that one-third of the world population will die." She went on saying that "one of their strategies is to help the state of Israel oppress Palestinian people indiscriminately. So I truly don't like this trick."

The second recurring theme in my interviews was that Israelis are enemies of Islam and have viciously treated Muslims, especially in Palestine. Whenever incidents of violence occurred between Israelis and Palestinians, many Indonesian Muslims pointed to the Jews as the culprits that caused the problem, chaos, or commotion without understanding the complexity of the issue at hand that triggered the conflict, tension, or violence. Many students adopted the view that Israel is responsible for the political instability in the Arab Middle East. They often perceived the Israeli-Palestinian conflict in religious terms, as a conflict between

Muslims and Jews. Framing the Middle Eastern conflict as a conflict between these two religious groups reinforces the perception that Jews are hostile to Islam. The Israel-Hezbollah dispute, for instance, is seen as a war between Judaism and Islam. One student expressed this sentiment bluntly, saying "It is obvious that Israelis want to kill the Muslims." Seeing Israel as the clear evidence of a Jewish attempt to destroy the Muslim *ummah* is a recurrent theme that emerged from my interviews with Indonesian students.

This finding is in line with that of the ADL survey that the majority of Indonesians (56 percent) think that Jews are more loyal to Israel than to the country they live in. For many Indonesians, the Israeli-Palestinian conflict is a threat from the Jews despite the fact that many Jewish factions—Rabbis, academics, activists, politicians, and so on—in various countries have openly opposed the racial politics of Zionism and rejected the brutal policies of hardliners within the Israeli government. Many Jewish academics are critical of the state of Israel. Judith Butler, a professor of rhetoric and literature at the University of California at Berkeley, for instance, is one of the 3,700 American Jews who opposed the Israeli "occupation" and urged the U.S. government to cut financial aid to Israel.[55] In 2002, a group of scholars at MIT and Harvard drafted a petition opposing Israel's current occupation and its treatment of Palestinians. Responding to the reaction of the president of Harvard University, Lawrence Summers, to the initiatives as "advocating and taking actions that are antisemitic in their effect if not in their intent," Butler writes, "No, it's not antisemitic."[56] Concerns about the growth of anti-Israeli sentiments on American campuses have been expressed by some scholars, including Asaf Romirowsky, who writes that "making a case for Israel becomes increasingly more difficult when Israelis and Jews decide to adopt a Palestinian agenda that detracts from the real issue behind the conflict."[57]

Most students who expressed their resentment against Israelis in my interviews either defended Palestinians on religious grounds or expressed concerns for humanity. One student said: "I don't like Israelis because they attacked our brothers in Palestine. As Muslims we have to express our solidarity [with Palestinians]." For him, rephrasing a prophetic tradition, Muslims are all brothers. The Muslim *ummah* is like one body: If one organ is in pain, the whole body will suffer. The student admitted that the barbaric actions of Israelis in their treatment of Muslims in Palestine have caused him, a Muslim, to feel sorry and to develop negative sentiment toward Israelis. While concern for the brutality of Israeli forces and the suffering of Palestinians seemed to be overwhelmingly shared by those whom I interviewed, a few others made connections with the American support for Israelis to accomplish their domination in the Middle Eastern conflicts. One student opined as follows: "I don't like Israelis because they hate Palestinians. They often terrorize other people, especially Muslims. I also don't like Americans because they financially help Israel. The United States did nothing when Israel attacked Palestine. As a superpower, the U.S. should punish Israel. The American silence and complacency make me believe that the U.S. actually funds the state of Israel."

The third identifiable theme that emerged during the interviews, related to the above sentiment, was the perception of Israelis as cruel people who treat Palestinians inhumanely. This is perhaps the most common sentiment I heard in my interviews and has often been portrayed by Islamist media outlets. Pictures of Israeli authorities demolishing Palestinian houses with a lack of humanity, of Palestinian children being gassed at checkpoints, or of unarmed men, women, and children being murdered by the Israeli military are widely circulated. My respondents referred to the cruelty of Israelis in various ways. One student expressed his anger, saying, "I strongly dislike Israelis because they seized the lands of Palestinians and forced them to leave their homes. Palestinian Muslims have been treated inhumanely by Israelis." Another student compared Israelis to members of ISIS, saying that Israelis and ISIS have treated the other cruelly and inhumanely. A Christian student said the following: "I am a non-Muslim but I also hate Israelis. The reason for that is because Israelis don't have sympathy towards other human beings and they kill innocent people, torture them, rape and deprive others of their happiness. I cannot imagine why they act so cruelly as if other people are not human. They have not treated other human beings as human beings." Another student expressed her support for the government not to establish any diplomatic relations with Israel. She argued that Israelis should not be permitted to enter Indonesia: "In my view, Israelis have gone too far. They have no idea who they are. They came to Palestine as visitors (*pendatang*), but then they treated their hosts unfairly. They misbehaved, killed, and expelled Palestinians. As a *Muslimah*, I will not be happy if Israelis are around in this country. They deserve to be rejected from entering any Muslim countries for their treatment of Palestinian Muslims."

The above discussion shows the extent to which Israel's atrocities and apartheid against Palestinians, as well as the United States' uncritical support for Israel, have created a breeding ground for antisemitism in Indonesia. My interviews provide insights into the rationales used by educated youths to justify their negative views of Jews. It appears that the popularity of antisemitism in Indonesia cannot be understood without a close examination of the public antipathy toward Israel in the Israeli-Palestinian conflict. The conflict seems to shape Indonesians' perceptions of Jews. For Indonesians, Jews and Israelis are conflated in various ways. First, the "Jews" are not seen as "real Jews," but as an imagined force of the Israeli power capable of destroying the Muslim *ummah* in general and of suppressing Indonesia in particular. Second, related to the above point, the Jews are also seen as a unitary category. All Jews are seen as the same, and their evil and heartless character is thought to be embodied in Israeli actions against Palestinians. Günther Jikeli finds a similar pattern of antisemitic discourse among European Muslim youths, who "explicitly said that they do not see any differences. The Israelis were described as 'the Jews' and generalizations were drawn from Israel to all Jews."[58] Third, as a consequence, the Israeli-Palestinian conflict is seen as a war between Jews and Muslims. As Jikeli notes, "Israel is portrayed as evil, represented by cruel soldiers, and Palestinians are seen as poor and innocent."[59] Fourth, the prolonged conflict between Israel and Palestine has led a number of Indonesian Muslims as well as Muslims around the world to perceive the conflict as an attack on their religion. By stressing the influence of the Israeli intelligence agencies on world politics, they have come to see the whole world as a threat and obstacle to the Muslim *ummah*.

While Jews have often been presented as rich, influential, and powerful, my informants rarely used Jews' ethnic identity to justify their hatred against them. Religious identity was used more often than ethnic identity. When asked why he or she aligned with Palestinians, my respondent would say, "Obviously, as a Muslim, I side with another Muslim to defend our religion." Palestinians are seen first and foremost as members of the Muslim nation. Thus, the Middle Eastern conflict is conflated with the enmity between Jews and Muslims. However, absent from the Indonesian framing of the conflict in religious terms is a direct reference to foundational texts of Islam or the depiction of conflicts with Jews in history. No one makes references to the polemics of the Qur'an against Jews, for instance, or the Prophet's conflict with Jews in Medina. It seems that modern antisemitism in Indonesia is mostly expressed in terms of hostility toward Israel in which Indonesians conflate Jews with Israelis in the context of the Middle Eastern conflict. It must be added that antisemitism was present in Indonesia even before the establishment of Israel. While the negative views of Jews with reference to the Israeli-Palestinian conflict seem to suggest that there has been a Middle Eastern influence on antisemitic discourses in Indonesia, antisemitism in the Arab Middle East also preceded its conflict with Israel, as will be discussed in the following section.

SOURCES OF ANTISEMITISM

It is worth noting that the nonexistence of diplomatic relations between Indonesia and Israel has a long history. The country's first president, Sukarno, adopted a zealously anti-colonial foreign policy, which is manifested in the first paragraph of the country's constitution of 1945: "Whereas independence is the inalienable right of all nations, therefore, all colonialism must be abolished in this world as it is not in conformity with humanity and justice."[60] Because Israel is viewed as a colonizer of Palestine, the Indonesian government refuses to recognize Israel, despite the fact that Israel recognized Indonesia after Indonesia's independence. Sukarno's opposition was expressed openly during the Asian-African Conference in 1955, known as the "Bandung Conference," whose purpose was to discuss peace and the role of the Third World in the Cold War, economic development, and decolonization. Moreover, in 1962, at the behest of Arab Middle Eastern allies, the Indonesian government refused to issue entry visas for Israeli athletes to participate in the Asian Games.[61]

In the early New Order period, President Suharto reoriented Indonesian foreign policy and brought about a closer partnership with the United States. Relations between Indonesia and Israel slowly improved. Following Israel's victories in the 1967 Arab-Israeli War, Suharto's stand toward Israel softened, as exemplified by arms and commercial deals between the two countries. He was perhaps impressed by Israeli military capabilities. To counteract domestic and Middle Eastern opposition, Suharto displayed diplomatic skills by sending his foreign minister, Adam Malik, to several Arab countries in 1972 to reassure them of Indonesia's support for the Palestinian cause. Malik expressed his willingness to allow the PLO (Palestine Liberation Organization) to open an office in Jakarta. At the same time, Indonesia began to establish cooperation with Israel. In the late 1970s, Indonesia purchased sixteen A4 fighter-bombers and eleven helicopters from the Israeli Air Force.[62] Perhaps the most significant breakthrough occurred in 1993 after the signing of the Oslo Accords, when Prime Minister Yitzhak Rabin visited Suharto at his home in Jakarta. Despite years of positive signals, including bilateral trade agreements and the visits of several key NGO leaders such as Abdurrahman Wahid, the chairman of Nahdlatul Ulama (NU) and later president of Indonesia, productive Israeli-Indonesian relations remain unlikely.

Domestic political considerations will likely keep Indonesia from rapprochement with Israel, even though some Arab countries have begun to normalize relations with Israel. According to a 2017 BBC World Service Poll, 64 percent of Indonesians viewed Israel's influence negatively, compared to only 9 percent who expressed a positive view.[63] Several Islamic groups have criticized the current government for being insufficiently attentive to the Islamist agenda. As a reaction to the growing conservatism in the country, President Jokowi decided to choose a conservative Muslim cleric, Ma'ruf Amin, as his vice president when seeking reelection in 2019. This situation, coupled with the rise of religious intolerance, will keep popular anti-Israel sentiment high. As a result, Indonesians are often more intransigent in their opposition to normalization than are the former Arab adversaries of Israel. The political analyst Johannes Nugroho is correct when he says: "While Indonesia's status as a middle power means that it cannot realistically hope to effect real strides in resolving the Israeli-Palestinian conflict, its politicians continue to use the issue conveniently to score points with the Muslim majority."[64]

It is commonly assumed that the Arab-Israel conflict is the cause of antisemitism in the Middle East. However, antisemitism existed in the Arab Middle East before the establishment of Israel. The question of whether antisemitic attitudes among Arab Muslims are the cause of their hostility toward Israel or whether the Arab enmity toward Israel is rather a phenomenon resulting from the conflict is debatable.[65] While the Middle Eastern conflict is certainly a fuel igniting the intensity of antisemitism, no single factor in and of itself has necessarily led to antisemitic attitudes. Before identifying some factors that have influenced these attitudes, it can be argued that antisemitism existed in Indonesia long prior to Indonesia's independence in 1945 (and, obviously, before the establishment of Israel). According to Jeffrey Hadler, antisemitism was introduced to Indonesia by European Nazi sympathizers as a reaction to pro-Zionist Jews in the Dutch East Indies in the 1930s. In the early twentieth century, a number of Jews attempted to establish Zionist organizations to connect with the global Zionist movement, such as the Nederlands Indie Zionistenbond (The Netherlands-Indies Union of Zionists) and the Vereenging van Joodsche Belangen (Association of Jewish Affairs). The first Zionist newspaper, *Erets Israel*, ran for thirteen years, from 1926 to 1939, and often published local features on Jewish holiday-making and less Zionist propaganda. Inspired by the Zionists, the Association for Jewish Interests in the Netherlands Indies (Vereeniging voor Joodsche Belangen in Nederlandsche Indie) was founded in 1927.[66] These Zionist activities, according to Hadler, served as a trigger for the arrival of Nazis in the Dutch East Indies, a theory that has been challenged by Eva Mirela Suciu, who argues that Nazism in the Dutch East Indies arrived independently of local Zionist activities.[67]

Another source of exposure to antisemitism was the propaganda against Jews disseminated by the Japanese Empire. As discussed earlier, the Japanese adopted some Nazi anti-Jewish propaganda and introduced the idea of a global Jewish conspiracy to Indonesians. The effect of Japanese propaganda seems to have been long-lasting and to have had a deep impact on Indonesian leaders; the latter looked at the Japanese as possible liberators from Western imperialism. An interest in Japan predated Japanese advances in Indonesia. Following the Russo-Japanese War (1904–5), many Indonesian Muslims sided with Japan for two reasons. First, Russia was viewed unfavorably due to its hostility toward the Ottoman Empire. Second, in contrast to Russia, Japan did not show antagonism to Islam, perhaps in order to win the hearts and minds of Muslims.[68] In fact, during Japan's occupation of the archipelago, the Japanese sought to win allies among Muslim leaders. In particular, they exploited the deep resentment against the Dutch and presented themselves as liberators and defenders of Indonesian Islam. Thus, they created the long-established anti-Westernism as a common thread between them and the colonized people.[69] While some of Indonesia's key national figures were rightly skeptical of the intentions of Japan, Japanese propaganda against Jews has had a profound impact on Indonesians' antisemitic attitudes.[70]

Despite the fact that antisemitism existed in Indonesia before its independence, contemporary antisemitic discourse has mostly taken the form of anti-Israel sentiments fomented by Middle Eastern literature. It goes without saying that antisemitism has been attractive to Middle Easterners for a number of reasons. First, Muslim scripture includes several passages that describe Jews negatively. For instance, Jews (or Israelites) are portrayed as disobeying God (Q 2:93), rejecting their own covenant (Q 2:100; 5:12), failing to follow their own Torah (Q 5:66), and distorting or twisting the meaning of the divine revelation they received (Q 2:101, 174). Muslim scripture also uses the language of the curse to condemn Jews (Q 2:88; 4:51–52; 5:12), and on occasion it calls on believers to fight them (Q 9:29). These negative portrayals of Jews should not necessarily lead one to think of the Qur'an as being "antisemitic," since all scriptures, be they the Qur'an, the Hebrew Bible, or the New Testament, include a significant amount of negative rhetoric directed against the communities they considered threatening.[71] However, those polemical passages have been understood by some Muslims to support their antisemitic rhetoric. In addition to the foundational texts, other alleged sources of Muslim hatred of Jews include references to historical narratives of the past to show the rivalry between Muslims and Jews. However, as Mark Cohen has shown, Jews were treated much better under the crescent than under the cross in the Middle Ages.[72]

The second source of antisemitism in the Middle East is Nazi propaganda that has been disseminated since the 1920s. Several studies show the fascist attraction to Middle Eastern leaders as due, in part, to their shared antagonism toward Britain and France. In his *Nazi Propaganda for the Arab World*, Jeffrey Herf argues that Nazi propagandists tried to prevent "British influence and . . . the Zionist project in the Middle East,"[73] partly by "export[ing] the regime's ideology in ways that they hoped would strike a nerve among Arabs and Muslims."[74] Herf also shows close links and similarities between Nazism and Islamism in their hatred of Jews. For his part, Matthias Küntzel contends that modern antisemitic attitudes were unknown to the Arab world until they were imported from Nazi Germany by the mufti of Jerusalem, al-Ḥajj Amīn al-Ḥusaynī, and the Egyptian Muslim Brotherhood.[75] Perhaps, the most comprehensive treatment of the close connection between Nazi Germany and the Arab world is that composed by Klaus-Michael Mallmann and Martin Cüppers titled *Halbmond und Hakenkreuz: Das Dritte Reich, die Araber und Palästina.*[76] This book examines, among other things, the role the mufti of Jerusalem played in transporting antisemitism and also the Nazi policy change from supporting German Jewish emigration to Palestine to supporting Arab opposition to Zionism.

Other scholars call into question this seemingly close link between Nazism and Arab nationalism/Islamism, with antisemitism the common denominator. In his 2012 article titled "The Arabs as Nazis?," Alexander Flores argues that there is no solid evidence to show that "a massive majority of Arabs took a pro-Nazi stand during the Third Reich and especially during World War II."[77] Tracing the root of today's Arab antisemitism to Nazi Germany is, according to Flores, "an enormous distortion of the origins and history of Arab anti-Semitism."[78] He believes that antisemitism entered the Arab world before its encounter with fascism. Flores writes, "It is true that explicit anti-Semitism European style is relatively new in the Middle East. It was imported from Europe, but the import began long before Küntzel claims it did."[79] Flores makes no assertion as to when exactly European-style antisemitism entered the Arab world. It is Richard Breitman who argues that antisemitism was imported by Christians from Europe before World War I. He writes:

European Christians brought modern forms of anti-Semitism into some Arab communities during the nineteenth century. Monks and European authorities living in the Middle East spread accusations of Jewish ritual murder, which led to sporadic outbursts of violence in Damascus and other cities. Direct contact between Christians and Muslims, I believe, was of considerable significance in transferring implausible charges against Jews and instilling intense emotions—creating extreme anti-Semites.[80]

At any rate, religious prejudice and mistrust marked not only relations between Muslims and non-Muslims, but also those between Christians and Jews. Throughout much of European history, Christian authorities sustained antisemitism, which was then exported to the Arab Middle East. As Gudrun Krämer puts it succinctly, "Core features of Christian anti-Judaism and modern anti-Semitism entered the Middle East through contact with Europe, be it that visitors from the Middle East became acquainted with them during their stay in Europe, be it that Europeans brought them to their countries."[81] Anti-Jewish and antisemitic materials and texts were transmitted and translated into non-European languages, including Arabic. Research on the dissemination of European antisemitic sources in the Arab world mostly focuses on the *Protocols of the Elders of Zion* and Hitler's *Mein Kampf* and their Arabic translations. *Mein Kampf* has never been fully translated into Arabic, in part because of the racist attitude of Hitler toward non-"Aryan" people. In *Mein Kampf*, Breitman writes, "Hitler had written insultingly about Arab peoples and had dismissed the idea of working with such racial inferiors."[82] Partial Arabic translations of *Mein Kampf* appeared in Beirut, Baghdad, and Cairo, but those translations "had failed to produce an Arabic translation of *Mein Kampf* which satisfied the standards of the German authorities," according to Stefan Wild.[83] The translator of the Arabic edition in Cairo, 'Alī Muḥammad Maḥbūb, often mistranslated phrases from the German original version. Although Hitler is reported to have given permission to change the derogatory racial remarks of *Mein Kampf*, as Stefan notes, "The report that the Egyptian translator had suppressed passages in his translation which implied Arab racial inferiority reached other areas of the Arab world and was an obstacle to German propaganda."[84]

Unlike *Mein Kampf*, *The Protocols of the Elders of Zion* has enjoyed remarkable success in terms of its reception among Arab Middle Easterners. *The Protocols* represents what Rochard Landes and Steven T. Katz refer to as "one of the most malicious forgeries in history—'an atrocity-producing narrative'—and the most widely distributed forgery in the world."[85] The booklet, written by an unnamed author and first published in 1905, recounts the alleged secret protocols from the first Zionist Congress in Basel in 1897 describing the plans of Jewish leaders to dominate the world. Written as a first person-narrative, the twenty-four sections of *The Protocols* begin with the seemingly candid discussion of how a secret Jewish cabal aimed at conquering the Christian world through the control of politics, media, and the marketplace. Soon after it was brought by Russian émigrés to western Europe and the United States in the 1920s, *The Protocols* became a global sensation, with millions of copies circulated by "propagandists and others who searched for conspiratorial explanations of the massive national, industrial, and urban changes that were taking place around them."[86] The first German translation appeared in 1920s, published by Theodor Fritsch, and it reached its thirteenth printing in 1933, after which the edition published by the Nazi Party dominated the market.[87]

The Protocols first appeared in Arabic translation in Palestine in 1921, although it may have reached there a few years earlier.[88] The earliest Arabic translations were done by Christians, including the priest Antūn Yamīn, who translated it from French in Cairo in the mid-1920s under the title *Mu'āmarāt al-Yahūdiyyah 'alā al-Shu'ūb* (Jewish Plots against the Nations).[89] Esther Webman writes: "By the 1967 Six Day War, at least nine Arabic translations had been printed, and between 1965 and 1967 fifty political books based on *The Protocols* were issued in Egypt alone."[90] Arguably, the Arab defeat during the Six-Day War and subsequent conflicts have intensified Arab and Muslim reliance on this inflammatory text, leading to a spate of antisemitic expressions using religious language. *The Protocols* is now used to explain the perception that Jews have power not only to establish Israel and rule the world but, more specifically, to disperse and divide the Muslim *ummah*. Newer Arabic translations of *The Protocols* continue to surface. In 2002, Akhbār al-Yaum, a respected publishing house in Egypt, published a new translation in the *Book of the Day* series. The booklet is also serialized in newspapers, such as the Saudi weekly *Akhbār al-'ālam al-Islāmī* and the Egyptian opposition weekly *al-'Arabi*.[91] One of the most popular television series, broadcast on numerous Arab stations, is "Fāris bilā Jawād" (Knight without a Horse), based in part on *The Protocols*. This forty-one-part Egyptian production by Muhammad Subhī, advertised as a chronicle of the Arab struggle against both colonial rule and the establishment of Israel, went on air on November 6, 2002, despite protests from all over the world, in particular the United States and Israel.[92]

It is most likely that Indonesians were introduced to *The Protocols* through networks of scholars between the Middle East and Indonesia.

Aḥmad Shalabī, an Egyptian professor from al-Azhar University who in the 1950s taught at the State Institute of Islamic Studies (IAIN) in Yogyakarta (Indonesia), was one of the great admirers of *The Protocols*. His book *Muqāranāt al-Adyān: Al-Yahūdiyah* (Comparative Religions: Judaism), relies heavily on *The Protocols* for its argument. According to Martin van Bruinessen, Shalabī may have introduced *The Protocols* to Indonesians.[93] While the Indonesian translation of his book appeared only in 1990 (the Malay translation was published in 1977 in Singapore), it is not unlikely that he introduced the content of *The Protocols* to his students and the general public during his stay in the country. It is worth noting that Muhammadiyah, the second-largest Muslim organization in Indonesia, had already published its "studies" on the booklet in the 1970s. The Research Unit of the Muhammadiyah (Lembaga Penelitian dan Pengembangan Agama) published a summary of Professor Mustafa Sa'dany's work under the title "Sorotan terhadap Protokolat" (Highlights on *The Protocols*) in 1978.[94] In addition, al-Azhar, at which Shalabī studied and taught, is the most popular university for Indonesian students studying in the Middle East. In 2003, the Azhari professor Ahmad Ḥijāzī al-Saqā (along with the journalist Hishām Khadr) published a book claiming to trace the origins of *The Protocols* in Biblical and Talmudic sources, which stirred some controversies. Al-Saqā's book *Brūtūkūl ḥukamā' ṣahyūn wa uṣūluhā al-Tawrātiyyah wa'l-Talmūtiyyah* (The Protocols of the Elders of Zion and Their Biblical and Talmudic Origins), includes a foreword written by the then–grand mufti of Egypt, 'Alī Jum'ah. In the foreword, Jum'ah writes:

> If there are any disagreements over the book *The Protocols of the Elders of Zion* regarding the Jewish wise men—whether they wrote it themselves or is it only attributed to them—the plausible conclusion [is that] they [did] write it. [This conclusion] relies on the fact that its [the book's] contents coincide perfectly with the contents of the Torah, which was written with their own hands, i.e.: "That the nations and the peoples [of] them are as unclean dogs.[95]

Interestingly, about three years later, in 2007, Jum'ah denied that he ever wrote such a foreword for al-Saqā's book. In his piece published by the national newspaper *al-Ahram* (January 1, 2007) titled "Taḥdhir wājib" (A Necessary Warning), the grand muftī was not only "surprised [to discover] my name on it, with my original title—a lecturer in the esteemed university of al-Azhar," but also questioned the authenticity of *The Protocols*, saying, "The book contains no truth, as we have believed for a long time."

Notwithstanding, al-Saqā's work continues to enjoy wide readership. In addition to publishing a complete translation of *The Protocols*, al-Saqā wrote another book, titled *Ṭabā'i' al-Yahūd fī al-Tawrāh wa'l-Talmud* (The Characters of Jews in the Torah and the Talmud). In this book the author quotes verses from the Qur'an and Jewish scriptures, as well as from *The Protocols* to demonstrate the vile character of the Jews and their ambitions to take over the world, noting that the themes found in *The Protocols* are also reflected in the Torah and the Talmud. Antisemitic publications from al-Azhar University are widely circulated in Indonesia. One example is from Dr. 'Abdullah al-Thail, whose dissertation written at al-Azhar has been translated into the Indonesian language under the title *Yahudi Sang Penghancur Dunia* (Jews: The Destroyers of the World). In this publication al-Thail presents common antisemitic arguments and cites *The Protocols* extensively. Al-Azhar has become a significant source for Indonesians to consult to learn about contemporary antisemitic conspiracy theories.

Of course, Egyptian antisemites are not the only sources for Indonesians. Antisemitic literature from other Arab countries has played its own role in shaping prejudice against Jews and Israel in Indonesia. It is particularly the case of Saudi publications, whose influence in Indonesia has been increasingly more visible in the past few decades. A work of the Jordanian-born scholar Majīd al-Kailānī, *Al-Khaṭar al-Ṣahyūnī 'ala al-'Ālam al-Islāmī* (The Dangers of Zionism to the Muslim World), which was published by a Saudi publisher in 1969, appeared in Indonesian translation in 1984. This book, like that of the Azhari professor al-Saqā, introduces the common alleged scenarios involving a Jewish Zionist takeover of the world along with Biblical references.[96] Like other Arab antisemites, al-Kailānī relies heavily on *The Protocols*, with emphasis on a Jewish desire to control the world and to corrupt the Muslim nations. My quick online search shows that Kailānī's book has been cited frequently by Indonesian authors. Another outdated book that demonstrates fascination with *The Protocols* and major themes of antisemitic sentiments is the work of Palestinian scholar Muhammad Izzat Darwazah, *Al-Judhūr al-Qadīmah li-Aḥdāth Banī Isrā'il wa'l-Yahūd wa Sulūkuhum wa Akhlāquhum* (The Original Roots of Israeli and Jewish Problems: Their Attitudes and Characters), first published in 1969 in Damascus, Syria. It was translated by an Indonesian student (Hamali) at the Umm al-Qurā University in Mecca and published in 1982.[97] As Bruinessen rightly notes, none of the above-mentioned publications casts any doubt on the authenticity of *The Protocols*.[98]

It should be added that sources for the growth of antisemitic discourse in Indonesia are not limited to translations of antisemitic works that rely on the fraudulent document. Nor is antisemitic literature mainly transmitted from the Arab world. In addition to being shaped by the works of respected Muslim scholars such as Shaykh Muṣṭafā al-Marāghī, Yūsuf al-Qaraḍāwī, Jalāl 'Ālam, Muhammad Ṭanṭāwī, Muhammad Nāmir al-Khaṭīb, Ahmad 'Ustmān, and As'ad Bayuḍ al-Tamīmī,[99] Indonesian conspiracy theories about Jews have also been shaped by the works of several Western authors, such as William Carr, Jerry Gray, and Andrew Hitchcock.[100] Despite the absence of references to *The Protocols* therein, these books promote conspiracy theories and antisemitic rhetoric. When one peruses these publications, one cannot help but notice that the scope of anti-Jewish propaganda has been expanding beyond obscurantist Muslim clerics. To insist that Indonesian antisemitism stemmed purely from the Arab Middle East would be exaggerating, since the works of Western antisemites have also been translated into the Indonesian language. Of course, the forgery *The Protocols* finds popularity.

Several publications about Jewish conspiracies recently produced by Indonesian authors make frequent references to *The Protocols*. In addition to Muhammad Thalib's works mentioned earlier, many other antisemitic publications describe *The Protocols* as a blueprint for Jewish domination that allows for the exploitation and mistreatment of all non-Jews. Like their Arab counterparts, Indonesian authors seldom raise questions concerning the authenticity of the forged text. As Ibnu Burdah notes, Indonesian authors continue "reproducing *The Protocols* by quoting, multiplying, expounding, and emphasizing it without taking into account the opinions that say that *The Protocols* are a forgery."[101] Ibnu Burdah goes on, arguing that "the absence of adequate discussion on the authenticity of *The Protocols* simply reinforces the perception of the existence of a

Jewish conspiracy that threatens Muslims."[102] Most Arab authors simply ignore the issue of authenticity because it does not matter whether *The Protocols* was written to discredit Jews or not. Adopting the ostensibly neutral stand, the Egyptian 'Abbās Maḥmūd al-'Aqqād contends that even if *The Protocols* is counterfeit, the fact of the matter is that "all decisions taken by the elders of Zion have been implemented literally in different parts of the world during the twentieth century since the book appeared."[103] It is true that, although following the controversy over the anti-Jewish television series the authenticity of *The Protocols* began to be questioned,[104] that has not caused Muslim attraction to it to cease.

Of course, antisemitic discourse among Indonesian authors extends beyond their reliance on *The Protocols*. Some authors address specific concerns in the country, including political and economic liberalization, and accuse international Jewish networks of manipulating human rights issues for their own advantage. In his *Membongkar Jaringan Bisnis Yahudi di Indonesia* (Exposing the Networks of Jewish Business in Indonesia), Anton Ramdan contends that Jewish corporations have been able to control the Indonesian marketplace through their deceitful tactics, lobbying, and capital.[105] Others blame their opponents, especially political leaders, for being powerless to stand up against the Jewish domination. Eggi Sudjana and J. W. Lotz, for instance, accuse former president Susilo Bambang Yudhoyono (SBY) of being an agent of American Jews.[106] While these are not serious publications, there is almost no scholarly discussion on Jews or Zionism in Indonesia, despite the fact that the "Jewish/Israeli issue" has been a source of interest. This lack of scholarly attention is, perhaps, due to the fact that Judaism is not recognized as an official religion. As Judaism is generally not the subject of study in religious textbooks, no balanced or alternative views are presented to the public, readers, and students.

When speaking to students in Indonesia I found that most have never heard of *The Protocols*, although its main argument for Jewish power and control in the world seems to be widely circulated among them. This suggests that the major themes of anti-Jewish conspiracy theories have been adopted by the Indonesian public and become part of their antisemitic discourse. The three recurring themes I identified from my interviews echo the sentiments of *The Protocols*: Jews are seen to be intelligent and powerful in a global context; they are also perceived to be deceitful and aggressive. Similarly, Israel is seen as an aggressor or colonizer, supported by the United States in its suppression of weaker powers. Undoubtedly, the content of antisemitic literature pervades the overwhelmingly negative views of Jews and Israel held by Indonesian youth.

CONCLUDING REMARKS

In this chapter I have discussed Indonesian perceptions of Jews and Israel despite the lack of a Jewish presence and have traced the sources of antisemitism to both the colonial period and Middle Eastern influence. James Siegel and Jeffrey Hadler refer to Indonesia as a case of antisemitism without Jews.[107] The fear of "the imagined Jew" projected by Indonesians shows their continued struggle to situate themselves within a global society that is continuously changed by foreign influences. In antisemitic discourse, Jews are seen as politically powerful and economically influential. Authors of antisemitic materials in the Middle East and Indonesia develop conspiracy theories about Jews and every other conceivable foreign influence not only to support their image of a global Jewish conspiracy, but also to promote various stereotypes of Jews. Among Indonesians, a strong belief in a global Jewish conspiracy correlates with both hatred toward Israel and simultaneous support for Palestine. Opposing Israel and siding with Palestine in the Israeli-Palestinian conflict is not necessarily antisemitic. However, much anti-Israel activity crosses the line to antisemitism when it invokes Jewish stereotypes or includes traditional antisemitic imagery, such as portraying Israel or Israelis as part of a Jewish conspiracy to dominate the world. It is in this context that Indonesian antisemitism seems to take a new form. Instead of openly expressing hostility toward Jewish people, Indonesians tend to express such sentiments by being anti-Israel.

Students I interviewed for this study developed perceptions of Jews that resonate with *The Protocols*, even though they may not have read this forgery. The influence of *The Protocols* pervades mainstream Indonesian thinking to a certain extent, because Jews are generally seen in a negative light. There is no single factor to account for why antisemitism is strong in Indonesia. While the seeds of antisemitism must have been planted before Indonesia's independence through the arrival of Nazi sympathizers during the Dutch occupation and the Japanese propaganda against Jews thereafter, modern antisemitism in Indonesia developed because of both internal and external factors. Internally, state negligence to recognize Judaism and the lack of diplomatic relations with the Jewish state imply that discriminatory attitudes toward Jews receive no attention. The country's growing religious conservatism has certainly contributed to the spread of antisemitic sentiment. The external factor in the spread of antisemitism is related to the ways in which Middle Eastern antisemitic literature has been transmitted to Indonesia through scholarly networks that make the translation of Arabic works possible. It is worth noting that in Indonesian antisemitic discourse, the Islamic aspects of the arguments are largely left out, which seems to suggest that modern antisemitism is primarily politically motivated.[108]

Conclusion and Suggestions
for Future Research

The data I have provided in this book and my analysis of the recent scholarship show that educational institutions have become potentially risky areas where students could be drawn into radical networks by active recruiters. Warnings about the attractiveness of school and university students as potential recruits, and of university campuses as places for radical groups to spread their ideologies, have featured in worldwide discussions about contemporary terrorist threats. Both in the United States and in Europe, especially the United Kingdom, several studies have explored how certain groups have exploited this pool of educated individuals by recruiting them into organizations regarded as terrorist organizations, or galvanized them into joining radical groups, and thus given rise to concerns about universities as breeding grounds for terrorism in policy circles.[1] Similarly, in Indonesia, the National Agency for Combating Terrorism (BNPT, Badan Nasional Penanggulangan Terorisme) has been active in preventing youth, including university students, from falling into the hands of terrorists. Recently the Ministry of Religious Affairs has also developed various initiatives to resist the wave of radicalization among Indonesian youth, including the establishment of a "Religious Moderation House" (Rumah Moderasi Beragama) on every state university campus. Given the global character of student radicalism, the findings reported in this book will contribute to an ongoing discussion about the relationship of education to radicalization. One obvious contribution of this book is that it provides empirical evidence on this relationship and indicates that the link is quite complicated. Another significant contribution consists of identifying some manifestations of religious intolerance and radicalism among the youth.

The first three chapters focus on high school students and the ways in which they navigated encounters with diversity and pluralism, be they religious, cultural, racial, ethnic, ideological, or something other. Chapter 1 discusses the research findings that school-aged adolescents tended to embrace religious tolerance half-heartedly, which is evident in their strong support for engagement with people of other faiths as well as their rejection of Islamic radicalism, but when it came to sensitive issues such as non-Muslim leadership in a Muslim society, they tended to hold back. That chapter investigates views of students toward the other and the extent to which interreligious contact or a lack thereof transformed their attitudes toward religious tolerance. Chapter 2 examines the role of social networks, including friends, parents, schoolteachers, and religious preachers, in shaping the views of young people toward the other. Compared to demographic issues such as ethnicity, religion, race, or ideology, the findings show that common interests, hobbies, worldviews, and social compatibility seemed to be more important considerations in the social relationships of youth. Additionally, interactions with non-formal religious authorities outside of schools and with social media played important roles in shaping students' views and attitudes of openness or hostility toward others. Chapter 3 addresses the question of civility and incivility among high school students. This study showed the fragility of their views toward the other, which is evident in the prevalence of bullying against minority groups, including the leveling of stereotypes against ethnic Chinese.

The next three chapters explore the phenomenon of religious radicalization among university students. Chapter 4 illuminates how educated youth became radicalized in the first place or how they converted to radical ideologies. On the basis of their own testimonies, I identify common patterns of their conversion experiences, which can help us better understand the driving forces of radicalization. Insights developed in this chapter can also contribute to a possible refinement of our conceptualization of the contested term "radicalization." Chapter 5 identifies those students who have been attracted to radical ideologies as "newbies" because they recently embraced a radical viewpoint and were not firmly grounded in an extreme religious viewpoint that justified militant attitudes and violent actions. The findings of this study call into question the presumed causal connection between radicalization and violent terrorism. Chapter 6 navigates the way in which self-radicalization among educated youth took place. This study shows that their exposure to extremist religious ideologies led them to question the impact of their involvement in the radical networks on themselves and others. As a result, they deradicalized themselves without necessarily subscribing to the kind of religious understanding promoted by the state.

The final two chapters examine the role the internet has played in shaping the views of high school and university students, as well as their attitudes toward antisemitic discourse. Chapter 7 demonstrates that the internet and numerous social media platforms have significantly impacted students, although they are not the only factors that drove youth toward religious intolerance and radicalism. Unlike other studies, this research shows that the dichotomy between online and offline or top-down and bottom-up influences is not as straightforward as has generally been assumed. One of the key findings discussed in this chapter is that university students were more susceptible to radical ideas than high school students. Various explanations have been offered to account for such an interesting phenomenon. The final chapter further illustrates how religious intolerance and radicalism among youth resonates with the tendency of Indonesian Muslims toward religious conservatism. The Israeli-Palestinian conflict has often been viewed as a religious war to enhance Muslim solidarity with the Palestinians and reinforce hatred of Jews and Israel. While the influence of Middle Eastern antisemitic literature should not be overlooked, Islamic arguments against Jews in the Indonesian antisemitic rhetoric are not as dominant as have generally been assumed.

As in other parts of the world, religious intolerance and radicalism in Indonesia are causes for state concern. Although in this book I have attempted to situate the findings of my study alongside broader debates concerning the nature of radicalization and deradicalization, I did not make any attempt to examine the efficacy of either state or non-state interventions to counter youth radicalization. My research does not go as far as to explore preventive measures against radicalization through education. There is no question that universities—across a range of national settings—have been both sites of radical political activity and arenas in which states have intervened and surveilled for the purpose of public safety and security.[2] In the United Kingdom, for instance, the British Parliament passed the Counter-Terrorism and Security Act in 2015, including the creation of a legal duty to prevent people from being drawn into terrorism that is applied to a range of public institutions, including institutions of higher education. A key pillar within the U.K. counter-terrorism strategy is the counter-radicalization initiative known as Prevent, which is comprised of what Catherine McGlynn and Shaun McDaid refer to as "a mixture of educational and community initiatives conceived with the aim of building capacities within communities to deter radicalization as a pathway to violence."[3] Similarly, in the same year, as Mayssoun Sukarieh and Stuart Tannock report, "Over ninety educators from across Europe met at a conference on radicalization and education in Manchester, where they drafted a *Manifesto for Education* as a 'call for action' for schools in Europe to work together to prevent radicalization of students."[4] Since then, several studies have examined the role of the state interventions in preventing radicalization at European universities.[5]

At the heart of these studies is how education is positioned in the current concerns about security and extremism. On the one hand, critics of state interventions argue that such measures could lead to "undue state interference in an arena where it is perfectly normal for radical, and even potentially offensive ideas, to be explored, debated or researched."[6] On the other hand, advocates of university counter-radicalization initiatives like McGlynn and McDaid contend that "it is particularly important to have policies and procedures in place during what for many young adults is a transitional period in their lives."[7] Thus schools and universities have become a key site of contestation in the debates about radicalization and deradicalization initiatives. Given the implications of these counter-radicalization strategies for schools and universities, further research needs to be done on the kinds of initiatives that have been introduced into educational institutions in Indonesia and their effectiveness. To what extent can education counter religious radicalism? Or under what circumstances can certain counter-radicalization initiatives be effective in halting violent radicalization processes?

It should be noted that counter-terrorism initiatives in Indonesia have been relatively successful in preventing major terrorist attacks. The law on counter-terrorism that was amended in 2018 has strengthened the powers of the BNPT to take a strong lead and coordinate initiatives among all relevant stakeholders, including youth. It is worth noting, however, that most studies on counter-radicalization in Indonesia, including the BNPT counter-terrorism strategies, are not concerned with anti-radicalization policies in education.[8] There is little doubt that anti-radicalization policies are imposed on schools and higher education institutions in the country. Schools and universities are required to actively promote civic education and Indonesian values in their teaching and curricula and to keep an eye on signs of radical tendencies in students. In the past few years, mosque activities on campuses have also been under close monitoring by university leadership.

It remains to be studied how and to what extent these counter-radicalization measures have been able to address key factors that may lead youth to radicalization in the first place. Of course, educational institutions can become recruiting grounds for extremism. As this book has shown, radical groups have been targeting campuses to disseminate extremist ideology. It should come as little surprise, therefore, that the government has regarded schools and universities as an arena for scrutiny, which complicates the common wisdom that educational institutions are seen as arenas in which free speech and expression should be the norm and no one can play the role of "thought police." I believe it is necessary for us to reexamine the relationship between education and radicalization/deradicalization and to think creatively about how to safeguard young people without compromising civil rights in educational institutions.

NOTES

INTRODUCTION

1. Mayssoun Sukarieh and Stuart Tannock, "The Deradicalization of Education: Terror, Youth, and the Assault on Learning," *Race and Class* 57, no. 4 (2015): 22–38.

2. Ibid., 25. For a discussion on mixed reactions to Britain's Prevent program, see, for instance, Paul Thomas, "Youth, Terrorism and Education: Britain's Prevent Programmes," *International Journal of Lifelong Education* 35, no. 1 (2016): 171–87; Catherine McGlynn and Shaun McDaid, "Radicalisation and Higher Education: Students' Understanding and Experience," *Terrorism and Political Violence* 31, no. 3 (2019): 559–76.

3. Reflecting on the existing literature, Jamie Bartlett and Carl Miller write, "Research on radicalization, acting on each or many of these levels, has however often focused solely on the small number of known terrorists from which most conclusions about the conditions likely to conduce their actions are drawn, omitting a comparison group of non-terrorist radicals." See Bartlett and Miller, "The Edge of Violence: Towards Telling the Difference between Violent and Non-Violent Radicalization," *Terrorism and Political Violence* 24 (2012): 1–21; 1. They suggest that a distinction needs to be made between radicalization that leads to violence and radicalization that does not lead to violence. The former is a process by which individuals come to undertake or directly aid or abet terrorist activity, and the latter refers to the process by which individuals come to hold radical views about the status quo but do not undertake, aid, or abet terrorist activity.

4. *Pancasila* is the official ideology of the Indonesian state. The word means "five principles," namely, monotheism, humanitarianism, unity, democracy, and justice.

5. Cameron Sumpter, "Countering Violent Extremism in Indonesia: Priorities, Practice and the Role of Civil Society," *Journal for Deradicalization* 11 (2017): 112–46.

6. Clifford Geertz, *The Religion of Java* (Chicago: University of Chicago Press, 1960).

7. M. C. Ricklefs, *A History of Modern Indonesia since c. 1200* (London: Palgrave, 2001).

8. Lilis Sri Handayani, "Jumlah Madrasah Negeri Masih Minim," *Republika*, September 14, 2018. See https://republika.co.id/berita/pf10gi366/jumlah-madrasah-negeri-masih-minim.

9. Ibid.

10. Agung Purwadi and Suhero Muljoatmodjo, "Education in Indonesia: Coping with Challenges in the Third Millennium," *Journal of Southeast Asian Education* 1, no. 1 (2000): 79–102.

11. Badan Pusat Statistik, "Jumlah Sekolah, Guru, dan Murid Madrasah Aliyah (MA) di Bawah Kementerian Agama Menurut Provinsi, 2019/2020." See https://www.bps.go.id/indikator/indikator/view_data_pub/0000/api_pub/80/da_04/1.

12. Lyn Parker and R. Raihani, "Democratizing Indonesia through Education? Community Participation in Islamic Schooling," *Educational Management Administration and Leadership* 39, no. 6 (2011): 712–32; 716.

13. Muhammad Zuhri, "The 1975 Three-Minister Decree and the Modernization of Indonesian Islamic Schools," *American Educational History Journal* 32, no. 1 (2005): 36–43; 39.

14. Robert Kingham and Jemma Parsons, "Integrating Islamic Schools into the Indonesian National Education System: A Case of Architecture over Implementation," in *Education in Indonesia*, ed. Daniel Suryadarma and Gavin W. Jones, 68–81 (Singapore: Institute of Southeast Asian Studies, 2013), 79.

15. Badan Pusat Statistik, "Jumlah Perguruan Tinggi, Mahasiswa dan Tenaga Pendidik." See https://www.bps.go.id/indikator/indikator/view_data_pub/0000/api_pub/82/da_04/1.

16. Ian Whitman and Team of Review of National Policies for Education, *Education in Indonesia: Rising to the Challenge* (Paris: OECD Publishing, 2015), 184.

17. Daniel Suryadarma and Gavin W. Jones, "Meeting the Education Challenge," in *Education in Indonesia*, ed. Suryadarma and Jones, 1–14 (Singapore: Institute of Southeast Asian Studies, 2013), 10.

18. Rivandra Royono and Diastika Rahwidiati, "Beating the Odds: Locally Relevant Alternatives to World-Class Universities," in *Education in Indonesia*, ed. Daniel Suryadarma and Gavin Jones, 180–202 (Singapore: Institute of Southeast Asian Studies, 2013), 197.

19. Hal Hill and Thee Kian Wie, "Indonesian Universities: Rapid Growth, Major Challenges," in *Education in Indonesia*, ed. Daniel Suryadarma

and Gavin W. Jones, 160–79 (Singapore: Institute of Southeast Asian Studies, 2013), 165.

20. According to the *Review of National Policies for Education*: Annually thirty thousand Indonesian higher education students study abroad, about 0.8 percent of the total, compared with 6.1 percent for Malaysia, 0.9 percent for Thailand, and 1.9 percent for Vietnam. There are about three thousand international students in Indonesia, an inbound mobility rate of 0.1 percent compared with 3.3 percent in Malaysia, 0.5 percent in Thailand, and 0.2 percent in Vietnam (figures from Irandoust, 2014). See Ian Whitman and Team of Review of National Policies for Education, *Education in Indonesia: Rising to the Challenge* (Paris: OECD Publishing, 2015), 197.

21. Hill and Wie, "Indonesian Universities," 168.

22. See https://www.topuniversities.com/university-rankings/asian -university-rankings/.

23. John W. Creswell and Vicki L. Plano Clark, *Designing and Conducting Mixed Methods Research* (Thousand Oaks, CA: SAGE Publications, 2011); Charles Teddlie and Abbas Tashakkori, *Foundations of Mixed Methods Research: Integrating Qualitative and Quantitative Approaches in the Social and Behavioral Sciences* (Thousand Oaks, CA: SAGE Publications, 2009); Bronwyn Hall and Kirsten Howard, "A Synergistic Approach: Conducting Mixed Methods Research with Typological and Systemic Design Considerations," *Journal of Mixed Methods Research* 2, no. 3 (2008): 1–22.

24. Alan Bryman, "Integrating Quantitative and Qualitative Research: How Is It Done?" *Qualitative Research* 6, no. 1 (2006), 97–113; 106. For a more detailed discussion, see David L. Morgan, *Integrating Qualitative and Quantitative Methods: A Pragmatic Approach* (Thousand Oaks, CA: SAGE Publications, 2014).

25. According to Edmund Husserl, phenomenology examines the perception of what the objective and cognitive elements mean to the individuals. See Husserl, *The Phenomenology of Internal Time-Consciousness*, trans. James S. Churchill (Bloomington: Indiana University Press, 1964). Jonathan Smith, Paul Flowers, and Michael Larkin define phenomenology "as a philosophical approach to the study of experience … [that] shares a particular interest in thinking about what the experience of being human is like, in all of its various aspects, but especially in terms of the things that matter to us, and which constitute our lived world." See Smith, Flowers, and Larkin, *Interpretative Phenomenological Analysis: Theory, Method, and Research* (London: SAGE Publications, 2009), 11.

26. The grounded theory, a qualitative design developed by Barney G. Glaser and Anselm L. Strauss in *The Discovery of Grounded Theory: Strategies for Qualitative Research* (Chicago: Aldine Publishing, 1967), is intended to

generate data that will generate a theory. According to Danica G. Hays and Chris Wood, "The purpose of a grounded theory approach is to generate data that is based or grounded in participant experiences and perspectives with the ultimate goal of theory development." See Hays and Wood, "Infusing Qualitative Traditions in Counseling Research Designs," *Journal of Counseling and Development* 89, no. 3 (2011), 288–95; 288.

27. Lynn Davies, "Educating against Extremism: Towards a Critical Politicisation of Young People," *International Review of Education* 55, nos. 2–3 (2008): 183–203.

28. Marc Sageman, *Understanding Terror Networks* (Philadelphia: University of Pennsylvania Press, 2004), 75.

29. Ibid., 76.

30. Diego Gambetta and Steffen Hertog, *Engineers of Jihad: The Curious Connection between Violent Extremism and Education* (Princeton, NJ: Princeton University Press, 2016), 33.

31. Mitchell D. Silber and Arvin Bhatt, *Radicalization in the West: The Homegrown Threat* (New York: New York City Police Department, 2007).

32. Alan B. Krueger and Jitka Maleckova, *Education, Poverty, Political Violence and Terrorism: Is There a Causal Connection?* (Cambridge, MA: National Bureau of Economic Research, 2002).

33. See Olawale Ismail, "Radicalisation and Violent Extremism in West Africa: Implications for African and International Security," *Conflict Security and Development* 31, no. 2 (2013): 209–30.

34. For a discussion of these theories, see Mina Al-Lami, "Studies of Radicalization: State of the Field Report," Politics and International Working Paper, University of London, 2009.

35. Diab M. Al-Badayneh, "University under Risk: The University as Incubator for Radicalization," in *Multi-Faceted Approach to Radicalization in Terrorist Organizations*, ed. Ihsan Bal, Suleyman Ozeren, and Mehmet Sozer (Clifton, VA: IOS Press, 2011), 32–41.

36. In 2007, Greg Fealy wrote a short piece in *Inside Indonesia*, titled "Conservative Turn," in which he discussed religious trends that unravel the recent development in the country, such as the closure of unregistered churches; attacks on the Ahmadi community; the election of conservative Muslim figures in the two largest Muslim organizations, Nahdlatul Ulama (NU) and Muhammadiyah; and the passing of shari'ah-based regulations in local districts. See Fealy, "Conservative Turn," *Inside Indonesia*, July 15, 2007. Six years later, Martin van Bruinessen published an edited volume titled *Contemporary Developments in Indonesian Islam: Explaining the "Conservative Turn"* (Singapore: Institute of Southeast Asian Studies, 2013).

CHAPTER 1

1. See https://www.pewresearch.org/religion/2014/01/14/religious -hostilities-reach-six-year-high/. For detailed discussions on the Pew Research Center's findings, see, for instance, Brian J. Grim and Roger Finke, *The Price of Freedom Denied: Religious Persecution and Conflict in the 21st Century* (New York: Cambridge University Press, 2010).

2. See Natalia Widiasari, "Media Reviews," *Asian Politics and Policy* 10, no. 1 (2018): 145–49; Dicky Sofjan, "Religious Diversity and Politico-Religious Intolerance in Indonesia and Malaysia," *Review of Faith and International Affairs* 14, no. 4 (2016): 53–64; Ihsan Ali-Fauzi, Samsu Rizal Panggabean, Nathanael Gratias Sumaktoyo, Husni Mubarak, Anick H. T. Testriono, and Siti Nurhayati, *Disputed Churches in Jakarta* (Jakarta: PUSAD Paramadina, 2011).

3. Greg Fealy, "A Conservative Turn," *Inside Indonesia*, July 15, 2007; Martin van Bruinessen, ed., *Contemporary Developments in Indonesian Islam: Explaining the "Conservative Turn"* (Singapore: Institute of Southeast Asian Studies, 2013); Kikue Hamayotsu, "Conservative Turn? Religion, State and Conflict in Indonesia," *Pacific Affairs* 87, no. 4 (2014): 815–25.

4. Andrée Feillard and Remy Madinier, *The End of Innocence? Indonesian Islam and the Temptations of Radicalism*, trans. Wong Wee (Singapore: NUS Press, 2011).

5. Martin van Bruinessen, "Introduction: Contemporary Developments in Indonesian Islam and the 'Conservative Turn' in the Twenty-First Century" in *Contemporary Developments in Indonesian Islam*, ed. Martin van Bruinessen, 1–20 (Singapore: Institute of Southeast Asian Studies, 2013), 3. See also idem, "What Happened to the Smiling Face of Indonesian Islam? Muslim Intellectualism and the Conservative Turn in Post-Suharto Indonesia," RSIS Working Paper No. 222, 2011.

6. For a discussion on this fatwa, see Piers Gillespie, "Current Issues in Indonesian Islam: Analysing the 2005 Council of Indonesian Ulama Fatwa No. 7 Opposing Pluralism, Liberalism, and Secularism," *Journal of Islamic Studies* 18, no. 2 (2007): 202–40; see also Mun'im Sirry, "Fatwas and Their Controversies: The Case of the Council of Indonesian Ulama (MUI)," *Journal of Southeast Asian Studies* 44, no. 1 (2013): 100–17.

7. Kikue Hamayotsu, "Conservative Turn? Religion, State, and Conflict in Indonesia," *Pacific Affairs* 87, no. 4 (2014): 815–25.

8. For detailed discussions on PPIM research findings, see Didin Syafruddin, Dadi Darmadi, Saiful Umum, and Ismatu Ropi, eds., *Potret Guru Agama: Pandangan tentang Toleransi dan Isu-Isu Kehidupan Keagamaan* (Jakarta: Kencana, 2018).

9. Ben K. C. Laksana and Bronwyn E. Wood, "Navigating Religious Diversity: Exploring Young People's Lived Religious Citizenship in Indonesia," *Journal of Youth Studies* 22, no. 6 (2018): 807–23.

10. Gordon W. Allport, *The Nature of Prejudice* (Oxford: Addison-Wesley, 1954).

11. For a detailed discussion on the question of diversity, conflict, and national unity in Indonesia, see, for instance, Risa J. Toha, "Ethnic Riots in Democratic Transition: A Lesson from Indonesia," Ph.D. dissertation, University of California, Los Angeles, 2012.

12. Chiara Logli, "Bhinneka Tunggal Ika (Unity in Diversity): Nationalism, Ethnicity and Religion in Indonesian Higher Education," Ph.D. dissertation, University of Hawai'i, Honolulu, 2015; Terance W. Bigalke, "Ten Keys to Understanding Indonesia," *Education about Asia* 12, no. 1 (2007): 12–16.

13. To remind the reader, these principles are monotheism, humanitarianism, unity, democracy, and justice.

14. Mirjam Künkler and Alfred C. Stepan, eds., *Democracy and Islam in Indonesia* (New York: Columbia University Press, 2013).

15. Zakyudin Baidhawy is correct when writing: "As noted by both Indonesian and foreign observers, the tenor of relations among religious communities in Indonesia was at its best during the New Order era (1966–1998). Pancasila (the state ideology) was successful in playing a unifying role in the nation-state. Unfortunately, these conditions, built by the top-down policy, failed even before the New Order regime's downfall under Suharto. The following period was marked by an increasing violence scale—direct and indirect, structural, and cultural. Riots and conflicts caused by different religions, ethnic and social groups, and politics became common everywhere in Indonesia from Aceh to East Timor, as well as Sanggau Ledo, Situbondo, Jakarta, Solo, Sampit, Maluku, and Poso, continuing throughout the last decade." See Zakiyuddin Baidhawy, "Building Harmony and Peace through Multiculturalist Theology-Based Religious Education: An Alternative for Contemporary Indonesia," *British Journal of Religious Education* 29, no. 1 (2007): 15–30; 17.

16. Sidney Jones, "Indonesian Government Approaches to Radical Islam Since 1998," in *Democracy and Islam in Indonesia*, ed. Mirjam Künkler and Alfred Stepan, 109–25 (New York: Columbia University Press, 2013), 125.

17. Karen Bryner, *Piety Project: Islamic Schools for Indonesia's Urban Middle Class*, Ph.D. dissertation, Columbia University, 2013, 3.

18. Muhammad Zuhri, "Political and Social Influences on Religious Schools: A Historical Perspective on Indonesian Islamic School Curricula," Ph.D. dissertation, McGill University, Toronto, 2006, 209–10.

19. Baidhawy, "Building Harmony and Peace through Multiculturalist Theology-Based Religious Education," 18.

20. Ibid., 19.

21. Erica Larson, "Civic and Religious Education in Manado, Indonesia: Ethical Deliberation about Plural Coexistence." Ph.D. dissertation, Boston University, 2019, 11.

22. Muhammad Zuhri, "Challenging Moderate Muslims: Indonesia's Muslim Schools in the Midst of Religious Conservatism," *Religion* 9, no. 310 (2018): 1–15; 13.

23. Laksana and Wood, "Navigating Religious Diversity," 808.

24. Nancy Tatom Ammerman, *Everyday Religion: Observing Modern Religious Lives* (Oxford: Oxford University Press, 2007); Meredith McGuire, *Lived Religion: Faith and Practice in Everyday Life* (Oxford: Oxford University Press, 2008); Daniel H. Levine, *Politics, Religion, and Society in Latin America* (Boulder, CO: Lynne Rienner Publishers, 2012).

25. Laksana and Wood, "Navigating Religious Diversity," 816.

26. Thomas Pettigrew and Linda Tropp, "A Meta-Analytic Test of Intergroup Contact Theory," *Journal of Personality and Social Psychology* 90, no. 5 (2006): 751–83.

27. Gordon Allport, *The Nature of Prejudice* (Oxford: Addison-Wesley, 1954).

28. Ibid., 267.

29. Pettigrew and Tropp, "A Meta-Analytic Test of Intergroup Contact Theory."

30. Ananthi Al-Ramiah and Miles Hewstone, "Intergroup Contact as a Tool for Reducing, Resolving, and Preventing Intergroup Conflict: Evidence, Limitations, and Potential," *American Psychologist* 68 (2013): 527–42; Lindsey Cameron, Adam Rutland, Rosa Hossain, and Rebecca Petley, "When and Why Does Extended Contact Work? The Role of High-Quality Direct Contact and Group Norms in the Development of Positive Ethnic Intergroup Attitudes amongst Children," *Group Processes and Intergroup Relations* 14, no. 2 (2011): 193–206; Agostino Mazziotta, Amelie Mummendey, and Stephen C. Wright, "Vicarious Intergroup Contact Effects: Applying Social-Cognitive Theory to Intergroup Contact Research," *Group Processes and Intergroup Relations* 14 (2011): 255–74; Jeanne Novak, Kelsey Jo Feyes, and Kimberly A. Christensen, "Application of Intergroup Contact Theory to the Integrated Workplace: Setting the Stage for Inclusion," *Journal for Vocational Rehabilitation* 35 (2011): 211–26; Pettigrew and Tropp, "A Meta-Analytic Test of Intergroup Contact Theory."

31. Cathryn Berger Kaye, *The Complete Guide to Service Learning: Proven, Practical Ways to Engage Students in Civic Responsibility, Academic Curriculum, and Social Action* (Minneapolis, MN: Free Spirit Publishing, 2010).

32. Amy Marcus-Newhall and Timothy R. Heindl, "Coping with Interracial Stress in Ethnically Diverse Classrooms: How Important are Allport's Contact Conditions?" *Journal of Social Issues* 54, no. 4 (1998): 813–30.

33. Michele Wittig and Sheila A. Grant-Thompson, "The Utility of Allport's Conditions of Intergroup Contact for Predicting Perceptions of Improved Racial Attitudes and Beliefs," *Journal of Social Issues* 54 (1998): 795–812; 795.

34. Nicolas Sorensen, Biren A. Nagda, Patricia Gurin, and Kelly E. Maxwell, "Taking a Hands-on Approach to Diversity in Higher Education: A Critical-Dialogic Model for Effective Intergroup Interaction," *Analyses of Social Issues and Public Policy* 9:1 (2009): 3–35; Biren A. Nagda and Patricia Gurin, "Intergroup Dialogue: A Critical-Dialogic Approach to Learning about Difference, Inequality, and Social Justice," *New Directions for Teaching and Learning* 111 (2007): 35–45; Rona Tamiko Halualani, Anu Chitgopekarb, Jennifer Huynh Thi Ahn Morrison, and Patrick Shaou-Whea Dodge, "Who's Interacting? And What are They Talking About? Intercultural Contact and Interaction among Multicultural University Students," *International Journal of Intercultural Relations* 28 (2004): 353–72; Patricia Gurin, Eric L. Dey, Sylvia Hurtado, and Gerard Gurin, "Diversity and Higher Education: Theory and Impact on Educational Outcomes," *Harvard Educational Review* 72, no. 3 (2002): 330–67.

35. Laksana and Wood, "Navigating Religious Diversity."

36. Brian Leiter, *Why Tolerate Religion?* (Princeton, NJ: Princeton University Press, 2012).

37. Leiter, *Why Tolerate Religion?*; Stan D. Gaede, *When Tolerance Is No Virtue: Political Correctness, Multiculturalism and the Future of Truth and Justice* (Downers Grove, IL: InterVarsity Press, 1993).

38. Torsten Knauth, "Tolerance—A Key Concept for Dealing with Cultural and Religious Diversity in Education," in *The European Wergeland Centre Statement Series*, ed. F. Tibbitts, R. Jackson, D. Kerr, T. Knauth, and P. Kirchschlager, 18–21 (Oslo: The European Wergeland Centre, 2014).

39. Leiter, *Why Tolerate Religion?*; Bernard Williams, "Toleration: An Impossible Virtue?" in *Toleration: An Elusive Virtue*, ed. David Heyd (Princeton, NJ: Princeton University Press, 1996).

40. Jacob Neusner and Bruce David Chilton, eds., *The Golden Rule: Analytical Perspectives* (Lanham, MD: University Press of America, 2008); Charles Steward Goodwin, *Satan's Cauldron: Religious Extremism and the Prospects for Tolerance* (Lanham, MD: University Press of America, 2006).

41. Walter Cardinal Kasper, "The Uniqueness and Universality of Jesus Christ," in *The Uniqueness and Universality of Jesus Christ: In Dialogue with the Religions*, ed. Massimo Serretti, 6–18 (Grand Rapids, MI: William B. Eerdmans Publishing, 2004), 7.

42. See CNN Indonesia, "Anti-Pemimpin Non-Muslim Meningkat Usai Kasus Ahok," https://www.cnnindonesia.com/nasional/20180924195859-32 -332825/anti-pemimpin-nonmuslim-meningkat-usai-kasus-ahok.

43. Emmanuel Agius and Jolanta Ambrosewicz, *Towards a Culture of Tolerance and Peace* (Montreal: International Bureau for Children's Rights, 2005).

44. Maitumeleng Albertina Ntho-Ntho and Jan F. Nieuwenthuis, "Religious Intolerance: The Case of Principals in Multi-faith Schools," *Journal for the Study of Religion* 29, no. 1 (2016): 167–86; 170.

45. Catherine Cornille, "Conditions for Inter-Religious Dialogue," in *The Wiley-Blackwell Companion to Inter-Religious Dialogue*, ed. Catherine Cornille, 20–33 (Malden, MA: Wiley-Blackwell, 2013), 28.

46. Christopher G. Ellison and Daniel A. Powers, "The Contact Hypothesis and Racial Attitudes among Black Americans," *Social Science Quarterly* 75, no. 2 (1994): 385–400.

47. Anthony Lising Antonio, "When Does Race Matter in College Friendships? Exploring Men's Diverse and Homogeneous Friendship Groups," *Review of Higher Education* 27, no. 4 (2004): 553–75; 572.

48. Baidhawy, "Building Harmony and Peace through Multiculturalist Theology-Based Religious Education."

49. Mun'im Sirry, "The Public Role of Non-Muslim *Dhimmī*s during 'Abbāsid Times," *Bulletin of the School of Oriental and African Studies* 72, no. 2 (2011): 187–204.

50. Charles Y. Glock, Robert Wuthnow, Jane Piliavin, and Metta Spencer, *Adolescent Prejudice* (New York: Harper and Row, 1975); Eric H. Erikson, *Identity: Youth and Crisis* (New York: W. W. Norton, 1980).

51. Stephen Borgatti and Brandon Ofem, "Overview: Social Network Theory and Analysis," in *Social Network Theory and Educational Change*, ed. A. Daly, 17–29 (Cambridge, MA: Harvard Education Press, 2010); David DuBois and Barton Hirsch, "School/Nonschool Friendship Patterns in Early Adolescence," *Journal of Early Adolescence* 13, no. 1 (1993): 102–22; Stephen Hansell, "Adolescent Friendship Networks and Distress in School," *Social Forces* 63, no. 3 (1985): 698–715; Shyamala Nada-Raja, Rob McGee, and Warren R. Stanton, "Perceived Attachment to Parents and Peers and Psychological Well-being in Adolescence," *Journal of Youth and Adolescence* 21 (1992): 471–85.

52. Sharon Rae Jenkins, Kelly Goodness, and Duane Buhrmester, "Gender Differences in Early Adolescents' Relationship Qualities, Self-efficacy, and

Depression Symptoms," *Journal of Early Adolescence* 22, no. 3 (2002): 277–309; Kenneth H. Rubin, Kathleen M. Dwyer, Cathryn Booth-LaForce, Angel K. Kim, Kim B. Burgess, and Linda Rose-Krasnor, "Attachment, Friendship, and Psychosocial Functioning in Early Adolescence," *Journal of Early Adolescence* 24, no. 4 (2002): 326–56.

53. Kathryn A. Kerns, Lisa Klepac, and AmyKay Cole, "Peer Relationships and Preadolescents' Perceptions of Security in the Child–Mother Relationship," *Developmental Psychology* 32 (1996): 457–66; Barbara L. Weimer, Kathryn Kerns, and Christopher Oldenburg, "Adolescents' Interactions with a Best Friend: Associations with Attachment Style," *Journal of Experimental Child Psychology* 88, no. 1 (2004): 102–20.

54. Andrea M. Hussong, "Distinguishing Mean and Structural Sex Differences in Adolescent Friendship Quality," *Journal of Social and Personal Relationships* 17, no. 2 (2000): 223–43; Laurie McNelles and Jennifer A. Connoly, "Intimacy between Adolescent Friends: Age and Gender Differences in Intimate Affect and Intimate Behaviors," *Journal of Research on Adolescence* 9 (1999): 143–59; Barry H. Schneider, Sharon S. Woodburn, Maria del Pilar Soteras del Toro, and Stephen J. Udvari, "Cultural and Gender Differences in the Implications of Competition for Early Adolescent Friendship," *Merrill-Palmer Quarterly* 51, no. 2 (2005): 163–91; James Youniss and Denise Haynie, "Friendship in Adolescence," *Journal of Developmental and Behavioral Pediatrics* 13, no. 1 (1992): 59–66.

55. Miles Hewstone, Ed Cairns, Alberto Voci, Juergen Hamberger, and Ulrike Niens, "Intergroup Contact, Forgiveness, and Experience of 'The Troubles' in Northern Ireland," *Journal of Social Issues* 62 (2006): 99–120; Shana Levin, Colette van Laar, and Jim Sidanius, "The Effects of Ingroup and Outgroup Friendship on Ethnic Attitudes in College: A Longitudinal Study," *Group Processes and Intergroup Relations* 6 (2003): 76–92; Rhiannon N. Turner and Lindsey Cameron, "Confidence in Contact: A New Perspective on Promoting Cross-Group Friendship among Children and Adolescents," *Social Issues and Public Policy* 10 (2016): 212–46.

56. Laksana and Wood, "Navigating Religious Diversity," 819.

57. Bruce Robert Norquist, "An Exploration of the Relationship between Student Engagement with Otherness and Development of Faith in Evangelical Higher Education," Ph.D. dissertation, Loyola University, Chicago, 2008, 40.

58. Gay Lin Holcomb, "Faithful Change: Exploring the Faith Development of Students Who Attend Christian Liberal Arts Institutions," Ph.D. dissertation, University of Kentucky, Lexington, 2004.

CHAPTER 2

1. Elisabetta Crocetti, "Identity Dynamics in Adolescence: Processes, Antecedents, and Consequences," *European Journal of Developmental Psychology* 15, no. 1 (2018): 11–23; Alessandro Bergamaschi, "Adolescents and Prejudice: A Comparative Study of the Attitudes of Two European Adolescent Populations Regarding the Issues That Are Raised by Increasing Cultural and Religious Pluralism," *International Journal of Intercultural Studies* 37 (2013): 302–12.

2. Kazumi Sugimura, Kobo Matsushima, Shogo Hirara, Mahami Takahashi, and Elisabetta Crocetti, "A Culturally Sensitive Approach to the Relationships between Identity Formation and Religious Beliefs in Youth," *Journal of Youth and Adolescence* 48 (2019): 668–79; Jeffrey Jensen Arnett, *Adolescence and Emerging Adulthood* (Upper Saddle River, NJ: Pearson Education, 2001); Arnett, *Emerging Adulthood: The Winding Road from the Late Teens through the Twenties* (New York: Oxford University Press, 2014).

3. Eric H. Erikson, *Identity: Youth and Crisis* (New York: W. W. Norton, 1980).

4. Vassilis Saroglou, "Adolescents' Social Development and the Role of Religion," in *Values, Religion, and Culture in Adolescent Development: Coherence at the Detriment of Openness*, ed. G. Trommsdorff and X. Chen, 391–423 (New York: Cambridge University Press, 2012).

5. See, for example, Robert W. Hefner, *Civil Islam: Muslims and Democratization in Indonesia* (Princeton, NJ: Princeton University Press, 2011); Carool Kersten, *Islam in Indonesia: The Contest for Society, Ideas and Values* (Oxford: Oxford University Press, 2015); Jeremy Menchik, *Islam and Democracy in Indonesia: Tolerance without Liberalism* (Cambridge: Cambridge University Press, 2016).

6. Mun'im Sirry, "The Public Expression of Traditional Islam," *The Muslim World* 100, no. 1 (2010): 60–77; Florian Pohl, *Islamic Education and the Public Sphere: Today's Pesantren in Indonesia* (New York: Waxmann, 2009); Ronald Lukens-Bull, *A Peaceful Jihad: Negotiating Identity and Modernity in Muslim Java* (New York: Palgrave Macmillan, 2005).

7. Pohl, *Islamic Education and the Public Sphere.*

8. Lukens-Bull, *A Peaceful Jihad.*

9. Teguh Wijaya Mulya and Anindito Aditomo, "Researching Religious Tolerance Education Using Discourse Analysis: A Case Study from Indonesia," *British Journal of Religious Education* 41, no. 4 (2019): 446–57; Muhammad Zuhri, "Challenging Moderate Muslims: Indonesia's Muslim Schools in the Midst of Religious Conservatism," *Religion* 9, no. 310 (2018): 1–15;

Mirjam Künkler and Hanna Lerner, "A Private Matter? Religious Education and Democracy in Indonesia and Israel," *British Journal of Religious Education* 38, no. 3 (2016): 279–307; Y. Yustiani, "Penanaman Nilai-Nilai Karakter Bangsa Melalui Mata Pelajaran Pendidikan Agama Islam di SMA Negeri," *Analisa Journal of Social Science and Religion* 22, no. 1 (2015): 135–47; Lyn Parker, "Religious Education for Peaceful Coexistence in Indonesia?" *South East Asia Research* 22, no. 4 (2014): 487–504; Zakiyuddin Baidhawy, "Building Harmony and Peace through Multiculturalist Theology-Based Religious Education: An Alternative for Contemporary Indonesia," *British Journal of Religious Education* 29, no. 1 (2007): 15–30.

10. Ben K. C. Laksana and Bronwyn E. Wood, "Navigating Religious Diversity: Exploring Young People's Lived Religious Citizenship in Indonesia," *Journal of Youth Studies* 22, no. 6 (2018): 807–23; 808.

11. Ibid., 819.

12. Mulya and Aditomo, "Researching Religious Tolerance Education Using Discourse Analysis."

13. Künkler and Lerner, "A Private Matter?"

14. Zuhri, "Challenging Moderate Muslims: Indonesia's Muslim Schools in the Midst of Religious Conservatism," 13.

15. Baidhawy, "Building Harmony and Peace through Multiculturalist Theology-Based Religious Education," 20.

16. Ibid., 27.

17. Ibid.

18. Ibid.

19. Parker, "Religious Education for Peaceful Coexistence in Indonesia?" 489.

20. Ibid., 494.

21. Ibid.

22. Azyumardi Azra, Kees van Dijk, and Nico J. G. Kaptein, eds., *Varieties of Religious Authority: Changes and Challenges in 20ᵗʰ-Century Islam* (Singapore: Institute of Southeast Asian Studies, 2010); Gudrun Krämer and Sabine Schmidtke, eds., *Speaking for Islam: Religious Authorities in Muslim Societies* (Leiden: Brill, 2006).

23. Ibid., 1.

24. Shana Levin, Colette van Laar, and Jim Sidanius, "The Effects of Ingroup and Outgroup Friendship on Ethnic Attitudes in College: A Longitudinal Study," *Group Processes and Intergroup Relations* 6 (2003): 76–92; Rhiannon Turner and Lindsey Cameron, "Confidence in Contact: A New Perspective on Promoting Cross-Group Friendship among Children and Adolescents," *Social Issues and Public Policy* 10 (2016): 212–46.

25. Stanley Wasserman and Katherine Faust, *Social Network Analysis: Methods and Applications* (Cambridge: Cambridge University Press, 1994).

26. Stephen Borgatti and Brandon Ofem, "Overview: Social Network Theory and Analysis," in *Social Network Theory and Educational Change*, ed. A. Daly, 17–29 (Cambridge, MA: Harvard Education Press, 2010).

27. Megan O'Bryan, Harold D. Fishbein, and D. Neal Ritche, "Intergenerational Transmission of Prejudice, Gender Role Stereotyping, and Intolerance," *Adolescence* 39 (2004): 407–25.

28. Levin, van Laar, and Sidanius, "The Effects of Ingroup and Outgroup Friendship in Ethnic Attitudes in College"; Drew Nesdale, Judith Griffith, Kevin Durkin, and Anne Maass, "Empathy, Group Norms and Children's Ethnic Attitudes," *Applied Developmental Psychology* 26 (2005): 623–37.

29. Bergamaschi, "Adolescents and Prejudice," 304; see also Chris Baerveld, Marijtje van Duijn, Lotte Vermeij, and Dianne van Hemert, "Ethnic Boundaries and Personal Choice: Assessing the Influence of Individual Inclinations to Choose Intra-Ethnic Relationships on Pupils' Networks," *Social Networks* 26, no. 1 (2004): 55–74.

30. Colleen Ward, Anne-Marie Masgoret, and Michelle Gezentsvey, "Investigating Attitudes toward International Students: Implications for Social Integration and International Education," *Social Issues and Policy Review* 3, no. 1 (2009): 79–102; 83.

31. Walter G. Stephan, C. Lausanne Renfro, Victoria Esses, Cookie White Stephan, and Tim Martin, "The Effects of Feeling Threatened on Attitudes towards Immigrants," *International Journal of Intercultural Relations* 29: (2005): 1–19; Donald R. Kinder, "The Continuing American Dilemma: Whites' Resistance to Racial Change 40 Years after Myrdal," *Journal of Social Issues* 42, no. 2 (1986): 151–71.

32. Rebecca S. Bigler, John M. Rohrbach, and Kiara S. Sanchez, "Children's Intergroup Relations and Attitudes," *Advances in Child Development and Behavior* 51 (2016): 131–69; 132.

33. Kenneth H. Rubin, William M. Bukowski, and Jeffrey Parker, "Peer Relations, Relationships, and Groups," in *Handbook of Child Psychology*, ed. William Damon, 619–700 (New York: Wiley, 2006); William M. Bukowski, Andrew F. Newcomb, and Willard W. Hartup, *The Company They Keep: Friendship in Childhood and Adolescence* (New York: Cambridge University Press, 1998).

34. Wyndol Furman and Duane Buhrmester, "Age and Sex Differences in Perceptions of Networks and Personal Relationships," *Child Development* 63 (1992): 103–15.

35. John W. Santrock, *Adolescence*, 13th ed. (New York: McGraw-Hill, 2009), 314; Jane Waldfogel, *What Children Need* (Cambridge, MA: Harvard University Press, 2006), 166.

36. Arnett, *Adolescence and Emerging Adulthood*, 239.

37. Nienke Moolenaar and Peter Sleegers, "Social Networks, Trust, and Innovation: The Role of Relationships in Supporting an Innovative Climate in Dutch Schools," in *Social Network Theory and Educational Change*, ed. A. Daly, 97–114 (Cambridge, MA: Harvard Education Press, 2010).

38. Penelope Eckert, "Vowels and Nail Polish: The Emergence of Linguistic Style in the Preadolescent Heterosexual Marketplace," in *Gender and Belief Systems*, ed. N. Warner, J. Ahlers, L. Bilmes, M. Oliver, S. Wertheim, and M. Chen, 183–90 (Berkeley: Berkeley Women and Language Group, 1996).

39. Menchik, *Islam and Democracy in Indonesia*, 66–67.

40. Mun'im Sirry, "Fatwas and Their Controversies: The Case of the Council of Indonesian Ulama (MUI)," *Journal of Southeast Asian Studies* 44, no. 1 (2013): 100–117.

41. Dadi Darmadi, "Guru Agama Makin Tak Toleran," *Koran Tempo*, December 25, 2016; see also Monique Rijkers, "Darurat Intoleransi Guru dan Buku Ajar Agama Islam," November 1, 2018. See https://www.dw.com/id /darurat-intoleransi-guru-dan-buku-ajar-agama-islam/a-45764686.

42. Pusat Pengkajian Islam dan Masyarakat (PPIM), *Sikap dan Perilaku Keberagamaan Guru dan Dosen Pendidikan Agama Islam* (Jakarta: UIN Syarif Hidayatullah, 2018), 8.

43. William Costanza, "Adjusting Our Gaze: An Alternative Approach to Understanding Youth Radicalization," *Journal of Strategic Security* 8, no. 1 (2015): 1–15; 12.

44. Mary E. Procidano and Kenneth Heller, "Measures of Perceived Social Support from Friends and from Family: Three Validation Studies," *American Journal of Community Psychology* 11, no. 1 (1983): 1–24.

45. Thomas W. Valente, *Social Networks and Health: Models, Methods, and Applications* (New York: Oxford University Press, 2010).

46. Bigler, Rohrbach, and Sanchez, "Children's Intergroup Relations and Attitudes," 131–69.

47. Ibid., 161.

48. Muhammad Qasim Zaman, *Modern Islamic Thought in A Radical Age* (Cambridge: Cambridge University Press, 2012).

49. Andrée Feillard, "From Handling Water in a Glass to Coping with an Ocean: Shifts in Religious Authority in Indonesia," in *Varieties of Religious*

Authority: Changes and Challenges in 20th-Century Islam, ed. Azyumardi Azra, A. van Dijk, and Kaptein, 157–76 (Singapore: Institute of Southeast Asian Studies, 2010).

50. Zaman, *Modern Islamic Thought in a Radical Age*, 33.

51. Frances E. Aboud and Anna-Beth Doyle, "Parental and Peer Influences on Children's Racial Attitudes," *International Journal of Intercultural Relations* 20, no. 3 (1996): 371–83; 381.

CHAPTER 3

1. Leo Suryadinata, Evi Nurvidya Arifin, and Aris Ananta, *Indonesia's Population: Ethnicity and Religion in a Changing Political Landscape* (Singapore: Institute of Southeast Asian Studies, 2003).

2. Badan Pusat Statistik, "Jumlah Sekolah, Guru, dan Murid Madrasah Aliyah (MA) di Bawah Kementerian Agama Menurut Provinsi, 2019/2020," https://www.bps.go.id/indikator/indikator/view_data_pub/0000/api_pub/80 /da_04/1.

3. Ouda Teda Ena, "Visual Analysis of E-Textbooks for Senior High School in Indonesia," Ph.D. dissertation, Loyola University, Chicago, 2013, 10.

4. Ibid.

5. Amy Huneck, "Bullying: A Cross-Cultural Comparison of One American and One Indonesian Elementary School," Ph.D. dissertation, Union Institute and University, Cincinnati, OH, 2007.

6. Ibid., 79.

7. Farah Aulia, Bullying Experience in Primary School Children," *Indonesian Journal of School Counseling* 1, no. 1 (2016): 28–32; 30.

8. Irvan Usman, "Perilaku Bullying Ditinjau dari Peran Kelompok Teman Sebaya dan Iklim Sekolah pada Siswa SMA di Kota Gorontalo," unpublished paper (2008) that can be found at https://repository.ung.ac.id/get/simlit_res /1/245/Perilaku-Bulliying-Ditinjau-Dari-Peran-Kelompok-Teman-Sebaya -dan-Iklim-Sekolah-Pada-Siswa-SMA-di-Kota-Gorontalo.pdf; Sugiariyanti, "Perilaku Bullying pada Anak dan Remaja," *Jurnal Ilmiah Psikologi* (2009): 101–8; Kadek Ayu Erika, Dian Atma Pertiwi, and Tuti Seniwati, "Bullying Behavior of Adolescents Based on Gender, Gang and Family," *Jurnal Ners* 12, no. 1 (2017): 126–32.

9. Lucy Bowes, Farida Aryani, Faridah Ohan, Rina Herlina Haryanti, Sri Winarna, Yuli Arsianto, Hening Budiyawati, Evi Widowati, Rika Saraswati, Yuliana Kristianto, Yulinda Erma Suryani, Derry Fahrizal Ulum, and Emilie Minnick, "The Development and Pilot Testing of an Adolescent Bullying

Intervention in Indonesia—The ROOTS Indonesia Program," *Global Health Action* 12, no. 1 (2019): 1–13.

10. Huneck, "Bullying," 34.

11. See Christopher S. Hazeltine, "Understanding Teachers' Perceptions of Bullying for Developing Teacher Detection and Intervention," Ph.D. dissertation, Walden University, Minneapolis, 2018; Khaerannisa Cortes and Becky Kochenderfer-Ladd, "To Tell or Not to Tell: What Influences Children's Decisions to Report Bullying to Their Teachers?" *School Psychology Quarterly* 29, no. 3 (2014): 336–48; Leanne Lester, Donna Cross, Therese Shaw, and Julian Dooley, "Adolescent Bully-Victims: Social Health and the Transition to Secondary School," *Cambridge Journal of Education* 42, no. 2 (2012): 213–33.

12. Chiaki Konishi, Shelley Hymel, Bruno D. Zumbo, and Zhen Li, "Do School Bullying and Student–Teacher Relationships Matter for Academic Achievement? A Multilevel Analysis," *Canadian Journal of School Psychology* 25, no. 1 (2010): 19–39; Hsi-Sheng Wei and Melissa Jonson-Reid, "Friends Can Hurt You: Examining the Coexistence of Friendship and Bullying among Early Adolescents," *School Psychology International* 32, no. 3 (2011): 244–62.

13. Helen Sarah Everett, "Faith Schools and Tolerance: A Comparative Study of the Influence of Faith Schools on Students' Attitudes of Tolerance," Ph.D. dissertation, University of London, 2012.

14. Rebecca M. Puhl, Jamie Lee Peterson, and Joerg Luedicke, "Weight-Based Victimization: Bullying Experiences of Weight Loss Treatment–Seeking Youth," *Pediatrics* 131, no. 1 (2013): 1–9.

15. Philip C. Rodkin, Dorothy L. Espelage, and Laura D. Hanish, "A Relational Framework for Understanding Bullying: Developmental Antecedents and Outcomes," *American Psychologist* 70, no. 4 (2015): 311–21; Laura S. Tenenbaum, Kris Varjas, Joel Meyers, and Leandra Parris, "Coping Strategies and Perceived Effectiveness in Fourth through Eighth Grade Victims of Bullying," *School Psychology International* 32, no. 3 (2011): 263–87.

16. Dan Olweus, *Bullying at School: What We Know and What We Can Do* (Cambridge, MA: Blackwell, 1993); idem, *Aggression in the Schools: Bullies and Whipping Boys* (Washington, DC: Wiley, 1978).

17. Rebekah Heinrichs, *Perfect Targets: Asperger Syndrome and Bullying* (Shawnee, KS: Autism Asperger Publishing, 2003).

18. E. W. deLara, "Why Adolescents Don't Disclose Incidents of Bullying and Harassment," *Journal of School Violence* 11, no. 4 (2012): 288–305.

19. Lori M. Weaver, James Brown, Dan Weddle, and Mathew Aalsma, "A Content Analysis of Protective Factors within States' Antibullying Laws," *Journal of School Violence* 12, no. 2 (2012): 156–73.

20. Huneck, "Bullying," 92.

21. Ibid.

22. Ibid., 34.

23. Doris Bender and Friedrich Losel, "Bullying at School as a Predictor of Delinquency, Violence and Other Anti-Social Behaviour in Adulthood," *Criminal Behaviour and Mental Health* 21, no. 2 (2011): 99–106; Tony Cassidy, "Bullying and Victimisation in School Children: The Role of Social Identity, Problem-Solving Style, and Family and School Context," *Social Psychology of Education* 12 (2009): 63–76; Billie Gastic, "School Truancy and the Disciplinary Problems of Bullying Victims," *Educational Review* 60, no. 4 (2008): 391–404.

24. Sheri Bauman and Jessica Summers, "Peer Victimization and Depressive Symptoms in Mexican American Middle School Students: Including Acculturation as a Variable of Interest," *Hispanic Journal of Behavioral Sciences* 31, no. 4 (2009): 515–35; Anne Mari Undheim and Anne Mari Sund, "Prevalence of Bullying and Aggressive Behavior and Their Relationship to Mental Health Problems among 12- to 15-Year-Old Norwegian Adolescents," *European Child and Adolescent Psychiatry* 19, no. 11 (2010): 803–11; Erling Roland, "Bullying, Depressive Symptoms and Suicidal Thoughts," *Educational Research* 44, no. 1 (2002): 55–67; Bender and Losel, "Bullying at School as a Predictor of Delinquency, Violence and Other Anti-Social Behaviour in Adulthood."

25. Susan M. Swearer, Dorothy L. Espelage, Tracy Vaillancourt, and Shelly Hymel, "What Can Be Done about School Bullying? Linking Research to Educational Practice," *Educational Researcher* 39, no. 1 (2010): 38–47.

26. Maria M. Ttofi and David P. Farrington, "Effectiveness of School-Based Programs to Reduce Bullying: A Systematic and Meta-analytic Review," *Journal of Experimental Criminology* 7 (2011): 27–56; Patricia Leavy and Kathryn P. Maloney, "American Reporting of School Violence and 'People Like Us': A Comparison of Newspaper Coverage of the Columbine and Red Lake School Shootings," *Critical Sociology* 35, no. 2 (2009): 273–92.

27. See https://www.kpai.go.id/utama/bahaya-mana-bully-fisik-atau-bully-kata-pada-anak.

28. Kusumasari Kartika, Hima Darmayanti, and Farida Kurniawati, "Fenomena Bullying di Sekolah: Apa dan Bagaimana?," *Pedagogia Jurnal Ilmu Pendidikan* 17, no. 1 (2019): 55–66.

29. See https://www.kpai.go.id/berita/sejumlah-kasus-bullying-sudah-warnai-catatan-masalah-anak-di-awal-2020-begini-kata-komisioner-kpai.

30. See https://jabar.tribunnews.com/2020/02/15/fakta-terbaru-kasus-bully-siswi-smp-purworejo-kepsek-ingin-masalah-diselesaikan-kekeluargaan?page=all.

31. Mona Solberg and Dan Olweus, "Prevalence Estimation of School Bullying with the Olweus Bully/Victim Questionnaire," *Aggressive Behavior* 29 (2003): 239–68.

32. Hannah Smith, Keja Polenik, Shamin Nakasita, and Alice Jones, "Profiling Social, Emotional and Behavioural Difficulties of Children Involved in Direct and Indirect Bullying Behaviours," *Emotional and Behavioural Difficulties* 17, nos. 3–4 (2012): 243–57.

33. Victor Sbarbaro and M. Enyeart Smith, "An Exploratory Study of Bullying and Cyberbullying Behaviors among Economically/Educationally Disadvantaged Middle School Students," *American Journal of Health Studies* 26, no. 3 (2011): 139–51.

34. Jami-Leigh Sawyer, Faye Mishna, Debra Pepler, and Judith Wiener, "The Missing Voice: Parents' Perspectives of Bullying," *Children and Youth Services Review* 33, no. 10 (2011): 1795–1803; Wendy M. Craig, Debra Pepler, and Andona R. Atlas, "Observations of Bullying in the Playground and in the Classroom," *School Psychology International* 21, no. 1 (2000): 22–36; Laura D. Hanish and Nancy G. Guerra, "The Roles of Ethnicity and School Context in Predicting Children's Victimization by Peers," *American Journal of Community Psychology* 28 (2000): 201–23.

35. Christina Salmivalli, "Participant Role Approach to School Bullying: Implications for Interventions," *Journal of Adolescence* 22, no. 4 (1999): 453–59.

36. Nancy Eisenberg and Richard A. Fabes, "Prosocial Development," in *Handbook of Child Psychology: Social, Emotional, and Personality Development,* ed. N. Eisenberg, 701–78 (New York: Wiley), 701.

37. Kent Weeks, *In Search of Civility: Confronting Incivility on the College Campus* (New York: Morgan James Publishing, 2011), 6.

38. Ibid.

39. Jennifer L. Aranda, "Educational Leadership, Adult and Higher Education," Ph.D. dissertation, University of South Dakota, Vermillion, 2018, 30.

40. Lynne M. Andersson and Christine M. Pearson, "Tit for Tat? The Spiraling Effect of Incivility in the Workplace," *Academy of Management Review* 24, no. 3 (1999): 452–71; 457.

41. Pier M. Forni, *The Civility Solution: What to Do When People Are Rude* (New York: St. Martin's Press, 2010), 21.

42. Ruth Braunstein, "Boundary-Work and the Demarcation of Civil from Uncivil Protest in the United States: Control, Legitimacy, and Political Inequality," *Theory and Society* 47, no. 5 (2018): 603–33.

43. See https://news.gallup.com/poll/157073/corruption-continues -plague-indonesia.aspx.

44. Mike Elsea, Ersilia Menesini, Yohji Morita, and Mona O'Moore, "Friendship and Loneliness among Bullies and Victims: Data from Seven Countries," *Aggressive Behavior* 30, no. 1 (2004): 71–83.

45. Ah Yusuf, Aziz Nashiruddin Habibie, Ferry Efendi, Iqlima Dwi Kurnia, and Anna Kurniati, "Prevalence and Correlates of Being Bullied among Adolescents in Indonesia: Results from the 2015 Global School-Based Student Health Survey," *International Journal of Adolescent Medicine and Health* 34, no. 1 (2019): 1–7.

46. UNICEF, *Laporan Tahunan Indonesia 2015*, https://www.medbox.org /document/unicef-laporan-tahunan-indonesia-2015#GO.

47. Mark Anderson, Joanne Kaufman, Thomas Simon, and Lisa Barrios, "School Associated Violent Deaths in the United States, 1994–1999," *JAMA* 286, no. 21 (2001): 2695–2702; J. P. McGee and C. R. DeBernardo, "The Classroom Avenger: A Behavioral Profile of School-Based Shootings," *The Forensic Examiner* 8 (1999): 16–18.

48. Richard Boyd, "The Value of Civility," *Urban Studies* 43, nos. 5–6 (2006): 863–78; Nicole Billante and Peter Saunders, "Why Civility Matters," *Policy* 18, no. 3 (2002): 32–36.

49. Giovinella Gonthier and Kevin Morrissey, *Rude Awakenings: Overcoming the Civility Crisis in the Workplace* (Chicago: Kaplan Publishing, 2002).

50. Stephanie Ferraro Oppel, "The Complexity of Civility (and Incivility) Development: Identity and the Challenge of Civility in the United States," Ph.D. dissertation, Drake University, Des Moines, IA, 2019, 120.

51. Daniel Coleman, *White Civility: The Literary Project of English Canada* (Toronto: University of Toronto Press, 2006), 11.

52. Oppel, *The Complexity of Civility (and Incivility) Development*, 109.

53. Robert Sutton, *The No Asshole Rule* (New York: Warner Business Books, 2007).

54. Harriette A. Scott, "In Search of Civility: A Community College Perspective," Ph.D. dissertation, Morgan State University, Baltimore, MD, 2009, 64.

55. Rudy H. Fichtenbaum, "Civility," *Academe* 6, no. 56 (2014), 27.

56. Keenly Wilkins, Paul Caldarella, Rachel Crook-Lyon, and K. Richard Young, "The Implications of Civility for Children and Adolescents: A Review of the Literature," *Issues in Religion and Psychotherapy* 33, no. 1 (2010): 37–45; 40.

CHAPTER 4

1. See, for instance, Emilia Aiello, Lidia Puigvert, and Tinka Schubert, "Preventing Violent Radicalization of Youth through Dialogic Evidence-Based Policies," *International Sociology* 33, no. 4 (2018): 435–53; Willy Pedersen, Viggo Vestel, and Anders Bakken, "At Risk for Radicalization and Jihadism? A Population-Based Study of Norwegian Adolescents," *Cooperation and Conflict* 53, no. 1 (2018): 61–83; William A. Costanza, "Adjusting Our Gaze: An Alternative Approach to Understanding Youth Radicalization," *Journal of Strategic Security* 1, no. 8 (2015): 1–15.

2. Lembaga Ilmu Pengetahuan Indonesia (LIPI), "Radikalisme Ideologi Menguasai Kampus," http://lipi.go.id/berita/single/Radikalisme-Ideologi -Menguasi-Kampus/15082.

3. Anas Saidi expressed his view during a seminar on radicalism's infiltration into university campuses, which was held at LIPI on February 18, 2016. See https://www.uinjkt.ac.id/id/peneliti-lipi-anak-muda-indonesia-makin -radikal/.

4. Andita Rahma, "Kemenristekdikti Akui Kampus Rentan Terpapar Radikalisme," *Tempo.co,* June 5, 2018, https://nasional.tempo.co/read/1095480 /Kemenristek-dikti-kampus-rentan-terpapar-radikalisme/full&view=ok.

5. For a discussion of BNPT research findings, see Suhardi Alius, *Pemahaman Membawa Bencara: Bunga Rampai Penanggulangan Terorisme* (Jakarta: Gramedia Pustaka Utama, 2019); idem, *Memimpin dengan Hati: Pengalaman sebagai Kepala BNPT* (Jakarta: Gramedia Pustaka Utama, 2019). The author of these books is the head of BNPT.

6. Nur Aini, "Survei BNPT: 39 Persen Mahasiswa Tertarik Paham Radikal," *Republika,* July 26, 2017.

7. The main purpose of HTI is to revive the caliphate system. Before it was banned, HTI was active in promoting their ideology in public settings, including schools, universities, mosques, and public arenas. In August 2007, more than eighty thousand people gathered in the Bung Karno Stadium in Jakarta, calling for the re-establishment of the caliphate system. The gathering was attended by several prominent public figures. For a detailed discussion, see Mohamed Nawab Mohamed Osman, *Hizbut Tahrir Indonesia and Political Islam: Identity, Ideology, and Religio-Political Mobilization* (London: Routledge, 2018).

8. Randy Borum, "Radicalization into Violent Extremism I: A Review of Social Science Theories." *Journal of Strategic Security* 4, no. 4 (2011): 7–36; idem, "Understanding the Terrorist Mindset." *FBI Law Enforcement Bulletin* (2003): 7–10; Quintan Wiktorowicz, "Introduction: Islamic Activism and Social Movement Theory," in *Islamic Activism: A Social Movement Theory*

Approach, ed. Quintan Wiktorowicz, 1–35 (Bloomington: Indiana University Press, 2004); Fathali M. Moghaddam, "The Staircase to Terrorism: A Psychological Exploration," *American Psychologist* 60, no. 2 (2005): 161–69; Thomas Precht, "Home Grown Terrorism and Islamist Radicalization in Europe: From Conversion to Terrorism," research report funded by the Danish Ministry of Justice, 2007; Mitchell D. Silber and Arvin Bhatt, *Radicalization in the West: The Homegrown Threat* (New York: New York City Police Department, 2007), http://www.nyc.gov/html/nypd/downloads/ pdf/public information/NYPD Report-Radicalization in the West.pdf.

9. Borum, "Radicalization into Violent Extremism I."

10. Andrew Silke, "Holy Warriors: Exploring the Psychological Processes of Jihadi Radicalization," *European Journal of Criminology* 5, no. 1 (2008): 99–123; Marc Sageman, *Understanding Terror Networks* (Philadelphia: University of Pennsylvania Press, 2004).

11. Asta Maskaliunaite, "Exploring the Theories of Radicalization," *International Studies: Interdisciplinary Political and Cultural Journal* 17, no. 1 (2015): 9–26; Jeffrey Monaghan and Adam Molnar, "Radicalisation Theories, Policing Practices, and the Future of Terrorism?" *Critical Studies on Terrorism* 9, no. 3 (2016): 393–413.

12. Quoted by Peter R. Neumann, "The Trouble with Radicalisation," *International Affairs* 89, no. 4 (2013): 873–93; 876.

13. John Horgan, "Lessons Learned since the Terrorist Attacks of September 11, 2001," part of the National Consortium for the Study of Terrorism and Responses to Terrorism (START), C-SPAN video, September 1, 2011, http://www.c-spanvideo.org/program/TenYearA.

14. Maskaliunaite, "Exploring the Theories of Radicalization," 12.

15. Alex Schmid, *Radicalisation, De-Radicalisation, Counter-Radicalisation: A Conceptual Discussion and Literature Review* (The Hague: International Centre for Counter-Terrorism, 2013), 217.

16. Peter R. Neumann, "Introduction," in *Perspectives on Radicalization and Political Violence*, edited by Peter Neumann (London: International Centre for the Study of Radicalization and Political Violence, 2008), 10.

17. Chuck Crossett and Jason A. Spitaletta, "Radicalization: Relevant Psychological and Sociological Concepts," U.S. Army Asymmetric Warfare Group, Ft. Meade, MD, 2010, 10.

18. Alex S. Wilner and Claire-Jehanne Dubouloz, "Homegrown Terrorism and Transformative Learning: An Interdisciplinary Approach to Understanding Radicalization," *Global Change, Peace & Security* 22, no. 1 (2010): 33–51; 38.

19. Maskaliunaite, "Exploring the Theories of Radicalization," 14.

20. Ibid.

21. Silber and Bhatt, *Radicalization in the West.*

22. Thomas Precht, *Home Grown Terrorism and Islamist Radicalization in Europe*; Quintan Wiktorowicz, "Introduction: Islamic Activism and Social Movement Theory"; idem, *Radical Islam Rising: Islamic Extremism in the West* (Lanham, MD: Rowman and Littlefield, 2005); Borum, "Understanding the Terrorist Mindset."

23. Precht, *Home Grown Terrorism and Islamist Radicalization in Europe*, 5.

24. Mohammed Hafez and Creighton Mullins, "The Radicalization Puzzle: A Theoretical Synthesis of Empirical Approaches to Homegrown Extremism," *Studies in Conflict & Terrorism* 38 (2015): 958–75; 960.

25. Ibid.

26. Marc Sageman, *Understanding Terror Networks* (Philadelphia: University of Pennsylvania Press, 2004).

27. Max Taylor and John Horgan, eds., *The Future of Terrorism* (London: Frank Cass, 2006); Arie W. Kruglanski and Shira Fishman, "The Psychology of Terrorism: Syndrome versus Tool Perspectives," *Journal of Terrorism and Political Violence* 18 (2009): 193–215; Clark McCauley and Sophia Moskalenko, "Mechanisms of Political Radicalization: Pathways toward Terrorism," *Terrorism and Political Violence* 20, no. 3 (2008): 415–33.

28. Michael King and Donald M. Taylor, "The Radicalization of Homegrown Jihadists: A Review of Theoretical Models and Social Psychological Evidence," *Terrorism and Political Violence* 23, no. 4 (2011): 602–22; 608.

29. Hafez and Mullins, "The Radicalization Puzzle," 961.

30. Alex P. Schmid, ed., *The Routledge Handbook on Terrorism Research* (London: Routledge, 2011), 217.

31. Tinka Velddhuis and Jorgen Staun, *Islamist Radicalisation: A Root Cause Model* (The Hague: Netherlands Institute of International Relations Clingendael, 2009), 6.

32. Maskaliunaite, "Exploring the Theories of Radicalization," 23.

33. Chares Demetriou, "Political Radicalization and Political Violence in Palestine (1920–1948), Ireland (1850–1921), and Cyprus (1914–1959)," *Social Science History* 36, no. 3 (2012): 391–420.

34. Neil Ferguson and Eve Binks, "Understanding Radicalization and Engagement in Terrorism through Religious Conversion Motifs," *Journal of Strategic Security* 8, nos. 1–2 (2015): 16–26.

35. Jose Vargas, *Understanding the Radicalization Process of U.S. Homegrown Terrorists* (Ph.D. dissertation, Walden University, Minneapolis, MN, 2017), 8.

36. For a summary of the debate on conversion, see Lewis R. Rambo, ed., *The Oxford Handbook of Religious Conversion* (Oxford: Oxford University Press, 2014).

37. David A. Snow and Richard Machalek, "The Sociology of Conversion," *Annual Review of Sociology* 10 (1984): 167–90; 171.

38. Lewis Rambo, *Understanding Religious Conversion* (New Haven, CT: Yale University Press, 1993).

39. Vargas, *Understanding the Radicalization Process of U.S. Homegrown Terrorists*, 50.

40. Ibid., 136.

41. Orla Lynch, "British Muslim Youth: Radicalization, Terrorism and the Construction of the 'Other,'" *Critical Studies on Terrorism* 6, no. 2 (2013): 241–61; Nick Hopkins, "Dual Identities and Their Recognition: Minority Group Members' Perspectives," *Political Psychology* 32, no. 2 (2011): 251–70; Laura Zahra McDonald, "Securing Identities, Resisting Terror: Muslim Youth Work in the UK and Its Implications for Security," *Religion, State and Society* 39, nos. 2–3 (2011): 177–89.

42. Damar Sinuko, *Diduga pro-HTI, Guru Besar Undip Prof. Suteki Dinonaktifkan*, CNN Indonesia, June 6, 2018, https://www.cnnindonesia.com /nasional/20180606222408-20-304123/diduga-pro-hti-guru-besar-undip -prof-suteki-dinonaktifkan.

43. Vargas, *Understanding the Radicalization Process of U.S. Homegrown Terrorists*, 92.

44. Costanza, "Adjusting Our Gaze," 1.

45. Ibid.

46. Hafez and Mullins, "The Radicalization Puzzle," 961.

47. Rambo, *Understanding Religious Conversion*, 20.

48. Borum, "Radicalization into Violent Extremism I," 23.

49. Lynch, "British Muslim Youth"; James Kirkup, "Muslims Must Embrace Our British Values," *Telegraph*, February 5, 2011; Toby Helm, Matthew Taylor, and Rowenna Davis, "David Cameron Sparks Fury from Critics Who Say Attack on Multiculturalism Has Boosted English Defense League," *Guardian Online*, February 5, 2011, http://www.guardian.co.uk/politics/2011 /feb/05/david-cameron-speech-criticised-edl.

50. Lynch, "British Muslim Youth," 244.

51. Ibid.

52. Ibid., 258.

53. Wiktorowicz, "Introduction: Islamic Activism and Social Movement Theory," 1–35.

CHAPTER 5

1. Charles Kurzman, *The Missing Martyrs: Why Are There So Few Muslim Terrorists?* (New York: Oxford University Press, 2019), 15.

2. See, for instance, William A. Costanza, "Adjusting Our Gaze: An Alternative Approach to Understanding Youth Radicalization," *Journal of Strategic Security* 8, no. 1 (2015): 1–15; Emilia Aiello, Lidia Puigvert, and Tinka Schubert, "Preventing Violent Radicalization of Youth through Dialogic Evidence-Based Policies," *International Sociology* 33, no. 4 (2018): 435–53; Willy Pedersen, Viggo Vestel, and Anders Bakken, "At Risk for Radicalization and Jihadism? A Population-Based Study of Norwegian Adolescents," *Cooperation and Conflict* 53, no. 1 (2008): 61–83.

3. Andrew Silke, "Holy Warriors: Exploring the Psychological Processes of Jihadi Radicalization," *European Journal of Criminology* 5, no. 1 (2008): 99–123.

4. Clark McCauley and Mary E. Segal, "Social Psychology of Terrorist Groups," in *Group Processes and Intergroup Relations*, ed. Clyde Hendrick (Beverly Hills, CA: SAGE Publications, 1987), 234; see also Marc Sageman, *Understanding Terror Networks* (Philadelphia: University of Pennsylvania Press, 2004).

5. Emily Corner and Paul Gill, "A False Dichotomy? Mental Illness and Lone-Actor Terrorism," *Law and Human Behavior* 39, no. 1 (2015): 23–34.

6. Jonas R. Kunst, Lisa S. Myhren, and Ivuoma N. Onyeador, "Simply Insane? Attributing Terrorism to Mental Illness (Versus Ideology) Affects Mental Representations of Race," *Criminal Justice and Behavior* 45, no. 12 (2018): 1888–1902.

7. Randy Borum, "Radicalization into Violent Extremism I: A Review of Social Science Theories," *Journal of Strategic Security* 4, no. 4 (2011): 7–36; Mohammed Hafez and Creighton Mullins, "The Radicalization Puzzle: A Theoretical Synthesis of Empirical Approaches to Homegrown Extremism," *Studies in Conflict and Terrorism* 38 (2015): 958–75; Asta Maskaliunaite, "Exploring the Theories of Radicalization," *International Studies: Interdisciplinary Political and Cultural Journal* 17, no. 1 (2015): 9–26.

8. Mark Sedgwick, "The Concept of Radicalization as a Source of Confusion," *Terrorism and Political Violence* 22, no. 4 (2010): 479–94; Arun Kundnani, "Radicalisation: The Journey of a Concept," *Institute of Race Relations* 54, no. 2 (2012): 3–25; Orla Lynch, "British Muslim Youth: Radicalization, Terrorism and the Construction of the 'Other,'" *Critical Studies on*

Terrorism 6, no. 2 (2013): 241–61; Maskaliunaite, "Exploring the Theories of Radicalization."

9. Donatella Della Porta and Gary LaFree, "Guest Editorial: Processes of Radicalization and De-Radicalization," *International Journal of Conflict and Violence* 6, no. 1 (2012): 5–10; 6.

10. Ibid.

11. Peter R. Neumann, "Introduction," in *Perspectives on Radicalization and Political Violence*, ed. Peter Neumann (London: International Centre for the Study of Radicalization and Political Violence, 2008).

12. Randy Borum, "Radicalization into Violent Extremism I."

13. Ibid., 8.

14. Ibid., 9.

15. Charlie Allen, "The Threat of Islamic Radicalization to the Homeland," written testimony to the U.S. Senate Committee on Homeland Security and Governmental Affairs, Washington, DC, March 14, 2007, 4.

16. Cited by Ines von Behr, Anaïs Reding, Charlie Edwards, and Luke Gribbon in *Radicalization in the Digital Era: RAND Europe* (Santa Monica, CA: RAND, 2013), 2.

17. Andrew Hoskins and Ben O'Loughlin, "Media and the Myth of Radicalization," *Media, War and Conflict* 2, no. 2 (2009): 107–10; 107.

18. Frank Furedi, "Muslim Alienation in the UK? Blame the Israelis!" *Spiked*, February 9, 2009, http://www.spikedonline.com/index.php?/site/article/6187/.

19. Peter R. Neumann, "The Trouble with Radicalisation," *International Affairs* 89, no. 4 (2013): 873–93; 873.

20. Peter Nesser, "Jihad in Europe: Exploring the Motivations for Salafi-Jihadi Terrorism in Europe Post-Millennium," Department of Political Science, University of Oslo, 2004.

21. Marieke Slootman and Jean Tillie, *Processes of Radicalisation: Why Some Amsterdam Muslims Become Radicals* (Universiteit van Amsterdam: Institute for Migration and Ethnic Studies, 2006).

22. Hafez and Mullins, "The Radicalization Puzzle," 960.

23. Angel Rabasa, Stacie L. Pettyjohn, Jeremy J. Ghez, Christopher Boucek, *Deradicalizing Islamist Extremists* (Santa Monica, CA: RAND, 2010), 23.

24. According to Robin Bush and Munawar-Rachman, 63 percent of NU and 76 percent of Muhammadiyah respondents object to having a non-Muslim house of worship in their neighborhoods. See Robin Bush and Budhy Munawar-Rachman, "NU and Muhammadiyah: Majority Views on Religious

Minority in Indonesia" in *Religious Diversity in the Muslim-Majority States in Southeast Asia*, ed. Bernhard Platzdasch and Johan Saravanamuttu, 16–50 (Singapore: Institute of Southeast Asian Studies, 2014); Jeremy Menchik, *Islam and Democracy in Indonesia: Tolerance without Liberalism* (Cambridge: Cambridge University Press, 2016), 66–67.

25. Michael King and Donald M. Taylor, "The Radicalization of Homegrown Jihadists: A Review of Theoretical Models and Social Phychological Evidence," *Terrorism and Political Violence* 23, no. 4 (2011): 602–22.

26. Mitchell Silber and Arvin Bhatt, *Radicalization in the West: The Homegrown Threat* (New York: New York City Police Department, 2007), https://seths.blog/wp-content/uploads/2007/09/NYPD_Report-Radicalization_in _the_West.pdf.

27. Fathali Moghaddam, "The Staircase to Terrorism: A Psychological Exploration," *American Psychologist* 60, no. 2 (2005): 161–69.

28. Marc Sageman, *Leaderless Jihad: Terror Networks in the Twenty-First Century* (Philadelphia: University of Pennsylvania Press, 2008).

29. King and Taylor, "The Radicalization of Homegrown Jihadists"; Lynch, "British Muslim Youth"; Jytte Klausen et al., "Toward a Behavioral Model of 'Homegrown' Radicalization Trajectories," *Studies in Conflict and Terrorism* 39 (2015): 67–83.

30. Brian M. Jenkins, "Foreword: Outside Expert's View," in *Homegrown Terrorism in the U.S. and U.K.: An Empirical Examination of the Radicalization Process*, ed. Daveed Gartenstein-Ross and Laura Grossman (Washington, DC: Foundation for the Defense of Democracies, 2009), 7.

31. Anne Aly and Jason-Leigh Striegher, "Examining the Role of Religion in Radicalization to Violent Islamist Extremism," *Studies in Conflict and Terrorism* 35 (2012): 849–62.

32. Ibid., 850.

33. Ibid., 849.

34. Mitchell Silber and Arvin Bhatt, *Radicalization in the West*.

35. Anne Aly, *Terrorism and Global Security: Historical and Contemporary Perspectives* (South Yarra, Australia: Palgrave Macmillan, 2011).

36. Borum, "Radicalization into Violent Extremism I"; Chares Demetriou, "Political Radicalization and Political Violence in Palestine (1920–1948), Ireland (1850–1921), and Cyprus (1914–1959)," *Social Science History* 36, no. 3 (2012): 391–420; Maskaliunaite, "Exploring the Theories of Radicalization."

37. Aly and Striegher, "Examining the Role of Religion in Radicalization to Violent Islamist Extremism," 860.

CHAPTER 6

1. Kate Barrelle, "Pro-Integration: Disengagement from and Life after Terrorism," *Behavioural Sciences of Terrorism and Political Aggression* 7, no. 2 (2015): 129–42.

2. Kira J. Harris, Eyal Gringart, and Deirdre Drake, "Leaving Ideological Groups Behind: A Model of Disengagement," *Behavioural Sciences of Terrorism and Political Aggression* (2017): 1–14.

3. John Horgan and Tore Bjorgo, *Leaving Terrorism Behind: Individual and Collective Disengagement* (London: Routledge, 2009).

4. Julie Chernov-Hwang, Rizal Panggabean, and Ihsan Ali-Fauzi, "The Disengagement of Indonesian Jihadists: Understanding the Pathways," *Terrorism and Political Violence* 29, no. 2 (2017): 277–95.

5. Daniel Koehler, "De-radicalization and Disengagement Programs as Counter-Terrorism and Prevention Tools: Insights from Field Experiences Regarding German Right-Wing Extremism and Jihadism," in *Countering Radicalisation and Violent Extremism among Youth to Prevent Terrorism*, ed. M. Lombardi et al., 120–50 (Washington, DC: IOS Press, 2015), 127.

6. Daniel Koehler, *Understanding Deradicalization: Methods, Tools and Programs for Countering Violent Extremism* (New York: Routledge, 2016).

7. Zora A. Sukabdi, "Terrorism in Indonesia: A Review on Rehabilitation and Deradicalization," *Journal of Terrorism Research* 6, no. 2 (2015): 36–56; Masdar Hilmy, "The Politics of Retaliation: The Backlash of Radical Islamists to Deradicalization Project in Indonesia," *Al-Jami'ah* 51, no. 1 (2013): 129–58.

8. Hilmy, "The Politics of Retaliation," 141.

9. Cameron Sumpter, "Countering Violent Extremism in Indonesia: Priorities, Practice and the Role of Civil Society," *Journal for Deradicalization* 11 (2017): 112–46; 119.

10. "Pasukan khusus ini dibiayai oleh pemerintah Amerika Serikat melalui bagian Jasa Keamanan Diplomatik (Diplomatic Security Service) Departemen Luar Negeri AS dan dilatih langsung oleh instruktur dari CIA, FBI, dan U.S. Secret Service. Kebanyakan staf pengajarnya adalah bekas anggota pasukan khusus AS." See Muhammad Nuh, "Propaganda Terorisme di Indonesia," *Era Muslim*, September 27, 2010, https://www.eramuslim.com/suara-kita/dialog/propaganda-terorisme-di-indonesia.htm#.X7seAapKjBI.

11. Sumpter, "Countering Violent Extremism in Indonesia," 121.

12. Hilmy, "The Politics of Retaliation," 144–45.

13. Sumpter, "Countering Violent Extremism in Indonesia," 129.

14. See Shaun Waterman, "Indonesia Tries Deradicalization," *Middle East Times*, July 22, 2008.

15. Ian Chalmers, "Countering Violent Extremism in Indonesia: Bringing Back the Jihadists," *Asian Studies Review* 41, no. 3 (2017): 1–21; 345.

16. Angel Rabasa, Stacie L. Pettyjohn, Jeremy J. Ghez, and Christopher Boueck, *Deradicalizing Islamist Extremists* (Santa Monica, CA: RAND, 2010), 1.

17. Ibid., 1–2.

18. John Horgan, *Walking Away from Terrorism: Accounts of Disengagement from Radical and Extremist Movements* (New York: Routledge, 2009), 152.

19. Ibid.

20. Naureen C. Fink and Ellie B. Hearne, *Beyond Terrorism: Deradicalization and Disengagement from Violent Extremism* (New York: International Peace Institute, 2008), 1; Basia Spalek, "Radicalisation, De-Radicalisation and Counter-Radicalisation in Relation to Families: Key Challenges for Research, Policy and Practice," *Security Journal* 29, no. 1 (2016): 39–52; 41.

21. Alex P. Schmid, *Radicalization, De-Radicalization, Counter-Radicalization: A Conceptual Discussion and Literature Review* (The Hague: International Centre for Counter-Terrorism, 2013).

22. Horgan, *Walking Away from Terrorism*.

23. Tore Bjorgo and John Horgan, *Leaving Terrorism Behind*, 5.

24. Tore Bjorgo, "The Process of Disengagement from Violent Groups of the Extreme Right," in Bjorgo and Horgan, *Leaving Terrorism Behind*.

25. Omar Ashour, "De-radicalization of Jihad? The Impact of Egyptian Islamist Revisionists on al Qaeda," *Perspectives on Terrorism* 11, no. 14 (2008): 11–14; 11.

26. Ashour, *The De-radicalization of Jihadists: Transforming Armed Islamist Movements* (New York: Routledge, 2009), 6.

27. Ibid.

28. Froukje Demant, Marieke Slootman, Frank Buijs, and Jean Tillie, *Decline and Disengagement: An Analysis of Processes of Deradicalisation* (Amsterdam: IMES, 2008), 13; Rabasa, Pettyjohn, Ghez, and Boueck, *Deradicalizing Islamist Extremists*, 2.

29. Rabasa, Pettyjohn, Ghez, and Boueck, *Deradicalizing Islamist Extremists*, 186.

30. Vivienne Chin, "Collateral Damage of Counter-Terrorism Measures and the Inevitable Consequence of the Social Exclusion and Marginalization of Vulnerable Groups" in *Countering Radicalisation and Violent Extremism among Youth to Prevent Terrorism*, M. Lombardi et al., 11–22 (Washington, DC: IOS Press, 2015).

31. Mohammed Elshimi, "De-Radicalisation Interventions as Technologies of the Self: A Foucauldian Analysis," *Critical Studies on Terrorism* 8, no. 1 (2015): 110–29; 116.

32. Michel Foucault, "Technologies of the Self: A Seminar with Michel Foucault," in *Technologies of the Self*, ed. L. Martin, H. Gutman, and P. Hutton, 16–49 (Amherst: University of Massachusetts Press, 1988), 18.

33. Nikolas Rose, "Identity, Genealogy, History," in *Questions of Cultural Identity*, ed. S. Hall and P. Du Gay, 128–49 (London: SAGE Publications, 1996), 132.

34. William E. Connolly, "Taylor, Foucault, and Otherness," *Political Theory* 13 (1985): 365–76; Lois McNay, *Foucault: A Critical Introduction* (Cambridge: Polity Press, 1994).

35. Michel Foucault, *Ethics: Essential Works of Foucault, 1954–1984*, ed. P. Rainbow (London: Penguin, 1997), 291.

36. Foucault, "Technologies of the Self," 18.

37. McNay, *Foucault: A Critical Introduction*, 4.

38. Ibid.

39. Elshimi, "De-Radicalisation Interventions as Technologies of the Self," 118.

40. Leonie Schmidt, "Cyberwarriors and Counterstars: Contesting Religious Radicalism and Violence on Indonesian Social Media," *Asiascape: Digital Asia* 5 (2018): 32–67.

41. Hamed El-Said, *New Approaches to Counter-Terrorism: Designing and Evaluating Counter Radicalization and De-radicalization* (New York: Palgrave Macmillan, 2015); Spalek, "Radicalization, De-Radicalization and Counter-Radicalization in Relation to Families."

42. Michael Jacobson, "Learning Counter-Narrative Lessons from the Cases of Terrorist Dropouts," in *Countering Violent Extremist Narratives*, ed. Eelco J. A. M. Kessels, 72–83 (The Hague: National Coordinator for Counterterrorism, 2010).

43. Daniel Koehler, "How and Why We Should Take Deradicalization Seriously," *Human Nature Behavior* 1 (2017): 1–3; 1.

44. Ibid., 1.

45. Bjorgo and Horgan, eds., *Leaving Terrorism Behind*; Arun Kundnani, *A Decade Lost: Rethinking Radicalization and Extremism* (London: Claystone, 2015).

46. Katherine Seifert, "Can Jihadis Be Rehabilitated? Radical Islam," *Middle East Quarterly* 17, no. 2 (2010): 21–30; Petter Nesser, "Joining Jihadi Terrorist Cells in Europe: Exploring Motivational Aspects of Recruitment and Radicalization" in *Understanding Violent Radicalization: Terrorist and Jihadist Movements*

in Europe, ed. Magnus Ranstorp, 87–114 (London: Routledge, 2010); John M. Venhaus, *Why Youth Join Al-Qaeda*, USIP Special Report 236 (Washington, DC: United States Institute of Peace, 2010), http://www.usip.org/files/resources/SR236Venhaus.pdf; Alex P. Schmid, *Radicalization, De-Radicalization, Counter-Radicalization*; Zora A. Sukabdi, "Terrorism in Indonesia."

47. Leila Ezzarqui, "De-Radicalization and Rehabilitation Program: The Case Study of Saudi Arabia," MA thesis, Georgetown University, Washington, DC, 2010.

48. Sumpter, "Countering Violent Extremism in Indonesia," 119.

49. Chalmers, "Countering Violent Extremism in Indonesia," 346.

50. Koehler, "How and Why We Should Take Deradicalization Seriously," 1.

51. Ashour, *The De-Radicalization of Jihadists*, 5.

52. Stefanie Mitchell, "Deradicalization: Using Triggers for the Development of a US Program," *Journal for Deradicalization* 17, no. 9 (2016): 101–25; 103.

53. Bjorgo and Horgan, *Leaving Terrorism Behind*; Ashour, *The De-Radicalization of Jihadists*; Andrew Silke, "Disengagement or Deradicalization? A Look at Prison Programs for Jailed Terrorists," *CTC Sentinel* 4, no. 1 (2011): 18–21.

54. Aitemad Muhanna-Matar, "The Limit-Experience and Self-Deradicalization: The Example of Radical Salafi Youth in Tunisia," *Critical Studies on Terrorism* 10, no. 3 (2017): 453–75; 454.

55. Ibid., 457

56. Ibid.

57. Ibid., 457–58.

58. Michel Foucault, "What Is Critique?" in *The Politics of Truth*, ed. Sylvère Lotringe and trans. Lysa Hochroth and C. Porter (Los Angeles, CA: Semiotext(e), 1997): 41–82.

59. Muhanna-Matar, "The Limit-Experience and Self-Deradicalization," 458.

60. Ibid.

61. Elshimi, "De-radicalization Interventions as Technologies of the Self," 125.

62. Ibid., 124.

CHAPTER 7

1. Till Baaken and Linda Schlegel, "Fishermen or Swarm Dynamics? Should We Understand Jihadist Online-Radicalization as a Top-Down or Bottom-Up Process?," *Journal for Deradicalization* 18, no. 13 (2018): 178–211,

184. Adam Bermingham and associates define online radicalization as follows: "a process whereby individuals, through their online interactions and exposures to various types of internet context, come to view violence as a legitimate method of solving social and political conflicts." See Bermingham et al., "Combining Social Network Analysis and Sentiment Analysis to Explore the Potential for Online Radicalisation," in *Conference Proceedings, 2009 International Conference on Advances in Social Network Analysis and Mining* (2009).

2. Pusat Studi Budaya dan Perubahan Social (PSBPS) Universitas Muhammadiyah Surakarta, PPIM UIN Jakarta—UNDP Indonesia, *Islamic Websites: Narrative Contestation between the Radical and the Moderate* (Jakarta: Convey Report, 2018), 9.

3. Ivany Atina Arbi, "Internet Contributes to Radicalism among Young RI Muslims," *Jakarta Post*, February 24, 2019. See also "Social Media Is Facilitating Islamic Radicalization in Indonesia," *ASEAN Today*, February 20, 2020.

4. Cited by Arbi in "Internet contributes to radicalism among young RI Muslims."

5. "Pelaku Bom Bunuh Diri Gereja Kepunton Tewas," *Tempo.com*, September 25, 2011, https://nasional.tempo.co/read/358115/pelaku-bom-bunuh -diri-gereja-kepunton-tewas/full&view=ok.

6. Nur Azlin Mohamed Yasin, "Online Indonesian Islamist Extremism: A Gold Mine of Information," S. Rajaratnam School of International Studies, Nanyang Technological University, October 7, 2011.

7. Haeri Halim and Hans Nicholas, "Govt Unblocks Radical Websites," *Jakarta Post*, April 1, 2015.

8. "Indonesia: New Counterterrorism Law Imperils Rights," Human Rights Watch, June 20, 2018, https://www.hrw.org/news/2018/06/20 /indonesia-new-counterterrorism-law-imperils-rights#.

9. Digital 2020 Indonesia, https://datareportal.com/reports/digital-2020 -indonesia.

10. Peter R. Neumann, "Options and Strategies for Countering Online Radicalization in the United States," *Studies in Conflict and Terrorism* 36 (2013): 431–59.

11. Luke Bertram, "Terrorism, the Internet and the Social Media Advantage: Exploring How Terrorist Organizations Exploit Aspects of the Internet, Social Media and How These Same Platforms Could Be Used to Counter-Violent Extremism," *Journal for Deradicalization* 16, no. 7 (2016): 225–52, 226.

12. Maura Conway, "Determining the Role of the Internet in Violent Extremism and Terrorism: Six Suggestions for Progressing Research," *Studies in Conflict and Terrorism* 40, no. 1 (2016): 77–98; Jytte Klausen, "Tweeting the

Jihad: Social Media Networks of Western Foreign Fighters in Syria and Iraq," *Studies in Conflict and Terrorism* 38 (2015): 1–22.

13. Bertram, "Terrorism, the Internet and the Social Media Advantage," 226.

14. Ibid., 229.

15. Catherine Bott, W. James Castan, Robertson Dickens, et al., *Recruitment and Radicalization of School-Aged Youth and International Terrorist Groups* (Arlington, VA: Homeland Security Institute, 2009), 5.

16. "Sepanjang 2019 Kominfo Blokir 1500 Konten Terorisme," *CNN Indonesia*, November 8, 2019, https://www.cnnindonesia.com/teknologi /20190810121926-192-420082/sepanjang-2019-kominfo-blokir-1500-konten -terorisme.

17. Judith Miller and David Samuels, "A Glossy Approach to Inciting Terrorism," *Wall Street Journal*, November 27, 2010.

18. Shawn Kaplan, "Three Prejudices against Terrorism," *Critical Studies on Terrorism* 2, no. 2 (2009): 181–99.

19. Merlyna Lim, *Islamic Radicalism and Anti-Americanism in Indonesia: The Role of the Internet* (Washington, DC: East–West Center, 2005), 3.

20. Tanja Dramac Jiries, "Rise of Radicalization in the Global Village: Online Radicalization vs. In-Person Radicalization—Is There a Difference," *Journal for Deradicalization* 6 (2016): 217.

21. Aaron Smith and Monica Anderson, "Social Media Use in 2018," Pew Research Center, March 1, 2018, https://www.pewresearch.org/internet /2018/03/01/social-media-use-in-2018/.

22. Gabriel Weimann, "Terror on Facebook, Twitter and YouTube," *Brown Journal of World Affairs* 16, no. 2 (2010): 45–54; Arab Salem, Etna Reid, and Hsiu-Chin Chen, "Multimedia Content Coding and Analysis: Unraveling the Content of Jihadi Extremist Groups' Videos," *Studies in Conflict and Terrorism* 31, no. 7 (2008): 605–26.

23. Weimann, "Terror on Facebook, Twitter and YouTube."

24. Christina Schori Liang, "Understanding and Countering Islamic State Propaganda," Geneva Center for Security Policy, February 1, 2015, https://www.gcsp.ch/publications/cyber-jihad; James P. Farwell, "The Media Strategy of ISIS," *Survival: Global Politics and Strategy* 56 (2014): 49–55.

25. Selena Larson, "Twitter Suspends 377,000 Accounts for Pro-Terrorism Content," CNN, March 21, 2017, https://money.cnn.com/2017/03 /21/technology/twitter-bans-terrorism-accounts/.

26. Ines von Behr, Anaïs Reding, Charlie Edwards, et al., "Radicalisation in the Digital Era," RAND Europe, 2013. https://www.rand.org/pubs /research_reports/RR453.html.

27. Ibid., 17. Italics in original.

28. Hanna Rogan, *Jihadism Online: A Study of How al-Qaida and Radical Islamist Groups Use the Internet for Terrorist Purposes* (Kjeller, Norway: Norwegian Defence Research Establishment [FFI], 2006), 30.

29. Joanne Hinds and Adam Joinson, "Radicalization, the Internet and Cybersecurity: Opportunities and Challenges for HCI," in *Human Aspects of Information Security, Privacy and Trust*, edited by Theo Tryfonas (New York: Springer, 2017), 486.

30. Ibid., 487.

31. Conway, "Determining the Role of the Internet in Violent Extremism and Terrorism," 80.

32. Ibid., 81.

33. Anne Aly, "Brothers, Believers, Brave Mujahideen: Focusing Attention on the Audience of Violent Jihadist Preachers," *Studies in Conflict and Terrorism* 40, no. 1 (2017): 62–76, 65.

34. von Behr et al., "Radicalisation in the Digital Era," 17. Italics in original.

35. Daniel Koehler, "The Radical Online: Individual Radicalization Processes and the Role of the Internet," *Journal for Deradicalization* 1 (2014): 116–34, 118.

36. Tom Holt, Joshua D. Freilich, Steven Chermak, et al., "Political Radicalization on the Internet: Extremist Content, Government Control, and the Power of Victim and Jihad Videos," *Dynamics of Asymmetric Conflict* 8, no. 2 (2015): 107–20, 108.

37. von Behr et al., "Radicalisation in the Digital Era," 21.

38. Marc Sageman, "The Next Generation of Terror," *Foreign Policy*, October 8, 2009, https://foreignpolicy.com/2009/10/08/the-next-generation-of-terror/.

39. Jason Burke, "Al-Shabab's Tweets Won't Boost Its Cause," *Guardian*, December 16, 2011, https://www.theguardian.com/commentisfree/2011/dec/16/al-shabab-tweets-terrorism-twitter.

40. von Behr, "Radicalization in the Digital Era," 16.

41. Koehler, "The Radical Online," 128. For a summary of the debate on this, see Daniele Valentini, Anna Maria Larusso, and Achim Stephan, "*Onlife* Extremism: Dynamic Integration of Digital and Physical Spaces in Radicalization," *Frontiers in Psychology*, March 24, 2020, https://www.frontiersin.org/articles/10.3389/fpsyg.2020.00524/full.

42. Baaken and Schlegel, "Fishermen or Swarm Dynamics."

43. Bruce Hoffman, *Inside Terrorism* (New York: Columbia University Press, 2006).

44. Marc Sageman, *Understanding Terror Networks* (Philadelphia: University of Pennsylvania Press, 2004).

45. Baaken and Schlegel, "Fishermen or Swarm Dynamics," 203.

46. Ibid., 181.

47. Paul Gill, Emily Corner, Maura Conway, et al., "Terrorist Use of the Internet by Numbers: Qualifying Behaviors, Patterns, and Processes," *Criminology and Public Policy* 16, no. 1 (2017): 99–117.

48. Scott Matthew Kleinmann, "Radicalization of Homegrown Sunni Militants in the United States: Comparing Converts and Non-Converts," *Studies in Conflict and Terrorism* 35, no. 4 (2012): 278–97.

49. Mehmet F. Bastug, Aziz Douai, and Davut Akca, "Exploring the 'Demand Side' of Online Radicalization: Evidence from the Canadian Context," *Studies in Conflict and Terrorism* 43, no. 7 (2020): 616–37.

50. Koehler, "The Radical Online," 131.

51. Séraphin Alava, Divina Frau-Meigs, and Ghayda Hassan, *Youth and Violent Extremism on Social Media: Mapping the Research* (Paris: UNESCO, 2017), 24–25.

52. Ghaffar Hussain and Erin Marie Saltman, *Jihad Trending: A Comprehensive Analysis of Online Extremism and How to Counter It* (London: Quilliam, 2014), 10.

53. Ibid.

54. Garth Davies, Christine Neudecker, Marie Ouellet, Martin Bouchard, and Benjamin Ducol, "Toward a Framework Understanding of Online Programs for Countering Violent Extremism," *Journal for Deradicalization* 6 (2016): 57. See also R. Briggs and Sebastien Feve, *Review of Programs to Counter Narratives of Violent Extremism: What Works and What Are the Implications for Government?* (London: Institute for Strategic Dialogue, 2013).

55. Davies et al., "Toward a Framework Understanding of Online Programs for Countering Violent Extremism," 57.

56. Tim Stevens and Peter T. Neumann, *Report on Countering Online Radicalization: A Strategy for Action* (London: International Centre for the Study of Radicalization and Political Violence, King's College, 2009).

57. Janjaap van Earten, Bertjan Doosje, Elly A. Konijn, et al., *Developing a Social Media Response to Radicalization: The Role of Counter-Narratives in Prevention of Radicalization and De-Radicalization* (Amsterdam: University of Amsterdam, 2017); Briggs and Feve, *Review of Programs to Counter Narratives of Violent Extremism*.

58. Davies et al., "Toward a Framework Understanding of Online Programs for Countering Violent Extremism," 59–60.

59. Cristina Archetti, *Understanding Terrorism in the Age of Global Media: A Communication Approach* (New York: Palgrave Macmillan, 2012); Steven R. Corman, "Understanding the Role of Narrative in Extremist Strategic Communication," in *Countering Violent Extremism: Scientific Methods and Strategies*, edited by L. Fenstermacher and S. Canna, 36–43 (Dayton, OH: Air Force Research Laboratory, 2011); Stevens and Neumann, *Report on Countering Online Radicalization*.

60. Yayah Khisbiyah, *Contestation of Islamic Discourse on the Internet* (Jakarta: PPIM-UIN, 2017), 66.

61. Bharath Ganesh and Jonathan Bright, "Countering Extremists on Social Media: Challenges for Strategic Communication and Content Moderation," *P&I: Policy and Internet* 12, no. 1 (2020): 6–19, 10.

62. Liam Sandford, "Exploring the Capabilities of Prevent in Addressing Radicalisation in Cyberspace within Higher Education," *Journal for Deradicalization* 19 (2019): 262–63.

63. Ibid., 279.

64. Ozen Odag, Anne Leiser, and Klaus Boehnke, "Reviewing the Role of the Internet in Radicalization Processes," *Journal for Deradizalization* 21 (2019–2020); Akil N. Awan, "Virtual Jihadist Media: Function, Legitimacy, and Radicalizing Efficacy," *European Journal of Cultural Studies* 10, no. 3 (2007), 389–408.

CHAPTER 8

1. Florette Cohen-Abady, Daniel Kaplin, Lee Jussim, et al., "The Modern Antisemitism-Israel Model (MASIM): Empirical Studies of North American Antisemitism," in *Antisemitism in North America: New World, Old Hate*, edited by Steven K. Baum, Neil J. Kressel, Florette Cohen-Abady, et al., 94–118 (Leiden: Brill, 2016), 102. Raphael Israeli follows a similar line of argument concerning Western Muslim attitudes toward Jews and Israel. He writes, for instance, that an "Islamic anti-Semitic heritage is not, unfortunately, the only luggage that Muslims bring with them to the West. Their conduct towards Jews, as towards westerners in general, has also been conditioned by patterns of behaviors that are cultivated in Arab and Muslim societies and have become part and parcel of the make-up of those societies." See Raphael Israeli, *Muslim Anti-Semitism in Christian Europe: Elemental and Residual Anti-Semitism* (New Brunswick, NJ: Transaction Publishers, 2009), 21.

2. Günther Jikeli, *European Muslim Antisemitism: Why Young Urban Males Say They Don't Like Jews* (Bloomington: Indiana University Press, 2015), 32.

3. See "footnote" 37 of the introduction.

4. Task Force on Antisemitism at the University of California, Irvine, "Report," n.d., https://www.brandeiscenter.com/wp-content/uploads/2017/11/ngo/ocirvine.pdf.

5. ADL is an advocacy organization established in 1913 with a mission "to stop the defamation of the Jewish people and to secure justice and fair treatment to all." See its mission statement at https://www.adl.org/about/mission-and-history. Since 1979, the ADL has produced an annual *Audit of Anti-Semitic Incidents*, which has been criticized for not distinguishing between legitimate and illegitimate criticisms. Emmaia Gelman, for instance, criticizes the ADL for counting calls for Palestinian rights and even criticism of the ADL itself as antisemitic incidents. She writes that "the ADL has consistently used the language of civil rights, and its position as an authority on them, to describe Israeli state military violence as liberatory and Palestinian resistance, including non-violent civil resistance, as extremist." See Emmaia Gelman, "The Anti-Defamation League Is Not What It Seems," *Boston Review*, May 23, 2019, https://www.bostonreview.net/articles/emmaia-gelman-anti-defamation-league/. In this chapter, I make it clear that defending Palestinian rights is not antisemitism. I am using the ADL survey data because they provide a general picture of worldwide antisemitism.

6. See Kenneth L. Marcus, "The Resurgence of Anti-Semitism on American College Campuses," *Current Psychology* 26, no. 3 (2007): 206–12. Since 2002, the ADL has reported an average of 88 antisemitic incidents each year on American university campuses. For discussion of this, see Kenneth Lasson, "Antisemitism in the Academic Voice" in *Antisemitism on the Campus: Past and Present*, edited by Eunice G. Pollack, 292–314 (Boston: Academic Studies Press, 2011), especially 294.

7. Andre Oboler, "Online Antisemitism: The Internet and the Campus" in *Antisemitism on the Campus*, edited by Eunice G. Pollack, 331.

8. Here I disagree with the ADL CEO, Jonathan Greenblatt, who contends that "anti-Zionism is antisemitism." See Ron Kampeas, "In Major Address, ADL Chief Focuses on Anti-Zionists and Threats to Orthodox Jews," *Times of Israel*, May 2, 2023, https://www.timesofisrael.com/in-major-address-adl-chief-focuses-on-anti-zionists-and-threats-to-orthodox-jews/.

9. Robert S. Wistrich, "A Deadly Mutation: Antisemitism and Anti-Zionism in Great Britain," in *Antisemitism on the Campus*, edited by Eunice G. Pollack, 58.

10. Theodor W. Adorno, Else-Frenkel-Brunswik, Daniel J. Levinson, and R. Nevitt Sanford, *The Authoritarian Personality* (New York: Harper and Row, 1950), 71.

11. James T. Siegel, "*Kiblat* and the Mediatic Jew," *Indonesia* 69 (2000): 9–40; Jeffrey Hadler, "Translations of Antisemitism: Jews, the Chinese, and Violence in Colonial and Post-Colonial Indonesia," *Indonesia and the Malay World* 32, no. 94 (2004), 291–313.

12. Bernard Glassman, *Anti-Semitic Stereotypes without Jews: Images of Jews in England, 1290–1700* (New York: Conference on Jewish Social Studies, 1976).

13. Sidik Jatmika, *Gerakan Zionis Berwajah Melayu* (Yogyakarta: Wihdah Press, 2001).

14. For a brief discussion about this volume and M. Thalib's other works, see Ibnu Burdah, "Indonesian Muslims' Perception of Jews and Israel," in *Muslim Attitudes to Jews and Israel: The Ambivalences of Rejection, Antagonism, Tolerance, and Cooperation*, edited by Moshe Ma'oz, 230–44 (Portland, OR: Sussex Academic Press, 2010), 234.

15. Eva Mirela Suciu, *Signs of Antisemitism in Indonesia*, B.A. Honours Thesis, University of Sydney, Camperdown, Australia, 2008, 35–36.

16. See Tim Peneliti, *Yahudi dan Jurus Maut Gus Dur* (Jakarta: Cidesindo, 1999).

17. Cited by James T. Siegel in "*Kiblat* and the Mediatic Jew," 16.

18. Ibid., 19.

19. Martin van Bruinessen, "Yahudi sebagai Simbol dalam Wacana Islam Indonesia Masa Kini," in *Spiritualitas Baru: Agama dan Aspirasi Rakyat*, edited by Y.B. Mangunwijaya et al., 253–68 (Yogyakarta: Dian/Interfidei, 1994), reprinted in Martin van Bruinessen, *Rakyat Kecil, Islam dan Politik* (Yogyakarta: Gading, 2013), 279.

20. Burhanuddin Muhtadi, "The Conspiracy of Jews: The Quest for Anti-Semitism in *Media Dakwah*," *Graduate Journal of Asia-Pacific Studies* 5, no. 2 (2007): 53–76, 60. Concerning Nurcholish Madjid, Siegel writes: "Some writers in the monthly magazine *Media Dakwah*, where much of the criticism of Nurcholish was published, no longer consider Nurcholish to be a Muslim, but no one claims he is a Jew. According to his critics, Nurcholish is the agent, more often than not unwitting, of orientalists." See Siegel, "*Kiblat* and the Mediatic Jew," 17.

21. Martin van Bruinessen, "Post-Suharto Muslim Engagements with Civil Society and Democratization," in *Indonesia in Transition: Rethinking "Civil Society," "Region" and "Crisis,"* edited by Hanneman Samuel and Henk Schulte Nordholt, 37–66 (Yogyakarta: Pustaka Pelajar, 2004), 37.

22. Anthony Reid, "Entrepreneurial Minorities, Nationalism, and the State," in *Essential Outsiders: Chinese and Jews in the Modern Transformation of*

Southeast Asia and Central Europe, edited by Daniel Chirot and Anthony Reid, 33–72 (Seattle: University of Washington Press, 1997), 55.

23. Neha Banka, "Inside the Secret World of Indonesia's Jewish Community," *Haaretz*, April 22, 2019; Tya Bilanhar, "Umat Yahudi-Indonesia Rayakan Paskah di Sinagoge Bekasi," *Satu Harapan*, April 7, 2018.

24. Debe Campbell, "Jewish Roots Stir Revival in World's Largest Muslim Nation," *Arizona Jewish Post*, August 30, 2019.

25. Hadler, "Translations of Antisemitism," 304.

26. See Gabriel Ferrand, *Relations de voyages et textes géographiques arabes, persans et turks relatifs a l'Extrême-Orient du VIIIe au XVIIIe siècles* (Paris: E. Leroux, 1913), 2: 582; André Wink, *Al-Hind: The Making of the Indo-Islamic World* (Leiden: Brill, 2002), 100; Geoff Wade, "An Early Age of Commerce in Southeast Asia, 900–1300 CE," *Journal of Southeast Asian Studies* 40, no. 2 (2009): 221–65, 232.

27. For discussion on this, see O. W. Walter, *Early Indonesian Commerce: A Study of the Origins of Śrivijaya* (Ithaca, NY: Cornell University Press, 1967).

28. Kingsley Garland Jayne, "Francis Xaverius," in *The Encyclopaedia Britannica*, 11th ed. (New York: Encyclopaedia Britannica Company, 1911), 28: 882–83.

29. Herbert Ivan Bloom, *The Economic Activities of the Jews of Amsterdam in the Seventeenth and Eighteenth Centuries* (Port Washington, NY: Kennikat Press, 1969).

30. John Jourdain, *The Journal of John Jourdain, 1608–1617, Describing His Experiences in Arabia, India, and the Malay Archipelago*, edited by William Foster (Cambridge: Hakluyt Society, 1905), 108.

31. See Hadler, "Translations of Antisemitism," 294.

32. J.C.H. Blom and J. J. Cahen, "Jewish Netherlanders, Netherlands Jews, and Jews in the Netherlands, 1870–1940," in *The History of the Jews in the Netherlands*, edited by J.C.H. Blom, R. G. Fuks-Mansfeld, and I Schoffer, translated by Arnold J. Pomerans and Erica Pomerans, 230–95 (Oxford: Littman Library of Jewish Civilization, 2002), 287–89. See also Hadler, "Translations of Antisemitism," 299.

33. Tudor Parfitt, *The Jews of Africa and Asia: Contemporary Anti-Semitism and Other Pressures,* Report No. 76 (London: Minority Rights, 1987), 9.

34. Cited by Hadler in "Translations of Antisemitism," 299.

35. Ibid., 300. For a detailed discussion of the role of Jews during the Dutch colonial period in Indonesia, see Romi Zarman, *Di Bawah Kuasa Anti-Semitisme: Orang Yahudi di Hindia Belanda (1861–1942)* (Pekanbaru: Tjatatan Indonesia, 2018).

36. L. de Jong, *The Collapse of a Colonial Society: The Dutch in Indonesia during the Second World War* (Leiden: KITLV Press, 2002), 453.

37. Harry Jindrich Benda, *The Crescent and the Rising Sun: Indonesian Islam under the Japanese Occupation, 1942–1945* (The Hague: W. van Hoeve, 1958), 254–55.

38. Leonard Chrysostomos Epafras, "Realitas Sejarah dan Dinamika Identitas Yahudi Nusantara," *Religio: Jurnal Agama-Agama* 2, no. 2 (2012), 223.

39. Ibid., 224–25.

40. Hadler, "Translations of Antisemitism," 306.

41. For a discussion of Jews and their synagogue in Surabaya, see Febby Risti Widjayanto, "Antisemitisme Modern dalam Pembongkaran Sinagog Surabaya: Psikologi Politik Multikulturalisme," *Jurnal Politik Muda* 3, no. 3 (2014): 103–17.

42. See ADL Global, https://global100.adl.org/country/indonesia/2014.

43. See Pew Research Center, "Mixed View of Hamas and Hezbollah in Largely Muslim Nations," chapter 3, https://www.pewresearch.org/global /2010/02/04/chapter-3-views-of-religious-groups/.

44. Wahid Institute and Indonesian Survey Circle (LSI, Lembaga Survei Indonesia). *Laporan Survei Nasional Tren Toleransi Sosial-Keagamaan di Kalangan Perempuan Muslim Indonesia.* Wahid Foundation 2018. See https:// drive.google.com/file/d/1mNy6TTISy9MSbAQ-iyfm_nJGXKNI6L88 /view.

45. The results of the survey were reported by SMRC in a press conference that was cited by Eben E. Siadari in "Survei SMRC: Kelompok Anti-Kristen/Tionghoa di RI Hanya 3,4 Persen," *Satu Harapan*, December 30, 2016, https://www.satuharapan.com/read-detail/read/survei-smrc-kelompok -anti-kristentionghoa-di-ri-hanya-34-persen.

46. See Saiful Mujani Research and Consulting (SMRC), "Sikap Publik atas Isu Kebangkitan PKI," Temuan Survei Nasional, updated 23–26 September 2020, https://saifulmujani.com/sikap-publik-atas-isu-kebangkitan-pki/, slides page 32.

47. John L. Sullivan, James Piereson, and George E. Marcus, *Political Tolerance and American Democracy* (Chicago: University of Chicago Press, 1982), 2, cited by Saiful Mujani in "Religious Democrats: Democratic Culture and Muslim Political Participation in Post-Suharto Indonesia," Ph.D. dissertation, Ohio State University, Columbus, 2003, 38.

48. Saiful Mujani, *Religious Democrats*, 166.

49. The SMRC research findings were presented by Saiful Mujani during his talk show, "Bedah Politik Bersama Saiful Mujani," on the SMRC YouTube

Channel from June to August 2022. See the SMRC YouTube channel, https://www.youtube.com/c/SMRCTV/videos.

50. For a brief discussion of Mujani's view, see Saidiman Ahmad, "Saiful Mujani: Intoleransi pada Yahudi Terkait dengan Sikap Diskriminatif Negara," *Saifulmujani.com,* July 7, 2022, https://saifulmujani.com/saiful-mujani-intoleransi-pada-yahudi-terkait-dengan-sikap-diskriminatif-negara/.

51. For discussion of this, see Neil J. Kressel, "How to Interpret American Poll Data on Jews, Israel and Antisemitism," in *Antisemitism in North America,* edited by Steven K. Baum, Neil J. Kressel, Florette Cohen-Abady, et al., 3–32 (Leiden: Brill).

52. Steven K. Baum et al., eds., *Antisemitism in North America,* 415.

53. Judit Bokser Liwerant and Yael Siman, "Antisemitism in Mexico and Latin America: Recurrences and Changes," in *Antisemitism in North America,* edited by Steven K. Baum et al., 124.

54. Ibid., 123.

55. For discussion of this, see Edward Alexander, "Antisemitism-Denial: The Berkeley School," in *Antisemitism on the Campus,* edited by Eunice G. Pollack.

56. Judith Butler, "No, It's Not Antisemitic," *London Review of Books* 25, no. 16 (August 21, 2003).

57. Asaf Romirowsky, "The Growth of Anti-Israeli Sentiment in the American Intellectual Community: Some Cautionary Tales," in *Antisemitism in North America,* edited by Steven K. Baum et al., 89.

58. Jikeli, *European Muslim Antisemitism,* 107.

59. Ibid., 106.

60. For the English translation of the Indonesian Constitution, see Wim Voermans, Maarten Stremler, and Paul Cliteur, *Constitutional Preambles: A Comparative Analysis* (Northampton, MA: Edward Elgar Publishing, 2017), 242–43.

61. Michael Singh, "How Does Indonesia View the Prospect of Normalization with Israel?," Washington Institute for Near East Policy, October 28, 2020, https://www.washingtoninstitute.org/policy-analysis/how-does-indonesia-view-prospect-normalization-israel.

62. Moshe Yegar, "The Republic of Indonesia and Israel," *Israel Affairs* 12, no. 1 (2006): 136–58; Greg Barton and Colin Rubenstein, "Indonesia and Israel: A Relationship in Waiting," *Jewish Political Studies Review* 17, nos. 1–2 (2005): 157–70.

63. Cited by Johannes Nugroho in "How Ghaza Occupies Indonesia's Identity Wars," New Zealand Institute of International Affairs, May 25, 2021, https://www.nziia.org.nz/articles/how-gaza-occupies-indonesias-identity-wars/.

64. Ibid.

65. See Alexander Flores, "Judeophobia in Context: Anti–Semitism among Modern Palestinians," *Die Welt des Islams* 46, no. 3 (2006), 307–30.

66. Hadler, "Translation of Antisemitism," 299–300.

67. Suciu, *Signs of Antisemitism in Indonesia*, 18.

68. Benda, *The Crescent and the Rising Sun*, 104.

69. Ibid., 201.

70. For a detailed discussion of the treatment of Jews under Japan, see Rotem Kowner, "The Japanese Internment of Jews in Wartime Indonesia and Its Causes," *Indonesia and the Malay World* 38 (2010): 349–71.

71. Steven Leonard Jacobs writes, "As is the case with both the Hebrew Bible and the New Testament, the Qur'an contains passages that alienate 'the Other' (in this case the Jews) as 'unbelievers' and 'infidels,' and that address the responsibilities of Muslims to pursue unto death these 'enemies of God.'" See Steven Leonard Jacobs, "Anti-Semitism in the Arab World," in *Encyclopedia of Race and Racism*, edited by John Hartwell Moore (Detroit: Macmillan, 2008), 1: 114.

72. See Mark R. Cohen, *Under Crescent and Cross: The Jews in the Middle Ages* (Princeton, NJ: Princeton University Press, 1994). In the same vein, Hyam Maccoby writes, "Opposition to Jews and Judaism at a deep level does not form an essential aspect of Islamic thought, but is a recent development in Islam arising from the shock of Judaism's emergence from an apparently accepted and prolonged position of general inferiority." See Hyam Maccoby, *Antisemitism and Modernity: Innovation and Continuity* (London: Routledge, 2006), 149.

73. Jeffrey Herf, *Nazi Propaganda for the Arab World* (New Haven, CT: Yale University Press, 2010), 262.

74. Ibid., 263.

75. Matthias Küntzel, *Djihad und Judenhaß: Über den neuen antijüdischen Krieg* (Freiburg: ça ira, 2003), English translation: *Jihad and Jew-Hatred: Islamism, Nazism and the Roots of 9/11* (New York: Telos Press, 2007).

76. Klaus-Michael Mallmann and Martin Cüppers, *Halbmond und Hakenkreuz: Das Dritte Reich, die Araber und Palästina* (Darmstadt: Wissenschaftliche Buchgesellschaft, 2006), English translation: *Nazi Palestine: The Plan for the Extermination of the Jews in Palestine*, translated by Krista Smith (New York: Enigma Books, 2010).

77. Alexander Flores, "The Arabs as Nazis? Some Reflections on 'Islamofascism' and Arab Anti-Semitism," *Die Welt des Islams* 52 (2012): 450–70; 450.

78. Ibid., 453.

79. Ibid., 454.

80. Richard Breitman, "Muslim Anti-Semitism: Historical Background," *Current Psychology* 26 (2007): 213–22; 214.

81. Gudrun Krämer, "Anti-Semitism in the Muslim World: A Critical Review," *Die Welt des Islams* 46 (2006): 255.

82. Breitman, "Muslim Anti-Semitism," 215.

83. Stefan Wild, "National Socialism in the Arab Near East between 1933 and 1939," *Die Welt des Islams* 25 (1985): 243–76; 163.

84. Ibid., 160.

85. Rochard Landes and Steven T. Katz, "Introduction: *The Protocols at the Dawn of the 21st Century*" in *The Paranoid Apocalypse: A Hundred-Year Retrospective on* The Protocols of the Elders of Zion, edited by Rochard Landes and Steven T. Katz, 1–20 (New York: New York University Press, 2012), 1.

86. Marouf Hasian Jr., "Understanding the Power of Conspiratorial Rhetoric: A Case of *The Protocols of the Elders of Zion*," *Communication Studies* 48, no. 3 (1997): 195–214; 196.

87. See Randall L. Bytwerk, "Believing in 'Inner Truth': *The Protocols of the Elders of Zion* in Nazi Propaganda, 1933–1945," *Holocaust and Genocide Studies* 29, no. 2 (2015): 212–29; 214.

88. According to David Dalin and John Rothmann, "In 1918, the cousin of the mayor of Jerusalem, Mūsā Kāsim Pasha al-Ḥusayini, who was also the cousin of Ḥajj Amīn al-Ḥusayni (the mufti of Jerusalem), told the Zionist leader Chaim Weismann that he had received a copy of *The Protocols of the Elders of Zion* from a British officer of the military administration of Palestine and asked whether the Zionist leaders were also 'the elders of Zion' and whether they shared the same conspiratorial program." See David G. Dalin and John F. Rothmann, *Icon of Evil: Hitler's Mufti and the Rise of Radical Islam* (New York: Random House, 2008), 111.

89. See Esther Webman, "Adoption of the Protocols in the Arab Discourse on the Arab–Israeli Conflict, Zionism, and the Jews," in *The Global Impact of* The Protocols of the Elders of Zion: *A Century-Old Myth*, edited by Esther Webman (London: Routledge, 2011), 176.

90. Ibid., 177.

91. Ibid., 178.

92. Jan Goldberg, "A Lesson from Egypt on the Origins of Modern Anti-Semitism in the Middle East," *Kirchliche Zeitgeschichte* 16, no. 1 (2003): 127–48; 129–130.

93. Bruinessen, "Yahudi sebagai Simbol dalam Wacana Islam Indonesia Masa Kini."

94. Lembaga Penelitian dan Pengembangan Agama, Muhammadiyah, *Sorotan terhadap Protokolat: Perjanjian dan Keputusan Muʿtamar Yahudi* (Jakarta: Yayasan Pengkhidmatan Islam, 1978).

95. 'Alī Jum'ah, "al-Taqdīm lil-kitāb," in *Brūtūkūl ḥukamā' ṣahyūn wa uṣūluhā al-Tawrātiyyah wa'l-Talmūtiyyah*, authored by Ahmad Ḥijāzī al-Saqā and Hishām Khadr (Cairo: Maktabat al-nāfidhah, 2003), 7.

96. See Majid Kailany, *Bahasa Zionisme terhadap Dunia Islam*, translated by Abdullah Baraja (Solo, Indonesia: Pustaka Mantiq, 1984).

97. M. Izzat Darouza, *Mengungkap tentang Yahudi: Watak, Jejak, Pijak, Kasus-Kasus Lama Bani Israel*, translated by Hamali (Surabaya: Pustaka Progresif, 1982).

98. Bruinessen, "Yahudi sebagai Simbol dalam Wacana Islam Indonesia Masa Kini."

99. Mustafa al-Maraghi, *76 Karakter Yahudi dalam al-Qur'an*, translated by Dr. M. Thalib (Solo, Indonesia: Pustaka Mantiq, 1993); Yusuf Qaradawi, *Bagaimana Islam Menilai Yahudi dan Nasrani*, trans. Abdul Hayyie al-Kattani (Jakarta: Gema Insani Press, 2000); Jalal 'Alam, Ali Thantawi, and Muhammad Namir al-Khatib, *Dendam Barat dan Yahudi terhadap Islam*, translated by Dr. M. Thalib dan Mustafa Mahdamy (Solo, Indonesia: Pustaka Mantiq, 1994); Ahmad Ustman, *Israel Siapa Mereka? Sejarah bangsa Israel dari Awal Kemunculannya hingga Terbentuknya Agama Yahudi*, translated by A. Halim (Jakarta: Fima Rodhet, 2008); As'ad Bayud al-Tamimi, *Impian Yahudi dan Kehancurannya Menurut al-Qur'an*, translated by H. Salim Basyarahil (Jakarta: Gema Insani Press, 1992).

100. William G. Carr, *Yahudi Menggenggam Dunia*, translated by Mushtolah Maufur (Jakarta: Penerbit al-Kautsar, 1991); Jerry D. Gray, *Art of Deception: Mereka Menipu Dunia*, translated by Testraswari (Jakarta: Sinergi Publishing, 2011); Andrew C. Hitchcock, *The Synagogue of Satan: Sejarah Rahasia Yahudi Menguasai Dunia dan Kehancuran Total yang Sudah Lama Dipersiapkan*, translated by Melody Violine (Jakarta: Ufuk Press, 2011).

101. Burdah, "Indonesian Muslims' Perception of Jews and Israel," 233.

102. Ibid., 134.

103. 'Abbās Maḥmūd al-'Aqqād, *Al-Ṣahyūniyyah wa Qaḍiyyat Falistīn* (Beirut: Al-Maktabah al-'Aṣriyyah, n.d.), 175.

104. For discussion of this, see Webman, "The Adoption of *The Protocols* in the Arab Discourse," 180–88.

105. Anton Ramdan, *Membongkar Jaringan Bisnis Yahudi di Indonesia: Menguak Strategi, Penopang, dan Berbagai Macam Bisnis di Indonesia* (Solo, Indonesia: IslamikArt, 2009). See also Fasial M. Sakri, *Melacak Yahudi Indonesia* (Jakarta: Bale Siasat, 2008). For a detailed discussion of Indonesian antisemitic literature, see Ismatu Ropi, Dadi Darmadi, and Rifqi Muhammad Fatkhi, *Dari Zionism eke Teori Konspirasi: Laporan Akhir Penelitian Kompetitif* (Jakarta: UIN Syarif Hidayatullah, 2013).

106. Eggi Sudjana, *SBY Antek Yahudi AS? Suatu Kondisional Menuju Revolusi* (Jakarta: Ummacom Press, 2011); J. W. Lotz, *Kepungan Yahudi di Cikeas* (Yogyakarta: Solomon, 2010).

107. Siegel, "*Kiblat* and the Mediatic Jew"; Hadler, "Translations of Antisemitism."

108. This is in line with Adelia Hanny Rachman's argument that "antisemitism prejudice against the Jews is not actually a resultant form of religious conflict but [rather] a religion, in this case, is used as a tool to create an arena of sentimental scrimmage. Political motive is very dominant for distinguishing them." See Adelia Hanny Rachman, "Jewish Existence in Indonesia: Identity, Recognition, and Prejudice," *IjoReSH: Indonesian Journal of Religion, Spirituality, and Humanity* 1, no. 1 (2022): 1–25; 18.

CONCLUSION AND SUGGESTIONS FOR FUTURE RESEARCH

1. See, for instance, Lorenzo Vidino and James Brandon, *Countering Radicalisation in Europe* (London: International Centre for Radicalisation and Political Violence, 2012); Tania Saeed and David Johnson, "Intelligence, Global Terrorism, and Higher Education: Neutralising Threats or Alienating Allies," *British Journal of Educational Studies* 64, no. 1 (2016): 37–51; Paul Thomas, "Youth, Terrorism, and Education: Britain's Prevent Programme," *International Journal of Lifelong Education* 35, no. 2 (2016), 171–87; Liam Sandford, "Exploring the Capabilities of Prevent in Addressing Radicalisation in Cyberspace within Higher Education," *Journal of Deradicalization* 19 (2019): 259–85.

2. Catherine McGlynn and Shaun McDaid, *Radicalisation and Counter-Radicalisation in Higher Education* (Bingley, UK: Emerald Publishing, 2019), 8.

3. Catherine McGlynn and Shaun McDaid, "Radicalisation and Higher Education: Students' Understanding and Experience," *Terrorism and Political Violence* 31, no. 3 (2019): 559–76, 562.

4. Mayssoun Sukarieh and Stuart Tannock, "The Deradicalisation of Education: Terror, Youth, and the Assault on Learning," *Race and Class* 57, no. 4 (2015): 22–38; 23.

5. See, for instance, Katherine E. Brown and Tania Saeed, "Radicalization and Counter-Radicalization at British Universities: Muslim Encounters and Alternatives," *Ethnic and Racial Studies* 38, no. 11 (2015): 1952–68; Sarah McNicol, "Responding to Concerns about Online Radicalization in UK Schools through a Radicalization Critical Digital Literacy Approach," *Computers in Schools* 33, no. 4 (2016): 227–38; Lynn Davies, "Security, Extremism, and Education: Safeguarding or Surveillance?," *British Journal of Educational Studies* 64, no. 1 (2016): 1–19; McGlynn and McDaid, "Radicalisation and

Higher Education"; Jose Antonio Rodriguez Garcia, "Islamic Religious Education and the Plan against Violent Radicalization in Spain," *British Journal of Religious Education* 41, no. 4 (2019): 412–21.

6. McGlynn and McDaid, *Radicalisation and Counter-Radicalisation in Higher Education*, 4.

7. Ibid.

8. See, for instance, Nuriyeni Kartika Bintarsari, "Countering Terrorism in Indonesia: A Study of Policy in Counter-Terrorism Measures of the Indonesia National Counter-Terrorism Agency (Badan Nasional Penanggulangan Terorisme/BNPT)," Ph.D. dissertation, Rutgers University, New Brunswick, NJ, 2022); Aria Nikissa, "Security, Islam, and Indonesia: An Anthropological Analysis of the National Counterterrorism Agency," *Bijdragen tot de Taal-, Land- en Volkenkunde* 176 (2020): 203–39; Alif Satria Fitriani, Pricilia Putri, Nirmala Sari, and Rebekha Adriana, "The Current State of Terrorism in Indonesia," CSIS (Center for Strategic and International Studies) working paper, 2018.

BIBLIOGRAPHY

Aboud, Frances E., and Anna-Beth Doyle. "Parental and Peer Influences on Children's Racial Attitudes." *International Journal of Intercultural Relations* 20, no. 3 (1996): 371–83.

Adorno, Theodor W., Else-Frenkel-Brunswik, Daniel J. Levinson, and R. Nevitt Sanford. *The Authoritarian Personality*. New York: Harper and Row, 1950.

Agius, Emmanuel, and Jolanta Ambrosewicz. *Towards a Culture of Tolerance and Peace*. Montreal: International Bureau for Children's Rights, 2005.

Ahmad, Saidiman. "Saiful Mujani: Intoleransi pada Yahudi Terkait dengan Sikap Diskriminatif Negara." *Saifulmujani.com*, July 7, 2022.

Aiello, Emilia, Lidia Puigvert, and Tinka Schubert. "Preventing Violent Radicalization of Youth through Dialogic Evidence-Based Policies." *International Sociology* 33, no. 4 (2018): 435–53.

Aini, Nur. "Survei BNPT: 39 Persen Mahasiswa Tertarik Paham Radikal." *Republika*, July 26, 2017.

'Alam, Jalal, Ali Thantawi, and Muhammad Namir al-Khatib. *Dendam Barat dan Yahudi terhadap Islam*. Translated by Dr. M. Thalib dan Mustafa Mahdamy. Solo, Indonesia: Pustaka Mantiq, 1994.

Alava, Séraphin, Divina Frau-Meigs, and Ghayda Hassan. *Youth and Violent Extremism on Social Media: Mapping the Research*. Paris: UNESCO, 2017.

Alexander, Edward. "Antisemitism-Denial: The Berkeley School." In *Antisemitism on the Campus: Past and Present*, edited by Eunice G. Pollack, 38–52. Boston: Academic Studies Press, 2011.

Ali-Fauzi, Ihsan, Samsu Rizal Panggabean, Nathanael Gratias Sumaktoyo, Anick H. T., Husni Mubarak, Testriono, and Siti Nurhayati. *Disputed Churches in Jakarta*. Jakarta: PUSAD Paramadina, 2011.

Alius, Suhardi. *Memimpin dengan Hati: Pengalaman sebagai Kepala BNPT*. Jakarta: Gramedia Pustaka Utama, 2019.

———. *Pemahaman Membawa Bencara: Bunga Rampai Penanggulangan Terorisme*. Jakarta: Gramedia Pustaka Utama, 2019.

Allen, Charlie. "The Threat of Islamic Radicalization to the Homeland." Written testimony to the U.S. Senate Committee on Homeland Security and Governmental Affairs, Washington, DC, March 14, 2007.

Allport, Gordon W. *The Nature of Prejudice.* Oxford: Addison-Wesley, 1954.

Aly, Anne. "Brothers, Believers, Brave Mujahideen: Focusing Attention on the Audience of Violent Jihadist Preachers." *Studies in Conflict and Terrorism* 40, no. 1 (2017): 62–76.

———. *Terrorism and Global Security: Historical and Contemporary Perspectives.* South Yarra, Australia: Palgrave Macmillan, 2011.

Aly, Anne, and Jason-Leigh Striegher. "Examining the Role of Religion in Radicalization to Violent Islamist Extremism." *Studies in Conflict and Terrorism* 35 (2012): 849–62.

Ammerman, Nancy Tatom. *Everyday Religion: Observing Modern Religious Lives.* Oxford: Oxford University Press, 2007.

Anderson, Mark, Joanne Kaufman, Thomas Simon, and Lisa Barrios. "School Associated Violent Deaths in the United States, 1994–1999." *JAMA* 286, no. 21 (2001): 2695–2702.

Andersson, Lynne M., and Christine M. Pearson. "Tit for Tat? The Spiraling Effect of Incivility in the Workplace." *Academy of Management Review* 24, no. 3 (1999): 452–71.

Antonio, Anthony Lising. "When Does Race Matter in College Friendships? Exploring Men's Diverse and Homogeneous Friendship Groups." *Review of Higher Education* 27, no. 4 (2004): 553–75.

Al-'Aqqād, 'Abbās Maḥmūd. *Al-Ṣahyūniyyah wa Qaḍiyyat Falisṭīn.* Beirut: Al-Maktabah al-'Aṣriyyah, n.d.

Aranda, Jennifer L. "Educational Leadership, Adult and Higher Education." Ph.D. dissertation, University of South Dakota, Vermillion, 2018.

Arbi, Ivany Atina. "Internet Contributes to Radicalism among Young RI Muslims." *Jakarta Post*, February 24, 2019.

Archetti, Cristina. *Understanding Terrorism in the Age of Global Media: A Communication Approach.* New York: Palgrave Macmillan, 2012.

Arnett, Jeffrey Jensen. *Adolescence and Emerging Adulthood.* Upper Saddle River, NJ: Pearson Education, 2001.

———. *Emerging Adulthood: The Winding Road from the Late Teens through the Twenties.* New York: Oxford University Press, 2014.

ASEAN Today. "Social Media Is Facilitating Islamic Radicalization in Indonesia." February 20, 2020.

Ashour, Omar. "De-radicalization of Jihad? The Impact of Egyptian Islamist Revisionists on al Qaeda." *Perspectives on Terrorism* 11, no. 14 (2008): 11–14.

————. *The De-radicalization of Jihadists: Transforming Armed Islamist Movements*. New York: Routledge, 2009.

Aulia, Farah. "Bullying Experience in Primary School Children." *Indonesian Journal of School Counseling* 1, no. 1 (2016): 28–32.

Awan, Akil N. "Virtual Jihadist Media: Function, Legitimacy, and Radicalizing Efficacy." *European Journal of Cultural Studies* 10, no. 3 (2007): 389–408.

Azra, Azyumardi, Kees van Dijk, and Nico J. G. Kaptein, eds. *Varieties of Religious Authority: Changes and Challenges in 20th-Century Islam*. Singapore: Institute of Southeast Asian Studies, 2010.

Baaken, Till, and Linda Schlegel. "Fishermen or Swarm Dynamics: Should We Understand Jihadist Online-Radicalization as a Top-Down or Bottom-Up Process?" *Journal for Deradicalization* 18, no. 13 (2018): 178–211.

Badan Pusat Statistik (BPS). "Jumlah Perguruan Tinggi, Mahasiswa dan Tenaga Pendidik." https://www.bps.go.id/indikator/indikator/view_data _pub/0000/api_pub/82/da_04/1.

————. "Jumlah Sekolah, Guru, dan Murid Madrasah Aliyah (MA) di Bawah Kementerian Agama Menurut Provinsi, 2019/2020." https://www.bps.go .id/indikator/indikator/view_data_pub/0000/api_pub/80/da_04/1.

Al-Badayneh, Diab M. "University under Risk: The University as Incubator for Radicalization." In *Multi-Faceted Approach to Radicalization in Terrorist Organizations*, edited by Ihsan Bal, Suleyman Ozeren, and Mehmet Sozer, 32–41. Clifton, VA: IOS Press, 2011.

Baerveld, Chris, Marijtje van Duijn, Lotte Vermeij, and Dianne van Hemert. "Ethnic Boundaries and Personal Choice: Assessing the Influence of Individual Inclinations to Choose Intra-Ethnic Relationships on Pupils' Networks." *Social Networks* 26, no. 1 (2004): 55–74.

Baidhawy, Zakiyuddin. "Building Harmony and Peace through Multiculturalist Theology-Based Religious Education: An Alternative for Contemporary Indonesia." *British Journal of Religious Education* 29, no. 1 (2007): 15–30.

Banka, Neha. "Inside the Secret World of Indonesia's Jewish Community." *Haaretz*, April 22, 2019.

Barrelle, Kate. "Pro-Integration: Disengagement from and Life after Terrorism." *Behavioural Sciences of Terrorism and Political Aggression* 7, no. 2 (2015): 129–42.

Bartlett, Jamie, and Carl Miller. "The Edge of Violence: Towards Telling the Difference between Violent and Non-Violent Radicalization." *Terrorism and Political Violence* 24 (2012): 1–21.

Barton, Greg, and Colin Rubenstein. "Indonesia and Israel: A Relationship in Waiting." *Jewish Political Studies Review* 17, nos. 1–2 (2005): 157–70.

Bastug, Mehmet F., Aziz Douai, and Davut Akca. "Exploring the 'Demand Side' of Online Radicalization: Evidence from the Canadian Context." *Studies in Conflict and Terrorism* 43, no. 7 (2020): 616–37.

Bauman, Sheri, and Jessica Summers. "Peer Victimization and Depressive Symptoms in Mexican American Middle School Students: Including Acculturation as a Variable of Interest." *Hispanic Journal of Behavioral Sciences* 31, no. 4 (2009): 515–35.

Benda, Harry Jindrich. *The Crescent and the Rising Sun: Indonesian Islam under the Japanese Occupation, 1942–1945.* The Hague: W. van Hoeve, 1958.

Bender, Doris, and Friedrich Losel. "Bullying at School as a Predictor of Delinquency, Violence and Other Anti-Social Behaviour in Adulthood." *Criminal Behaviour and Mental Health* 21, no. 2 (2011): 99–106.

Bergamaschi, Alessandro. "Adolescents and Prejudice: A Comparative Study of the Attitudes of Two European Adolescent Populations Regarding the Issues That Are Raised by Increasing Cultural and Religious Pluralism." *International Journal of Intercultural Studies* 37 (2013): 302–12.

Bermingham, Adam, Maura Conway, Lisa McInerner, Neil O'Hare, and Alan Smeaton. "Combining Social Network Analysis and Sentiment Analysis to Explore the Potential for Online Radicalisation." In *Conference Proceedings*, 2009 International Conference on Advances in Social Network Analysis and Mining (IEEE Computer Society, 2009), 231–36.

Bertram, Luke. "Terrorism, the Internet and the Social Media Advantage: Exploring How Terrorist Organizations Exploit Aspects of the Internet, Social Media and How These Same Platforms Could Be Used to Counter Violent Extremism." *Journal for Deradicalization* 16, no. 7 (2016): 225–52.

Bigalke, Terance W. "Ten Keys to Understanding Indonesia." *Education about Asia* 12, no. 1 (2007): 12–16.

Bigler, Rebecca S., John M. Rohrbach, and Kiara S. Sanchez. "Children's Intergroup Relations and Attitudes." *Advances in Child Development and Behavior* 51 (2016): 131–69.

Bilanhar, Tya. "Umat Yahudi-Indonesia Rayakan Paskah di Sinagoge Bekasi." *Satu Harapan*, April 7, 2018.

Billante, Nicole, and Peter Saunders. "Why Civility Matters." *Policy* 18, no. 3 (2002): 32–36.

Bintarsari, Nuriyeni Kartika. "Countering Terrorism in Indonesia: A Study of Policy in Counter-Terrorism Measures of the Indonesia National Counter-Terrorism Agency (Badan Nasional Penanggulangan Terorisme/BNPT)." Ph.D. dissertation, Rutgers University, New Brunswick, NJ, 2022.

Bjorgo, Tore. "The Process of Disengagement from Violent Groups of the Extreme Right." In *Leaving Terrorism Behind: Individual and Collective*

Disengagement, edited by T. Bjorgo and J. Horgan, 49–65. New York: Routledge, 2009.

Bjorgo, Tore, and John Horgan, eds. *Leaving Terrorism Behind: Individual and Collective Disengagement*. London: Routledge, 2009.

Blom, J.C.H., and J. J. Cahen. "Jewish Netherlanders, Netherlands Jews, and Jews in the Netherlands, 1870–1940." In *The History of the Jews in the Netherlands*, edited by J.C.H. Blom, R. G. Fuks-Mansfeld, and I. Schoffer and translated by Arnold J. Pomerans and Erica Pomerans, 230–95. Oxford: Littman Library of Jewish Civilization, 2002.

Bloom, Herbert Ivan. *The Economic Activities of the Jews of Amsterdam in the Seventeenth and Eighteenth Centuries*. Port Washington, NY: Kennikat Press, 1969.

Borgatti, Stephen, and Brandon Ofem. "Overview: Social Network Theory and Analysis." In *Social Network Theory and Educational Change*, edited by A. Daly, 17–29. Cambridge, MA: Harvard Education Press, 2010.

Borum, Randy. "Radicalization into Violent Extremism I: A Review of Social Science Theories." *Journal of Strategic Security* 4, no. 4 (2011): 7–36.

———. "Understanding the Terrorist Mindset." *FBI Law Enforcement Bulletin* (2003): 7–10.

Bott, Catherine, W. James Castan, Robertson Dickens, Thomas Rowley, Erik Smith, and Rosemary Lark. *Recruitment and Radicalization of School-Aged Youth and International Terrorist Groups*. Arlington, VA: Homeland Security Institute, 2009.

Bowes, Lucy, Farida Aryani, Faridah Ohan, Rina Herlina Haryanti, Sri Winarna, Yuli Arsianto, Hening Budiyawati, Evi Widowati, Rika Saraswati, Yuliana Kristianto, Yulinda Erma Suryani, Derry Fahrizal Ulum, and Emilie Minnick. "The Development and Pilot Testing of an Adolescent Bullying Intervention in Indonesia—The ROOTS Indonesia Program." *Global Health Action* 12, no. 1 (2019): 1–13.

Boyd, Richard. "The Value of Civility." *Urban Studies* 43, nos. 5–6 (2006): 863–78.

Braunstein, Ruth. "Boundary-Work and the Demarcation of Civil from Uncivil Protest in the United States: Control, Legitimacy, and Political Inequality." *Theory and Society* 47, no. 5 (2018): 603–33.

Breitman, Richard. "Muslim Anti-Semitism: Historical Background." *Current Psychology* 26 (2007): 213–22.

Briggs, R., and Sebastien Feve. *Review of Programs to Counter-Narratives of Violent Extremism: What Works and What Are the Implications for Government?* London: Institute for Strategic Dialogue, 2013.

Brown, Katherine E., and Tania Saeed. "Radicalization and Counter-Radicalization at British Universities: Muslim Encounters and Alternatives." *Ethnic and Racial Studies* 38, no. 11 (2015): 1952–68.

Bruinessen, Martin van. "Introduction: Contemporary Developments in Indonesian Islam and the 'Conservative Turn' in the Twenty-First Century." In *Contemporary Developments in Indonesian Islam*, edited by Martin van Bruinessen, 1–20. Singapore: Institute of Southeast Asian Studies, 2013.

———. "Post-Suharto Muslim Engagements with Civil Society and Democratization." In *Indonesia in Transition: Rethinking "Civil Society," "Region" and "Crisis,"* edited by Hanneman Samuel and Henk Schulte Nordholt, 37–66. Yogyakarta: Pustaka Pelajar, 2004.

———. *Rakyat Kecil, Islam dan Politik.* Yogyakarta: Gading, 2013.

———. "What Happened to the Smiling Face of Indonesian Islam? Muslim Intellectualism and the Conservative Turn in Post-Suharto Indonesia." RSIS Working Paper No. 222, 2011.

———. "Yahudi sebagai Simbol dalam Wacana Islam Indonesia Masa Kini." In *Spiritualitas Baru: Agama dan Aspirasi Rakyat,* edited by Y. B. Mangun-wijaya et al., 253–68. Yogyakarta: Dian/Interfidei, 1994.

———, ed. *Contemporary Developments in Indonesian Islam: Explaining the "Conservative Turn."* Singapore: Institute of Southeast Asian Studies, 2013.

Bryman, Alan. "Integrating Quantitative and Qualitative Research: How Is It Done?" *Qualitative Research* 6, no. 1 (2006): 97–113.

Bryner, Karen. "Piety Project: Islamic Schools for Indonesia's Urban Middle Class." Ph.D. dissertation, Columbia University, New York, 2013.

Bukowski, William M., Andrew F. Newcomb, and Willard W. Hartup. *The Company They Keep: Friendship in Childhood and Adolescence.* New York: Cambridge University Press, 1998.

Burdah, Ibnu. "Indonesian Muslims' Perception of Jews and Israel." In *Muslim Attitudes to Jews and Israel: The Ambivalences of Rejection, Antagonism, Tolerance, and Cooperation,* edited by Moshe Ma'oz, 230–44. Portland, OR: Sussex Academic Press, 2010.

Burke, Jason. "Al-Shabab's Tweets Won't Boost Its Cause." *Guardian,* December 16, 2011. https://www.theguardian.com/commentisfree/2011/dec/16/al-shabab-tweets-terrorism-twitter.

Bush, Robin, and Budhy Munawar-Rachman. "NU and Muhammadiyah: Majority Views on Religious Minority in Indonesia." In *Religious Diversity in the Muslim-Majority States in Southeast Asia,* edited by Bernhard Platzdasch and Johan Saravanamuttu, 16–50. Singapore: Institute of Southeast Asian Studies, 2014.

Butler, Judith. "No, It's Not Antisemitic." *London Review of Books* 25, no. 16 (August 21, 2003).

Bytwerk, Randall L. "Believing in 'Inner Truth': *The Protocols of the Elders of Zion* in Nazi Propaganda, 1933–1945." *Holocaust and Genocide Studies* 29, no. 2 (2015): 212–29.

Cameron, Lindsey, Adam Rutland, Rosa Hossain, and Rebecca Petley. "When and Why Does Extended Contact Work? The Role of High-Quality Direct Contact and Group Norms in the Development of Positive Ethnic Intergroup Attitudes amongst Children." *Group Processes and Intergroup Relations* 14, no. 2 (2011): 193–206.

Campbell, Debe. "Jewish Roots Stir Revival in World's Largest Muslim Nation." *Arizona Jewish Post*, August 30, 2019.

Carr, William G. *Yahudi Menggenggam Dunia*, translated by Mushtolah Maufur. Jakarta: Penerbit al-Kautsar, 1991.

Cassidy, Tony. "Bullying and Victimisation in School Children: The Role of Social Identity, Problem-Solving Style, and Family and School Context." *Social Psychology of Education* 12 (2009): 63–76.

Chalmers, Ian. "Countering Violent Extremism in Indonesia: Bringing Back the Jihadists." *Asian Studies Review* 41, no. 3 (2017): 1–21.

Chernov-Hwang, Julie, Rizal Panggabean, and Ihsan Ali-Fauzi. "The Disengagement of Indonesian Jihadists: Understanding the Pathways." *Terrorism and Political Violence* 29, no. 2 (2017): 277–95.

Chin, Vivienne. "Collateral Damage of Counter-Terrorism Measures and the Inevitable Consequence of the Social Exclusion and Marginalization of Vulnerable Groups." In *Countering Radicalisation and Violent Extremism among Youth to Prevent Terrorism*, edited by M. Lombardi, R. Ragab, V. Chin, Y. Dandurand, V. de Devitiis, and A. Burato, 11–22. Washington, DC: IOS Press, 2015.

CNN Indonesia. "Sepanjang 2019 Kominfo Blokir 1500 Konten Terorisme." November 8, 2019. https://www.cnnindonesia.com/teknologi /20190810121926-192-420082/sepanjang-2019-kominfo-blokir-1500 -konten-terorisme.

Cohen, Mark R. *Under Crescent and Cross: The Jews in the Middle Ages*. Princeton, NJ: Princeton University Press, 1994.

Cohen-Abady, Florette, Daniel Kaplin, Lee Jussim, and Rachel Rubinstein. "The Modern Antisemitism-Israel Model (MASIM): Empirical Studies of North American Antisemitism." In *Antisemitism in North America: New World, Old Hate*, edited by Steven K. Baum, Neil J. Kressel, Florette Cohen-Abady, and Steven Leonard Jacobs, 94–118. Leiden: Brill, 2016.

Coleman, Daniel. *White Civility: The Literary Project of English Canada.* Toronto: University of Toronto Press, 2006.

Connolly, William E. "Taylor, Foucault, and Otherness." *Political Theory* 13 (1985): 365–76.

Conway, Maura. "Determining the Role of the Internet in Violent Extremism and Terrorism: Six Suggestions for Progressing Research." *Studies in Conflict and Terrorism* 40, no. 1 (2016): 77–98.

Corman, Steven R. "Understanding the Role of Narrative in Extremist Strategic Communication." In *Countering Violent Extremism: Scientific Methods and Strategies*, edited by L. Fenstermacher and S. Canna, 36–43. Dayton, OH: Air Force Research Laboratory, 2011.

Corner, Emily, and Paul Gill. "A False Dichotomy? Mental Illness and Lone-Actor Terrorism." *Law and Human Behavior* 39, no. 1 (2015): 23–34.

Cornille, Catherine. "Conditions for Inter-Religious Dialogue." In *The Wiley-Blackwell Companion to Inter-Religious Dialogue*, edited by Catherine Cornille, 20–33. Malden, MA: Wiley-Blackwell, 2013.

Cortes, Khaerannisa, and Becky Kochenderfer-Ladd. "To Tell or Not to Tell: What Influences Children's Decisions to Report Bullying to Their Teachers?" *School Psychology Quarterly* 29, no. 3 (2014): 336–48.

Costanza, William A. "Adjusting Our Gaze: An Alternative Approach to Understanding Youth Radicalization." *Journal of Strategic Security* 8, no. 1 (2015): 1–15.

Craig, Wendy M., Debra Pepler, and Andona R. Atlas. "Observations of Bullying in the Playground and in the Classroom." *School Psychology International* 21, no. 1 (2000): 22–36.

Creswell, John W., and Vicki L. Plano Clark. *Designing and Conducting Mixed Methods Research.* Thousand Oaks, CA: SAGE Publications, 2011.

Crocetti, Elisabetta. "Identity Dynamics in Adolescence: Processes, Antecedents, and Consequences." *European Journal of Developmental Psychology* 15, no. 1 (2018): 11–23.

Crossett, Chuck, and Jason A. Spitaletta. "Radicalization: Relevant Psychological and Sociological Concepts." U.S. Army Asymmetric Warfare Group, Ft. Meade, MD, 2010.

Dalin, David G., and John F. Rothmann. *Icon of Evil: Hitler's Mufti and the Rise of Radical Islam.* New York: Random House, 2008.

Darmadi, Dadi. "Guru Agama Makin Tak Toleran." *Koran Tempo*, December 25, 2016.

Darouza, M. Izzat. *Mengungkap tentang Yahudi: Watak, Jejak, Pijak, Kasus-Kasus Lama Bani Israel.* Translated by Hamali. Surabaya: Pustaka Progresif, 1982.

Digital 2020 Indonesia. https://datareportal.com/reports/digital-2020 -indonesia.

Davies, Garth, Christine Neudecker, Marie Ouellet, et al. "Toward a Framework Understanding of Online Programs for Countering Violent Extremism." *Journal for Deradicalization* 6 (2016): 51–86.

Davies, Lynn. "Educating against Extremism: Towards a Critical Politicisation of Young People." *International Review of Education* 55, nos. 2–3 (2008): 183–203.

———. "Security, Extremism, and Education: Safeguarding or Surveillance?" *British Journal of Educational Studies* 64, no. 1 (2016): 1–19.

de Jong, L. *The Collapse of a Colonial Society: The Dutch in Indonesia during the Second World War.* Leiden: KITLV Press, 2002.

deLara, E. W. "Why Adolescents Don't Disclose Incidents of Bullying and Harassment." *Journal of School Violence* 11, no. 4 (2012): 288–305.

Della Porta, Donatella, and Gary LaFree. "Guest Editorial: Processes of Radicalization and De-Radicalization." *International Journal of Conflict and Violence* 6, no. 1 (2012): 5–10.

Demant, Froukje, Marieke Slootman, Frank Buijs, and Jean Tillie. *Decline and Disengagement: An Analysis of Processes of Deradicalisation.* Amsterdam: IMES, 2008.

Demetriou, Chares. "Political Radicalization and Political Violence in Palestine (1920–1948), Ireland (1850–1921), and Cyprus (1914–1959)." *Social Science History* 36, no. 3 (2012): 391–420.

DuBois, David, and Barton Hirsch. "School/Nonschool Friendship Patterns in Early Adolescence." *Journal of Early Adolescence* 13, no. 1 (1993): 102–22.

Earten, Janjaap van, Bertjan Doosje, Elly A. Konijn, and Beatrice de Graaf. *Developing a Social Media Response to Radicalization: The Role of Counter-Narratives in Prevention of Radicalization and De-Radicalization.* Amsterdam: University of Amsterdam, 2017.

Eckert, Penelope. "Vowels and Nail Polish: The Emergence of Linguistic Style in the Preadolescent Heterosexual Marketplace." In *Gender and Belief Systems,* edited by N. Warner, J. Ahlers, L. Bilmes, M. Oliver, S. Wertheim, and M. Chen, 183–190. Berkeley, CA: Berkeley Women and Language Group, 1996.

Eisenberg, Nancy, and Richard A. Fabes. "Prosocial Development." In *Handbook of Child Psychology: Social, Emotional, and Personality Development,* edited by N. Eisenberg, 701–78. New York: Wiley.

Ellison, Christopher G., and Daniel A. Powers. "The Contact Hypothesis and Racial Attitudes among Black Americans." *Social Science Quarterly* 75, no. 2 (1994): 385–400.

El-Said, Hamed. *New Approaches to Counter-Terrorism: Designing and Evaluating Counter Radicalization and De-radicalization.* New York: Palgrave Macmillan, 2015.

Elsea, Mike, Ersilia Menesini, Yohji Morita, and Mona O'Moore. "Friendship and Loneliness among Bullies and Victims: Data from Seven Countries." *Aggressive Behavior* 30, no. 1 (2004): 71–83.

Elshimi, Mohammed. "De-Radicalisation Interventions as Technologies of the Self: A Foucauldian Analysis." *Critical Studies on Terrorism* 8, no. 1 (2015): 110–29.

Ena, Ouda Teda. "Visual Analysis of E-Textbooks for Senior High School in Indonesia." Ph.D. dissertation, Loyola University, Chicago, 2013.

Epafras, Leonard Chrysostomos. "Realitas Sejarah dan Dinamika Identitas Yahudi Nusantara." *Religio: Jurnal Agama-Agama* 2, no. 2 (2012): 194–244.

Erika, Kadek Ayu, Dian Atma Pertiwi, and Tuti Seniwati. "Bullying Behavior of Adolescents Based on Gender, Gang and Family." *Jurnal Ners* 12, no. 1 (2017): 126–32.

Erikson, Eric H. *Identity: Youth and Crisis.* New York: W. W. Norton, 1980.

Everett, Helen Sarah. "Faith Schools and Tolerance: A Comparative Study of the Influence of Faith Schools on Students' Attitudes of Tolerance." Ph.D. dissertation, University of London, 2012.

Ezzarqui, Leila. "De-Radicalization and Rehabilitation Program: The Case Study of Saudi Arabia." M.A. thesis, Georgetown University, Washington, DC, 2010.

Farwell, James P. "The Media Strategy of ISIS." *Survival: Global Politics and Strategy* 56 (2014): 49–55.

Fealy, Greg. "Conservative Turn." *Inside Indonesia*, July 15, 2007.

Feillard, Andrée. "From Handling Water in a Glass to Coping with an Ocean: Shifts in Religious Authority in Indonesia." In *Varieties of Religious Authority: Changes and Challenges in 20th-Century Islam*, edited by Azyumardi Azra, A. van Dijk, and Nico J. G. Kaptein, 157–76. Singapore: Institute of Southeast Asian Studies, 2010.

Feillard, Andrée, and Remy Madinier. *The End of Innocence? Indonesian Islam and the Temptations of Radicalism.* Translated by Wong Wee. Singapore: NUS Press, 2011.

Ferguson, Neil, and Eve Binks. "Understanding Radicalization and Engagement in Terrorism through Religious Conversion Motifs." *Journal of Strategic Security* 8, nos. 1–2 (2015): 16–26.

Ferrand, Gabriel. *Relations de voyages et textes géographiques arabes, persans et turks relatifs a l'Extrême-Orient du VIIIe au XVIIIe siècles.* Paris: E. Leroux, 1913.

Fichtenbaum, Rudy H. "Civility." *Academe* 6, no. 56 (2014).

Fink, Naureen C., and Ellie B. Hearne. *Beyond Terrorism: Deradicalization and Disengagement from Violent Extremism*. New York: International Peace Institute, 2008.

Fitriani, Alif Satria, Pricilia Putri, Nirmala Sari, and Rebekha Adriana. "The Current State of Terrorism in Indonesia." CSIS (Center for Strategic and International Studies) Working Paper, 2018.

Flores, Alexander. "The Arabs as Nazis? Some Reflections on 'Islamofascism' and Arab Anti-Semitism." *Die Welt des Islams* 52 (2012): 450–70.

———. "Judeophobia in Context: Anti-Semitism among Modern Palestinians." *Die Welt des Islams* 46, no. 3 (2006): 307–30.

Forni, Pier M. *The Civility Solution: What to Do When People Are Rude*. New York: St. Martin's Press, 2010.

Foucault, Michel. *Ethics: Essential Works of Foucault, 1954–1984*. Edited by P. Rainbow. London: Penguin, 1997.

———. "Technologies of the Self: A Seminar with Michel Foucault." In *Technologies of the Self*, edited by L. Martin, H. Gutman, and P. Hutton, 16–49. Amherst: University of Massachusetts Press, 1988.

———. "What Is Critique?" In *The Politics of Truth*, edited by Sylvère Lotringe and translated by Lysa Hochroth and C. Porter, 41–82. Los Angeles, CA: Semiotext(e), 1997.

Furedi, Frank. "Muslim Alienation in the UK? Blame the Israelis!" *Spiked*, February 9, 2009.

Furman, Wyndol, and Duane Buhrmester. "Age and Sex Differences in Perceptions of Networks and Personal Relationships." *Child Development* 63 (1992): 103–15.

Gaede, Stan D. *When Tolerance Is No Virtue: Political Correctness, Multiculturalism and the Future of Truth and Justice*. Downers Grove, IL: InterVarsity Press, 1993.

Gambetta, Diego, and Steffen Hertog. *Engineers of Jihad: The Curious Connection between Violent Extremism and Education*. Princeton, NJ: Princeton University Press, 2016.

Ganesh, Bharath, and Jonathan Bright. "Countering Extremists on Social Media: Challenges for Strategic Communication and Content Moderation." *P&I: Policy and Internet* 12, no. 1 (2020): 6–19.

Garcia, Jose Antonio Rodriguez. "Islamic Religious Education and the Plan against Violent Radicalization in Spain." *British Journal of Religious Education* 41, no. 4 (2019): 412–21.

Gastic, Billie. "School Truancy and the Disciplinary Problems of Bullying Victims." *Educational Review* 60, no. 4 (2008): 391–404.

Geertz, Clifford. *The Religion of Java*. Chicago: University of Chicago Press, 1960.

Gelman, Emmaia. "The Anti-Defamation League Is Not What It Seems." *Boston Review*, May 23, 2019. https://www.bostonreview.net/articles/emmaia-gelman-anti-defamation-league/.

Gill, Paul, Emily Corner, Maura Conway, Amy Thornton, Mia Bloom, and John Horgan. "Terrorist Use of the Internet by Numbers: Qualifying Behaviors, Patterns, and Processes." *Criminology and Public Policy* 16, no. 1 (2017): 99–117.

Gillespie, Piers. "Current Issues in Indonesian Islam: Analysing the 2005 Council of Indonesian Ulama Fatwa No. 7 Opposing Pluralism, Liberalism, and Secularism." *Journal of Islamic Studies* 18, no. 2 (2007): 202–40.

Glaser, Barney G., and Anselm L. Strauss. *The Discovery of Grounded Theory: Strategies for Qualitative Research*. Chicago: Aldine Publishing, 1967.

Glassman, Bernard. *Anti-Semitic Stereotypes without Jews: Images of Jews in England, 1290–1700*. New York: Conference on Jewish Social Studies, 1976.

Glock, Charles Y., Robert Wuthnow, Jane Piliavin, and Metta Spencer. *Adolescent Prejudice*. New York: Harper and Row, 1975.

Goldberg, Jan. "A Lesson from Egypt on the Origins of Modern Anti-Semitism in the Middle East." *Kirchliche Zeitgeschichte* 16, no. 1 (2003): 127–48.

Gonthier, Giovinella, and Kevin Morrissey. *Rude Awakenings: Overcoming the Civility Crisis in the Workplace*. Chicago: Kaplan Publishing, 2002.

Goodwin, Charles Steward. *Satan's Cauldron: Religious Extremism and the Prospects for Tolerance*. Lanham, MD: University Press of America, 2006.

Gray, Jerry D. *Art of Deception: Mereka Menipu Dunia*. Translated by Testraswari. Jakarta: Sinergi Publishing, 2011.

Grim, Brian J., and Roger Finke. *The Price of Freedom Denied: Religious Persecution and Conflict in the 21st Century*. New York: Cambridge University Press, 2010.

Gurin, Patricia, Eric L. Dey, Sylvia Hurtado, and Gerard Gurin. "Diversity and Higher Education: Theory and Impact on Educational Outcomes." *Harvard Educational Review* 72, no. 3 (2002): 330–67.

Hadler, Jeffrey. "Translations of Antisemitism: Jews, the Chinese, and Violence in Colonial and Post-Colonial Indonesia." *Indonesia and the Malay World* 32, no. 94 (2004): 291–313.

Hafez, Mohammed, and Creighton Mullins. "The Radicalization Puzzle: A Theoretical Synthesis of Empirical Approaches to Homegrown Extremism." *Studies in Conflict and Terrorism* 38 (2015): 958–75.

Halim, Haeri, and Hans Nicholas. "Govt Unblocks Radical Websites." *Jakarta Post*, April 1, 2015.

Hall, Bronwyn, and Kirsten Howard. "A Synergistic Approach: Conducting Mixed Methods Research with Typological and Systemic Design Considerations." *Journal of Mixed Methods Research* 2, no. 3 (2008): 1–22.

Halualani, Rona Tamiko, Anu Chitgopekarb, Jennifer Huynh Thi Ahn Morrison, and Patrick Shaou-Whea Dodge. "Who's Interacting? And What Are They Talking About? Intercultural Contact and Interaction among Multicultural University Students." *International Journal of Intercultural Relations* 28 (2004): 353–72.

Hamayotsu, Kikue. "Conservative Turn? Religion, State, and Conflict in Indonesia." *Pacific Affairs* 87, no. 4 (2014): 815–25.

Handayani, Lilis Sri. "Jumlah Madrasah Negeri Masih Minim." *Republika*, September 14, 2018.

Hanish, Laura D., and Nancy G. Guerra. "The Roles of Ethnicity and School Context in Predicting Children's Victimization by Peers." *American Journal of Community Psychology* 28 (2000): 201–23.

Hansell, Stephen. "Adolescent Friendship Networks and Distress in School." *Social Forces* 63, no. 3 (1985): 698–715.

Harris, Kira J., Eyal Gringart, and Deirdre Drake. "Leaving Ideological Groups Behind: A Model of Disengagement." *Behavioural Sciences of Terrorism and Political Aggression* (2017): 1–14.

Hasian Jr., Marouf. "Understanding the Power of Conspiratorial Rhetoric: A Case of *The Protocols of the Elders of Zion*." *Communication Studies* 48, no. 3 (1997): 195–214.

Hays, Danica G., and Chris Wood. "Infusing Qualitative Traditions in Counseling Research Designs." *Journal of Counseling and Development* 89, no. 3 (2011): 288–95.

Hazeltine, Christopher S. "Understanding Teachers' Perceptions of Bullying for Developing Teacher Detection and Intervention." Ph.D. dissertation, Walden University, Minneapolis, 2018.

Hefner, Robert W. *Civil Islam: Muslims and Democratization in Indonesia*. Princeton, NJ: Princeton University Press, 2011.

Heinrichs, Rebekah. *Perfect Targets: Asperger Syndrome and Bullying*. Shawnee, KS: Autism Asperger Publishing, 2003.

Helm, Toby, Matthew Taylor, and Rowenna Davis. "David Cameron Sparks Fury from Critics Who Say Attack on Multiculturalism Has Boosted English Defense League." *Guardian Online*, February 5, 2011.

Herf, Jeffrey. *Nazi Propaganda for the Arab World*. New Haven, CT: Yale University Press, 2010.

Hewstone, Miles, Ed Cairns, Alberto Voci, Juergen Hamberger, and Ulrike Niens. "Intergroup Contact, Forgiveness, and Experience of 'The Troubles' in Northern Ireland." *Journal of Social Issues* 62 (2006): 99–120.

Hill, Hal, and Thee Kian Wie. "Indonesian Universities: Rapid Growth, Major Challenges." In *Education in Indonesia*, edited by Daniel Suryadarma and Gavin W. Jones, 160–79. Singapore: Institute of Southeast Asian Studies, 2013.

Hilmy, Masdar. "The Politics of Retaliation: The Backlash of Radical Islamists to Deradicalization Project in Indonesia." *Al-Jami'ah* 51, no. 1 (2013): 129–58.

Hinds, Joanne, and Adam Joinson. "Radicalization, the Internet and Cybersecurity: Opportunities and Challenges for HCI." In *Human Aspects of Information Security, Privacy and Trust*, edited by Theo Tryfonas, 481–93. New York: Springer, 2017.

Hitchcock, Andrew C. *The Synagogue of Satan: Sejarah Rahasia Yahudi Menguasai Dunia dan Kehancuran Total yang Sudah Lama Dipersiapkan*. Translated by Melody Violine. Jakarta: Ufuk Press, 2011.

Hoffman, Bruce. *Inside Terrorism*. New York: Columbia University Press, 2006.

Holcomb, Gay Lin. "Faithful Change: Exploring the Faith Development of Students Who Attend Christian Liberal Arts Institutions." Ph.D. dissertation, University of Kentucky, Lexington, 2004.

Holt, Tom, Joshua D. Freilich, Steven Chermak, and Clark McCauley. "Political Radicalization on the Internet: Extremist Content, Government Control, and the Power of Victim and Jihad Videos." *Dynamics of Asymmetric Conflict* 8, no. 2 (2015): 107–20.

Hopkins, Nick. "Dual Identities and Their Recognition: Minority Group Members' Perspectives." *Political Psychology* 32, no. 2 (2011): 251–70.

Horgan, John. *Lessons Learned since the Terrorist Attacks of September 11, 2001*. Part of the National Consortium for the Study of Terrorism and Responses to Terrorism. C-SPAN video, September 1, 2011. http://www.c-spanvideo.org/program/TenYearA.

———. *Walking Away from Terrorism: Accounts of Disengagement from Radical and Extremist Movements*. New York: Routledge, 2009.

Horgan, John, and Tore Bjorgo. *Leaving Terrorism Behind: Individual and Collective Disengagement*. London: Routledge, 2009.

Hoskins, Andrew, and Ben O'Loughlin. "Media and the Myth of Radicalization." *Media, War and Conflict* 2, no. 2 (2009): 107–10.

Human Rights Watch. "Indonesia: New Counterterrorism Law Imperils Rights." June 20, 2018. https://www.hrw.org/news/2018/06/20/indonesia -new-counterterrorism-law-imperils-rights#.

Huneck, Amy. "Bullying: A Cross-Cultural Comparison of One American and One Indonesian Elementary School." Ph.D. dissertation, Union Institute and University, Cincinnati, OH, 2007.

Hussain, Ghaffar, and Erin Marie Saltman. *Jihad Trending: A Comprehensive Analysis of Online Extremism and How to Counter.* London: Quilliam, 2014.

Husserl, Edmund. *The Phenomenology of Internal Time-Consciousness.* Translated by James S. Churchill. Bloomington: Indiana University Press, 1964.

Hussong, Andrea M. "Distinguishing Mean and Structural Sex Differences in Adolescent Friendship Quality." *Journal of Social and Personal Relationships* 17, no. 2 (2000): 223–43.

Indonesian Survey Circle (LSI). Lembaga Survei Indonesia. 2012.

———. Lembaga Survei Indonesia. 2019.

Ismail, Olawale. "Radicalisation and Violent Extremism in West Africa: Implications for African and International Security." *Conflict Security and Development* 31, no. 2 (2013): 209–30.

Israeli, Raphael. *Muslim Anti-Semitism in Christian Europe: Elemental and Residual Anti-Semitism.* New Brunswick, NJ: Transaction Publishers, 2009.

Jacobs, Steven Leonard. "Anti-Semitism in the Arab World." In *Encyclopedia of Race and Racism,* edited by John Hartwell Moore, 1: 112–14. Detroit: Macmillan, 2008.

Jacobson, Michael. "Learning Counter-Narrative Lessons from the Cases of Terrorist Dropouts." In *Countering Violent Extremist Narratives,* edited by Eelco J.A.M. Kessels, 72–83. The Hague: National Coordinator for Counterterrorism, 2010.

Jatmika, Sidik. *Gerakan Zionis Berwajah Melayu.* Yogyakarta: Wihdah Press, 2001.

Jayne, Kingsley Garland. "Francis Xaverius." In *The Encyclopaedia Britannica,* 11th ed., 28:882–83. New York: Encyclopaedia Britannica Company, 1911.

Jenkins, Brian M. "Foreword: Outside Expert's View." In *Homegrown Terrorism in the U.S. and U.K.: An Empirical Examination of the Radicalization Process,* edited by Daveed Gartenstein-Ross and Laura Grossman, 7–9. Washington, DC: Foundation for the Defense of Democracies, 2009.

Jenkins, Sharon Rae, Kelly Goodness, and Duane Buhrmester. "Gender Differences in Early Adolescents' Relationship Qualities, Self-efficacy, and Depression Symptoms." *Journal of Early Adolescence* 22, no. 3 (2002): 277–309.

Jikeli, Günther. *European Muslim Antisemitism: Why Young Urban Males Say They Don't Like Jews.* Bloomington: Indiana University Press, 2015.

Jiries, Tanja Dramac. "Rise of Radicalization in the Global Village: Online Radicalization vs. In-Person Radicalization—Is There a Difference?" *Journal for Deradicalization* 6 (2016): 206–30.

Jones, Sidney. "Indonesian Government Approaches to Radical Islam Since 1998." In *Democracy and Islam in Indonesia*, edited by Mirjam Künkler and Alfred Stepan, 109–25. New York: Columbia University Press, 2013.

Jourdain, John. *The Journal of John Jourdain, 1608–1617, Describing His Experiences in Arabia, India, and the Malay Archipelago.* Edited by William Foster. Cambridge: The Hakluyt Society, 1905.

Jumʿah, ʿAlī. "al-Taqdīm lil-kitāb." In *Brūtūkūl ḥukamāʾ ṣahyūn wa uṣūluhā al-Tawrātiyyah waʾl-Talmūtiyyah*, authored by Ahmad Ḥijāzī al-Saqā and Hishām Khadr. Cairo: Maktabat al-nāfidhah, 2003.

Kailany, Majid. *Bahasa Zionisme terhadap Dunia Islam.* Translated by Abdullah Baraja. Solo, Indonesia: Pustaka Mantiq, 1984.

Kampeas, Ron. "In Major Address, ADL Chief Focuses on Anti-Zionists and Threats to Orthodox Jews." *Times of Israel*, May 2, 2023.

Kaplan, Shawn. "Three Prejudices against Terrorism." *Critical Studies on Terrorism* 2, no. 2 (2009): 181–99.

Kartika, Kusumasari, Hima Darmayanti, and Farida Kurniawati. "Fenomena Bullying di Sekolah: Apa dan Bagaimana?," *Pedagogia Jurnal Ilmu Pendidikan* 17, no. 1 (2019): 55–66.

Kasper, Walter Cardinal. "The Uniqueness and Universality of Jesus Christ." In *The Uniqueness and Universality of Jesus Christ: In Dialogue with the Religions*, edited by Massimo Serretti, 6–18. Grand Rapids, MI: William B. Eerdmans Publishing, 2004.

Kaye, Cathryn Berger. *The Complete Guide to Service Learning: Proven, Practical Ways to Engage Students in Civic Responsibility, Academic Curriculum, and Social Action.* Minneapolis, MN: Free Spirit Publishing, 2010.

Kerns, Kathryn A., Lisa Klepac, and AmyKay Cole. "Peer Relationships and Preadolescents' Perceptions of Security in the Child–Mother Relationship." *Developmental Psychology* 32 (1996): 457–66.

Kersten, Carool. *Islam in Indonesia: The Contest for Society, Ideas and Values.* Oxford: Oxford University Press, 2015.

Khisbiyah, Yayah. *Contestation of Islamic Discourse on the Internet.* Jakarta: PPIM-UIN, 2017.

Kinder, Donald R. "The Continuing American Dilemma: Whites' Resistance to Racial Change 40 Years after Myrdal." *Journal of Social Issues* 42, no. 2 (1986): 151–71.

King, Michael, and Donald M. Taylor. "The Radicalization of Homegrown Jihadists: A Review of Theoretical Models and Social Psychological Evidence." *Terrorism and Political Violence* 23, no. 4 (2011): 602–22.

Kingham, Robert, and Jemma Parsons. "Integrating Islamic Schools into the Indonesian National Education System: A Case of Architecture over Implementation." In *Education in Indonesia*, edited by Daniel Suryadarma and Gavin W. Jones, 68–81. Singapore: Institute of Southeast Asian Studies, 2013.

Kirkup, James. "Muslims Must Embrace Our British Values." *Telegraph*, February 5, 2011.

Klausen, Jytte. "Tweeting the *Jihad*: Social Media Networks of Western Foreign Fighters in Syria and Iraq." *Studies in Conflict and Terrorism* 38 (2015): 1–22.

Klausen, Jytte, Selene Campion, Nathan Needle, Giang Nguyen, and Rosanne Libretti. "Toward a Behavioral Model of 'Homegrown' Radicalization Trajectories." *Studies in Conflict and Terrorism* 39 (2015): 67–83.

Kleinmann, Scott Matthew. "Radicalization of Homegrown Sunni Militants in the United States: Comparing Converts and Non-Converts." *Studies in Conflict and Terrorism* 35, no. 4 (2012): 278–97.

Knauth, Torsten. "Tolerance—A Key Concept for Dealing with Cultural and Religious Diversity in Education." In *The European Wergeland Centre Statement Series*, edited by F. Tibbitts, R. Jackson, D. Kerr, T. Knauth, and P. Kirchschlager. Oslo: The European Wergeland Centre, 2014.

Koehler, Daniel. "De-radicalization and Disengagement Programs as Counter-Terrorism and Prevention Tools: Insights from Field Experiences Regarding German Right-Wing Extremism and Jihadism." In *Countering Radicalisation and Violent Extremism among Youth to Prevent Terrorism*, edited by M. Lombardi, R. Ragab, V. Chin, Y. Dandurand, V. de Devitiis, and A. Burato, 120–50. Washington, DC: IOS Press, 2015.

———. "How and Why We Should Take Deradicalization Seriously." *Human Nature Behavior* 1 (2017): 1–3.

———. "The Radical Online: Individual Radicalization Processes and the Role of the Internet." *Journal for Deradicalization* 1 (2014): 116–34.

———. *Understanding Deradicalization: Methods, Tools and Programs for Countering Violent Extremism*. New York: Routledge, 2016.

Konishi, Chiaki, Shelley Hymel, Bruno D. Zumbo, and Zhen Li. "Do School Bullying and Student–Teacher Relationships Matter for Academic Achievement? A Multilevel Analysis." *Canadian Journal of School Psychology* 25, no. 1 (2010): 19–39.

Kowner, Rotem. "The Japanese Internment of Jews in Wartime Indonesia and Its Causes." *Indonesia and the Malay World* 38 (2010): 349–71.

Krämer, Gudrun. "Anti-Semitism in the Muslim World: A Critical Review." *Die Welt des Islams* 46 (2006): 243–76.

Krämer, Gudrun, and Sabine Schmidtke, eds. *Speaking for Islam: Religious Authorities in Muslim Societies.* Leiden: Brill, 2006.

Kressel, Neil J. "How to Interpret American Poll Data on Jews, Israel and Antisemitism." In *Antisemitism in North America: New World, Old Hate,* edited by Steven K. Baum, Neil J. Kressel, Florette Cohen-Abady, and Steven Leonard Jacobs, 3–32. Leiden: Brill, 2016.

Krueger, Alan B., and Jitka Maleckova. *Education, Poverty, Political Violence and Terrorism: Is There a Causal Connection?* Cambridge, MA: National Bureau of Economic Research, 2002.

Kruglanski, Arie W., and Shira Fishman. "The Psychology of Terrorism: Syndrome versus Tool Perspectives." *Journal of Terrorism and Political Violence* 18 (2009): 193–215.

Kundnani, Arun. *A Decade Lost: Rethinking Radicalization and Extremism.* London: Claystone, 2015.

———. "Radicalisation: The Journey of a Concept." *Institute of Race Relations* 54, no. 2 (2012): 3–25.

Künkler, Mirjam, and Alfred C. Stepan, eds. *Democracy and Islam in Indonesia.* New York: Columbia University Press, 2013.

Künkler, Mirjam, and Hanna Lerner. "A Private Matter? Religious Education and Democracy in Indonesia and Israel." *British Journal of Religious Education* 38, no. 3 (2016): 279–307.

Kunst, Jonas R., Lisa S. Myhren, and Ivuoma N. Onyeador. "Simply Insane? Attributing Terrorism to Mental Illness (Versus Ideology) Affects Mental Representations of Race." *Criminal Justice and Behavior* 45, no. 12 (2018): 1888–1902.

Küntzel, Matthias. *Djihad und Judenhaß: Über den neuen antijüdischen Krieg.* Freiburg: ça ira, 2003. English translation: *Jihad and Jew-Hatred: Islamism, Nazism and the Roots of 9/11.* New York: Telos Press, 2007.

Kurzman, Charles. *The Missing Martyrs: Why Are There So Few Muslim Terrorists?* New York: Oxford University Press, 2019.

Laksana, Ben K. C., and Bronwyn E. Wood. "Navigating Religious Diversity: Exploring Young People's Lived Religious Citizenship in Indonesia." *Journal of Youth Studies* 22, no. 6 (2018): 807–23.

Al-Lami, Mina. "Studies of Radicalization: State of the Field Report." Politics and International Working Paper, University of London, 2009.

Landes, Rochard, and Steven T. Katz. "Introduction: *The* Protocols *at the Dawn of the 21st Century.*" In *The Paranoid Apocalypse: A Hundred-Year Retrospective on* The Protocols of the Elders of Zion, edited by Rochard Landes and Steven T. Katz, 1–20. New York: New York University Press, 2012.

Larson, Erica. "Civic and Religious Education in Manado, Indonesia: Ethical Deliberation about Plural Coexistence." Ph.D. dissertation, Boston University, 2019.

Larson, Selena. "Twitter Suspends 377,000 Accounts for Pro-Terrorism Content." CNN, March 21, 2017. https://money.cnn.com/2017/03/21/technology/twitter-bans-terrorism-accounts/.

Lasson, Kenneth. "Antisemitism in the Academic Voice." In *Antisemitism on the Campus: Past and Present*, edited by Eunice G. Pollack, 292–314. Boston: Academic Studies Press, 2011.

Leavy, Patricia, and Kathryn P. Maloney. "American Reporting of School Violence and 'People Like Us': A Comparison of Newspaper Coverage of the Columbine and Red Lake School Shootings." *Critical Sociology* 35, no. 2 (2009): 273–92.

Leiter, Brian. *Why Tolerate Religion?* Princeton, NJ: Princeton University Press, 2012.

Lembaga Ilmu Pengetahuan Indonesia (LIPI). "Radikalisme Ideologi Menguasai Kampus." http://lipi.go.id/berita/single/Radikalisme-Ideologi-Menguasi-Kampus/15082.

Lembaga Penelitian dan Pengembangan Agama, Muhammadiyah. *Sorotan terhadap Protokolat: Perjanjian dan Keputusan Mu'tamar Yahudi*. Jakarta: Yayasan Pengkhidmatan Islam, 1978.

Lester, Leanne, Donna Cross, Therese Shaw, and Julian Dooley. "Adolescent Bully-Victims: Social Health and the Transition to Secondary School." *Cambridge Journal of Education* 42, no. 2 (2012): 213–33.

Levin, Shana, Colette van Laar, and Jim Sidanius. "The Effects of Ingroup and Outgroup Friendship on Ethnic Attitudes in College: A Longitudinal Study." *Group Processes and Intergroup Relations* 6 (2003): 76–92.

Levine, Daniel H. *Politics, Religion, and Society in Latin America*. Boulder, CO: Lynne Rienner Publishers, 2012.

Liang, Christina Schori. "Understanding and Countering Islamic State Propaganda." Geneva Center for Security Policy, February 1, 2015.

Lim, Merlyna. *Islamic Radicalism and Anti-Americanism in Indonesia: The Role of the Internet*. Washington, DC: East–West Center, 2005.

Liwerant, Judit Bokser, and Yael Siman. "Antisemitism in Mexico and Latin America: Recurrences and Changes." In *Antisemitism in North America:*

New World, Old Hate, edited by Steven K. Baum, Neil J. Kressel, Florette Cohen-Abady, and Steven Leonard Jacobs, 121–73. Leiden: Brill, 2016.

Logli, Chiara. "Bhinneka Tunggal Ika (Unity in Diversity): Nationalism, Ethnicity and Religion in Indonesian Higher Education." Ph.D. dissertation, University of Hawai'i, Honolulu, 2015.

Lotz, J. W. *Kepungan Yahudi di Cikeas*. Yogyakarta: Solomon, 2010.

Lukens-Bull, Ronald. *A Peaceful Jihad: Negotiating Identity and Modernity in Muslim Java*. New York: Palgrave Macmillan, 2005.

Lynch, Orla. "British Muslim Youth: Radicalization, Terrorism and the Construction of the 'Other.'" *Critical Studies on Terrorism* 6, no. 2 (2013): 241–61.

Maccoby, Hyam. *Antisemitism and Modernity: Innovation and Continuity*. London: Routledge, 2006.

Mallmann, Klaus-Michael, and Martin Cüppers. *Halbmond und Hakenkreuz: Das Dritte Reich, die Araber und Palästina*. Darmstadt: Wissenschaftliche Buchgesellschaft, 2006. English translation: *Nazi Palestine: The Plan for the Extermination of the Jews in Palestine*. Translated by Krista Smith. New York: Enigma Books, 2010.

Al-Maraghi, Mustafa. *76 Karakter Yahudi dalam al-Qur'an*. Translated by Dr. M. Thalib. Solo, Indonesia: Pustaka Mantiq, 1993.

Marcus, Kenneth L. "The Resurgence of Anti-Semitism on American College Campuses." *Current Psychology* 26, no. 3 (2007): 206–12.

Marcus-Newhall, Amy, and Timothy R. Heindl. "Coping with Interracial Stress in Ethnically Diverse Classrooms: How Important Are Allport's Contact Conditions?" *Journal of Social Issues* 54, no. 4 (1998): 813–30.

Maskaliunaite, Asta. "Exploring the Theories of Radicalization." *International Studies: Interdisciplinary Political and Cultural Journal* 17, no. 1 (2015): 9–26.

Mazziotta, Agostino, Amelie Mummendey, and Stephen C. Wright. "Vicarious Intergroup Contact Effects: Applying Social-Cognitive Theory to Intergroup Contact Research." *Group Processes and Intergroup Relations* 14 (2011): 255–74.

McCauley, Clark, and Mary E. Segal. "Social Psychology of Terrorist Groups." In *Group Processes and Intergroup Relations*, edited by Clyde Hendrick, 331–46. Beverly Hills, CA: SAGE Publications, 1987.

McCauley, Clark, and Sophia Moskalenko. "Mechanisms of Political Radicalization: Pathways toward Terrorism." *Terrorism and Political Violence* 20, no. 3 (2008): 415–33.

McDonald, Laura Zahra. "Securing Identities, Resisting Terror: Muslim Youth Work in the UK and Its Implications for Security." *Religion, State and Society* 39, nos. 2–3 (2011): 177–89.

McGee, J. P., and C. R. DeBernardo. "The Classroom Avenger: A Behavioral Profile of School-Based Shootings." *The Forensic Examiner* 8 (1999): 16–18.

McGlynn, Catherine, and Shaun McDaid. *Radicalisation and Counter-Radicalisation in Higher Education.* Bingley, UK: Emerald Publishing, 2019.

———. "Radicalisation and Higher Education: Students' Understanding and Experience." *Terrorism and Political Violence* 31, no. 3 (2019): 559–76.

McGuire, Meredith. *Lived Religion: Faith and Practice in Everyday Life.* Oxford: Oxford University Press, 2008.

McNay, Lois. *Foucault: A Critical Introduction.* Cambridge: Polity Press, 1994.

McNelles, Laurie, and Jennifer A. Connoly. "Intimacy between Adolescent Friends: Age and Gender Differences in Intimate Affect and Intimate Behaviors." *Journal of Research on Adolescence* 9 (1999): 143–59.

McNicol, Sarah. "Responding to Concerns about Online Radicalization in UK Schools through a Radicalization Critical Digital Literacy Approach." *Computers in Schools* 33, no. 4 (2016): 227–38.

Menchik, Jeremy. *Islam and Democracy in Indonesia: Tolerance without Liberalism.* Cambridge: Cambridge University Press, 2016.

Miller, Judith, and David Samuels. "A Glossy Approach to Inciting Terrorism." *Wall Street Journal*, November 27, 2010.

Mitchell, Stefanie. "Deradicalization: Using Triggers for the Development of a US Program." *Journal for Deradicalization* 17, no. 9 (2016): 101–25.

Moghaddam, Fathali M. "The Staircase to Terrorism: A Psychological Exploration." *American Psychologist* 60, no. 2 (2005): 161–69.

Monaghan, Jeffrey, and Adam Molnar. "Radicalisation Theories, Policing Practices, and the Future of Terrorism?" *Critical Studies on Terrorism* 9, no. 3 (2016): 393–413.

Moolenaar, Nienke, and Peter Sleegers. "Social Networks, Trust, and Innovation: The Role of Relationships in Supporting an Innovative Climate in Dutch Schools." In *Social Network Theory and Educational Change*, edited by A. Daly, 97–114. Cambridge, MA: Harvard Education Press, 2010.

Morgan, David L. *Integrating Qualitative and Quantitative Methods: A Pragmatic Approach.* Thousand Oaks, CA: SAGE Publications, 2014.

Muhanna-Matar, Aitemad. "The Limit-Experience and Self-Deradicalization: The Example of Radical Salafi Youth in Tunisia." *Critical Studies on Terrorism* 10, no. 3 (2017): 453–75.

Muhtadi, Burhanuddin. "The Conspiracy of Jews: The Quest for Anti-Semitism in *Media Dakwah*." *Graduate Journal of Asia-Pacific Studies* 5, no. 2 (2007): 53–76.

Mujani, Saiful. "Religious Democrats: Democratic Culture and Muslim Political Participation in Post-Suharto Indonesia." Ph.D. dissertation, Ohio State University, Columbus, 2003.

Mulya, Teguh Wijaya, and Anindito Aditomo. "Researching Religious Tolerance Education Using Discourse Analysis: A Case Study from Indonesia." *British Journal of Religious Education* 41, no. 4 (2019): 446–57.

Nada-Raja, Shyamala, Rob McGee, and Warren R. Stanton. "Perceived Attachment to Parents and Peers and Psychological Well-being in Adolescence." *Journal of Youth and Adolescence* 21 (1992): 471–85.

Nagda, Biren A., and Patricia Gurin. "Intergroup Dialogue: A Critical-Dialogic Approach to Learning about Difference, Inequality, and Social Justice." *New Directions for Teaching and Learning* 111 (2007): 35–45.

Nesdale, Drew, Judith Griffith, Kevin Durkin, and Anne Maass. "Empathy, Group Norms and Children's Ethnic Attitudes." *Applied Developmental Psychology* 26 (2005): 623–37.

Nesser, Petter. "Jihad in Europe: Exploring the Motivations for Salafi-Jihadi Terrorism in Europe Post-Millennium." M.A. thesis, Department of Political Science, University of Oslo, 2004.

———. "Joining Jihadi Terrorist Cells in Europe: Exploring Motivational Aspects of Recruitment and Radicalization." In *Understanding Violent Radicalization: Terrorist and Jihadist Movements in Europe*, edited by Magnus Ranstorp, 87–114. London: Routledge, 2010.

Neumann, Peter R. "Introduction." In *Perspectives on Radicalization and Political Violence*, edited by Peter Neumann, 3–7. London: International Centre for the Study of Radicalization and Political Violence, 2008.

———. "Options and Strategies for Countering Online Radicalization in the United States." *Studies in Conflict and Terrorism* 36 (2013): 431–59.

———. "The Trouble with Radicalisation." *International Affairs* 89, no. 4 (2013): 873–93.

Neusner, Jacob, and Bruce David Chilton, eds. *The Golden Rule: Analytical Perspectives*. Lanham, MD: University Press of America, 2008.

Nikissa, Aria. "Security, Islam, and Indonesia: An Anthropological Analysis of the National Counterterrorism Agency." *Bijdragen tot de Taal-, Land- en Volkenkunde* 176 (2020): 203–39.

Norquist, Bruce Robert. "An Exploration of the Relationship between Student Engagement with Otherness and Development of Faith in Evangelical Higher Education." Ph.D. dissertation, Loyola University, Chicago, 2008.

Novak, Jeanne, Kelsey Jo Feyes, and Kimberly A. Christensen. "Application of Intergroup Contact Theory to the Integrated Workplace: Setting the Stage for Inclusion." *Journal for Vocational Rehabilitation* 35 (2011): 211–26.

Ntho-Ntho, Maitumeleng Albertina, and Jan F. Nieuwenthuis. "Religious Intolerance: The Case of Principals in Multi-faith Schools." *Journal for the Study of Religion* 29, no. 1 (2016): 167–86.

Nugroho, Johannes. "How Ghaza Occupies Indonesia's Identity Wars." New Zealand Institute of International Affairs, May 25, 2021.

Nuh, Muhammad. "Propaganda Terorisme di Indonesia," *Era Muslim*, September 27, 2010. https://www.eramuslim.com/suara-kita/dialog/propaganda -terorisme-di-indonesia.htm#.X7seAapKjBI.

Oboler, Andre. "Online Antisemitism: The Internet and the Campus." In *Antisemitism on the Campus: Past and Present*, edited by Eunice G. Pollack, 330–52. Boston: Academic Studies Press, 2011.

O'Bryan, Megan, Harold D. Fishbein, and D. Neal Ritchey. "Intergenerational Transmission of Prejudice, Gender Role Stereotyping, and Intolerance." *Adolescence* 39 (2004): 407–25.

Odag, Ozen, Anne Leiser, and Klaus Boehnke. "Reviewing the Role of the Internet in Radicalization Processes." *Journal for Deradizalization* 21 (2019–2020): 261–300.

Olweus, Dan. *Aggression in the Schools: Bullies and Whipping Boys*. Washington, DC: Wiley, 1978.

———. *Bullying at School: What We Know and What We Can Do*. Cambridge, MA: Blackwell, 1993.

Oppel, Stephanie Ferraro. "The Complexity of Civility (and Incivility) Development: Identity and the Challenge of Civility in the United States." Ph.D. dissertation, Drake University, Des Moines, IA, 2019.

Osman, Mohamed Nawab Mohamed. *Hizbut Tahrir Indonesia and Political Islam: Identity, Ideology, and Religio-Political Mobilization*. London: Routledge, 2018.

Parfitt, Tudor. *The Jews of Africa and Asia: Contemporary Anti-Semitism and Other Pressures*. Report No. 76. London: Minority Rights, 1987.

Parker, Lyn. "Religious Education for Peaceful Coexistence in Indonesia?" *South East Asia Research* 22, no.4 (2014): 487–504.

Parker, Lyn, and R. Raihani. "Democratizing Indonesia through Education? Community Participation in Islamic Schooling." *Educational Management Administration and Leadership* 39, no. 6 (2011): 712–32.

Pedersen, Willy, Viggo Vestel, and Anders Bakken. "At Risk for Radicalization and Jihadism? A Population-Based Study of Norwegian Adolescents." *Cooperation and Conflict* 53, no. 1 (2018): 61–83.

Pettigrew, Thomas, and Linda Tropp. "A Meta-Analytic Test of Intergroup Contact Theory." *Journal of Personality and Social Psychology* 90, no. 5 (2006): 751–83.

Pohl, Florian. *Islamic Education and the Public Sphere: Today's Pesantren in Indonesia.* New York: Waxmann, 2009.

Precht, Thomas. "Home Grown Terrorism and Islamist Radicalization in Europe: From Conversion to Terrorism." Research report funded by the Danish Ministry of Justice, 2007.

Procidano, Mary E., and Kenneth Heller. "Measures of Perceived Social Support from Friends and from Family: Three Validation Studies." *American Journal of Community Psychology* 11, no. 1 (1983): 1–24.

Puhl, Rebecca M., Jamie Lee Peterson, and Joerg Luedicke. "Weight-Based Victimization: Bullying Experiences of Weight Loss Treatment–Seeking Youth." *Pediatrics* 131, no. 1 (2013): 1–9.

Purwadi, Agung, and Suhero Muljoatmodjo. "Education in Indonesia: Coping with Challenges in the Third Millennium." *Journal of Southeast Asian Education* 1, no. 1 (2000): 79–102.

Pusat Pengkajian Islam dan Masyarakat (PPIM). *Sikap dan Perilaku Keberagamaan Guru dan Dosen Pendidikan Agama Islam.* Jakarta: UIN Syarif Hidayatullah, 2018.

Pusat Studi Budaya dan Perubahan Social (PSBPS) Universitas Muhammadiyah Surakarta, PPIM UIN Jakarta—UNDP Indonesia. *Islamic Websites: Narrative Contestation between the Radical and the Moderate.* Jakarta: Convey Report, 2018.

Qaradawi, Yusuf. *Bagaimana Islam Menilai Yahudi dan Nasrani.* Translated by Abdul Hayyie al-Kattani. Jakarta: Gema Insani Press, 2000.

Rabasa, Angel, Stacie L. Pettyjohn, Jeremy J. Ghez, and Christopher Boucek. *Deradicalizing Islamist Extremists.* Santa Monica, CA: RAND, 2010.

Rachman, Adelia Hanny. "Jewish Existence in Indonesia: Identity, Recognition, and Prejudice." *IjoReSH: Indonesian Journal of Religion, Spirituality, and Humanity* 1, no. 1 (2022): 1–25.

Rahma, Andita. "Kemenristekdikti Akui Kampus Rentan Terpapar Radikalisme." *Tempo.co*, June 5, 2018. https://nasional.tempo.co/read/1095480/Kemenristek-dikti-kampus-rentan-terpapar-radikalisme/full&view=ok.

Rambo, Lewis R. *Understanding Religious Conversion.* New Haven, CT: Yale University Press, 1993.

———, ed. *The Oxford Handbook of Religious Conversion.* Oxford: Oxford University Press, 2014.

Ramdan, Anton. *Membongkar Jaringan Bisnis Yahudi di Indonesia: Menguak Strategi, Penopang, dan Berbagai Macam Bisnis di Indonesia.* Solo, Indonesia: IslamikArt, 2009.

Al-Ramiah, Ananthi, and Miles Hewstone. "Intergroup Contact as a Tool for Reducing, Resolving, and Preventing Intergroup Conflict: Evidence, Limitations, and Potential." *American Psychologist* 68 (2013): 527–42.

Reid, Anthony. "Entrepreneurial Minorities, Nationalism, and the State." In *Essential Outsiders: Chinese and Jews in the Modern Transformation of Southeast Asia and Central Europe*, edited by Daniel Chirot and Anthony Reid, 33–72. Seattle: University of Washington Press, 1997.

Ricklefs, M. C. *A History of Modern Indonesia since c. 1200.* London: Palgrave, 2001.

Rijkers, Monique. "Darurat Intoleransi Guru dan Buku Ajar Agama Islam." *dw.com*, November 1, 2018. https://www.dw.com/id/darurat-intoleransi -guru-dan-buku-ajar-agama-islam/a-45764686.

Rodkin, Philip C., Dorothy L. Espelage, and Laura D. Hanish. "A Relational Framework for Understanding Bullying: Developmental Antecedents and Outcomes." *American Psychologist* 70, no. 4 (2015): 311–21.

Rogan, Hanna. *Jihadism Online: A Study of How al-Qaida and Radical Islamist Groups Use the Internet for Terrorist Purposes.* Kjeller, Norway: Norwegian Defence Research Establishment (FFI), 2006.

Roland, Erling. "Bullying, Depressive Symptoms and Suicidal Thoughts." *Educational Research* 44, no. 1 (2002): 55–67.

Romirowsky, Asaf. "The Growth of Anti-Israeli Sentiment in the American Intellectual Community: Some Cautionary Tales." In *Antisemitism in North America: New World, Old Hate*, edited by Steven K. Baum, Neil J. Kressel, Florette Cohen-Abady, and Steven Leonard Jacobs, 81–93. Leiden: Brill, 2016.

Ropi, Ismatu, Dadi Darmadi, and Rifqi Muhammad Fatkhi. *Dari Zionism eke Teori Konspirasi: Laporan Akhir Penelitian Kompetitif.* Jakarta: UIN Syarif Hidayatullah, 2013.

Rose, Nikolas. "Identity, Genealogy, History." In *Questions of Cultural Identity*, edited by S. Hall and P. Du Gay, 128–49. London: SAGE Publications, 1996.

Royono, Rivandra, and Diastika Rahwidiati. "Beating the Odds: Locally Relevant Alternatives to World-Class Universities." In *Education in Indonesia*, edited by Daniel Suryadarma and Gavin Jones, 180–202. Singapore: Institute of Southeast Asian Studies, 2013.

Rubin, Kenneth H., William M. Bukowski, and Jeffrey Parker. "Peer Relations, Relationships, and Groups." In *Handbook of Childs Psychology*, edited by William Damon, 619–700. New York: Wiley, 2006.

Rubin, Kenneth H., Kathleen M. Dwyer, Cathryn Booth-LaForce, Angel K. Kim, Kim B. Burgess, and Linda Rose-Krasnor. "Attachment, Friendship, and Psychosocial Functioning in Early Adolescence." *Journal of Early Adolescence* 24, no. 4 (2002): 326–56.

Saeed, Tania, and David Johnson. "Intelligence, Global Terrorism, and Higher Education: Neutralising Threats or Alienating Allies." *British Journal of Educational Studies* 64, no. 1 (2016): 37–51.

Sageman, Marc. *Leaderless Jihad: Terror Networks in the Twenty-First Century.* Philadelphia: University of Pennsylvania Press, 2008. https://foreignpolicy.com/2009/10/08/the-next-generation-of-terror/.

———. "The Next Generation of Terror." *Foreign Policy*, October 8, 2009.

———. *Understanding Terror Networks.* Philadelphia: University of Pennsylvania Press, 2004.

Saiful Mujani Research and Consulting (SMRC). "Sikap Publik atas Isu Kebangkitan PKI." Temuan Survei Nasional. Updated September 23–26, 2020. https://saifulmujani.com/sikap-publik-atas-isu-kebangkitan-pki/, slides page 32.

Sakri, Fasial M. *Melacak Yahudi Indonesia.* Jakarta: Bale Siasat, 2008.

Salem, Arab, Etna Reid, and Hsiu-Chin Chen. "Multimedia Content Coding and Analysis: Unraveling the Content of Jihadi Extremist Groups' Videos." *Studies in Conflict and Terrorism* 31, no. 7 (2008): 605–26.

Salmivalli, Christina. "Participant Role Approach to School Bullying: Implications for Interventions." *Journal of Adolescence* 22, no. 4 (1999): 453–59.

Sandford, Liam. "Exploring the Capabilities of Prevent in Addressing Radicalisation in Cyberspace within Higher Education." *Journal for Deradicalization* 19 (2019): 259–85.

Santrock, John W. *Adolescence.* 13th ed. New York: McGraw-Hill, 2009.

Saroglou, Vassilis. "Adolescents' Social Development and the Role of Religion." In *Values, Religion, and Culture in Adolescent Development: Coherence at the Detriment of Openness*, edited by G. Trommsdorff and X. Chen, 391–423. New York: Cambridge University Press, 2012.

Sawyer, Jami-Leigh, Faye Mishna, Debra Pepler, and Judith Wiener. "The Missing Voice: Parents' Perspectives of Bullying." *Children and Youth Services Review* 33, no. 10 (2011): 1795–1803.

Sbarbaro, Victor, and M. Enyeart Smith. "An Exploratory Study of Bullying and Cyberbullying Behaviors among Economically/Educationally

Disadvantaged Middle School Students." *American Journal of Health Studies* 26, no. 3 (2011): 139–51.

Schmid, Alex P., *Radicalization, De-Radicalization, Counter-Radicalization: A Conceptual Discussion and Literature Review*. The Hague: International Centre for Counter-Terrorism, 2013.

———, ed. *The Routledge Handbook on Terrorism Research*. London: Routledge, 2011.

Schmidt, Leonie. "Cyberwarriors and Counterstars: Contesting Religious Radicalism and Violence on Indonesian Social Media." *Asiascape: Digital Asia* 5 (2018): 32–67.

Schneider, Barry H., Sharon S. Woodburn, Maria del Pilar Soteras del Toro, and Stephen J. Udvari. "Cultural and Gender Differences in the Implications of Competition for Early Adolescent Friendship." *Merrill-Palmer Quarterly* 51, no. 2 (2005): 163–91.

Scott, Harriette A. "In Search of Civility: A Community College Perspective." Ph.D. dissertation, Morgan State University, Baltimore, MD, 2009.

Sedgwick, Mark. "The Concept of Radicalization as a Source of Confusion." *Terrorism and Political Violence* 22, no. 4 (2010): 479–94.

Seifert, Katherine. "Can Jihadis Be Rehabilitated? Radical Islam." *Middle East Quarterly* 17, no. 2 (2010): 21–30.

Siadari, Eben E. "Survei SMRC: Kelompok Anti-Kristen/Tionghoa di RI Hanya 3,4 Persen." *Suara Harapan*, December 30, 2016. https://www.satuharapan.com/read-detail/read/survei-smrc-kelompok-anti-kristentionghoa-di-ri-hanya-34-persen.

Siegel, James T. "*Kiblat* and the Mediatic Jew." *Indonesia* 69 (2000): 9–40.

Silber, Mitchell D., and Arvin Bhatt. *Radicalization in the West: The Homegrown Threat*. New York: New York City Police Department, 2007. https://seths.blog/wp-content/uploads/2007/09/NYPD_Report-Radicalization_in_the_West.pdf.

Silke, Andrew. "Disengagement or Deradicalization? A Look at Prison Programs for Jailed Terrorists." *CTC Sentinel* 4, no. 1 (2011): 18–21.

———. "Holy Warriors: Exploring the Psychological Processes of Jihadi Radicalization." *European Journal of Criminology* 5, no. 1 (2008): 99–123.

Singh, Michael. "How Does Indonesia View the Prospect of Normalization with Israel?" Washington Institute for Near East Policy, Washington, DC, October 28, 2020. https://www.washingtoninstitute.org/policy-analysis/how-does-indonesia-view-prospect-normalization-israel.

Sinuko, Damar. *Diduga pro-HTI, Guru Besar Undip Prof. Suteki Dinonaktifkan.* CNN Indonesia, June 6, 2018. https://www.cnnindonesia.com/nasional

/20180606222408-20-304123/diduga-pro-hti-guru-besar-undip-prof
-suteki-dinonaktifkan.

Sirry, Mun'im. "Fatwas and Their Controversies: The Case of the Council of Indonesian Ulama (MUI)." *Journal of Southeast Asian Studies* 44, no. 1 (2013): 100–117.

———. "The Public Expression of Traditional Islam." *The Muslim World* 100, no. 1 (2010): 60–77.

———. "The Public Role of Non-Muslim *Dhimmī*s during 'Abbāsid Times." *Bulletin of the School of Oriental and African Studies* 72, no. 2 (2011): 187–204.

Slootman, Marieke, and Jean Tillie. *Processes of Radicalisation: Why Some Amsterdam Muslims Become Radicals.* Universiteit van Amsterdam: Institute for Migration and Ethnic Studies, 2006.

Smith, Aaron, and Monica Anderson. "Social Media Use in 2018." Pew Research Center, March 1, 2018. https://www.pewresearch.org/internet /2018/03/01/social-media-use-in-2018/.

Smith, Hannah, Keja Polenik, Shamin Nakasita, and Alice Jones. "Profiling Social, Emotional and Behavioural Difficulties of Children Involved in Direct and Indirect Bullying Behaviours." *Emotional and Behavioural Difficulties* 17, nos. 3–4 (2012): 243–57.

Smith, Jonathan, Paul Flowers, and Michael Larkin. *Interpretative Phenomenological Analysis: Theory, Method, and Research.* London: SAGE Publications, 2009.

Snow, David A., and Richard Machalek. "The Sociology of Conversion." *Annual Review of Sociology* 10 (1984): 167–90.

"Social Media Is Facilitating Islamic Radicalization in Indonesia." *ASEAN Today*, February 20, 2020.

Sofjan, Dicky. "Religious Diversity and Politico-Religious Intolerance in Indonesia and Malaysia." *Review of Faith and International Affairs* 14, no. 4 (2016): 53–64.

Solberg, Mona, and Dan Olweus. "Prevalence Estimation of School Bullying with the Olweus Bully/Victim Questionnaire." *Aggressive Behavior* 29 (2003): 239–68.

Sorensen, Nicolas, Biren A. Nagda, Patricia Gurin, and Kelly E. Maxwell. "Taking a 'Hands-on' Approach to Diversity in Higher Education: A Critical-Dialogic Model for Effective Intergroup Interaction." *Analyses of Social Issues and Public Policy* 9, no. 1 (2009): 3–35.

Spalek, Basia. "Radicalisation, De-Radicalisation and Counter-Radicalisation in Relation to Families: Key Challenges for Research, Policy and Practice." *Security Journal* 29, no. 1 (2016): 39–52.

Stephan, Walter G., C. Lausanne Renfro, Victoria Esses, Cookie White Stephan, and Tim Martin. "The Effects of Feeling Threatened on Attitudes towards Immigrants." *International Journal of Intercultural Relations* 29 (2005): 1–19.

Stevens, Tim, and Peter R. Neumann. *Report on Countering Online Radicalization: A Strategy for Action.* London: International Centre for the Study of Radicalization and Political Violence, King's College, 2009.

Suciu, Eva Mirela. "Signs of Antisemitism in Indonesia." B.A. Honours Thesis, University of Sydney, Camperdown, Australia, 2008.

Sudjana, Eggi. *SBY Antek Yahudi AS? Suatu Kondisional Menuju Revolusi.* Jakarta: Ummacom Press, 2011.

Sugiariyanti. "Perilaku Bullying pada Anak dan Remaja." *Jurnal Ilmiah Psikologi* (2009): 101–8.

Sugimura, Kazumi, Kobo Matsushima, Shogo Hirara, Mahami Takahashi, and Elisabetta Crocetti. "A Culturally Sensitive Approach to the Relationships between Identity Formation and Religious Beliefs in Youth." *Journal of Youth and Adolescence* 48 (2019): 668–79.

Sukabdi, Zora A. "Terrorism in Indonesia: A Review on Rehabilitation and Deradicalization." *Journal of Terrorism Research* 6, no. 2 (2015): 36–56.

Sukarieh, Mayssoun, and Stuart Tannock. "The Deradicalisation of Education: Terror, Youth, and the Assault on Learning." *Race and Class* 57, no. 4 (2015): 22–38.

Sullivan, John L., James Piereson, and George E. Marcus. *Political Tolerance and American Democracy.* Chicago: University of Chicago Press 1982.

Sumpter, Cameron. "Countering Violent Extremism in Indonesia: Priorities, Practice and the Role of Civil Society." *Journal for Deradicalization* 11 (2017): 112–46.

Suryadarma, Daniel, and Gavin W. Jones, "Meeting the Education Challenge." In *Education in Indonesia,* edited by Daniel Suryadarma and Gavin W. Jones, 1–14. Singapore: Institute of Southeast Asian Studies, 2013.

Suryadinata, Leo, Evi Nurvidya Arifin, and Aris Ananta. *Indonesia's Population: Ethnicity and Religion in a Changing Political Landscape.* Singapore: Institute of Southeast Asian Studies, 2003.

Sutton, Robert. *The No Asshole Rule.* New York: Warner Business Books, 2007.

Swearer, Susan M., Dorothy L. Espelage, Tracy Vaillancourt, and Shelly Hymel. "What Can Be Done about School Bullying? Linking Research to Educational Practice." *Educational Researcher* 39, no. 1 (2010): 38–47.

Syafruddin, Didin, Dadi Darmadi, Saiful Umum, and Ismatu Ropi, eds. *Potret Guru Agama: Pandangan tentang Toleransi dan Isu-Isu Kehidupan Keagamaan.* Jakarta: Kencana, 2018.

Al-Tamimi, As'ad Bayud. *Impian Yahudi dan Kehancurannya Menurut al-Qur'an.* Translated by H. Salim Basyarahil. Jakarta: Gema Insani Press, 1992.

Taylor, Max, and John Horgan, eds. *The Future of Terrorism.* London: Frank Cass, 2006.

Teddlie, Charles, and Abbas Tashakkori. *Foundations of Mixed Methods Research: Integrating Qualitative and Quantitative Approaches in the Social and Behavioral Sciences.* Thousand Oaks, CA: SAGE Publications, 2009.

Tenenbaum, Laura S., Kris Varjas, Joel Meyers, and Leandra Parris. "Coping Strategies and Perceived Effectiveness in Fourth through Eighth Grade Victims of Bullying." *School Psychology International* 32, no. 3 (2011): 263–87.

Thomas, Paul. "Youth, Terrorism and Education: Britain's Prevent Programmes." *International Journal of Lifelong Education* 35, no. 2 (2016): 171–87.

Tim Peneliti. *Yahudi dan Jurus Maut Gus Dur.* Jakarta: Cidesindo, 1999.

Toha, Risa J. "Ethnic Riots in Democratic Transition: A Lesson from Indonesia." Ph.D. dissertation, University of California, Los Angeles, 2012.

Ttofi, Maria M., and David P. Farrington. "Effectiveness of School-Based Programs to Reduce Bullying: A Systematic and Meta-analytic Review." *Journal of Experimental Criminology* 7 (2011): 27–56.

Turner, Rhiannon, and Lindsey Cameron. "Confidence in Contact: A New Perspective on Promoting Cross-Group Friendship among Children and Adolescents." *Social Issues and Public Policy* 10 (2016): 212–46.

Undheim, Anne Mari, and Anne Mari Sund. "Prevalence of Bullying and Aggressive Behavior and Their Relationship to Mental Health Problems among 12- to 15-Year-Old Norwegian Adolescents." *European Child and Adolescent Psychiatry* 19, no. 11 (2010): 803–11.

UNICEF. *Laporan Tahu Indonesia 2015.* https://www.medbox.org/document/unicef-laporan-tahunan-indonesia-2015#GO.

Usman, Irvan. "Perilaku Bullying Ditinjau dari Peran Kelompok Teman Sebaya dan Iklim Sekolah pada Siswa SMA di Kota Gorontalo." Unpublished paper, 2008.

Ustman, Ahmad. *Israel Siapa Mereka? Sejarah bangsa Israel dari Awal Kemunculannya hingga Terbentuknya Agama Yahudi.* Translated by A. Halim. Jakarta: Fima Rodhet, 2008.

Valente, Thomas W. *Social Networks and Health: Models, Methods, and Applications.* New York: Oxford University Press, 2010.

Valentini, Daniele, Anna Maria Larusso, and Achim Stephan. "*Onlife* Extremism: Dynamic Integration of Digital and Physical Spaces in

Radicalization." *Frontiers in Psychology*, March 24, 2020. https://www
.frontiersin.org/articles/10.3389/fpsyg.2020.00524/full.

Vargas, Jose. "Understanding the Radicalization Process of U.S. Homegrown
Terrorists." Ph.D. dissertation, Walden University, Minneapolis, MN,
2017.

Velddhuis, Tinka, and Jorgen Staun. *Islamist Radicalisation: A Root Cause
Model.* The Hague: Netherlands Institute of International Relations Clingendael, 2009.

Venhaus, John M. *Why Youth Join Al-Qaeda.* USIP Special Report 236. Washington, DC: United States Institute of Peace, 2010. http://www.usip.org
/files/resources/SR236Venhaus.pdf.

Vidino, Lorenzo, and James Brandon. *Countering Radicalisation in Europe.*
London: International Centre for Radicalisation and Political Violence,
2012.

Voermans, Wim, Maarten Stremler, and Paul Cliteur. *Constitutional Preambles: A
Comparative Analysis.* Northampton, MA: Edward Elgar Publishing, 2017.

von Behr, Ines, Anaïs Reding, Charlie Edwards, and Luke Gribbon. "Radicalisation in the Digital Era." RAND Europe. 2013.

Wade, Geoff. "An Early Age of Commerce in Southeast Asia, 900–1300 CE."
Journal of Southeast Asian Studies 40, no. 2 (2009): 221–65.

Wahid Institute and Indonesian Survey Circle (LSI, Lembaga Survei Indonesia). *Laporan Survei Nasional Tren Toleransi Sosial-Keagamaan di Kalangan
Perempuan Muslim Indonesia.* Wahid Foundation, 2018.

Waldfogel, Jane. *What Children Need.* Cambridge, MA: Harvard University
Press, 2006.

Walter, O. W. *Early Indonesian Commerce: A Study of the Origins of Śrīvijaya.*
Ithaca, NY: Cornell University Press, 1967.

Ward, Colleen, Anne-Marie Masgoret, and Michelle Gezentsvey. "Investigating Attitudes toward International Students: Implications for Social
Integration and International Education." *Social Issues and Policy Review*
3, no. 1 (2009): 79–102.

Wasserman, Stanley, and Katherine Faust. *Social Network Analysis: Methods
and Applications.* Cambridge: Cambridge University Press, 1994.

Waterman, Shaun. "Indonesia Tries Deradicalization." *Middle East Times*,
July 22, 2008.

Weaver, Lori M., James Brown, Dan Weddle, and Mathew Aalsma. "A Content Analysis of Protective Factors within States' Antibullying Laws."
Journal of School Violence 12, no. 2 (2012): 156–73.

Webman, Esther. "Adoption of the Protocols in the Arab Discourse on the
Arab–Israeli Conflict, Zionism, and the Jews." In *The Global Impact of*

The Protocols of the Elders of Zion: A Century-Old Myth, edited by Esther Webman, 175–95. London: Routledge, 2011.

Weeks, Kent. In Search of Civility: Confronting Incivility on the College Campus. New York: Morgan James Publishing, 2011.

Wei, Hsi-Sheng, and Melissa Jonson-Reid. "Friends Can Hurt You: Examining the Coexistence of Friendship and Bullying among Early Adolescents." School Psychology International 32, no. 3 (2011): 244–62.

Weimann, Gabriel. "Terror on Facebook, Twitter and YouTube." Brown Journal of World Affairs 16, no. 2 (2010): 45–54.

Weimer, Barbara L., Kathryn Kerns, and Christopher Oldenburg. "Adolescents' Interactions with a Best Friend: Associations with Attachment Style." Journal of Experimental Child Psychology 88, no. 1 (2004): 102–20.

Whitman, Ian, and Team of Review of National Policies for Education. Education in Indonesia: Rising to the Challenge. Paris: OECD Publishing, 2015.

Widiasari, Natalia. "Media Reviews." Asian Politics and Policy 10, no. 1 (2018): 145–49.

Widjayanto, Febby Risti. "Antisemitisme Modern dalam Pembongkaran Sinagog Surabaya: Psikologi Politik Multikulturalisme." Jurnal Politik Muda 3, no. 3 (2014): 103–17.

Wiktorowicz, Quintan. "Introduction: Islamic Activism and Social Movement Theory." In Islamic Activism: A Social Movement Theory Approach, edited by Quintan Wiktorowicz, 1–35. Bloomington: Indiana University Press, 2004.

———. Radical Islam Rising: Islamic Extremism in the West. Lanham, MD: Rowman and Littlefield, 2005.

Wild, Stefan. "National Socialism in the Arab Near East between 1933 and 1939." Die Welt des Islams 25 (1985): 126–70.

Wilkins, Keenly, Paul Caldarella, Rachel Crook-Lyon, and K. Richard Young. "The Implications of Civility for Children and Adolescents: A Review of the Literature." Issues in Religion and Psychotherapy 33, no. 1 (2010): 37–45.

Williams, Bernard. "Toleration: An Impossible Virtue?" In Toleration: An Elusive Virtue, edited by David Heyd, 18–27. Princeton, NJ: Princeton University Press, 1996.

Wilner, Alex S., and Claire-Jehanne Dubouloz. "Homegrown Terrorism and Transformative Learning: An Interdisciplinary Approach to Understanding Radicalization." Global Change, Peace and Security 22, no. 1 (2010): 1–26.

Wink, André. Al-Hind: The Making of the Indo-Islamic World. Leiden: Brill, 2002.

Wistrich, Robert S. "A Deadly Mutation: Antisemitism and Anti-Zionism in Great Britain." In *Antisemitism on the Campus: Past and Present,* edited by Eunice G. Pollack, 53–74. Boston: Academic Studies Press, 2011.

Wittig, Michele, and Sheila A. Grant-Thompson. "The Utility of Allport's Conditions of Intergroup Contact for Predicting Perceptions of Improved Racial Attitudes and Beliefs." *Journal of Social Issues* 54 (1998): 795–812.

Yasin, Nur Azlin Mohamed. "Online Indonesian Islamist Extremism: A Gold Mine of Information." S. Rajaratnam School of International Studies, Nanyang Technological University, Singapore. October 7, 2011.

Yegar, Moshe. "The Republic of Indonesia and Israel." *Israel Affairs* 12, no. 1 (2006): 136–58.

Youniss, James, and Denise Haynie. "Friendship in Adolescence." *Journal of Developmental and Behavioral Pediatrics* 13, no. 1 (1992): 59–66.

Yustiani, Y. "Penanaman Nilai-Nilai Karakter Bangsa Melalui Mata Pelajaran Pendidikan Agama Islam di SMA Negeri." *Analisa Journal of Social Science and Religion* 22, no. 1 (2015): 135–47.

Yusuf, Ah, Aziz Nashiruddin Habibie, Ferry Efendi, Iqlima Dwi Kurnia, and Anna Kurniati. "Prevalence and Correlates of Being Bullied among Adolescents in Indonesia: Results from the 2015 Global School-Based Student Health Survey." *International Journal of Adolescent Medicine and Health* 34, no. 1 (2019): 1–7.

Zaman, Muhammad Qasim. *Modern Islamic Thought in a Radical Age.* Cambridge: Cambridge University Press, 2012.

Zarman, Romi. *Di Bawah Kuasa Anti-Semitisme: Orang Yahudi di Hindia Belanda (1861–1942).* Pekanbaru: Tjatatan Indonesia, 2018.

Zuhri, Muhammad. "Challenging Moderate Muslims: Indonesia's Muslim Schools in the Midst of Religious Conservatism." *Religion* 9, no. 310 (2018): 1–15.

———. "The 1975 Three-Minister Decree and the Modernization of Indonesian Islamic Schools." *American Educational History Journal* 32, no. 1 (2005): 36–43.

———. "Political and Social Influences on Religious Schools: A Historical Perspective on Indonesian Islamic School Curricula." Ph.D. dissertation, McGill University, Montreal, 2006.

INDEX

MUN'IM SIRRY is an associate professor of theology at the University of Notre Dame and author of several books, including *The Qur'an with Cross-References*.

www.ingramcontent.com/pod-product-compliance
Lightning Source LLC
Chambersburg PA
CBHW071511281025
34597CB00028B/1193

www.ingramcontent.com/pod-product-compliance
Lightning Source LLC
Chambersburg PA
CBHW071511281025
34597CB00028B/1193